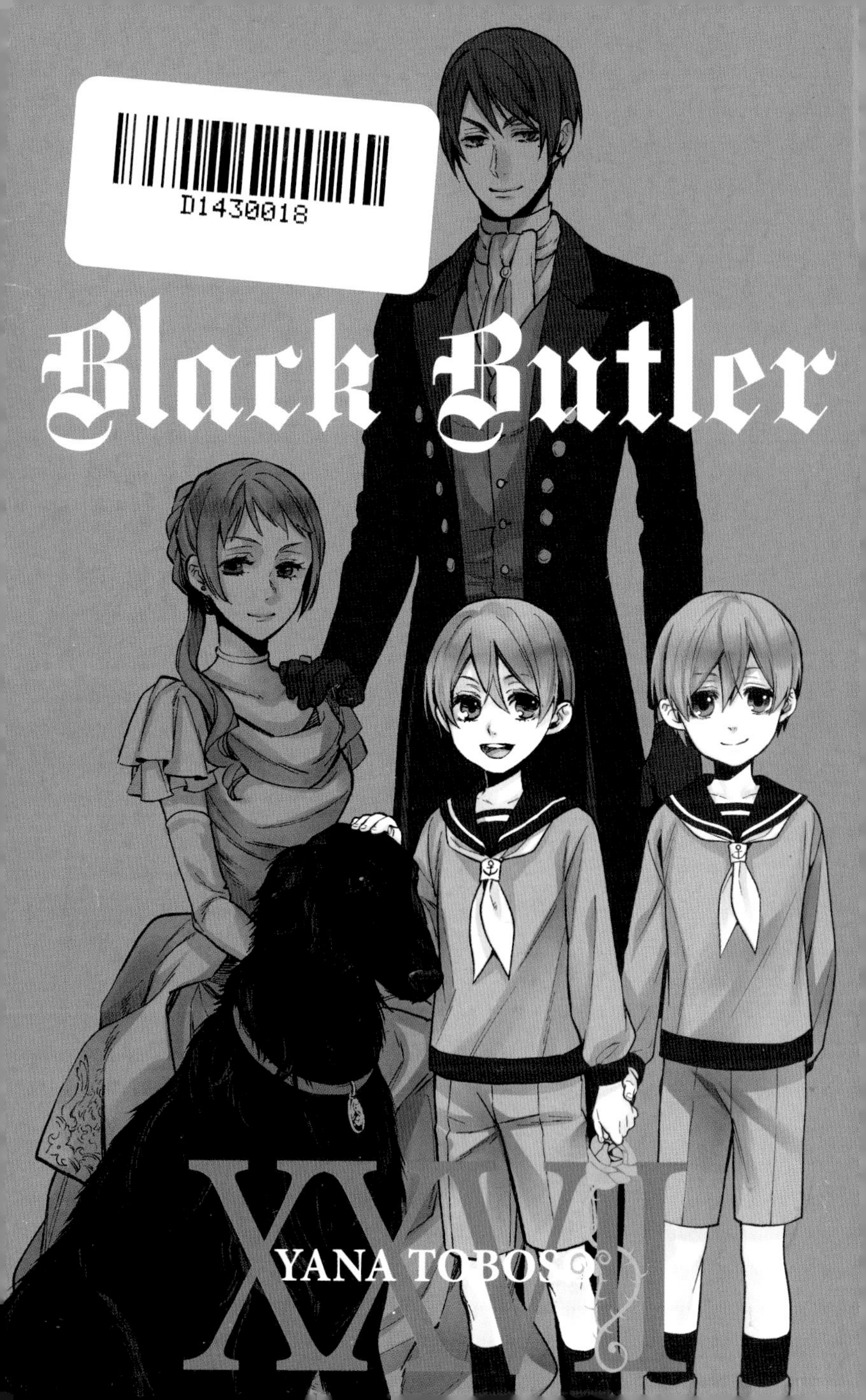
Black Butler
XXVII
YANA TOBOSO

# Contents

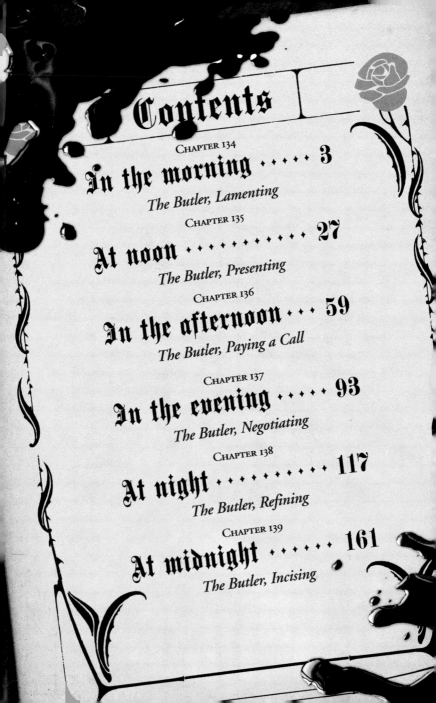

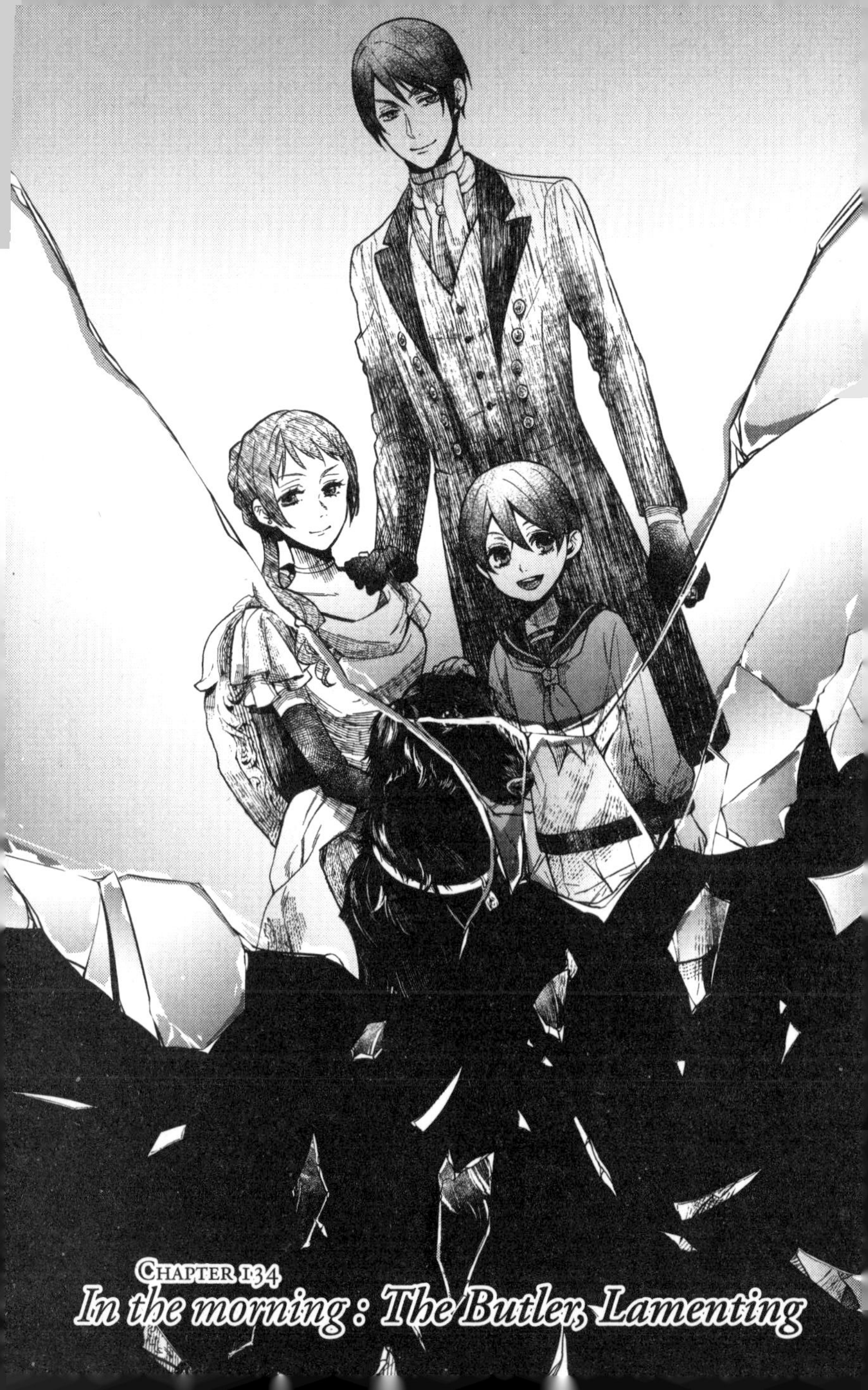

## Chapter 134
# In the morning : The Butler, Lamenting

HAPPY TENTH BIRTHDAY!
SAME TO YOU...
...CIEL!
OUR TENTH BIRTHDAY.
HAPPY BIRTHDAY...
...MY LITTLE ANGELS!
HAPPY BIRTHDAY!
I SHALL COME AND HELP YOU CHANGE FOR THE PARTY AROUND SIX.

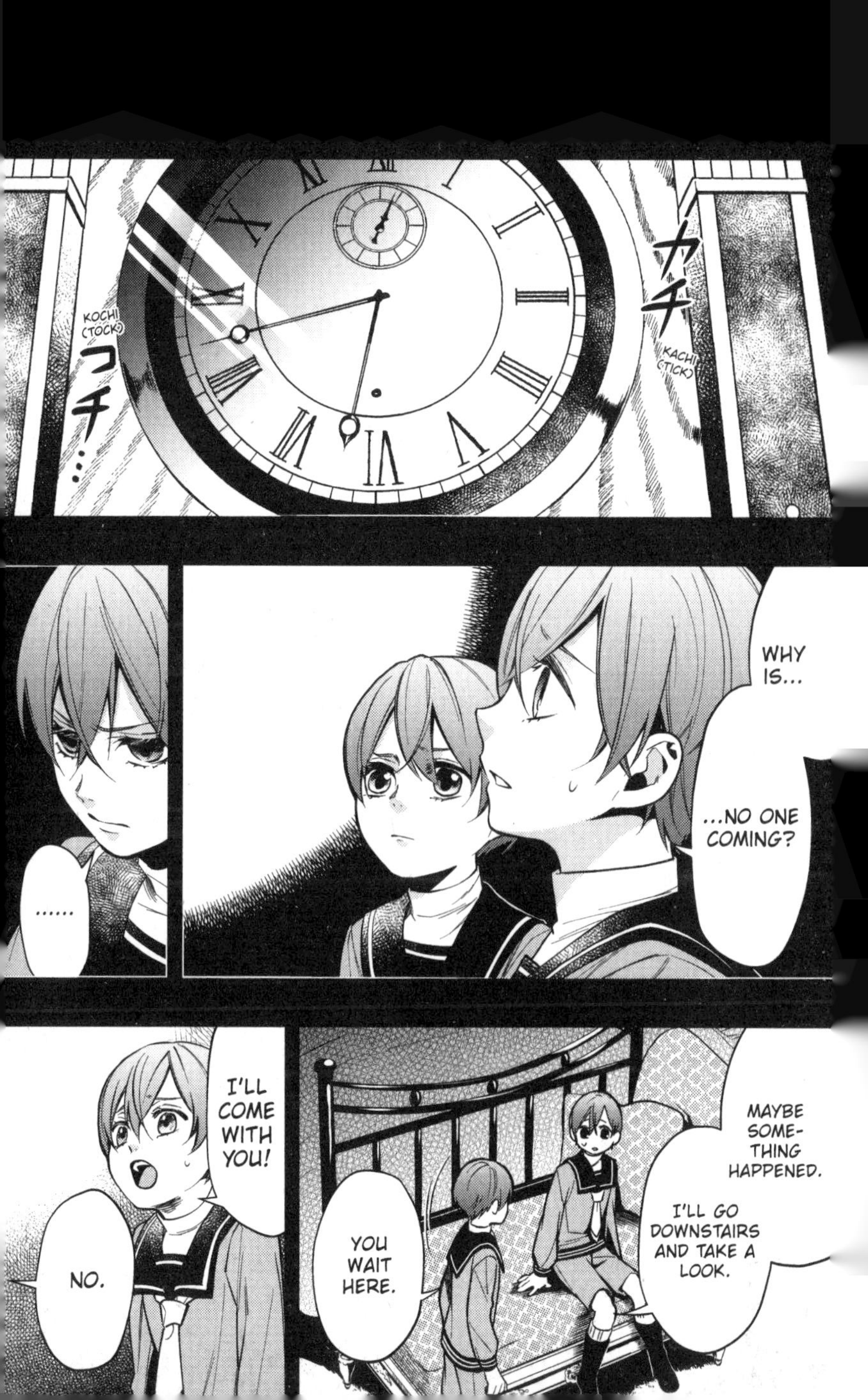
カチ
KACHI (TICK)
KOCHI (TOCK)
コチ…
WHY IS…
…NO ONE COMING?
……
MAYBE SOME-THING HAPPENED.
I'LL GO DOWNSTAIRS AND TAKE A LOOK.
YOU WAIT HERE.
I'LL COME WITH YOU!
NO.

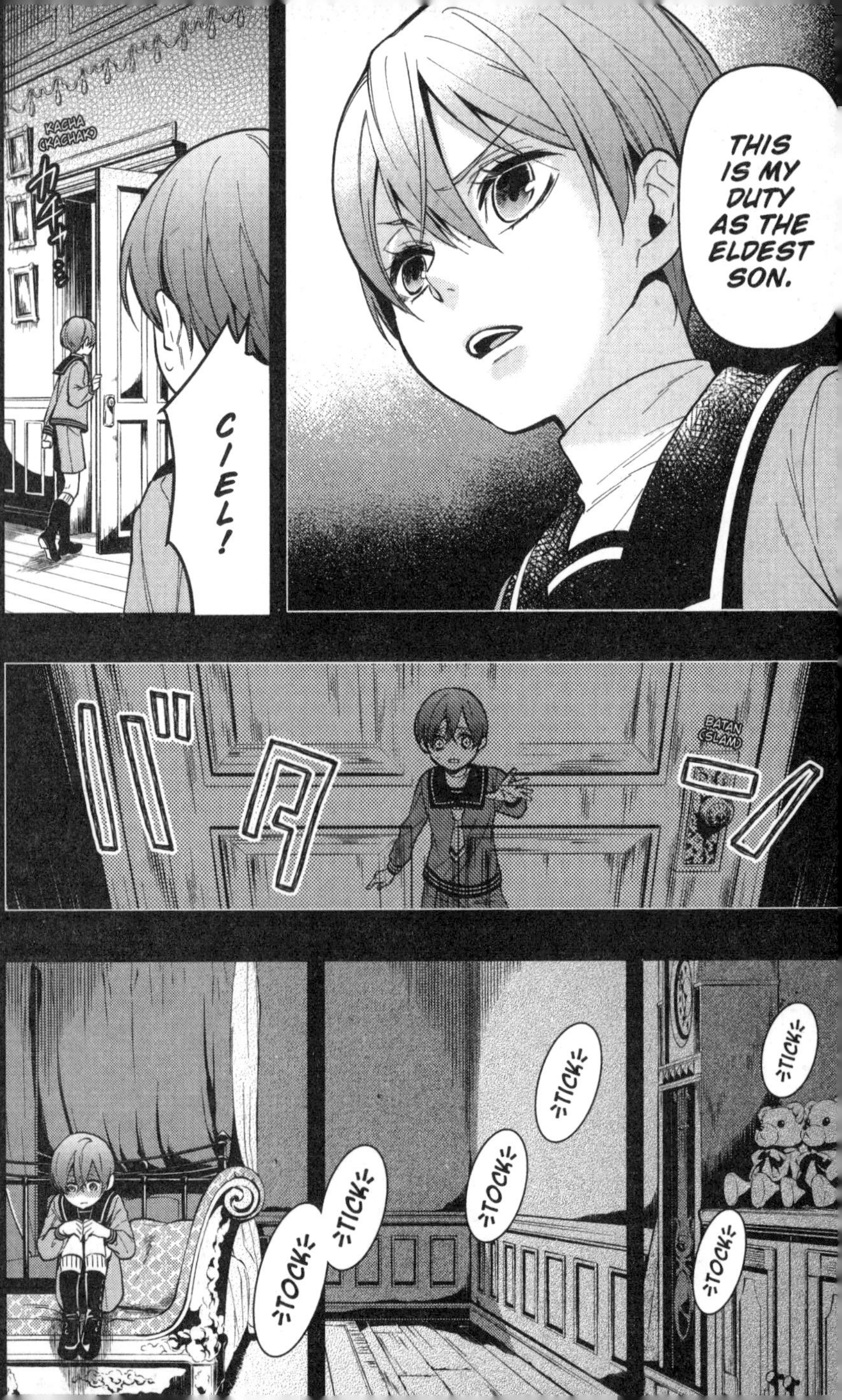
THIS IS MY DUTY AS THE ELDEST SON.
KACHA (KACHAK)
CIEL!
BATAN (SLAM)
TICK
TOCK
TICK
TOCK
TICK
TOCK

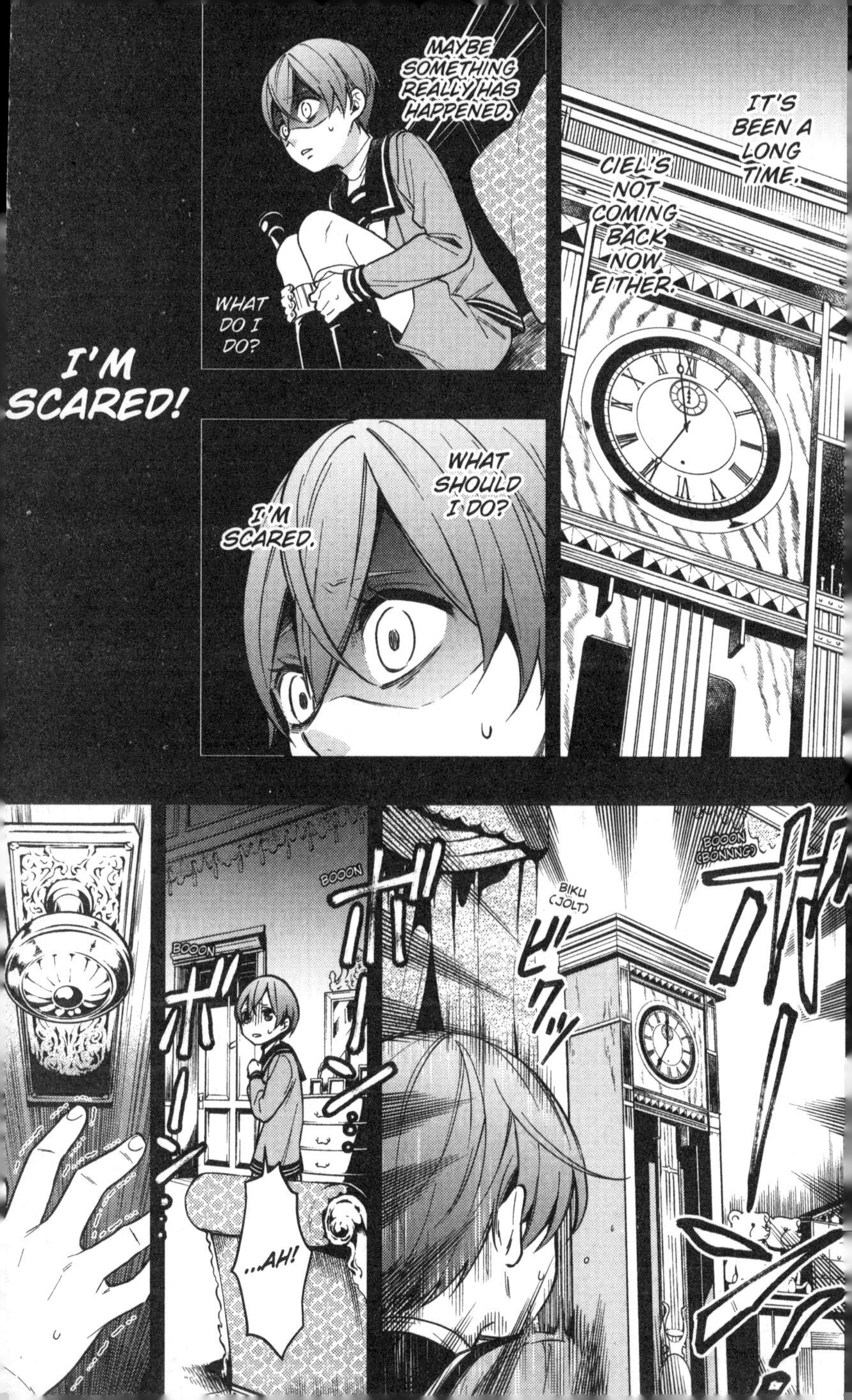
IT'S BEEN A LONG TIME.
CIEL'S NOT COMING BACK NOW EITHER.
MAYBE SOMETHING REALLY HAS HAPPENED.
WHAT DO I DO?
WHAT SHOULD I DO?
I'M SCARED.
I'M SCARED!
BOOON (BONNNG)
BIKU (JOLT)
BOOON
BOOON
...AH!

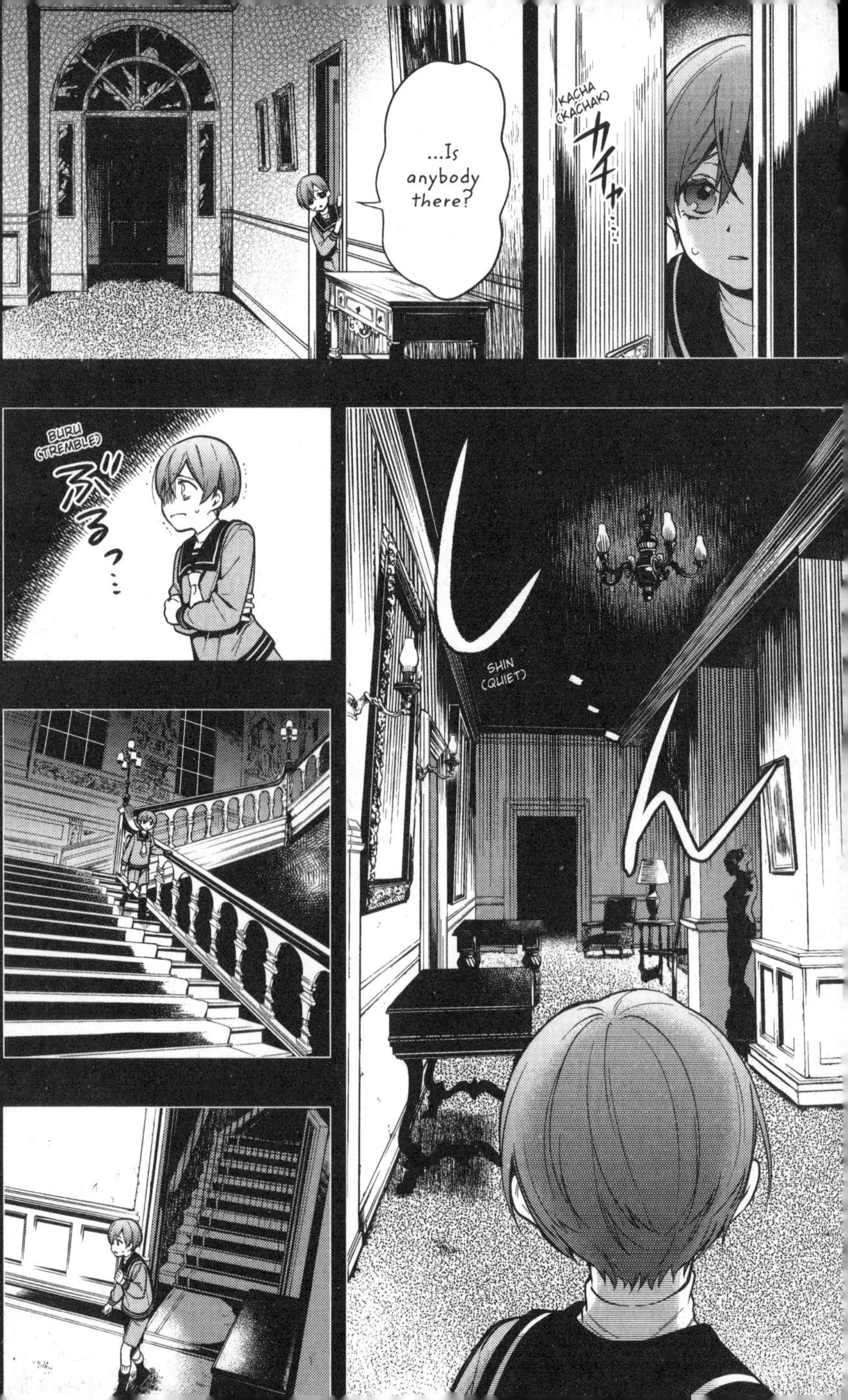
KACHA (KACHAK)
...Is anybody there?
SHIN (QUIET)
BURU (TREMBLE)

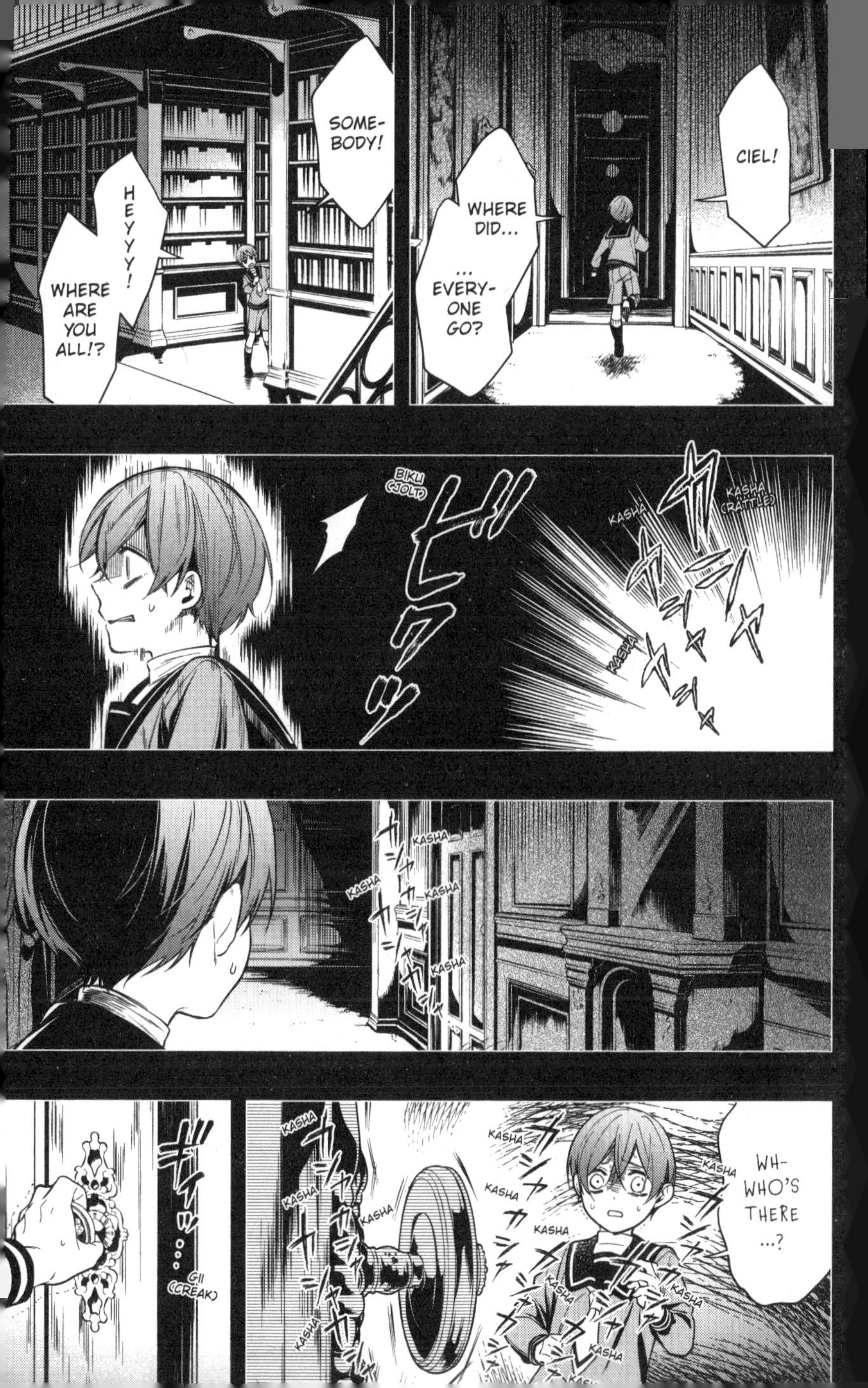
CIEL!
WHERE DID...
... EVERY-ONE GO?
SOME-BODY!
HEYYY!
WHERE ARE YOU ALL!?
KASHA (RATTLE)
KASHA
KASHA
BIKU (JOLT)
KASHA
KASHA
KASHA
KASHA
WH-WHO'S THERE ...?
KASHA
KASHA
KASHA
KASHA
KASHA
KASHA
KASHA
KASHA
KASHA
KASHA
KASHA
KASHA
GII (CREAK)

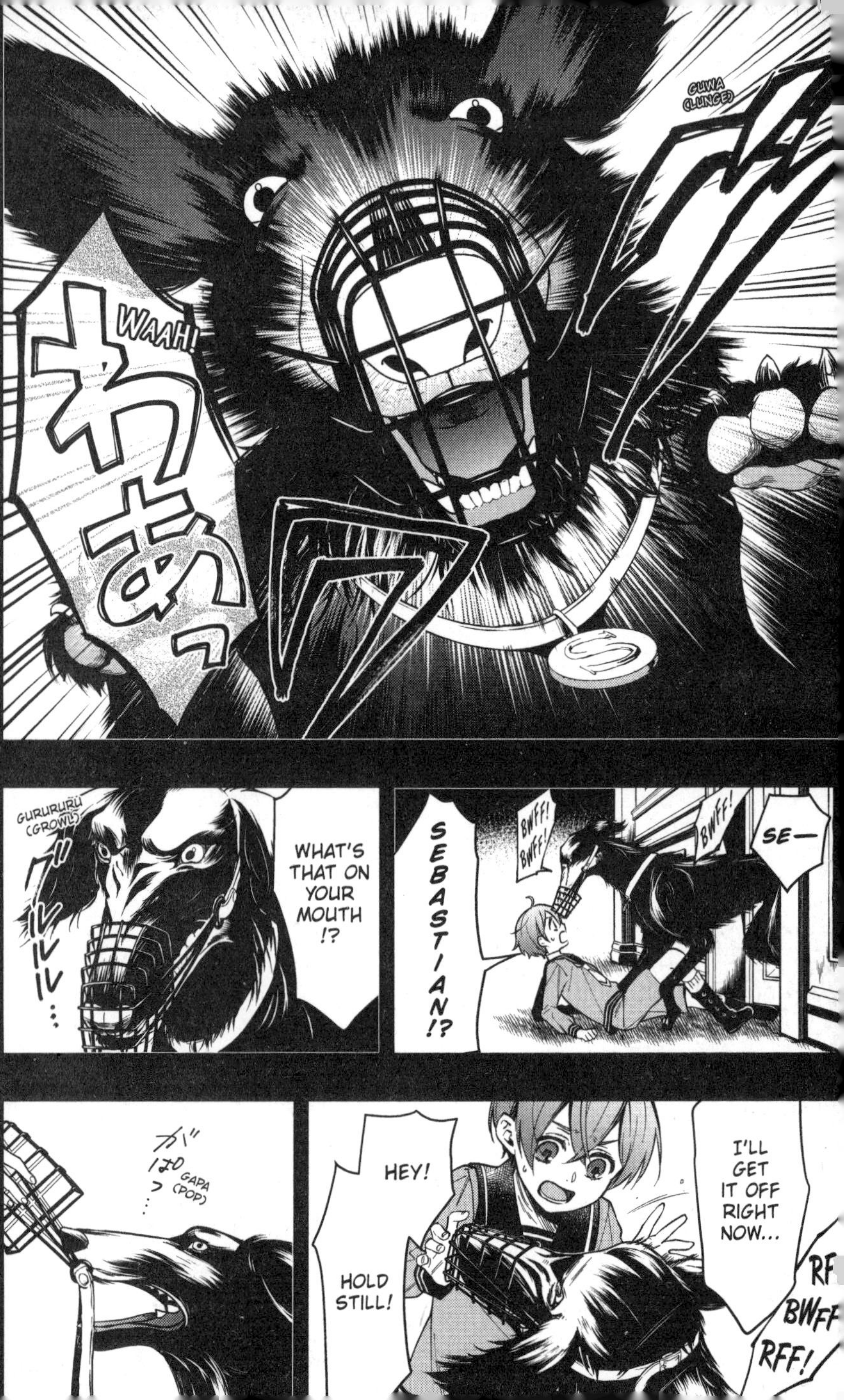
GUWA (LUNGED)
わあっ
WAAH!
SE—
BWFF!
BWFF! BWFF!
SEBASTIAN!?
GURURURU (GROWL)
WHAT'S THAT ON YOUR MOUTH!?
I'LL GET IT OFF RIGHT NOW...
RF BWFF RFF!
HEY!
HOLD STILL!
GAPA (POP)

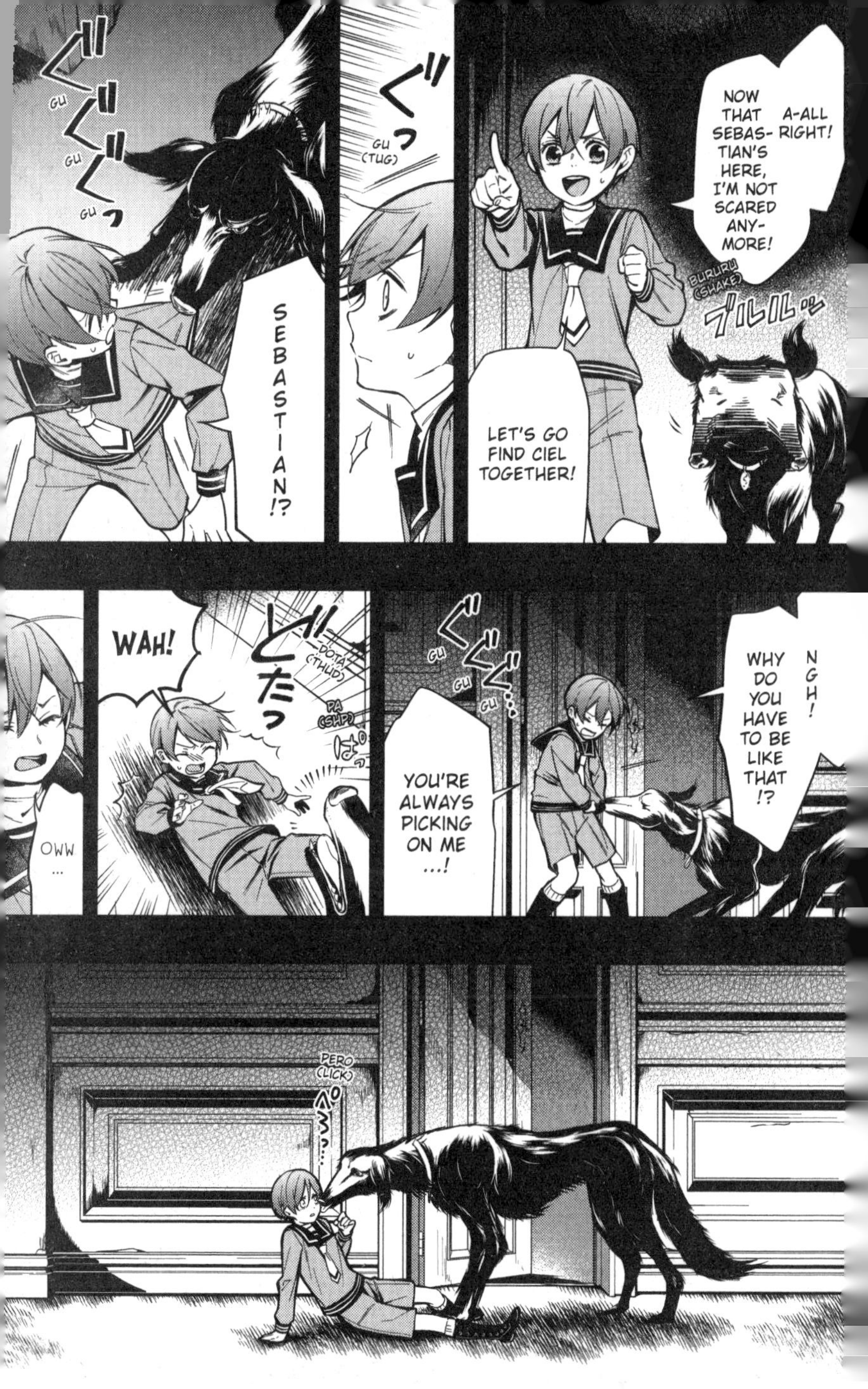
A-ALL RIGHT!
NOW THAT SEBASTIAN'S HERE, I'M NOT SCARED ANYMORE!
BURURU (SHAKE)
LET'S GO FIND CIEL TOGETHER!
GU (TUG)
GU
GU
GU
SEBASTIAN!?
NGH!
WHY DO YOU HAVE TO BE LIKE THAT!?
GU
GU
GU
YOU'RE ALWAYS PICKING ON ME...!
DOTA (THUD)
WAH!
PA (SHP)
OWW...
PERO (LICK)

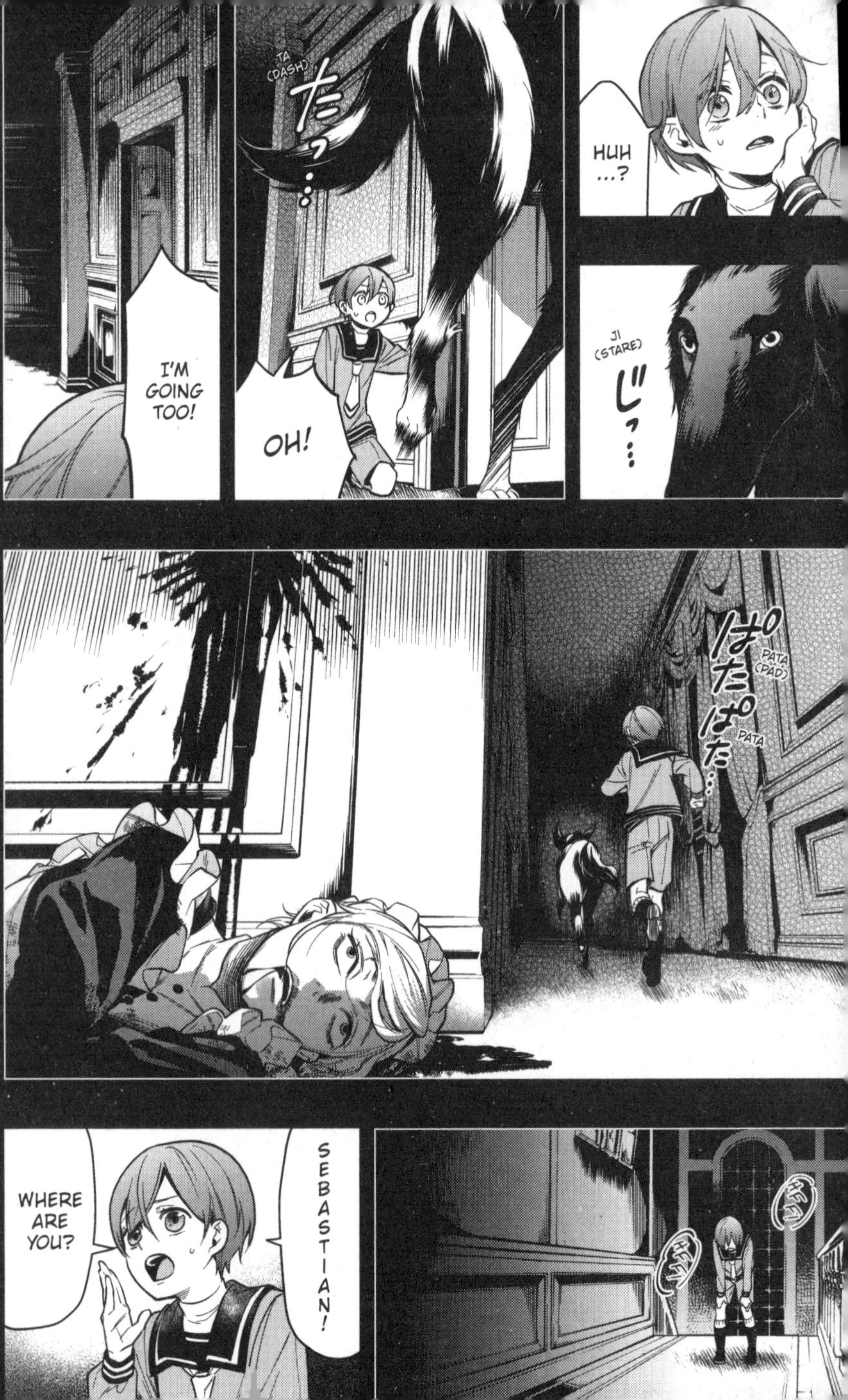
HUH ...?
JI (STARE)
じっ…
TA (DASH)
たっ…
OH!
I'M GOING TOO!
ぱたぱた…
PATA (PAD)
PATA
SEBASTIAN!
WHERE ARE YOU?

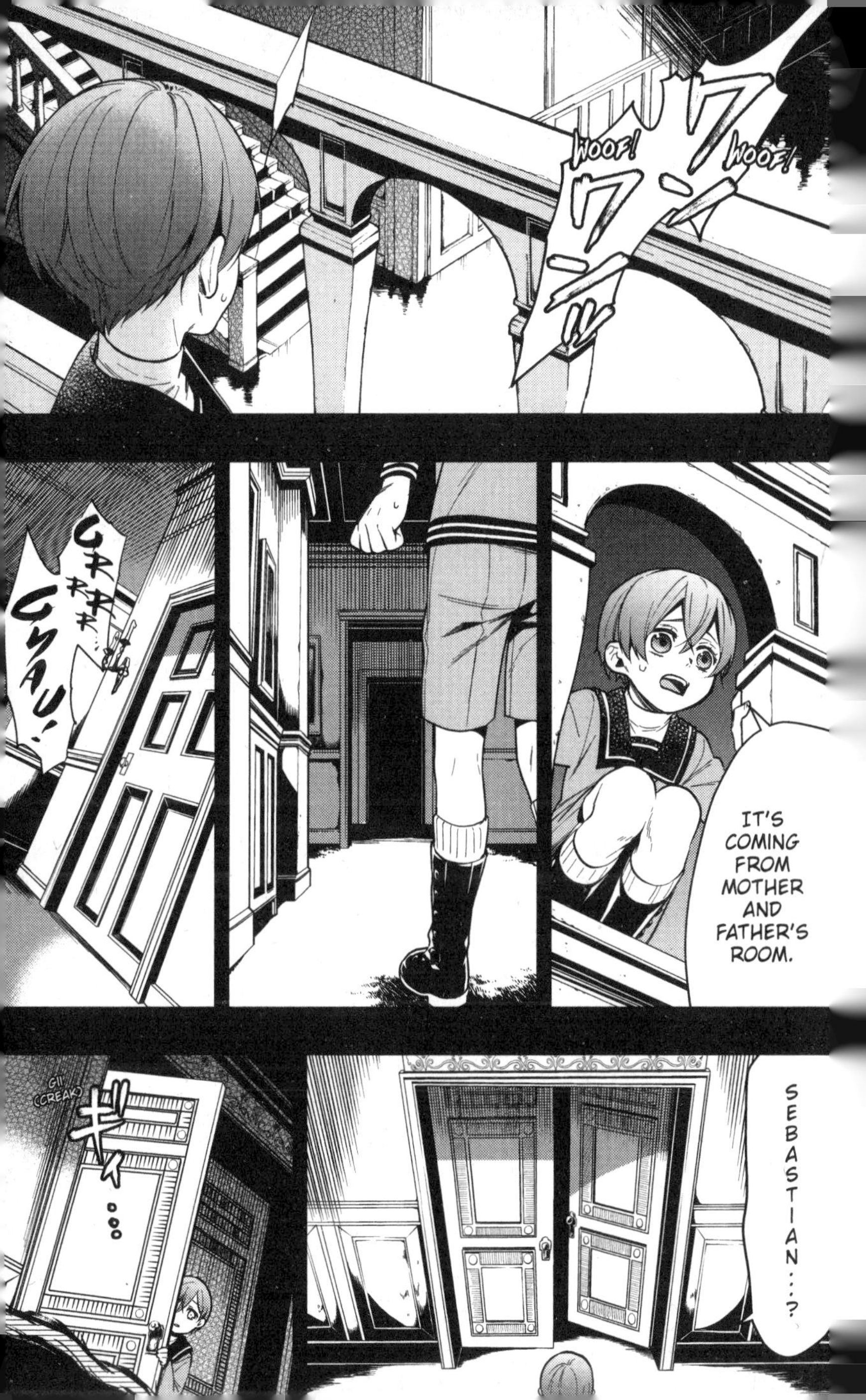
WOOF!
WOOF!
IT'S COMING FROM MOTHER AND FATHER'S ROOM.
GRRRRR...
GYAU!
SEBASTIAN...?
GII (CREAK)
...

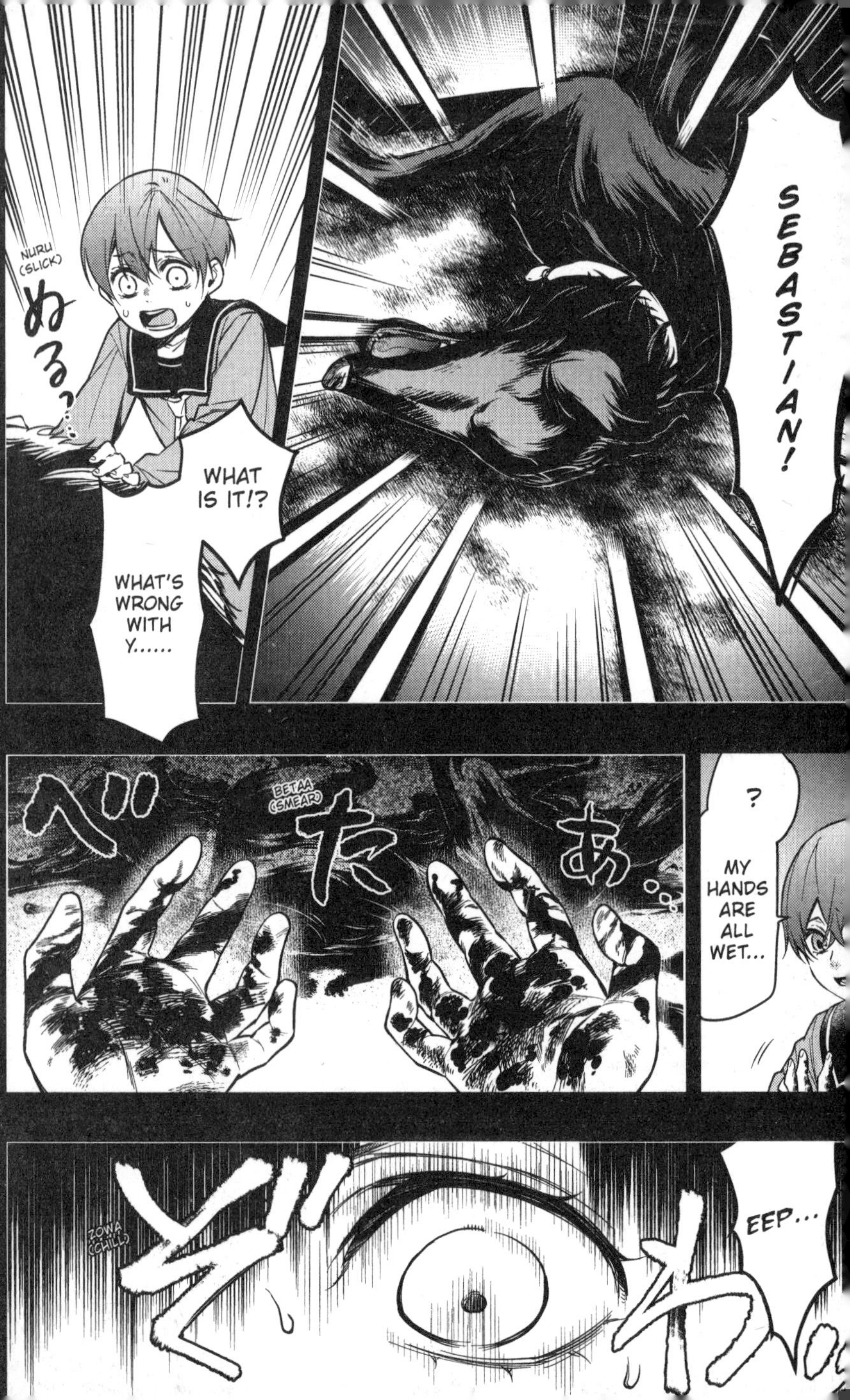
SEBASTIAN!
NURU (SLICK)
ぬるっ…
WHAT IS IT!?
WHAT'S WRONG WITH Y......
?
MY HANDS ARE ALL WET...
BETAA (SMEAR)
べたぁ…
EEP...
ZOWA (CHILL)
ゾワ…

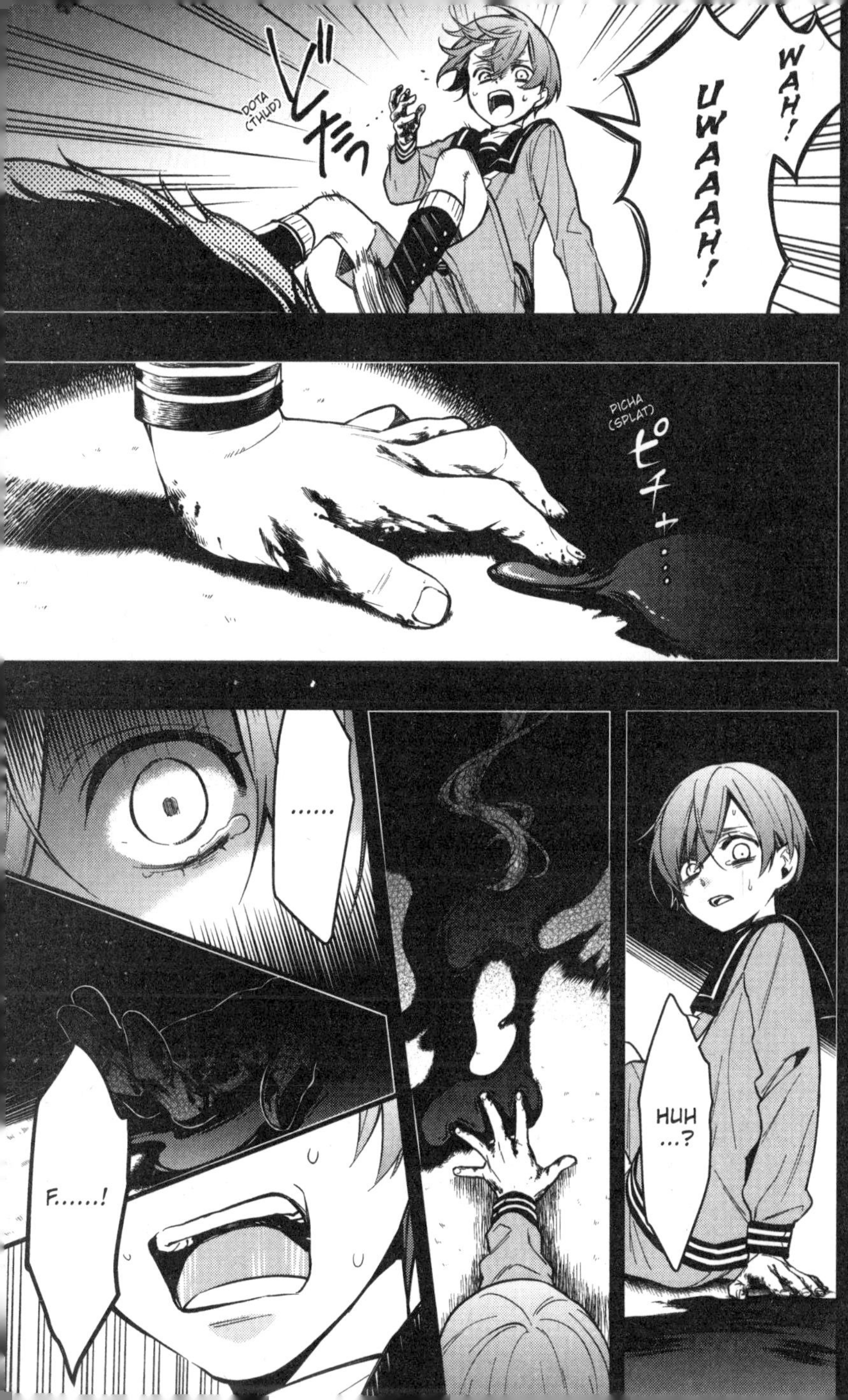
WAH! UWAAAAH!
DOTA (THUD)
PICHA (SPLAT)
HUH ...?
......
F......!

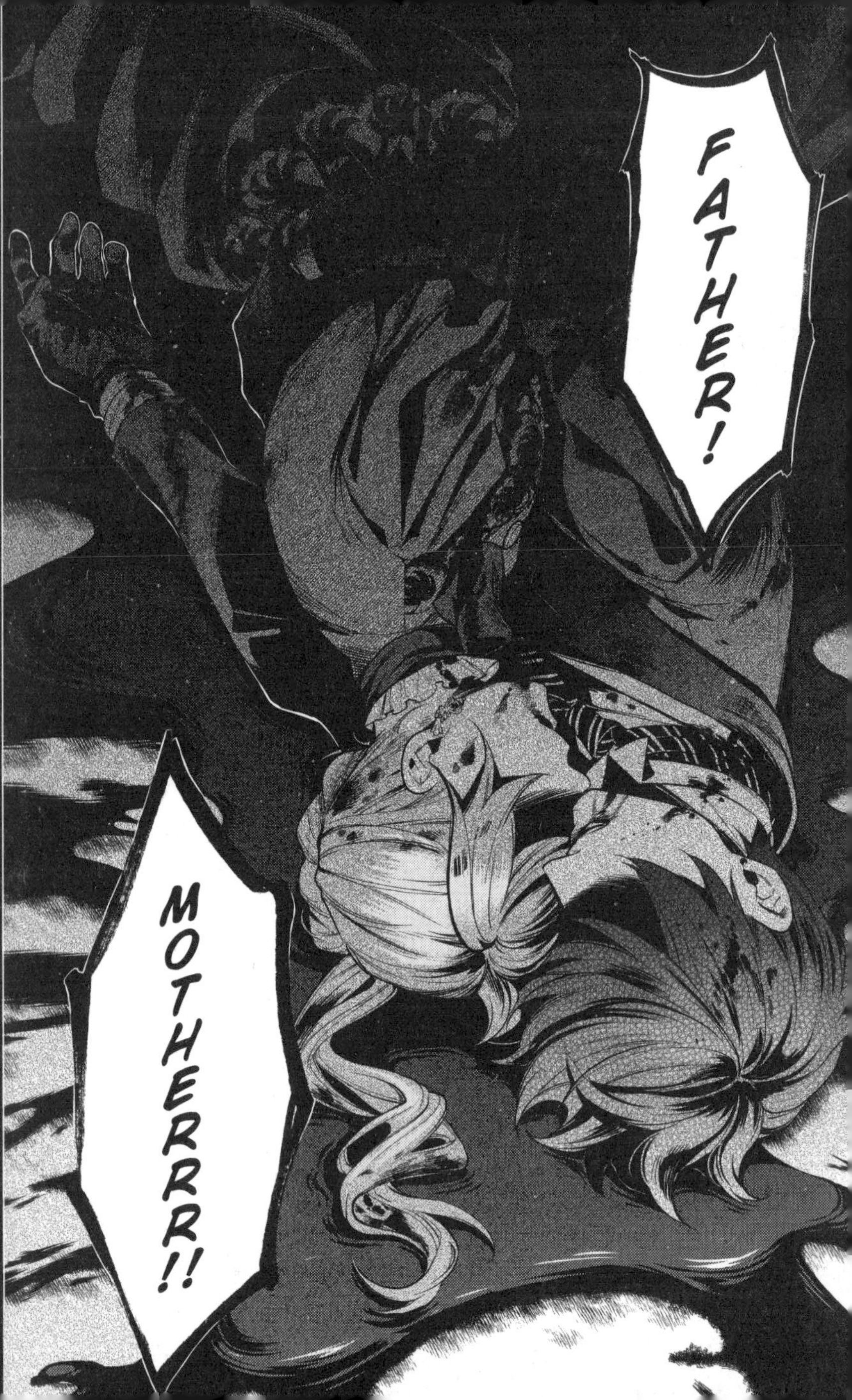
FATHER!
MOTHERRR!!

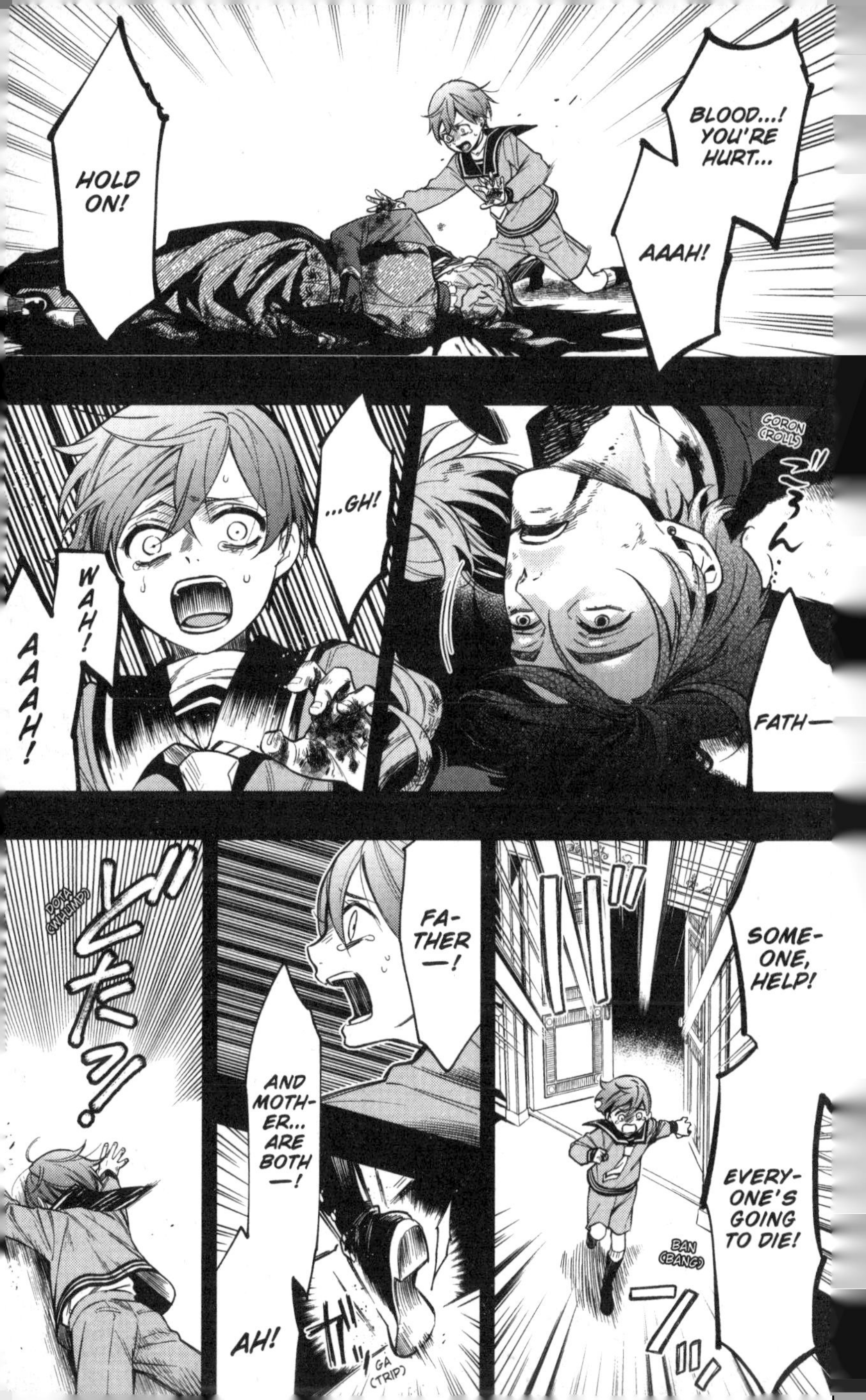
BLOOD...! YOU'RE HURT...
AAAH!
HOLD ON!
GORON (ROLL)
FATH—
...GH!
WAH!
AAAAH!
SOME-ONE, HELP!
EVERY-ONE'S GOING TO DIE!
BAN (BANG)
FA-THER—!
AND MOTH-ER... ARE BOTH—!
AH!
GA (TRIP)
DOTA (WHUMP)

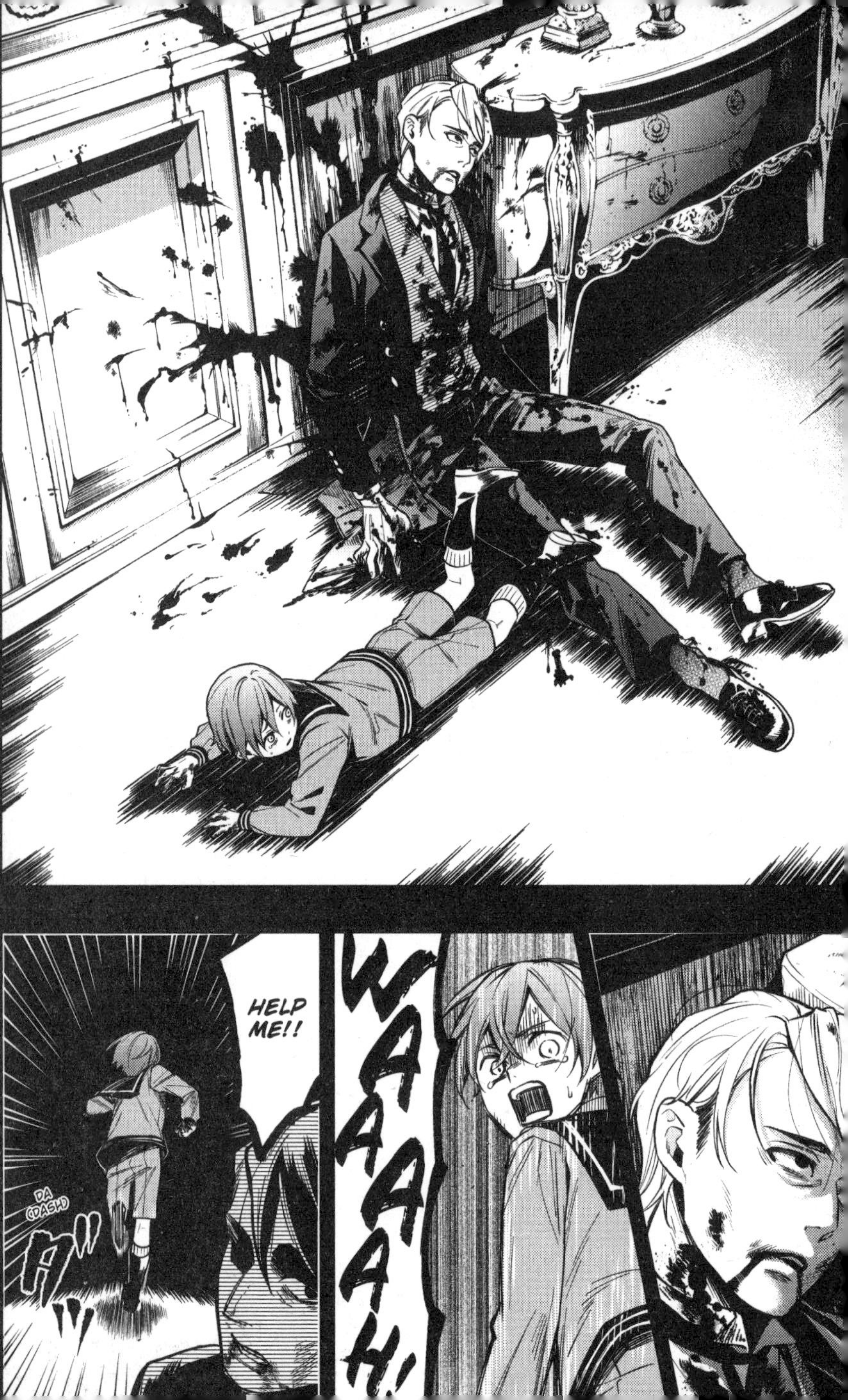
WAAAAH!
HELP ME!!
DA (DASH)

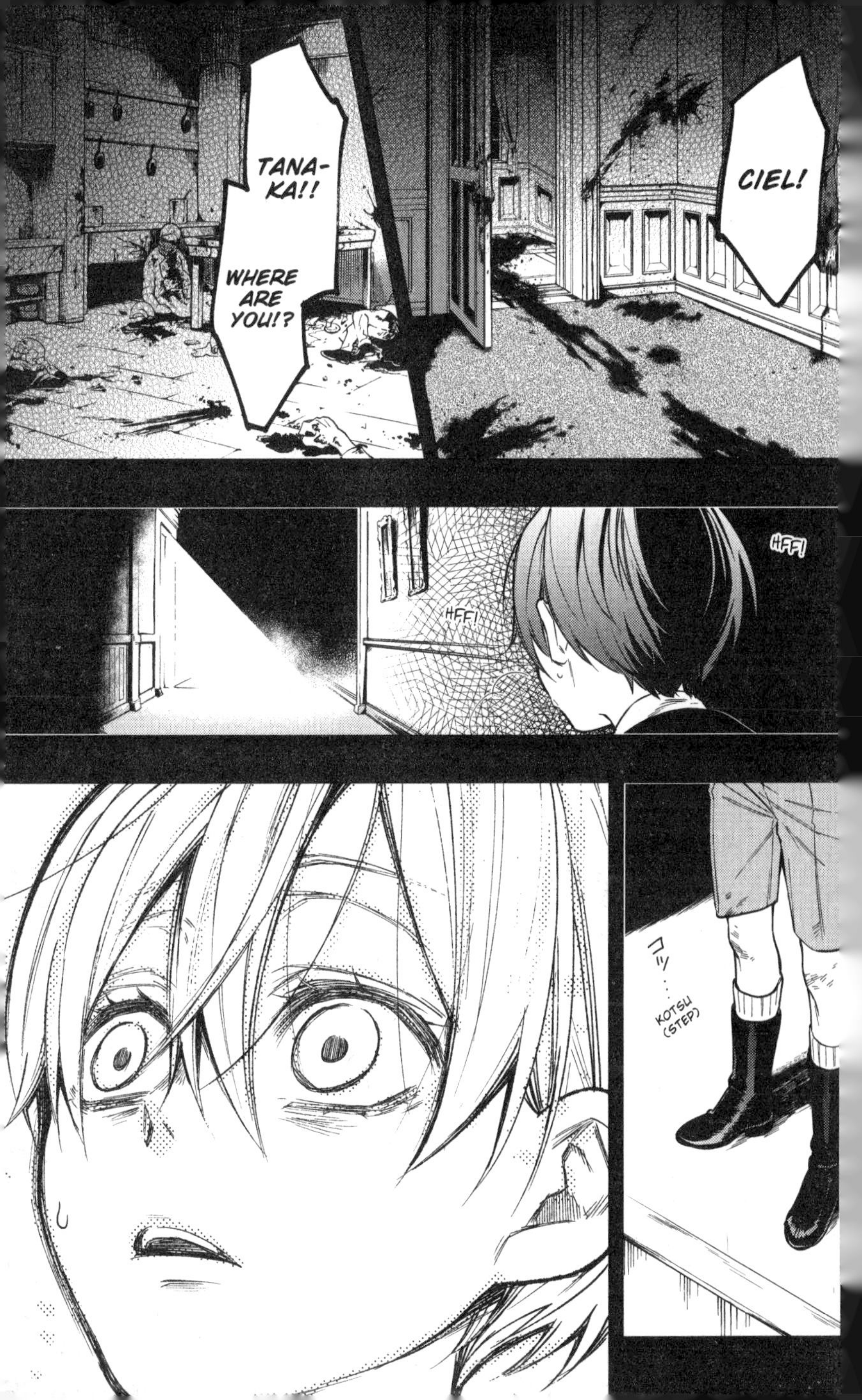
CIEL!
TANA-KA!!
WHERE ARE YOU!?
HFF!
HFF!
コツ…
KOTSU (STEP)

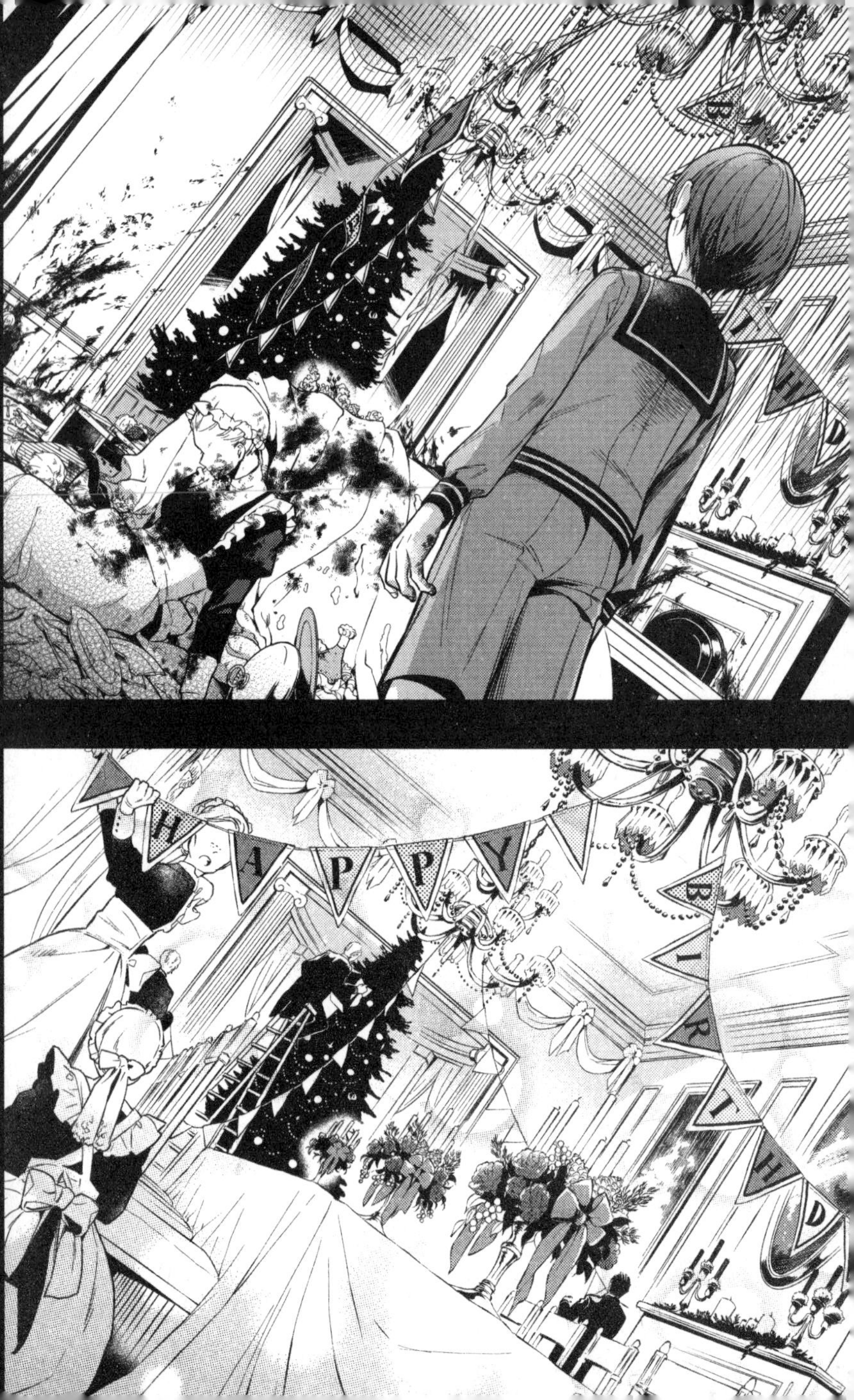
HAPPY
BIRTHD

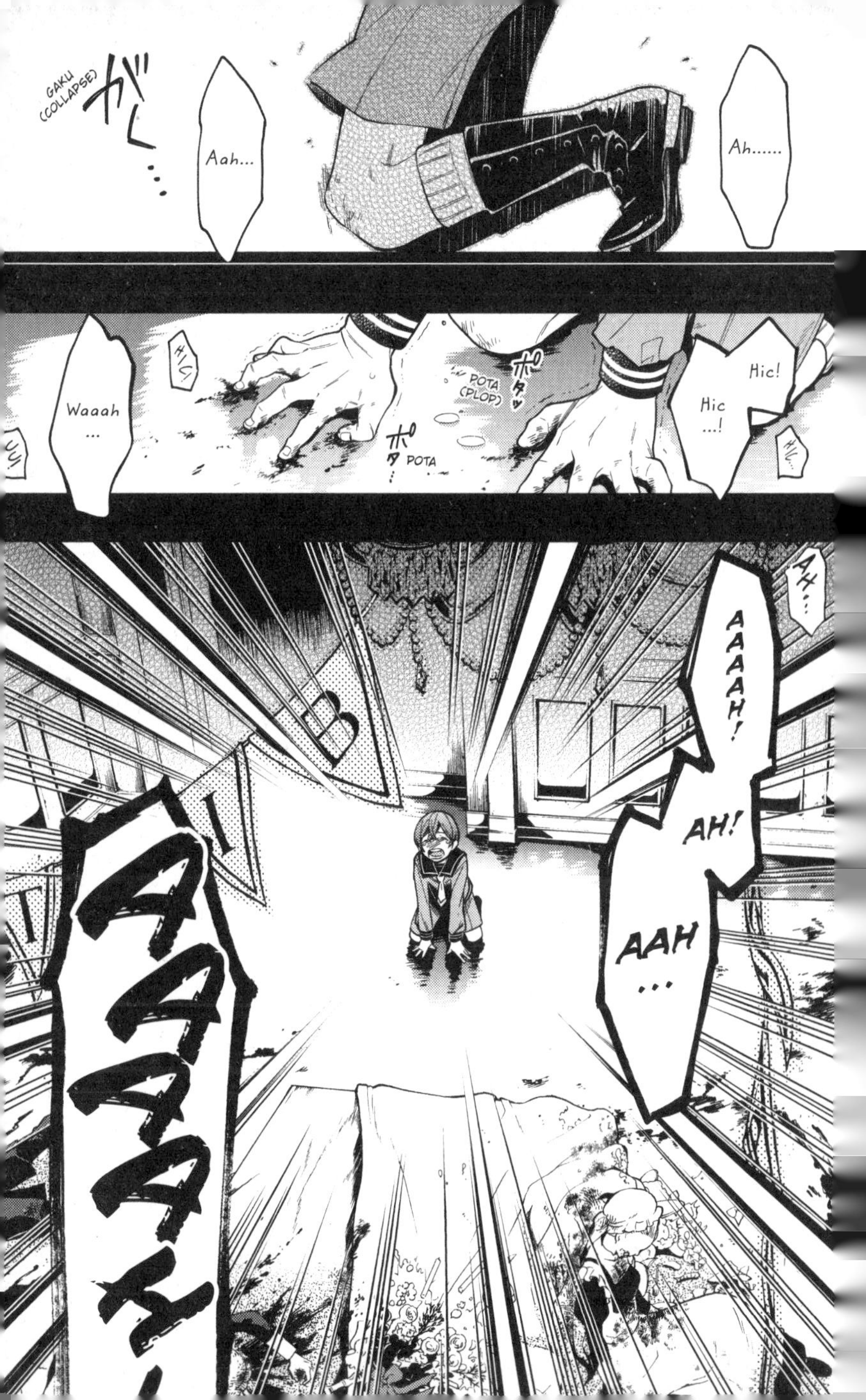

Ah......
Aah...
GAKU (COLLAPSE)
Hic! Hic ...!
POTA (PLOP)
POTA
Waaah ...
AAAAAH! AH! AAH ...
AAAAAH!

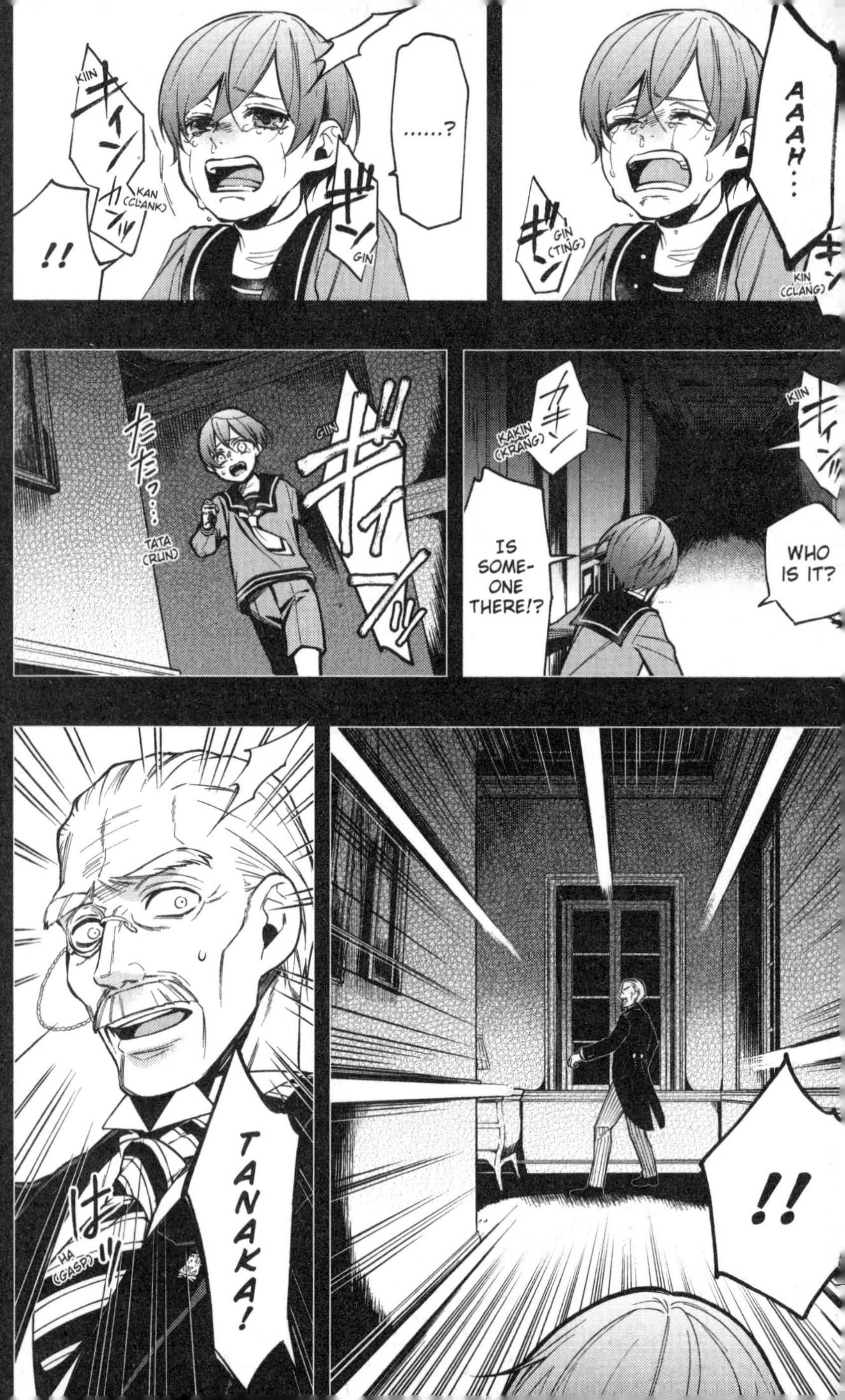

AAAH...
KIN (CLANG)
GIN (TING)
......?
KIIN
GIN
KAN (CLANK)
!!
KIIN
WHO IS IT?
KAKIN (KRANG)
IS SOME-ONE THERE!?
GIN
TATA (RUN)
!!
TANAKA!
HA (GASP)

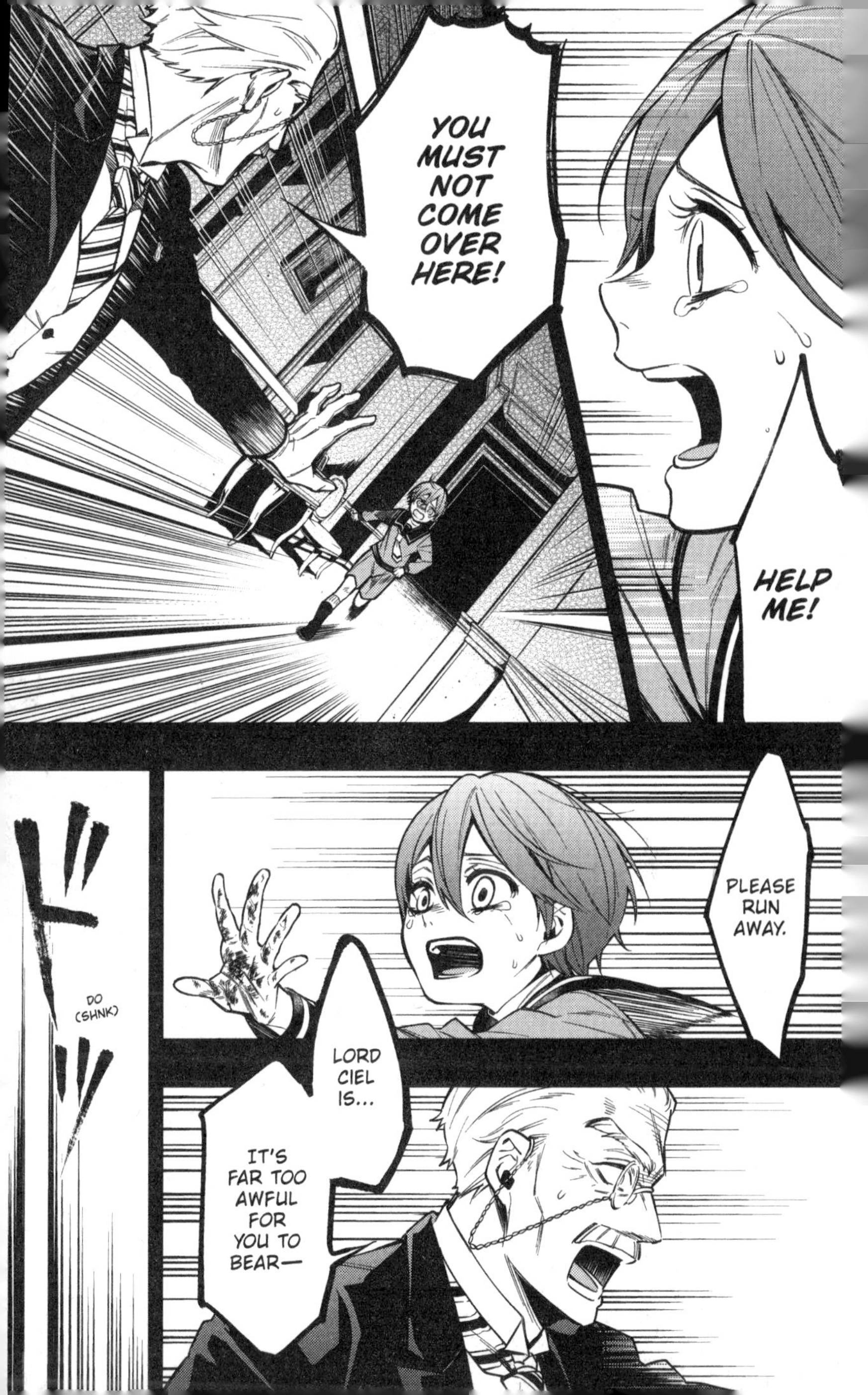
YOU MUST NOT COME OVER HERE!
HELP ME!
PLEASE RUN AWAY.
LORD CIEL IS...
IT'S FAR TOO AWFUL FOR YOU TO BEAR—
DO (SHNK)

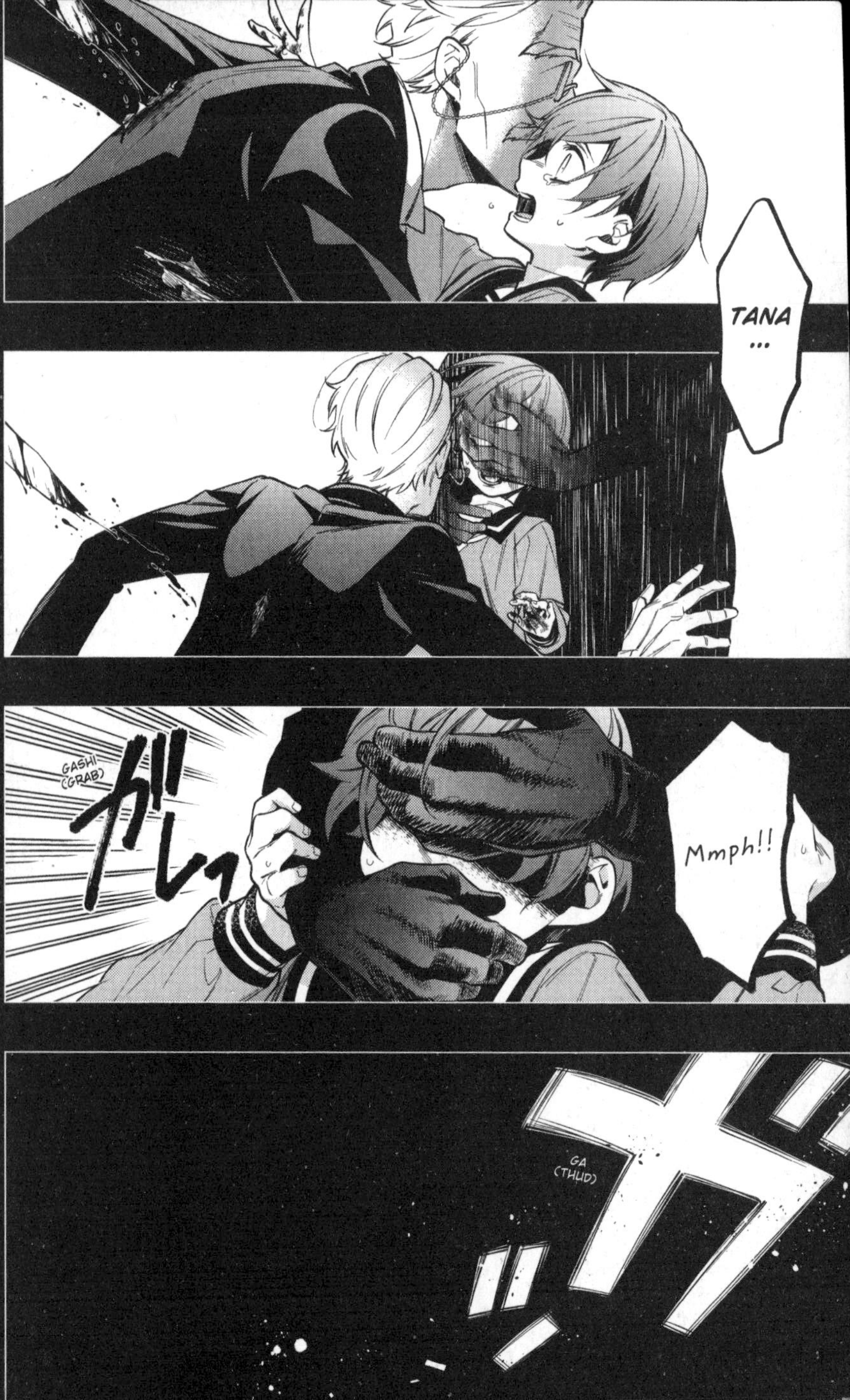
TANA
...
GASHI
(GRAB)
Mmph!!
GA
(THUD)

Black Butler

Chapter 135

# *At noon : The Butler, Presenting*

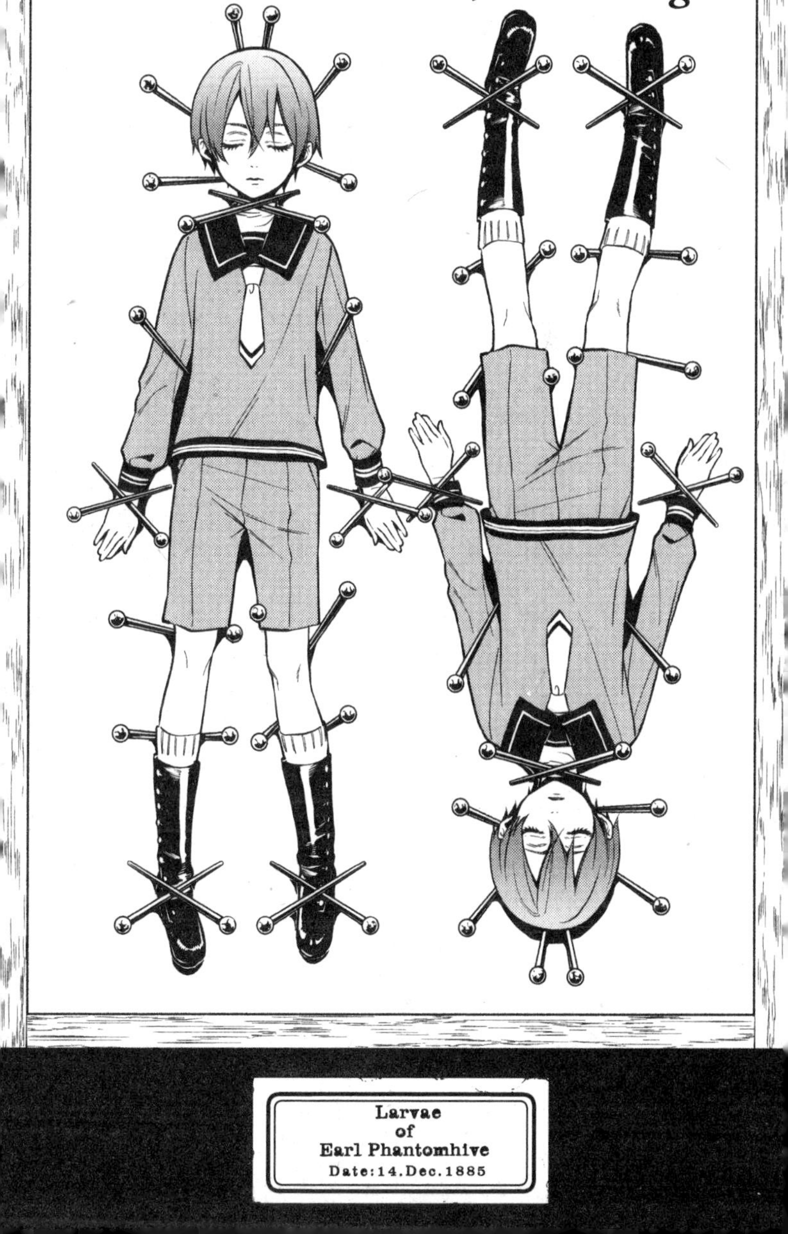

Larvae
of
Earl Phantomhive
Date:14.Dec.1885

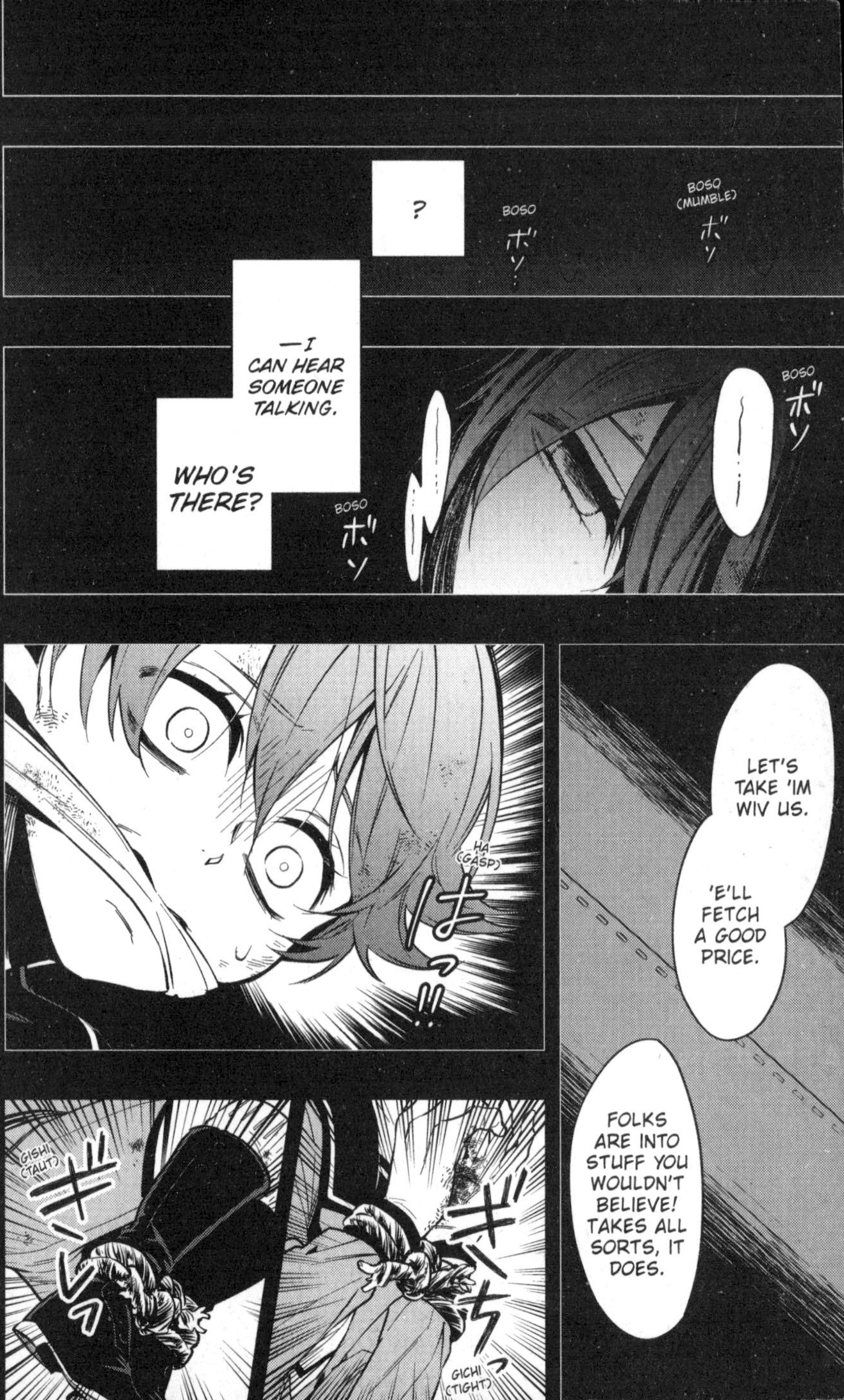
BOSO (MUMBLE)
ボソ
BOSO
ボソ
?
BOSO
ボソ
—I CAN HEAR SOMEONE TALKING.
WHO'S THERE?
BOSO
ボソ
LET'S TAKE 'IM WIV US.
'E'LL FETCH A GOOD PRICE.
FOLKS ARE INTO STUFF YOU WOULDN'T BELIEVE! TAKES ALL SORTS, IT DOES.
HA (GASP)
はっ!!
GICHI (TIGHT)
GISHI (TAUT)

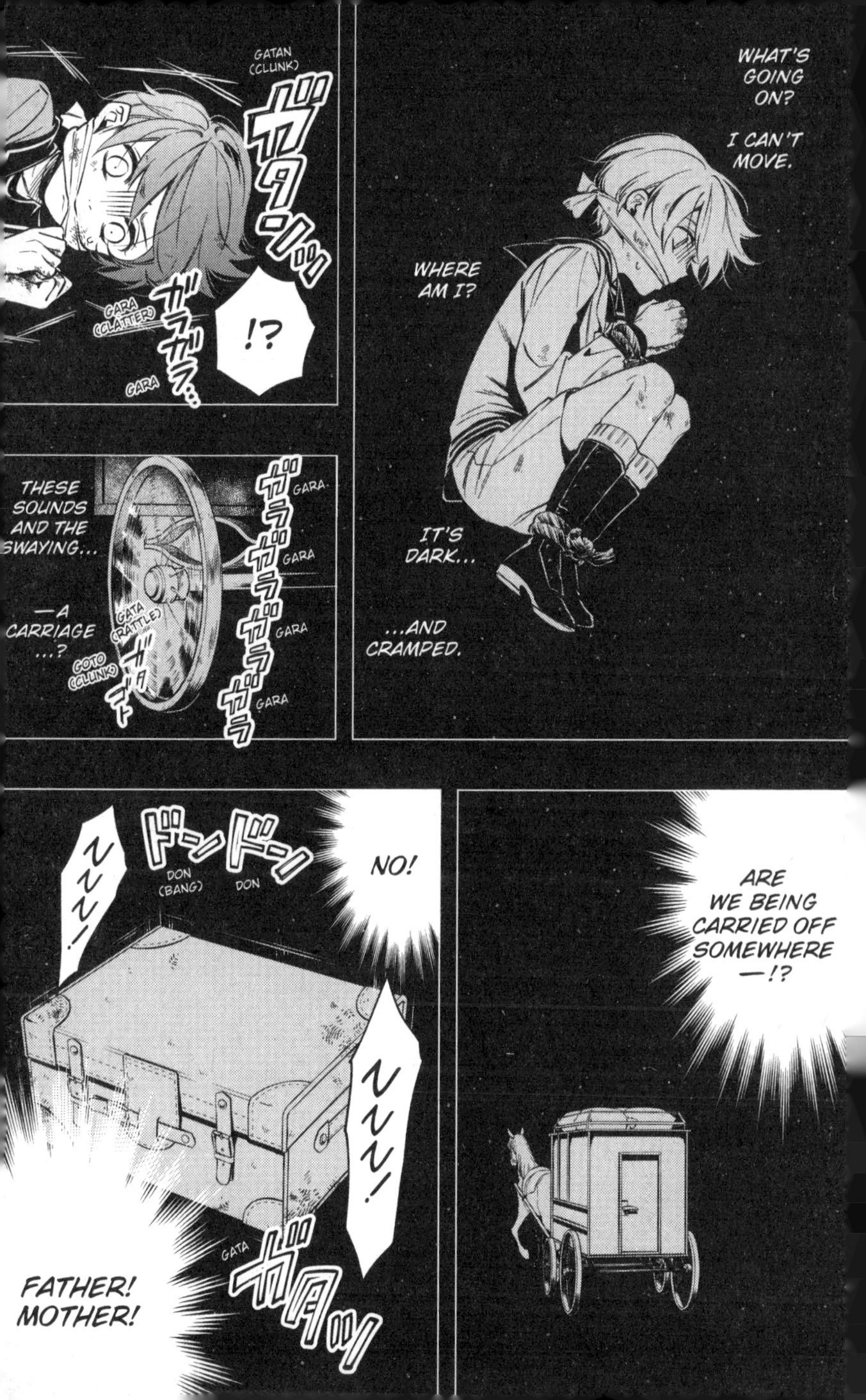
WHAT'S GOING ON?
I CAN'T MOVE.
WHERE AM I?
IT'S DARK...
...AND CRAMPED.
ガタンッ
GATAN (CLUNK)
!?
ガラガラ…
GARA (CLATTER)
GARA
THESE SOUNDS AND THE SWAYING...
ガラガラガラガラ
GARA
GARA
GARA
GARA
—A CARRIAGE ...?
GATA (RATTLE)
GOTO (CLUNK)
ARE WE BEING CARRIED OFF SOMEWHERE —!?
NO!
ドンドン
DON (BANG)
DON
NNNN!
NNNN!
ガタッ
GATA
FATHER! MOTHER!

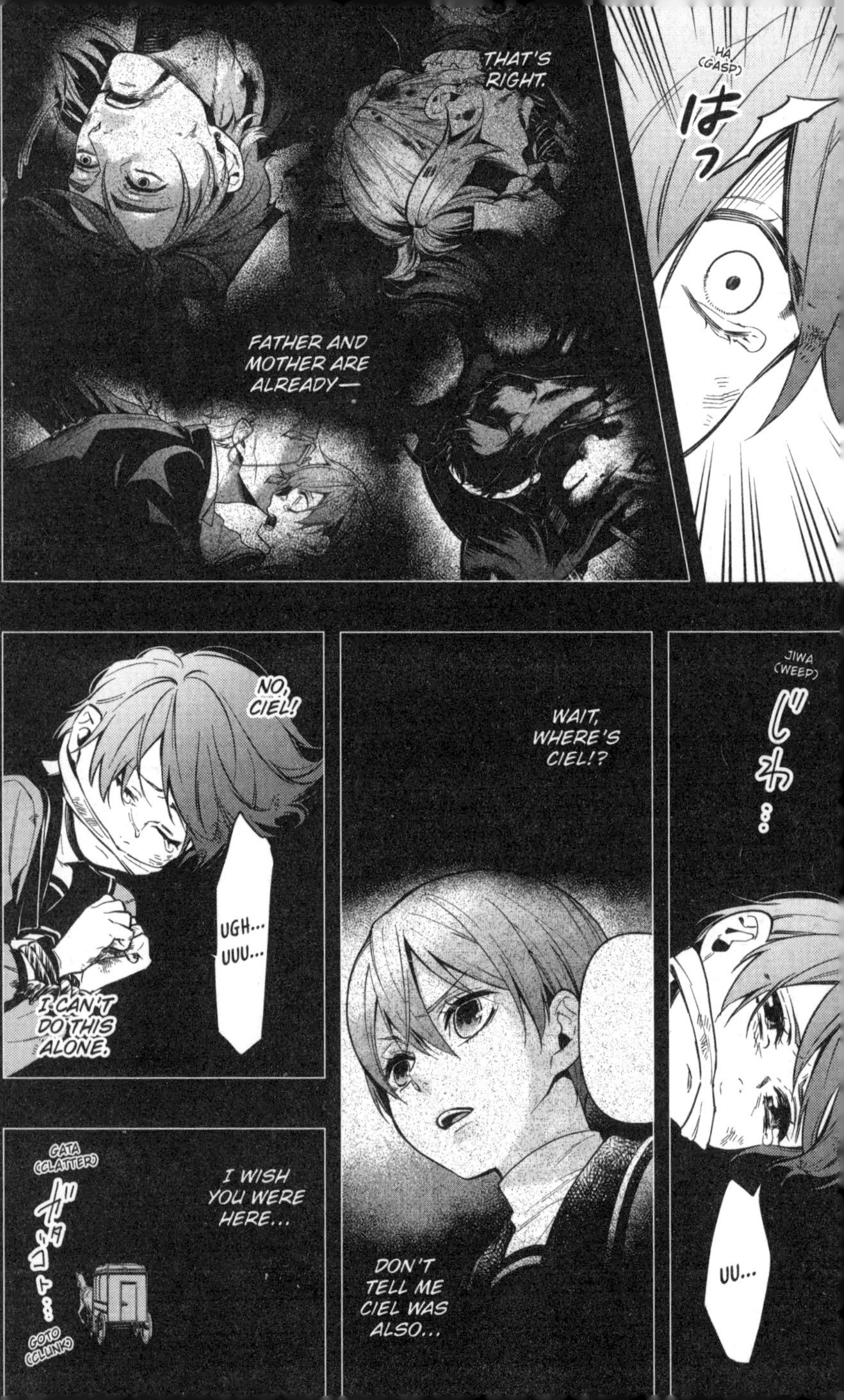
HA (GASP)
はっ
THAT'S RIGHT.
FATHER AND MOTHER ARE ALREADY—
JIWA (WEEP)
じわ…
UU...
WAIT, WHERE'S CIEL!?
DON'T TELL ME CIEL WAS ALSO...
NO, CIEL!
UGH... UUU...
I CAN'T DO THIS ALONE.
GATA (CLATTER)
ガタゴト…
GOTO (CLUNK)
I WISH YOU WERE HERE...

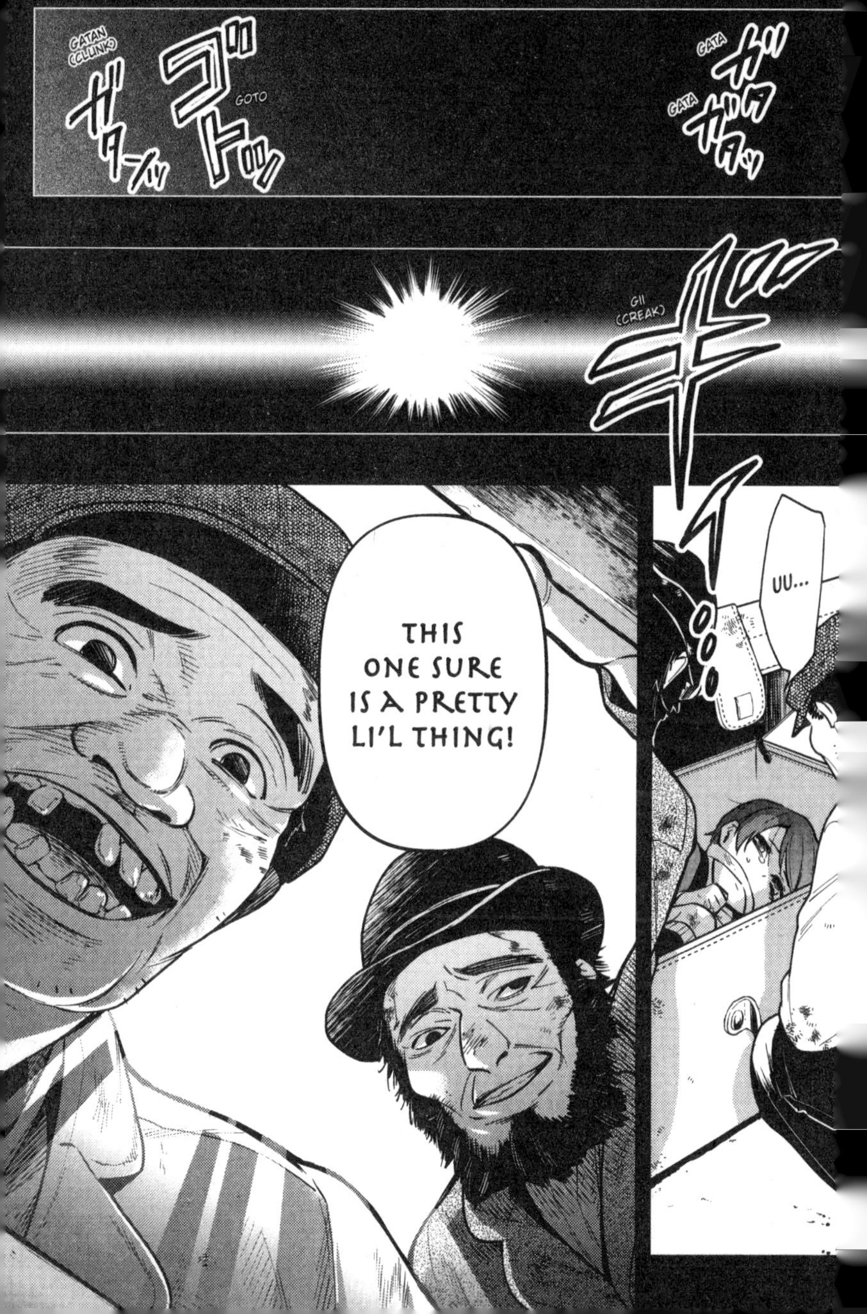
GATA
GATA
GATAN (CLUNK)
GOTO
GII (CREAK)
UU...
THIS ONE SURE IS A PRETTY LI'L THING!

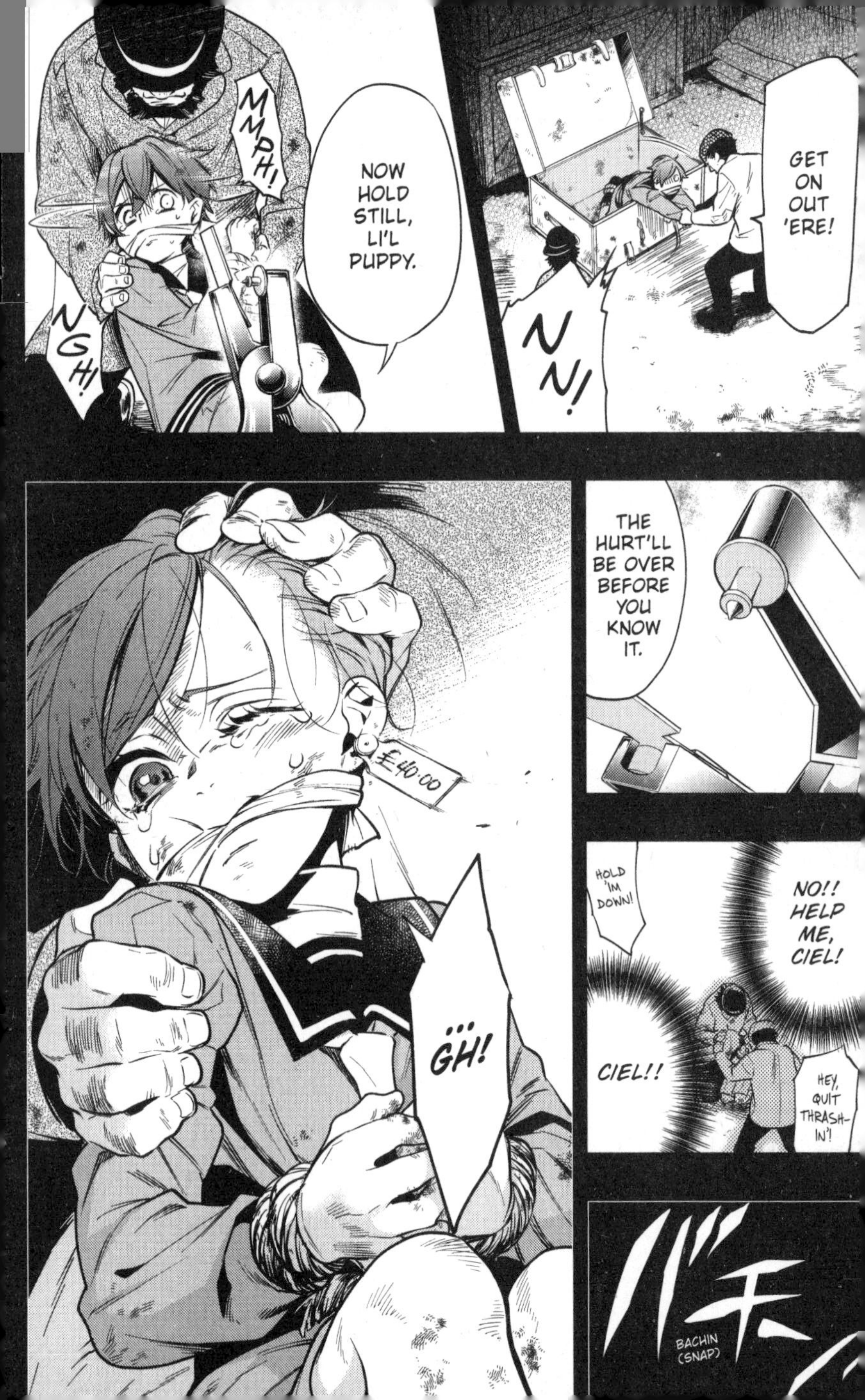
GET ON OUT 'ERE!
NN!
NOW HOLD STILL, LI'L PUPPY.
MMPH!
NGH!
THE HURT'LL BE OVER BEFORE YOU KNOW IT.
NO!! HELP ME, CIEL!
HOLD 'IM DOWN!
CIEL!!
HEY, QUIT THRASHIN'!
BACHIN (SNAP)
£40·00
...GH!

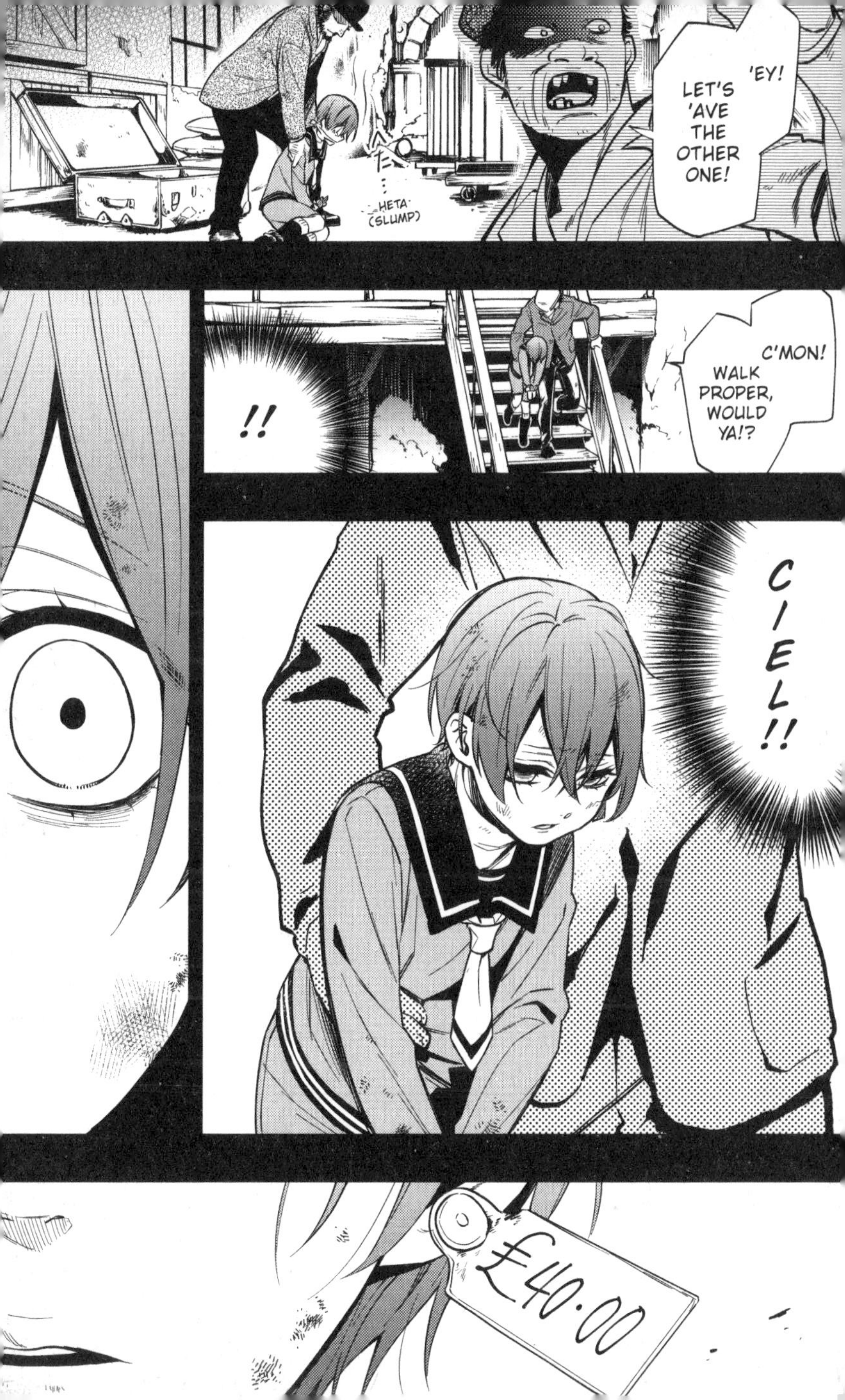
'EY! LET'S 'AVE THE OTHER ONE!
HETA (SLUMP)
C'MON! WALK PROPER, WOULD YA!?
!!
CIEL!!
£40.00

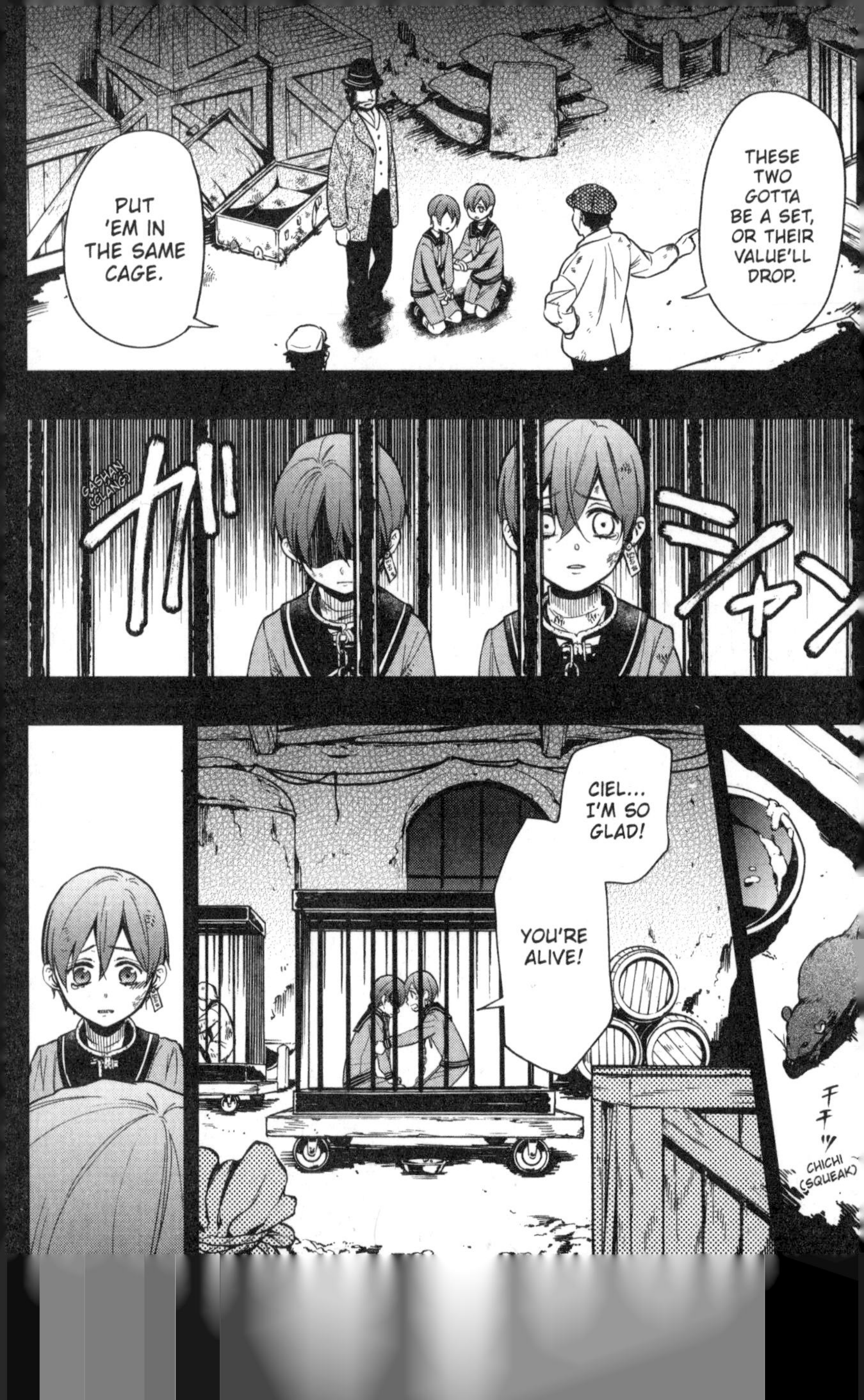
THESE TWO GOTTA BE A SET, OR THEIR VALUE'LL DROP.
PUT 'EM IN THE SAME CAGE.
ガシャン
GASHAN (CLANG)
チチッ
CHICHI (SQUEAK)
CIEL... I'M SO GLAD!
YOU'RE ALIVE!

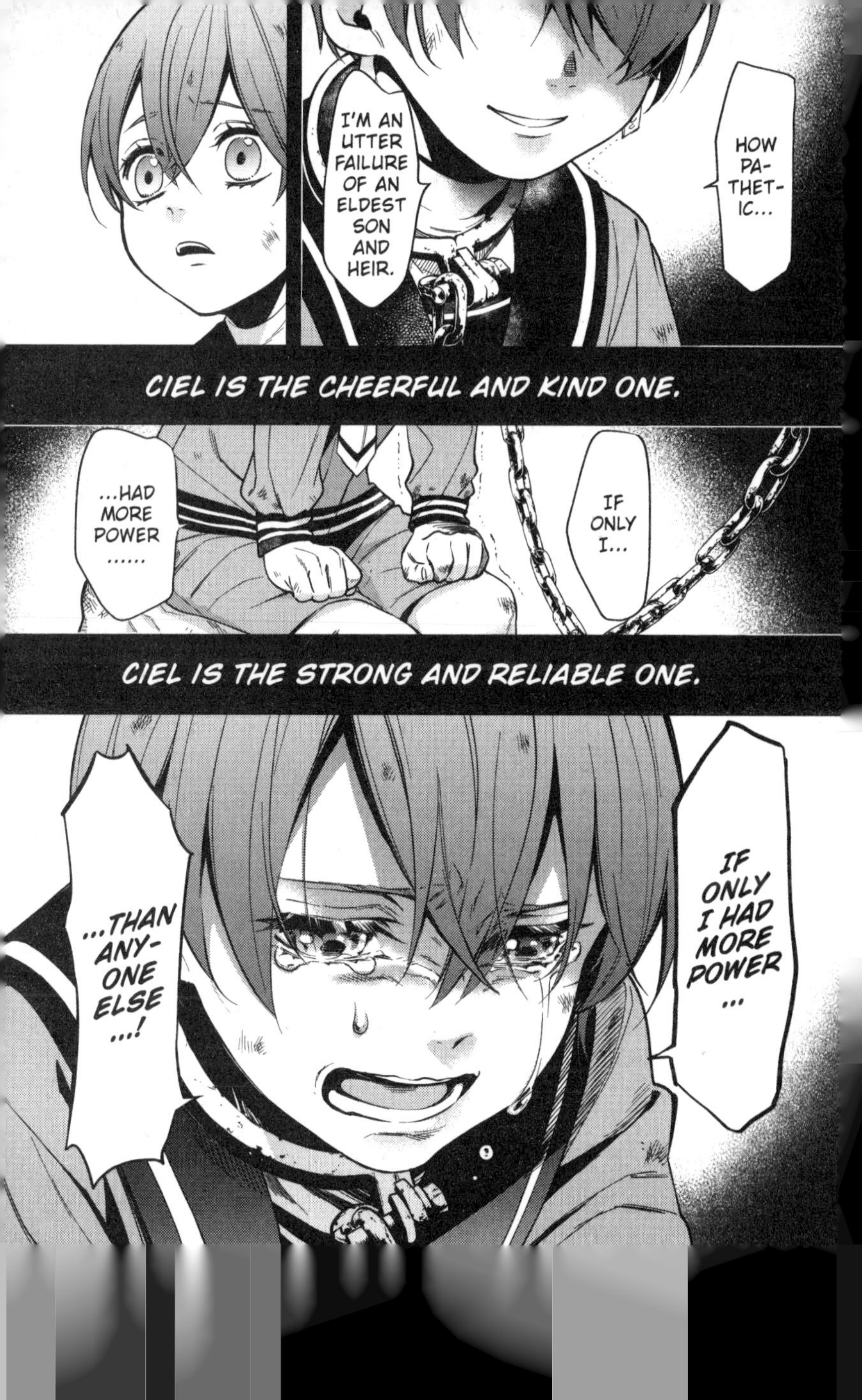
HOW PATHETIC...
I'M AN UTTER FAILURE OF AN ELDEST SON AND HEIR.
CIEL IS THE CHEERFUL AND KIND ONE.
IF ONLY I...
...HAD MORE POWER......
CIEL IS THE STRONG AND RELIABLE ONE.
IF ONLY I HAD MORE POWER...
...THAN ANYONE ELSE...!

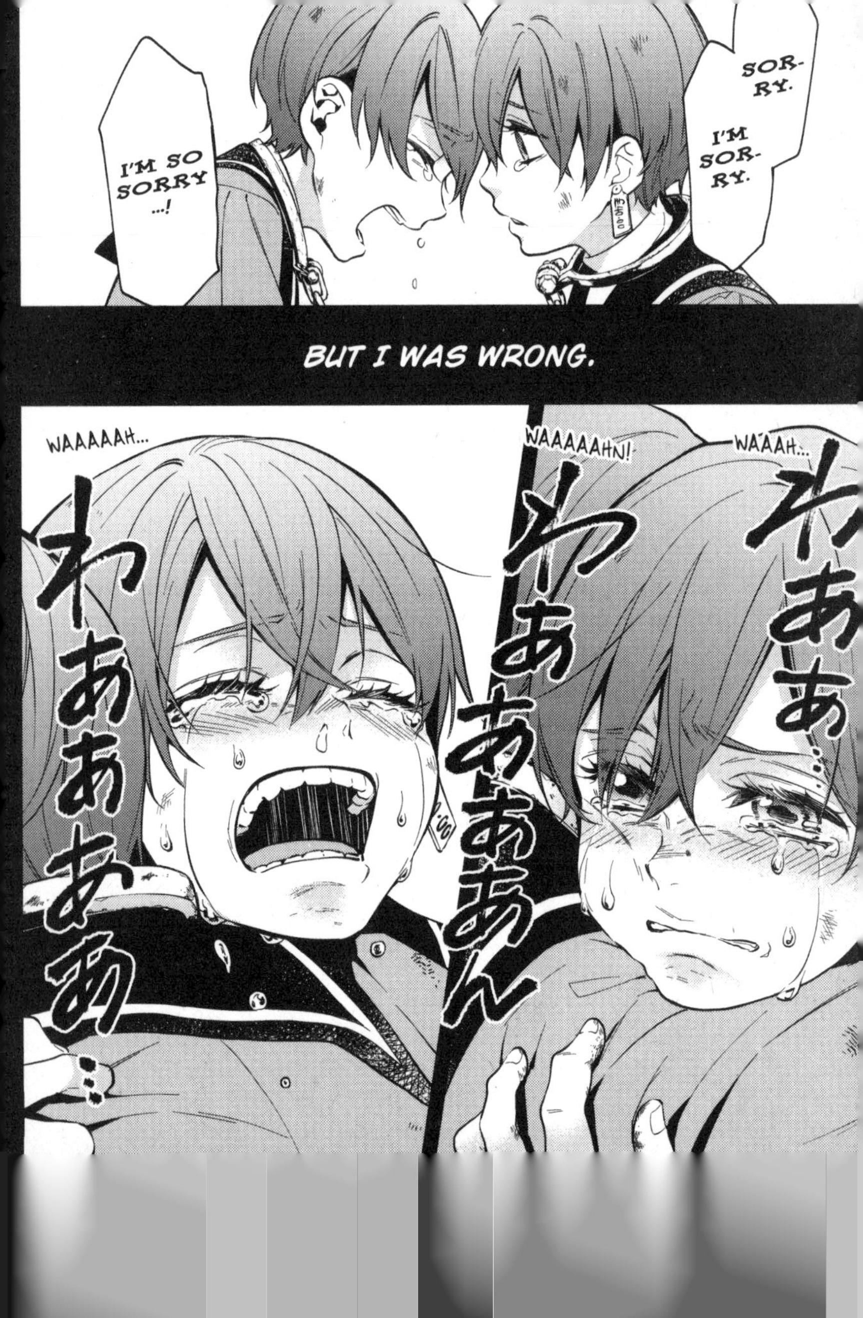
SORRY. I'M SORRY.
I'M SO SORRY...!
BUT I WAS WRONG.
WAAAH...
わああ…
WAAAAAHN!
わあああん
WAAAAAH...
わああああ…

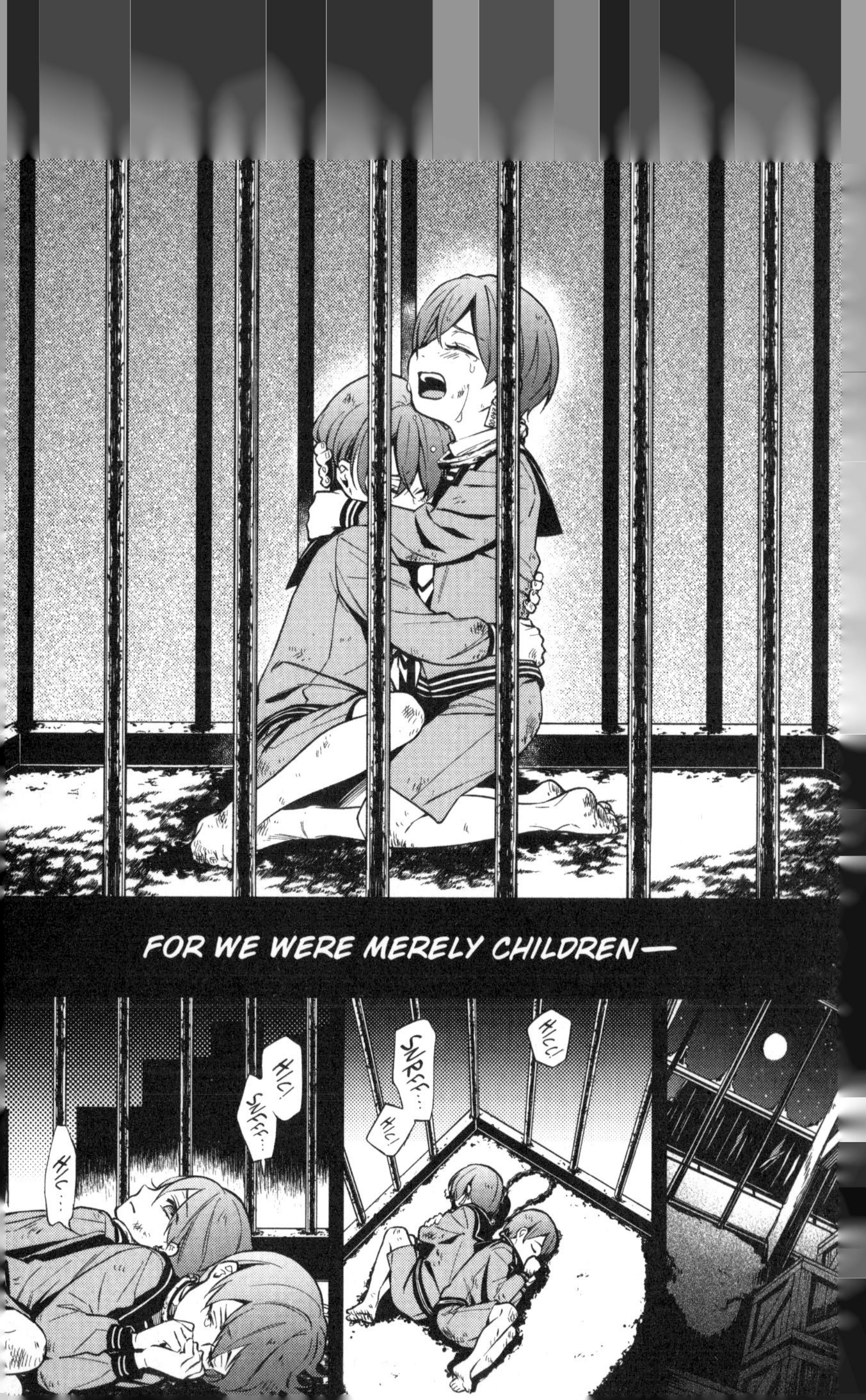
FOR WE WERE MERELY CHILDREN—
HIC!
SNRFF...
HIC!
HIC!
SNFF...
HIC...

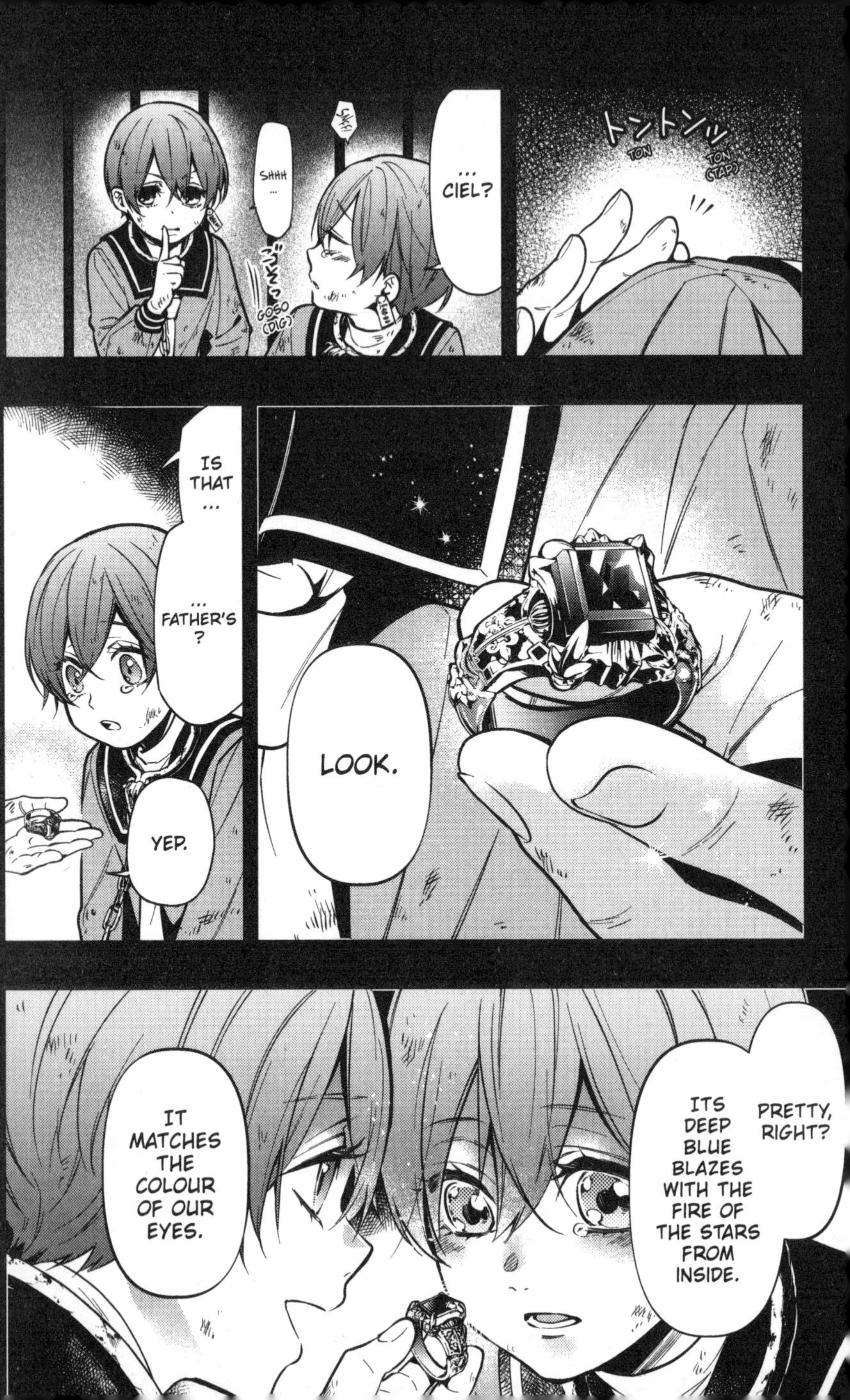
トントンッ
TON TON (TAP)
... CIEL?
SHHH ...
GOSO (DIG)
LOOK.
IS THAT ...
... FATHER'S ?
YEP.
PRETTY, RIGHT?
ITS DEEP BLUE BLAZES WITH THE FIRE OF THE STARS FROM INSIDE.
IT MATCHES THE COLOUR OF OUR EYES.

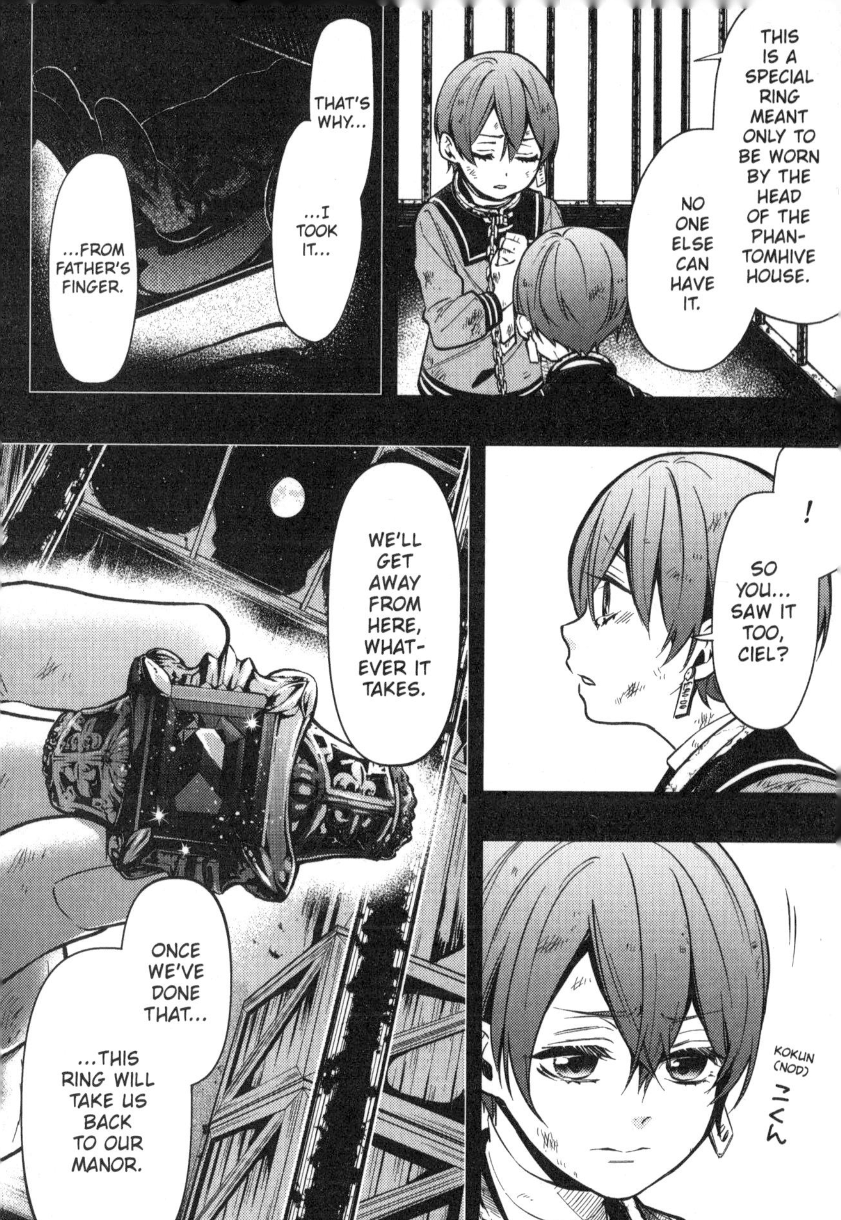
THIS IS A SPECIAL RING MEANT ONLY TO BE WORN BY THE HEAD OF THE PHANTOMHIVE HOUSE.
NO ONE ELSE CAN HAVE IT.
THAT'S WHY...
...I TOOK IT...
...FROM FATHER'S FINGER.
!
SO YOU... SAW IT TOO, CIEL?
KOKUN (NOD)
WE'LL GET AWAY FROM HERE, WHATEVER IT TAKES.
ONCE WE'VE DONE THAT...
...THIS RING WILL TAKE US BACK TO OUR MANOR.

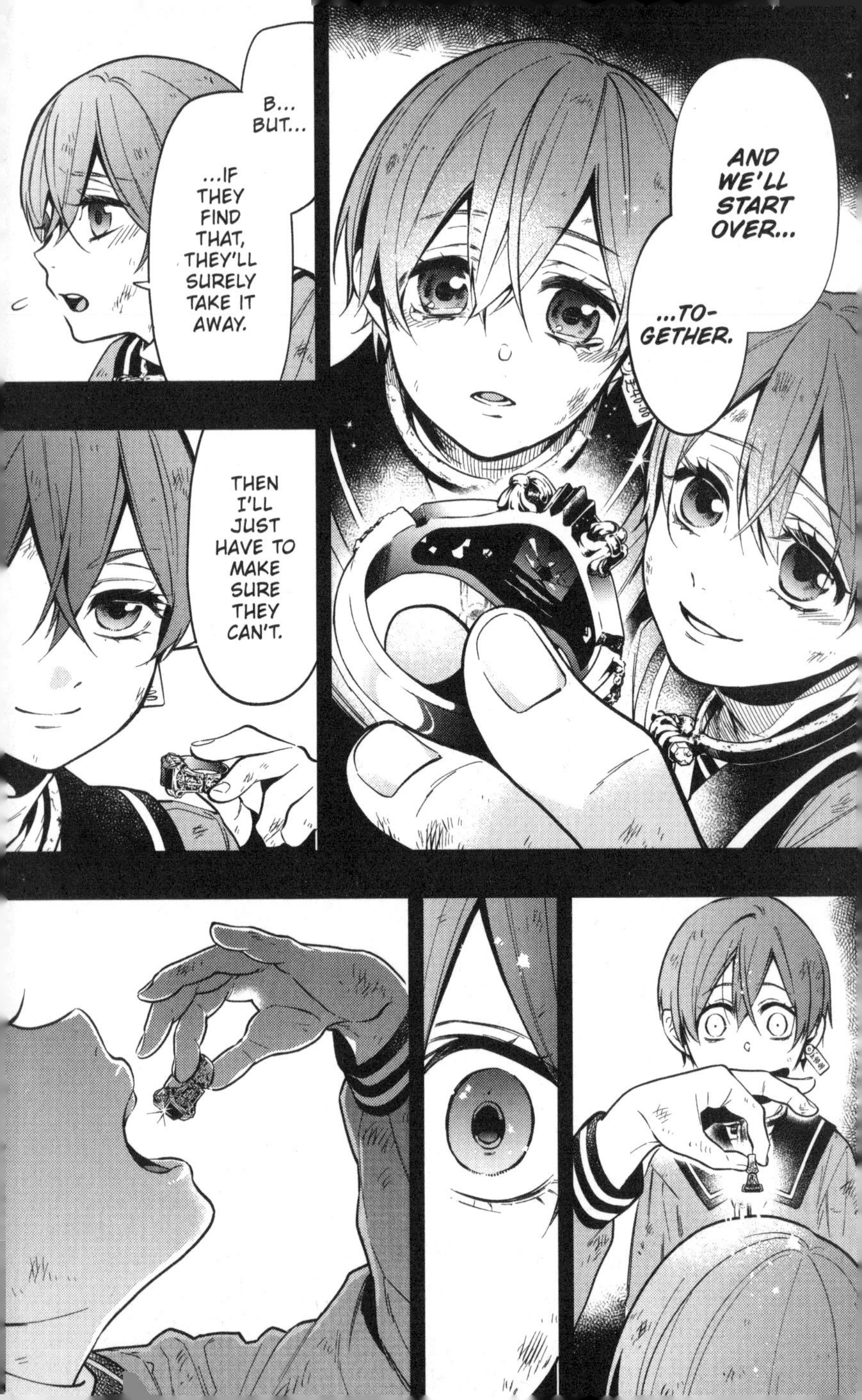
AND WE'LL START OVER...
...TO-GETHER.
B... BUT...
...IF THEY FIND THAT, THEY'LL SURELY TAKE IT AWAY.
THEN I'LL JUST HAVE TO MAKE SURE THEY CAN'T.

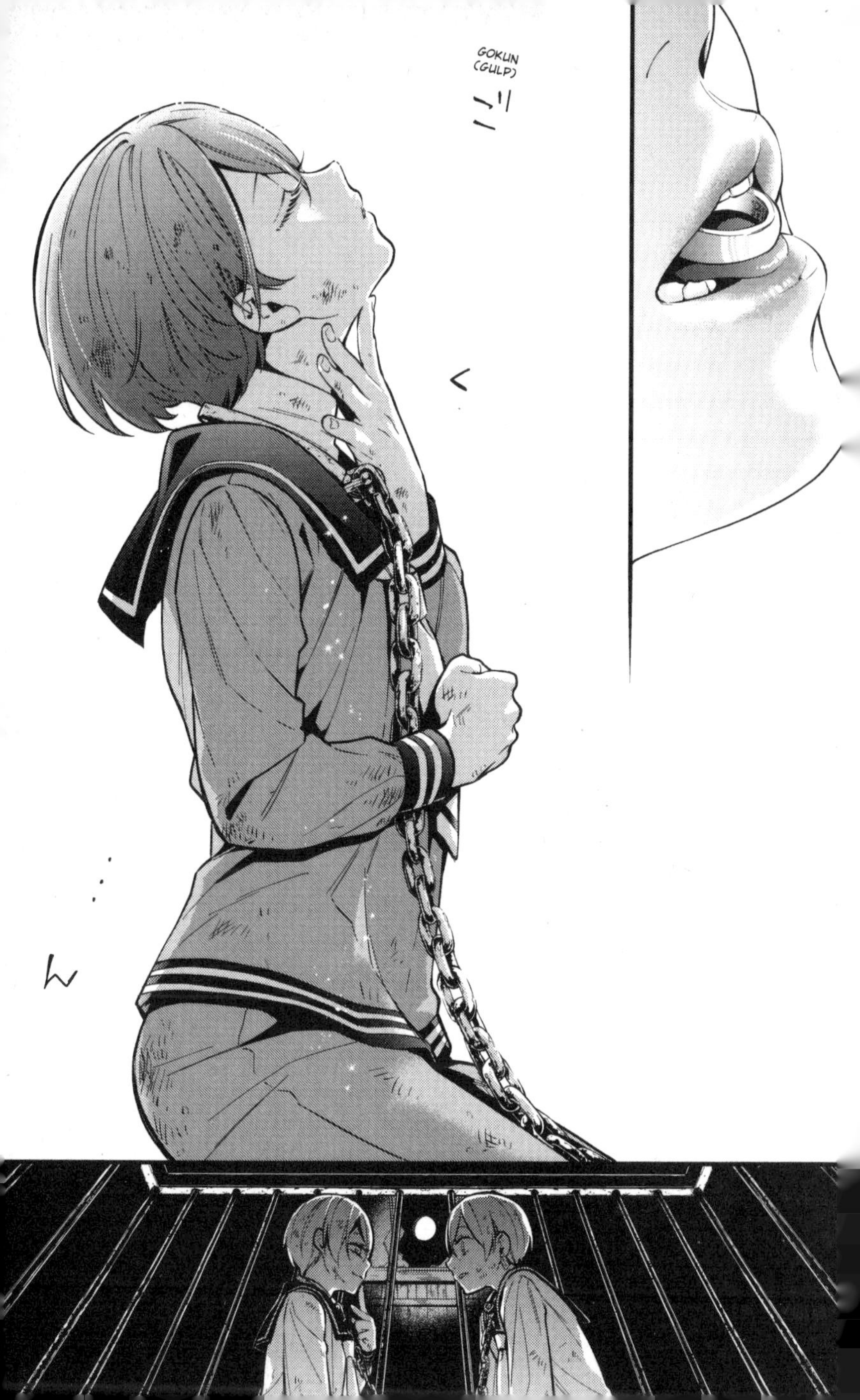
GOKUN
(GULP)

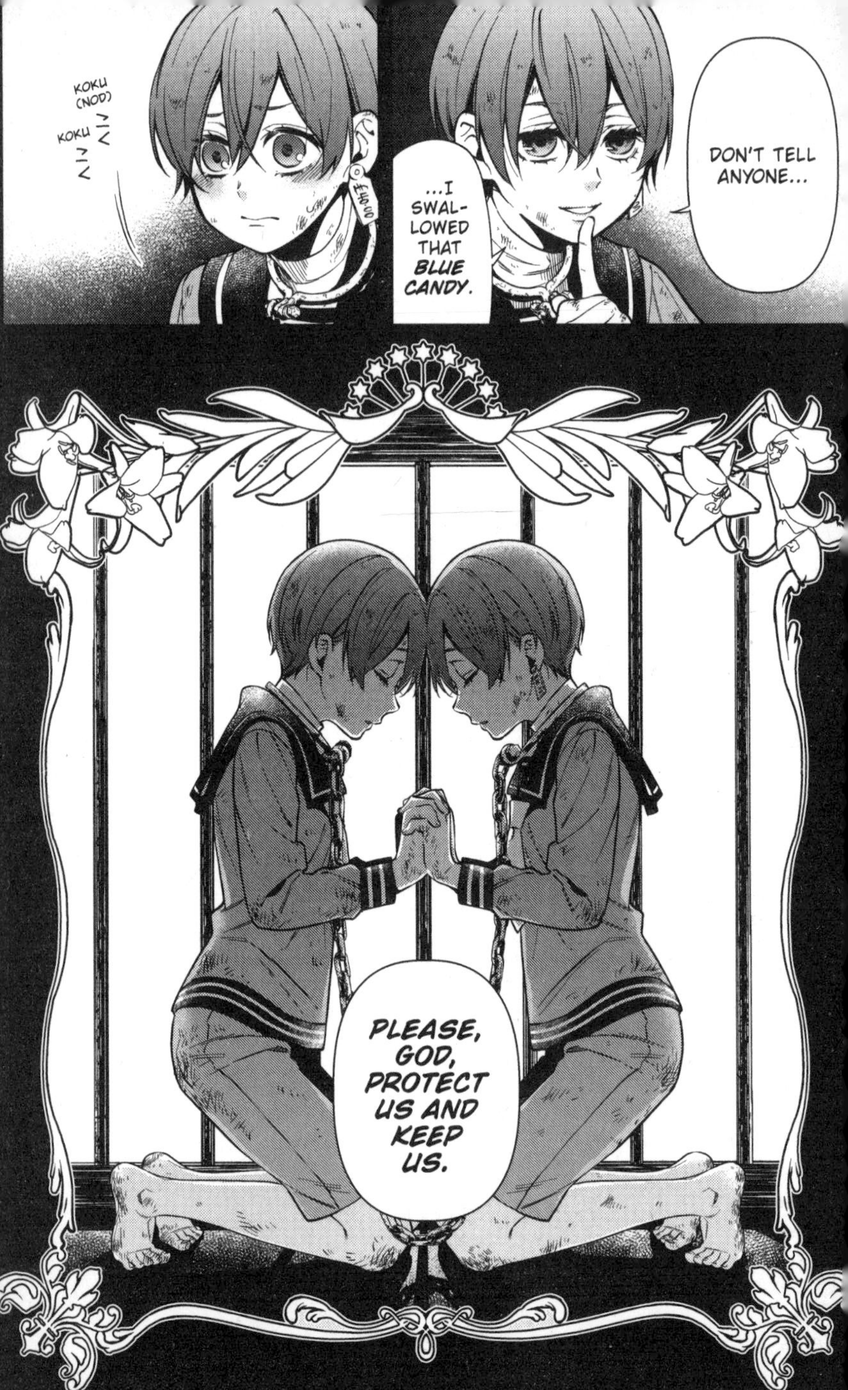
DON'T TELL ANYONE...
...I SWALLOWED THAT BLUE CANDY.
KOKU (NOD)
KOKU
PLEASE, GOD, PROTECT US AND KEEP US.

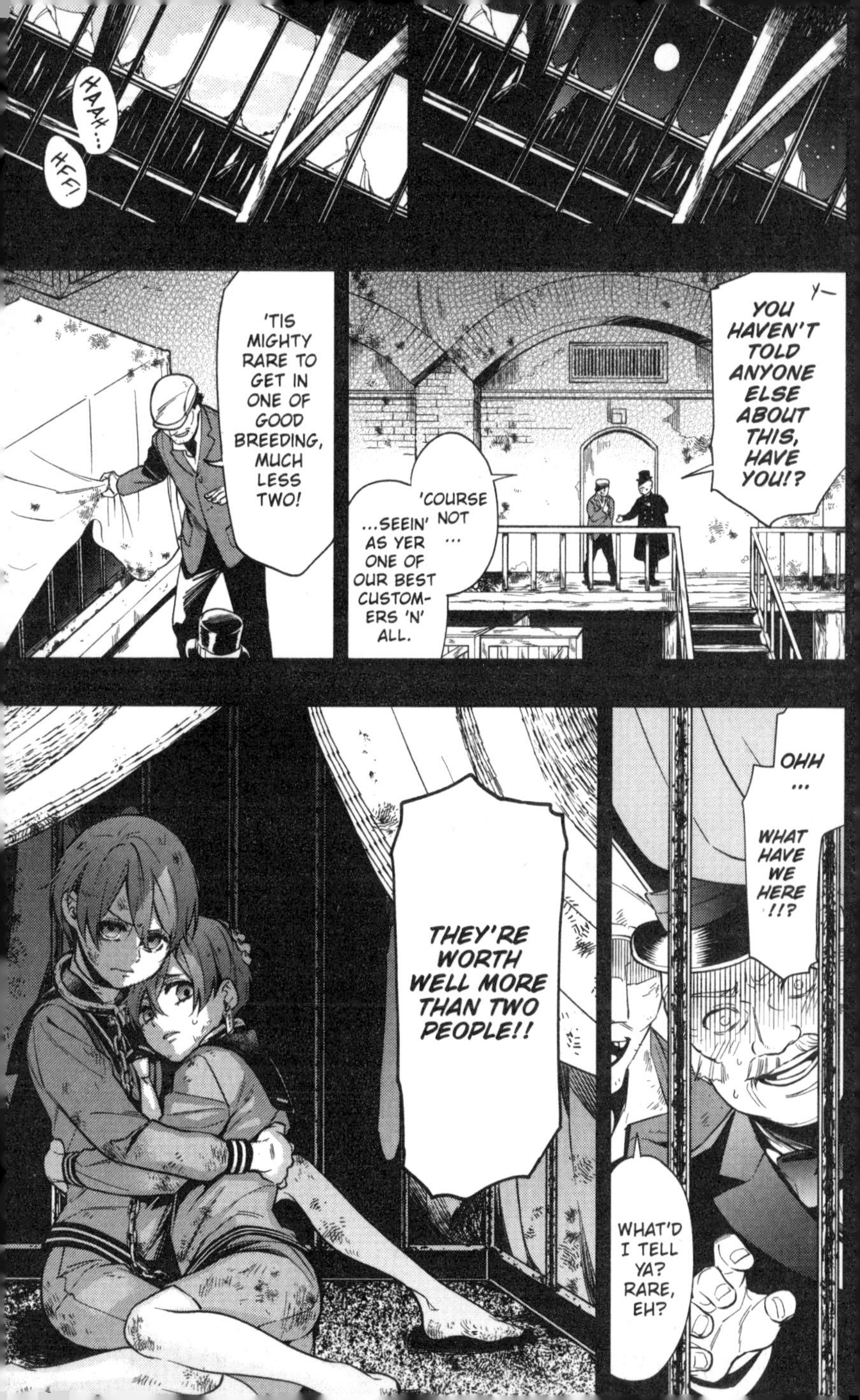
HAAH...
HFF!
Y—
YOU HAVEN'T TOLD ANYONE ELSE ABOUT THIS, HAVE YOU!?
'COURSE NOT ...
...SEEIN' AS YER ONE OF OUR BEST CUSTOMERS 'N' ALL.
'TIS MIGHTY RARE TO GET IN ONE OF GOOD BREEDING, MUCH LESS TWO!
OHH ...
WHAT HAVE WE HERE !!?
WHAT'D I TELL YA? RARE, EH?
THEY'RE WORTH WELL MORE THAN TWO PEOPLE!!

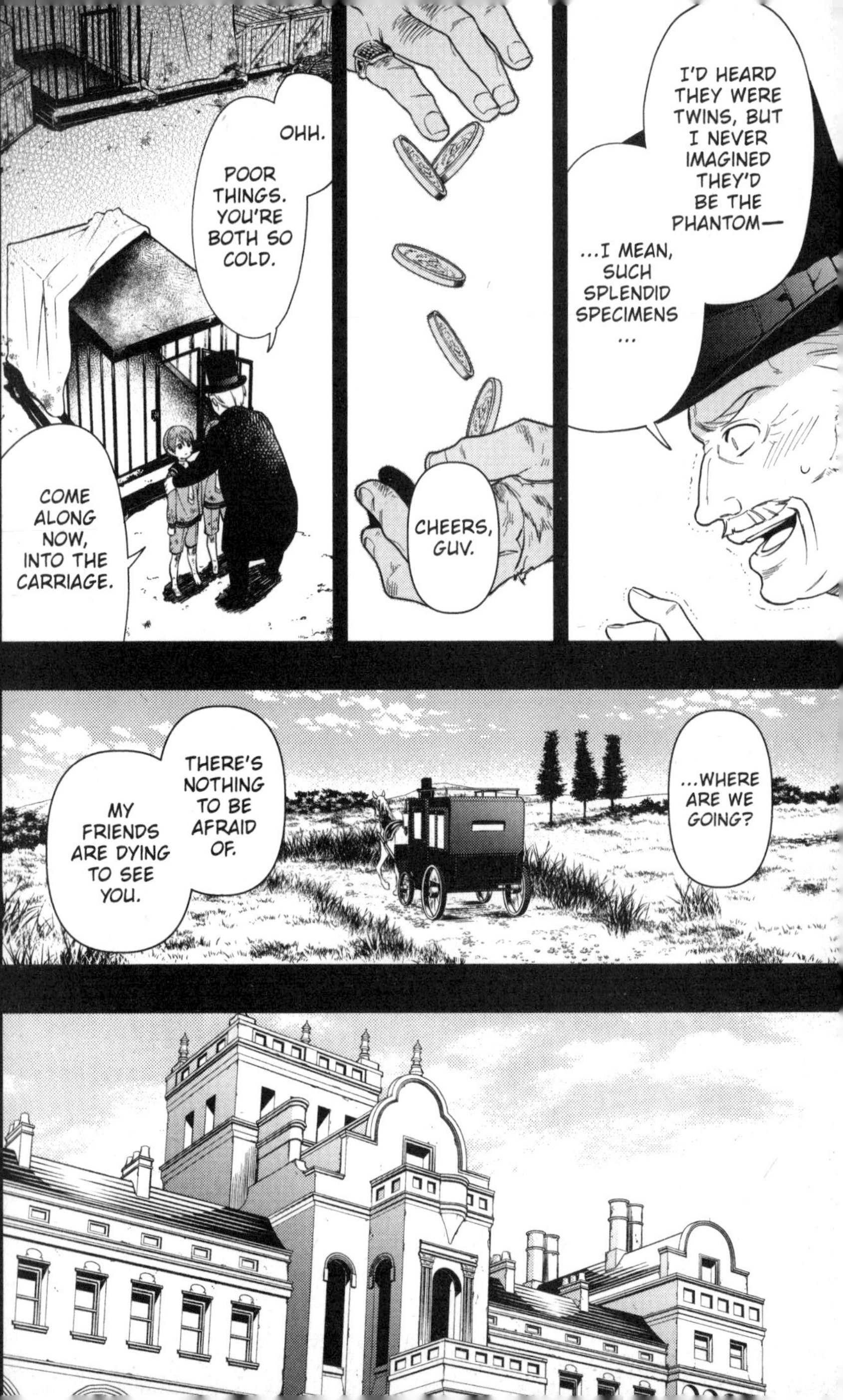
I'D HEARD THEY WERE TWINS, BUT I NEVER IMAGINED THEY'D BE THE PHANTOM—
...I MEAN, SUCH SPLENDID SPECIMENS...
CHEERS, GUV.
OHH.
POOR THINGS. YOU'RE BOTH SO COLD.
COME ALONG NOW, INTO THE CARRIAGE.
...WHERE ARE WE GOING?
THERE'S NOTHING TO BE AFRAID OF.
MY FRIENDS ARE DYING TO SEE YOU.

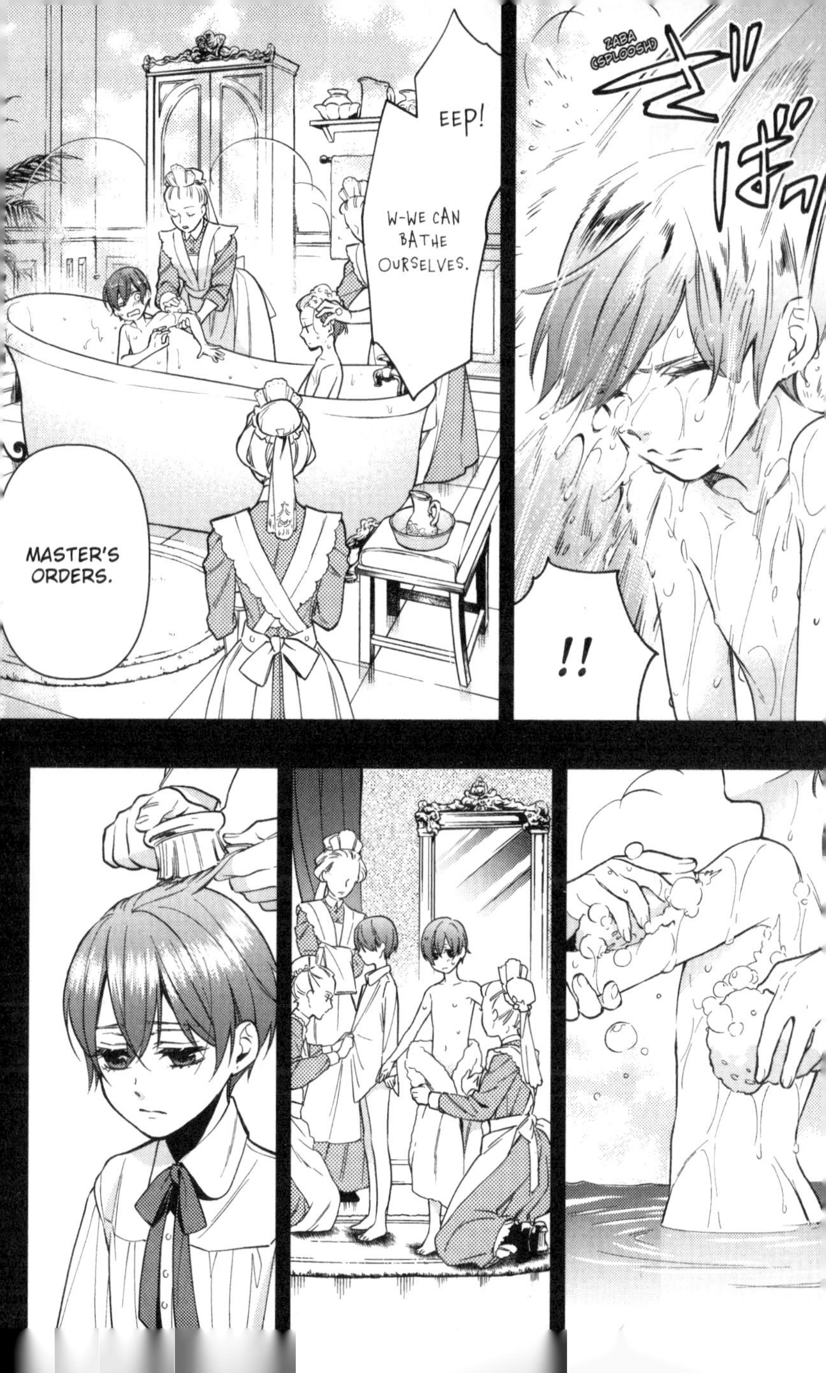
ZABA (SPLOOSH)
!!
EEP!
W-WE CAN BATHE OURSELVES.
MASTER'S ORDERS.

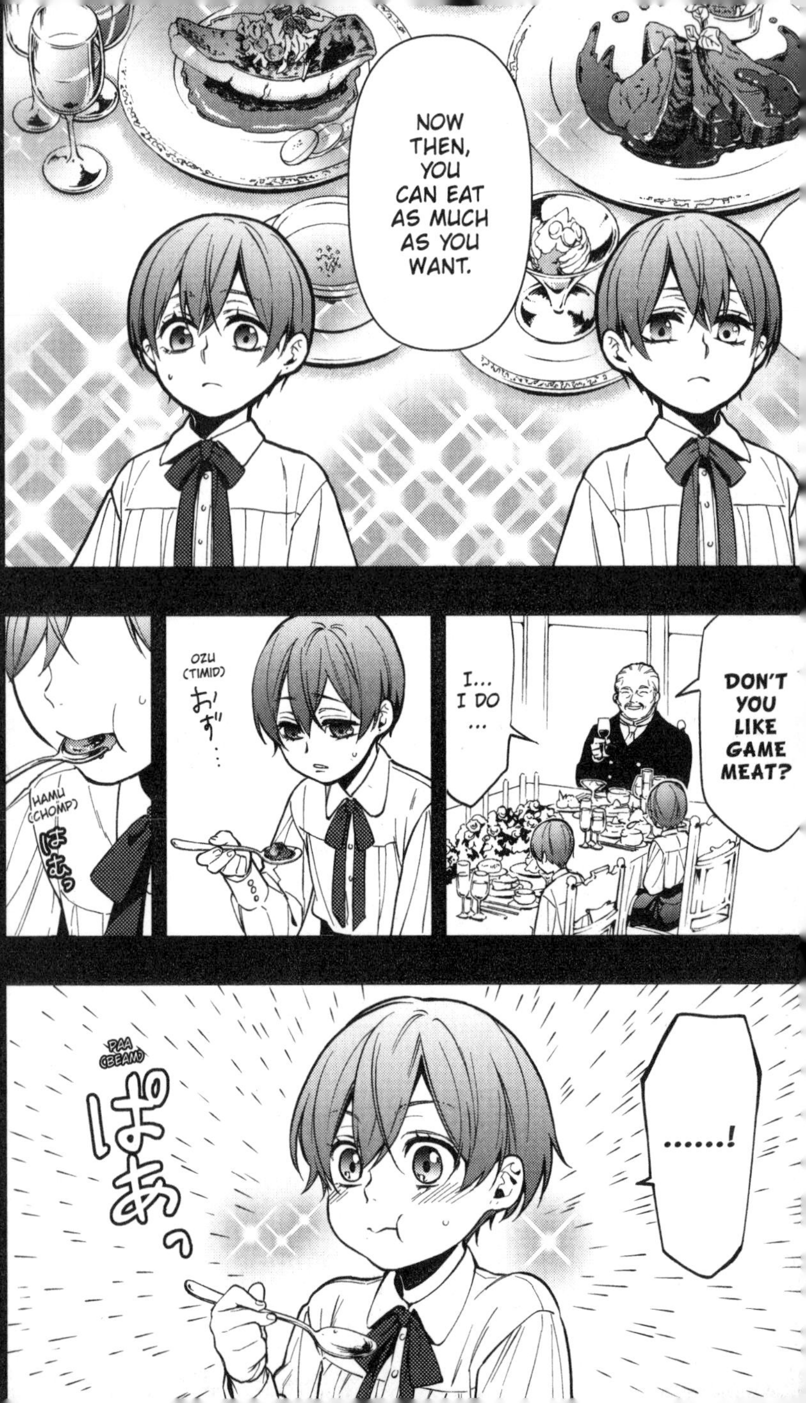
NOW THEN, YOU CAN EAT AS MUCH AS YOU WANT.
DON'T YOU LIKE GAME MEAT?
I... I DO ...
OZU (TIMID)
おず…
HAMU (CHOMP)
はむっ
......!
PAA (BEAM)
ぱあっ

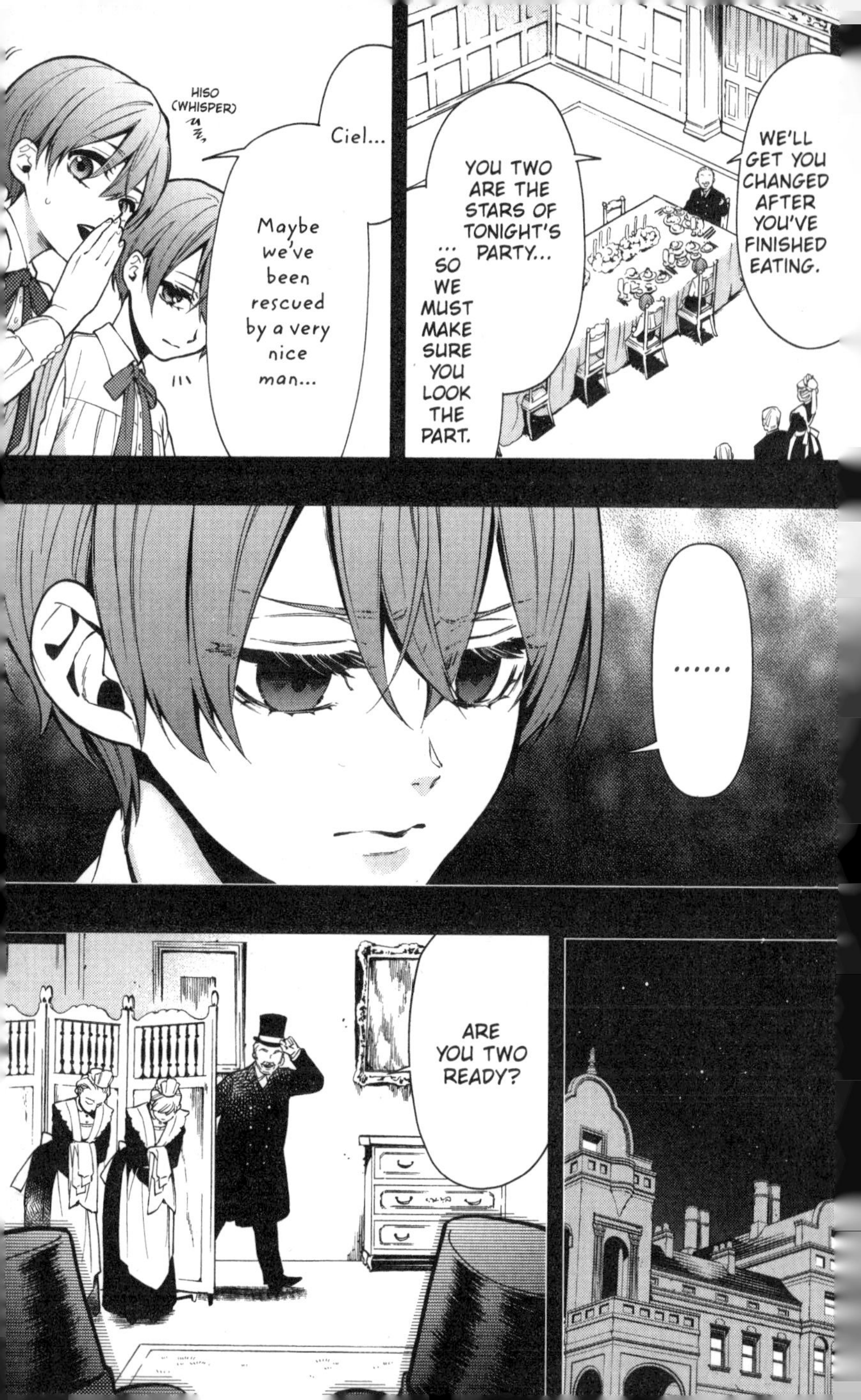
WE'LL GET YOU CHANGED AFTER YOU'VE FINISHED EATING.
YOU TWO ARE THE STARS OF TONIGHT'S PARTY...
...SO WE MUST MAKE SURE YOU LOOK THE PART.
HISO (WHISPER)
Ciel...
Maybe we've been rescued by a very nice man...
......
ARE YOU TWO READY?

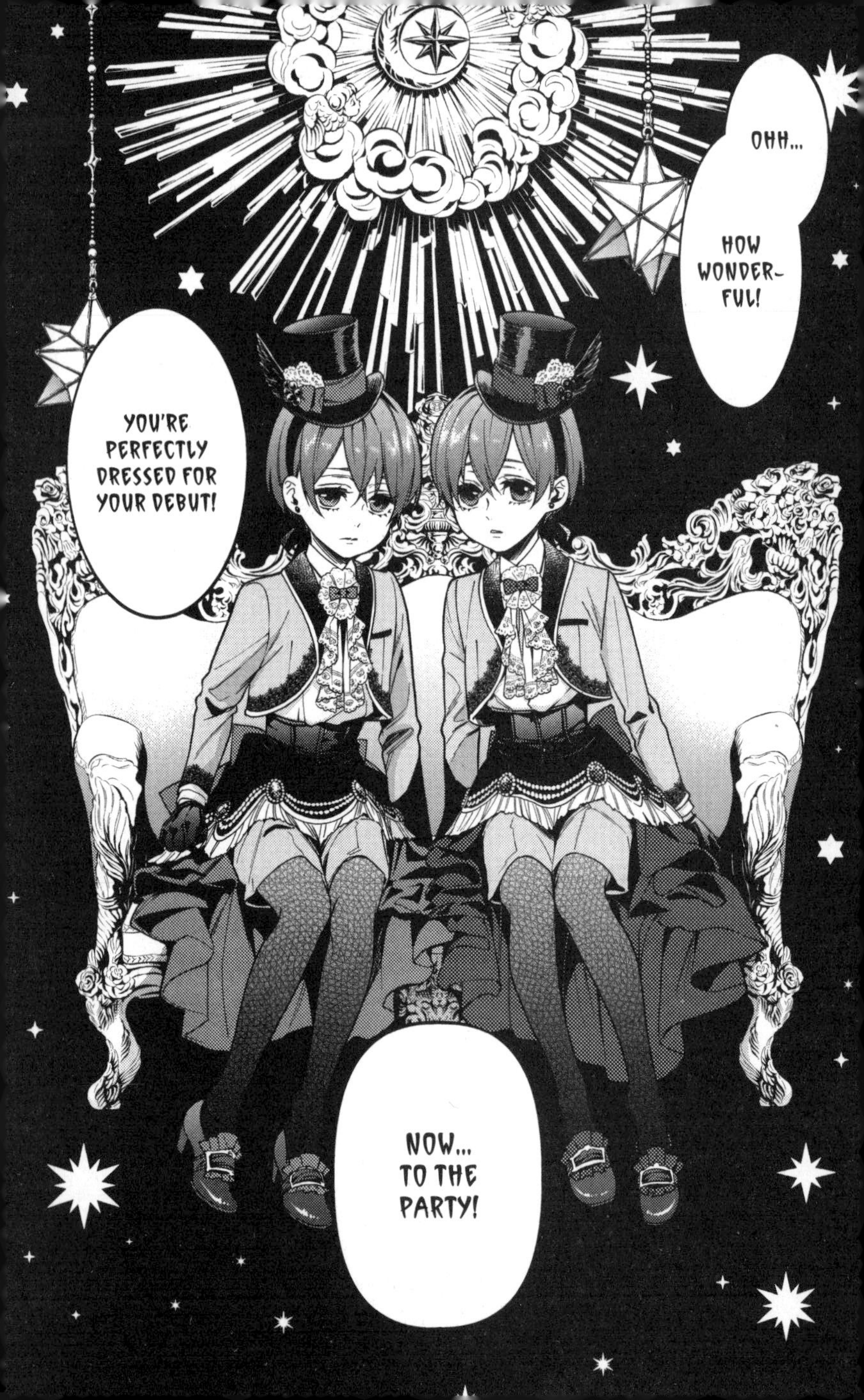
OHH...
HOW WONDER-FUL!
YOU'RE PERFECTLY DRESSED FOR YOUR DEBUT!
NOW... TO THE PARTY!

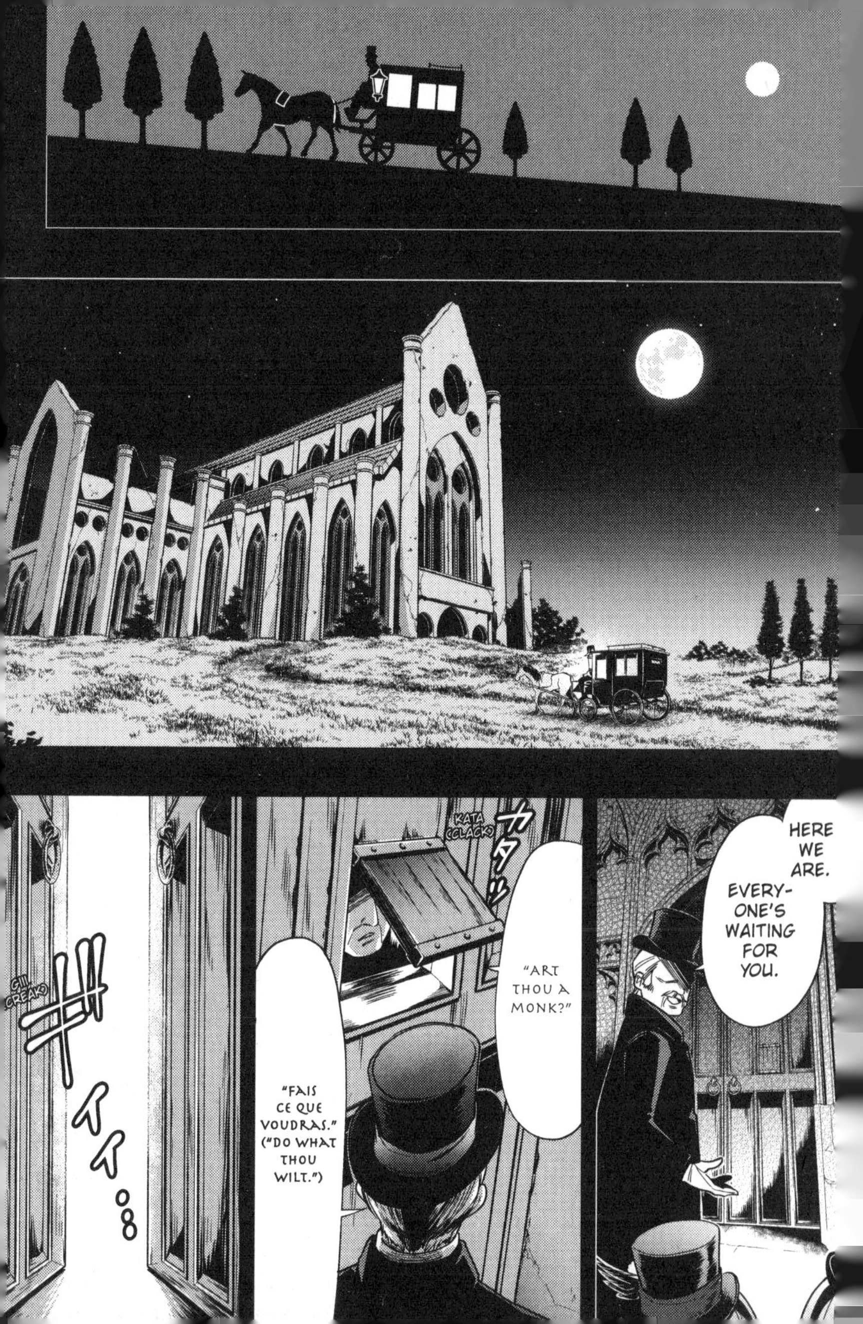
HERE WE ARE. EVERY-ONE'S WAITING FOR YOU.
KATA (CLACK)
カタッ
"ART THOU A MONK?"
"FAIS CE QUE VOUDRAS." ("DO WHAT THOU WILT.")
GIII (CREAK)
ギイイ。。

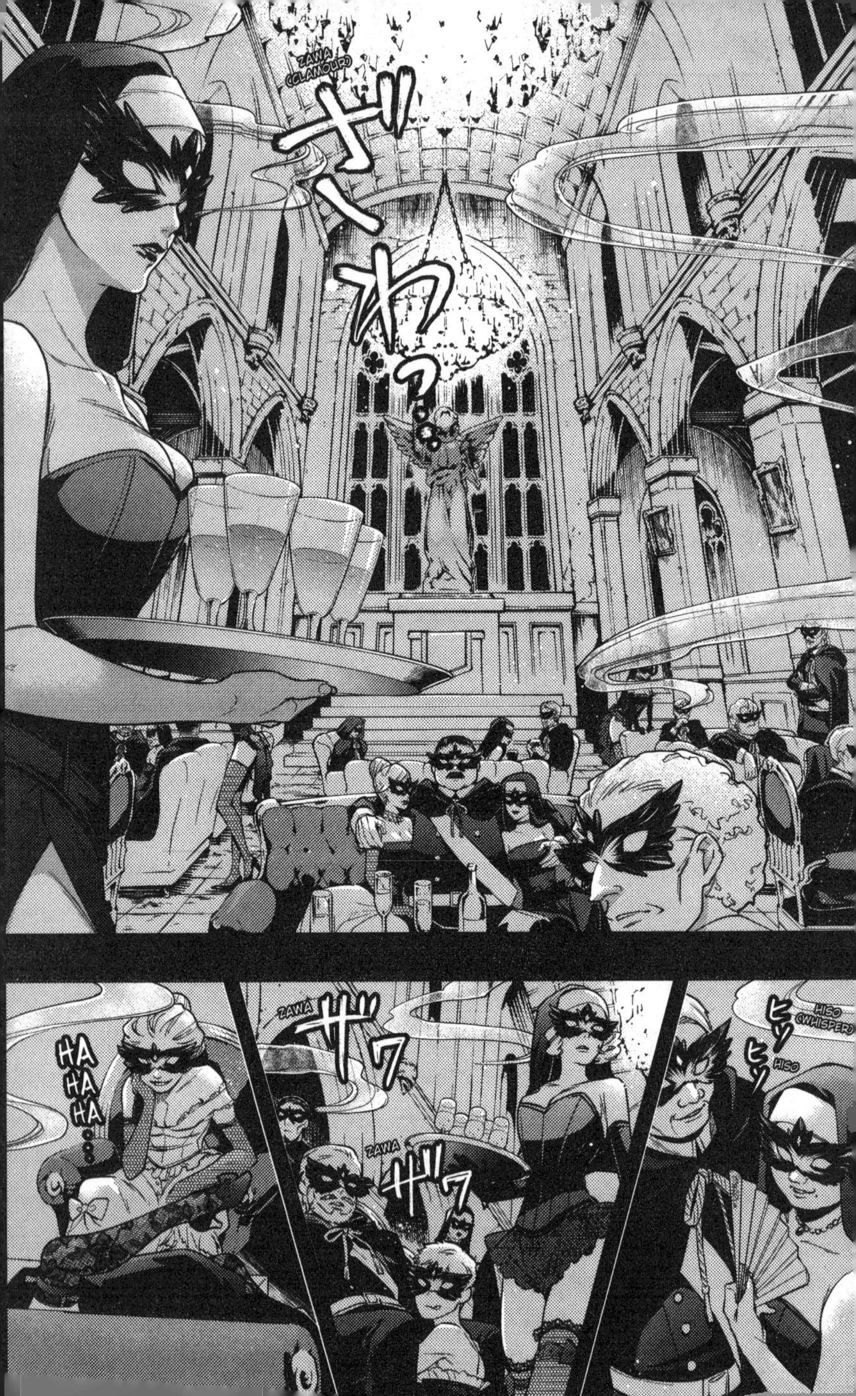
ZAWA (CLAMOUR)
ザわァ…
HISO (WHISPER)
ヒソ
HISO
ヒソ
ZAWA
ザワ
ZAWA
ザワ
HA HA HA…

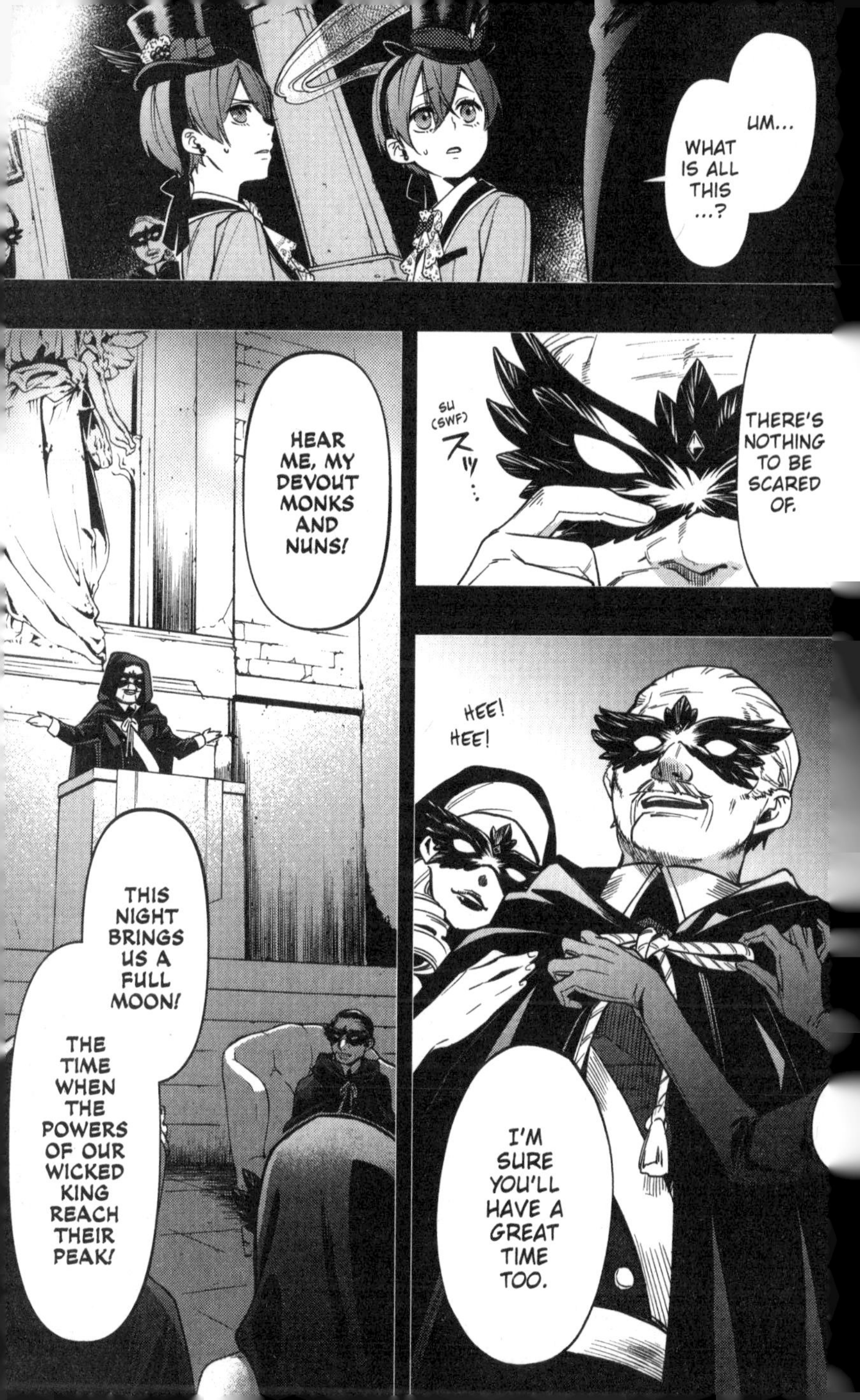
UM... WHAT IS ALL THIS ...?
THERE'S NOTHING TO BE SCARED OF.
SU (SWF)
スッ...
HEAR ME, MY DEVOUT MONKS AND NUNS!
HEE! HEE!
I'M SURE YOU'LL HAVE A GREAT TIME TOO.
THIS NIGHT BRINGS US A FULL MOON!
THE TIME WHEN THE POWERS OF OUR WICKED KING REACH THEIR PEAK!

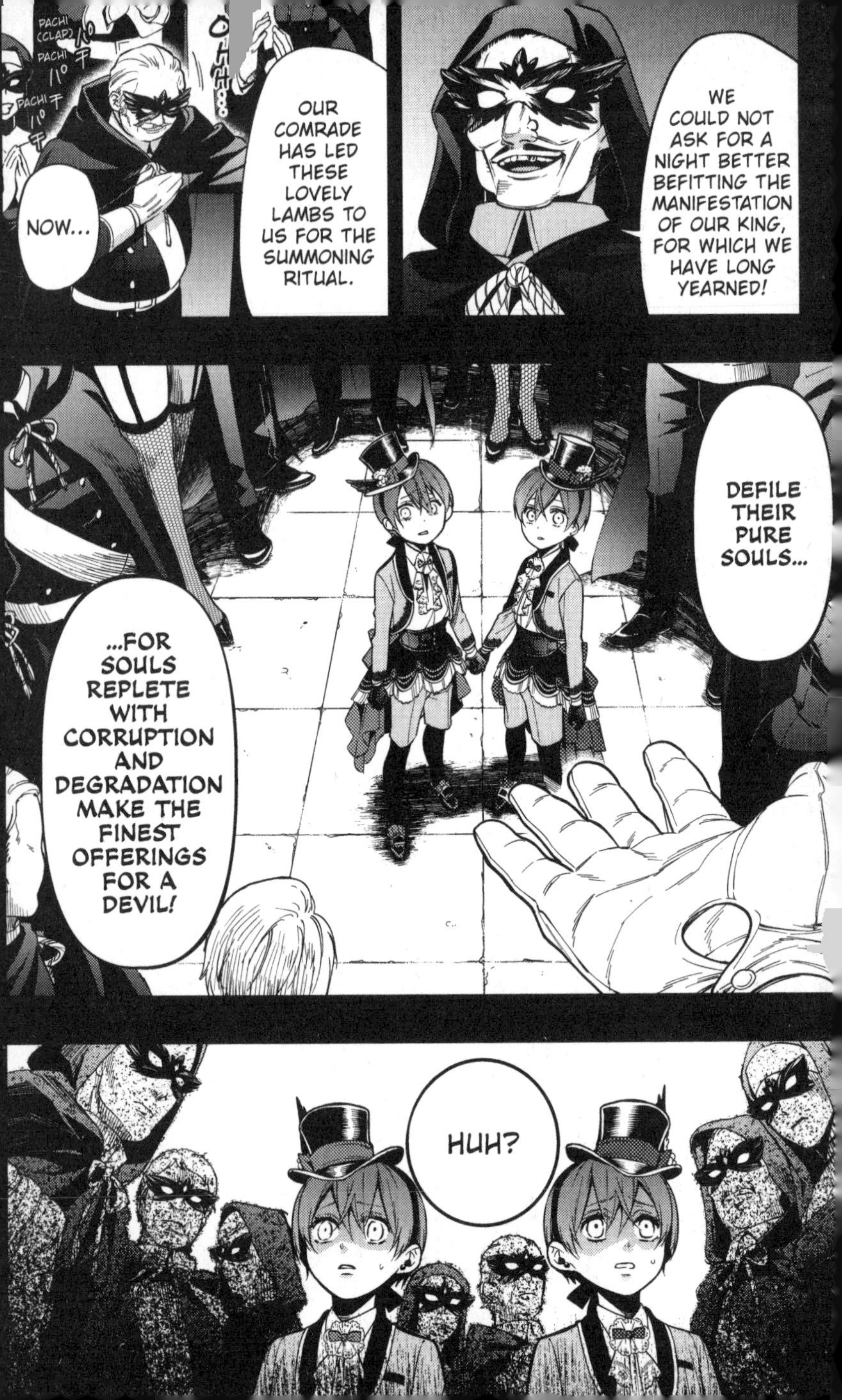
WE COULD NOT ASK FOR A NIGHT BETTER BEFITTING THE MANIFESTATION OF OUR KING, FOR WHICH WE HAVE LONG YEARNED!
OUR COMRADE HAS LED THESE LOVELY LAMBS TO US FOR THE SUMMONING RITUAL.
PACHI (CLAP)
PACHI
PACHI
NOW...
DEFILE THEIR PURE SOULS...
...FOR SOULS REPLETE WITH CORRUPTION AND DEGRADATION MAKE THE FINEST OFFERINGS FOR A DEVIL!
HUH?

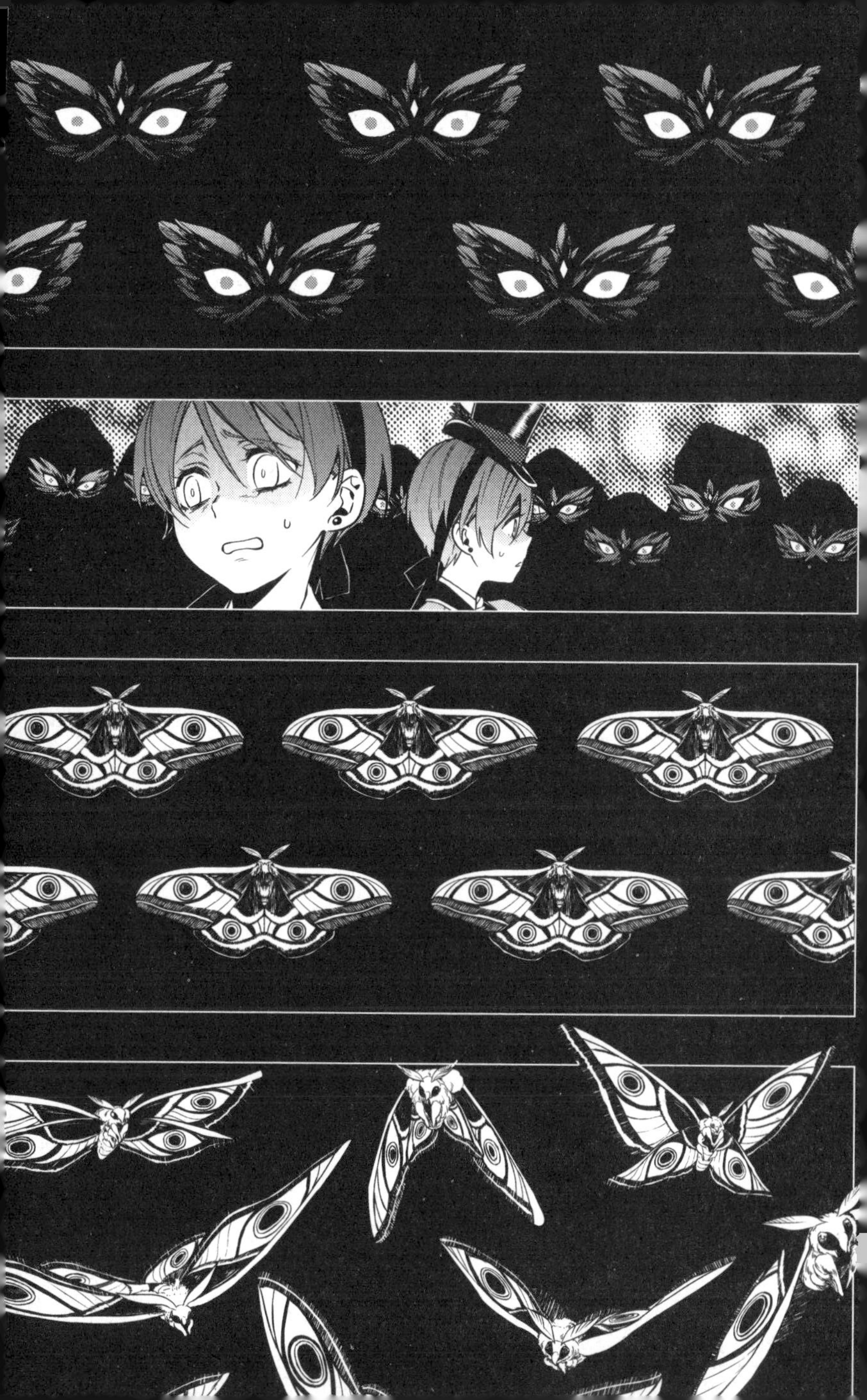

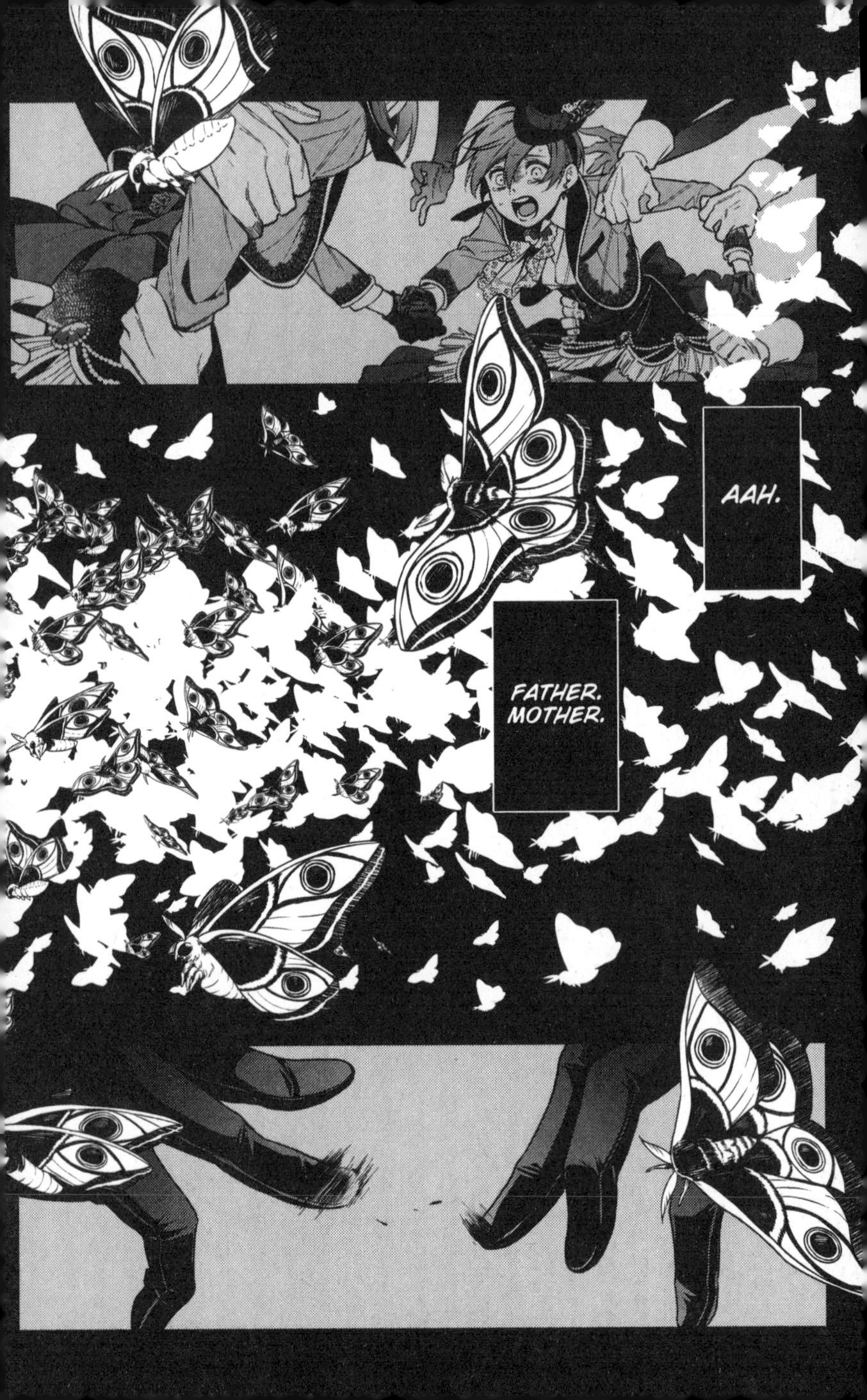
AAH.
FATHER. MOTHER.

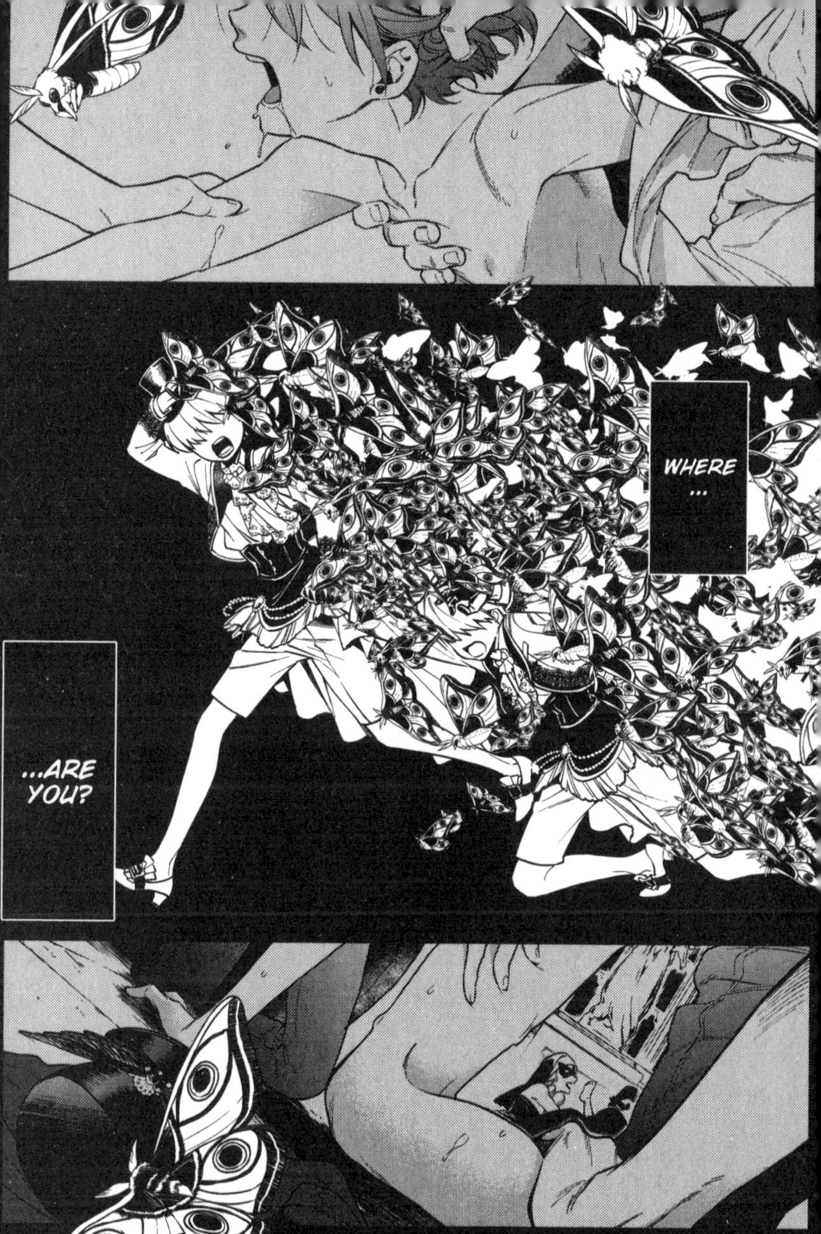
WHERE ...
...ARE YOU?

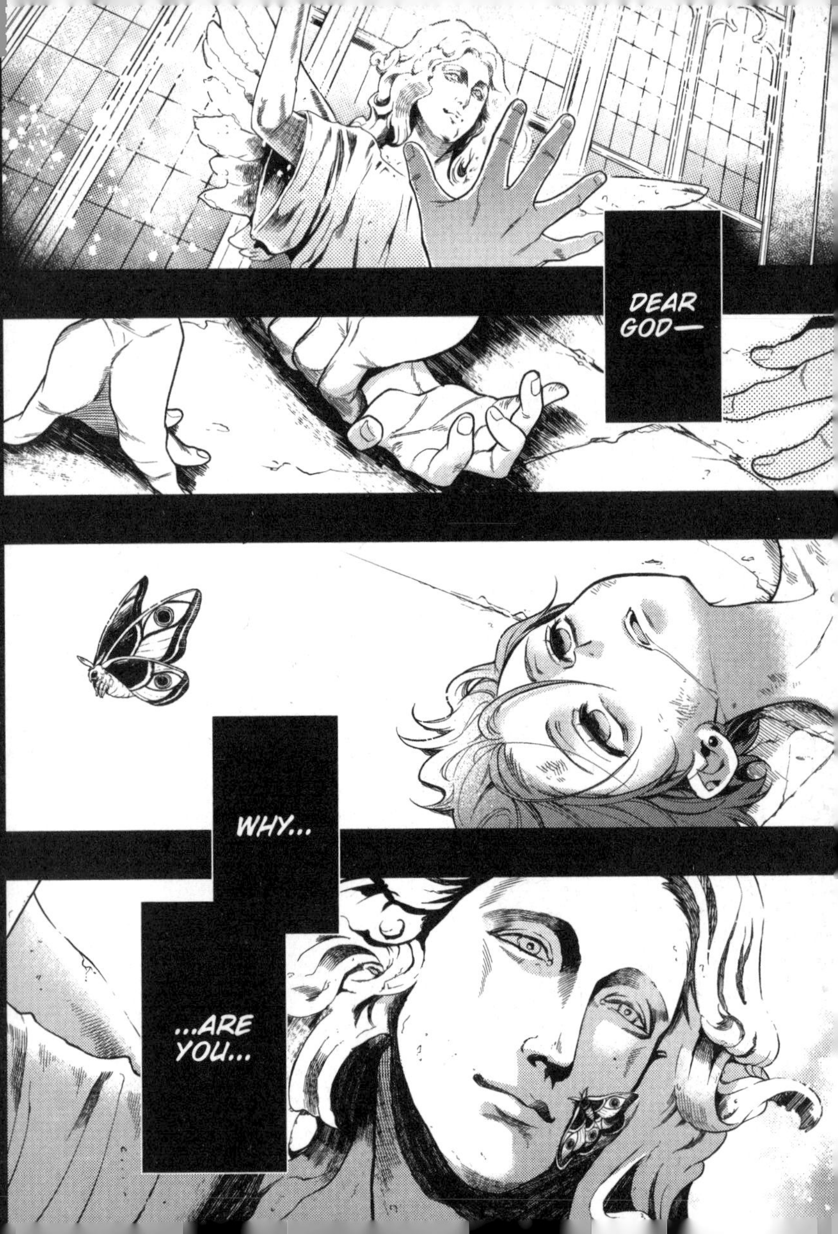
DEAR GOD—
WHY...
...ARE YOU...

**Black Butler**

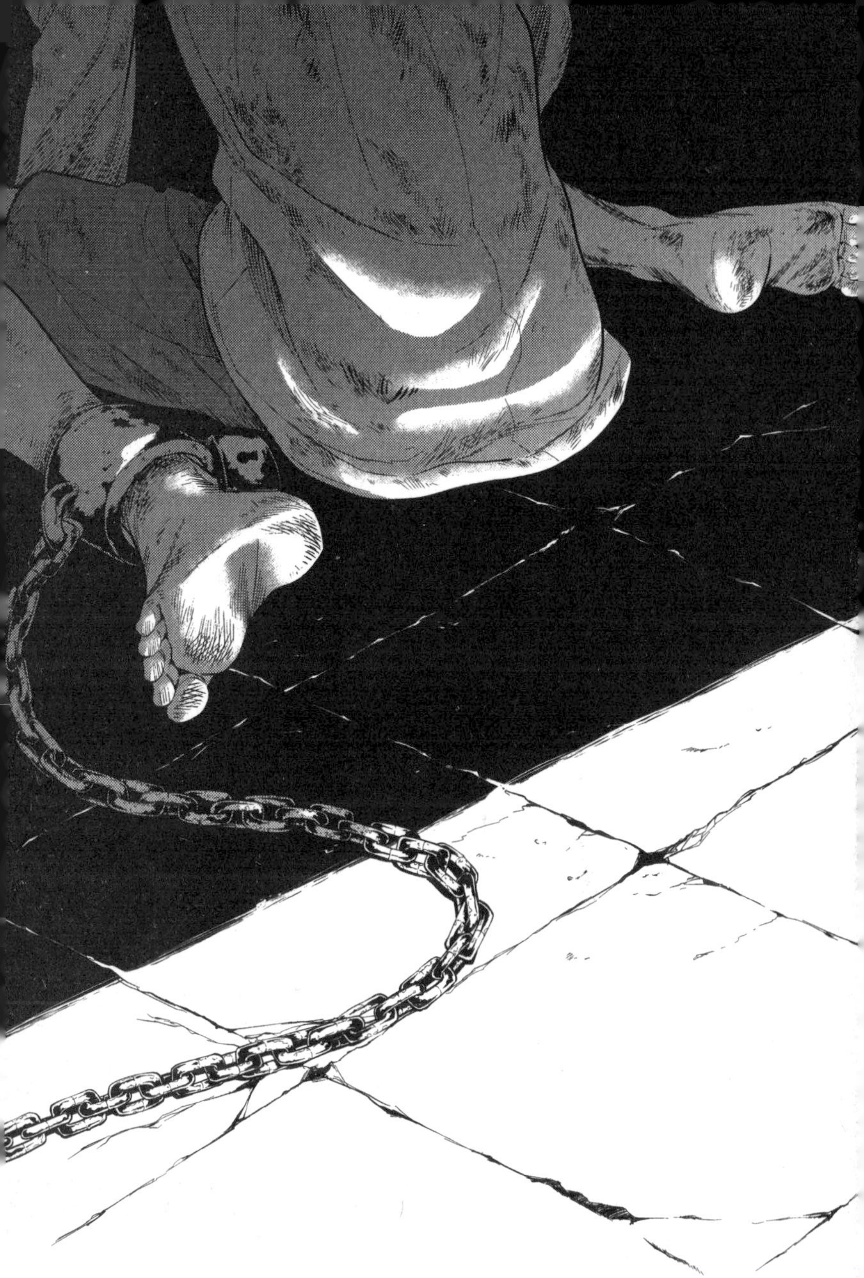

CHAPTER 136

# *In the afternoon : The Butler, Paying a Call*

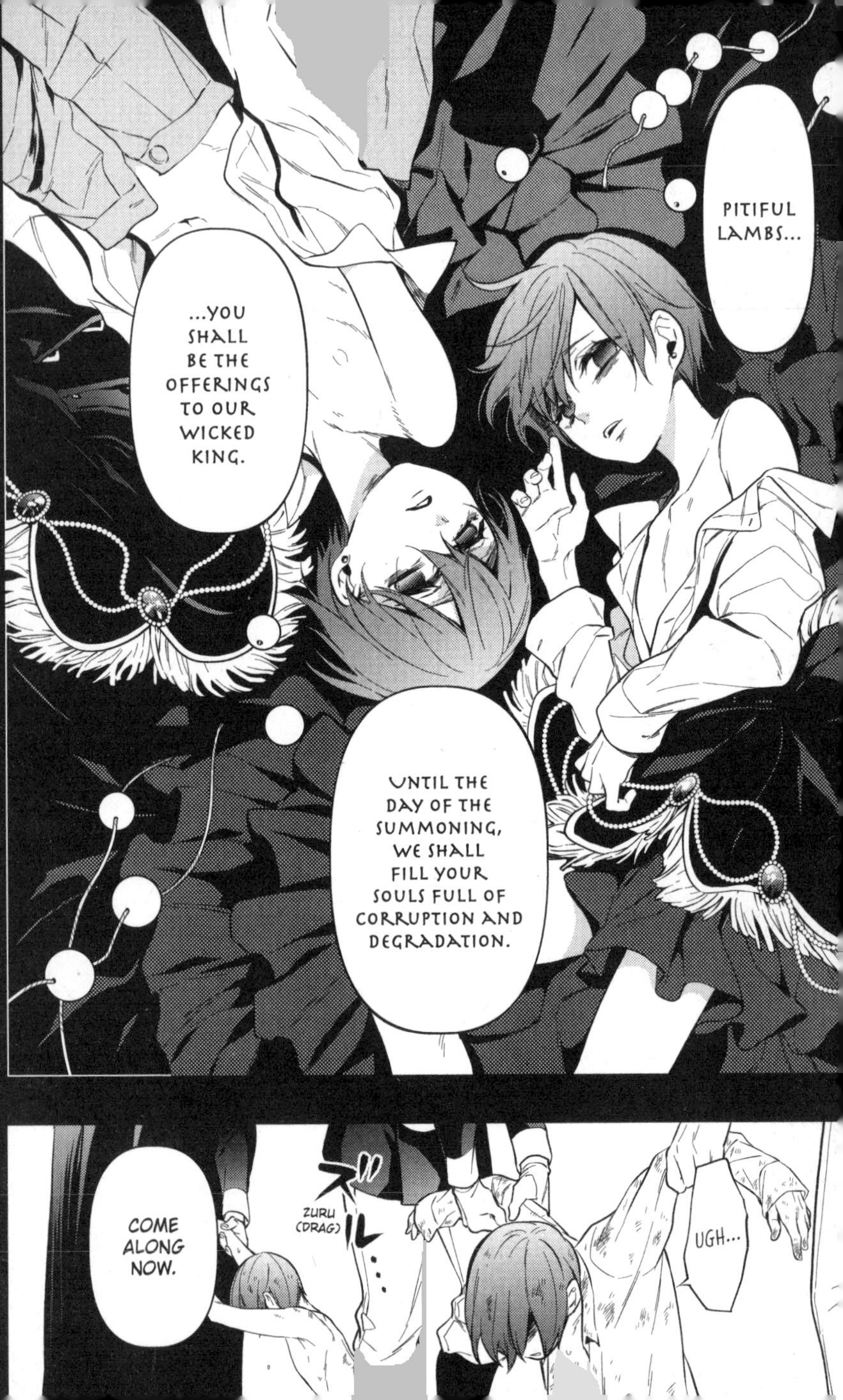
PITIFUL LAMBS...
...YOU SHALL BE THE OFFERINGS TO OUR WICKED KING.
UNTIL THE DAY OF THE SUMMONING, WE SHALL FILL YOUR SOULS FULL OF CORRUPTION AND DEGRADATION.
UGH...
ZURU (DRAG)
COME ALONG NOW.

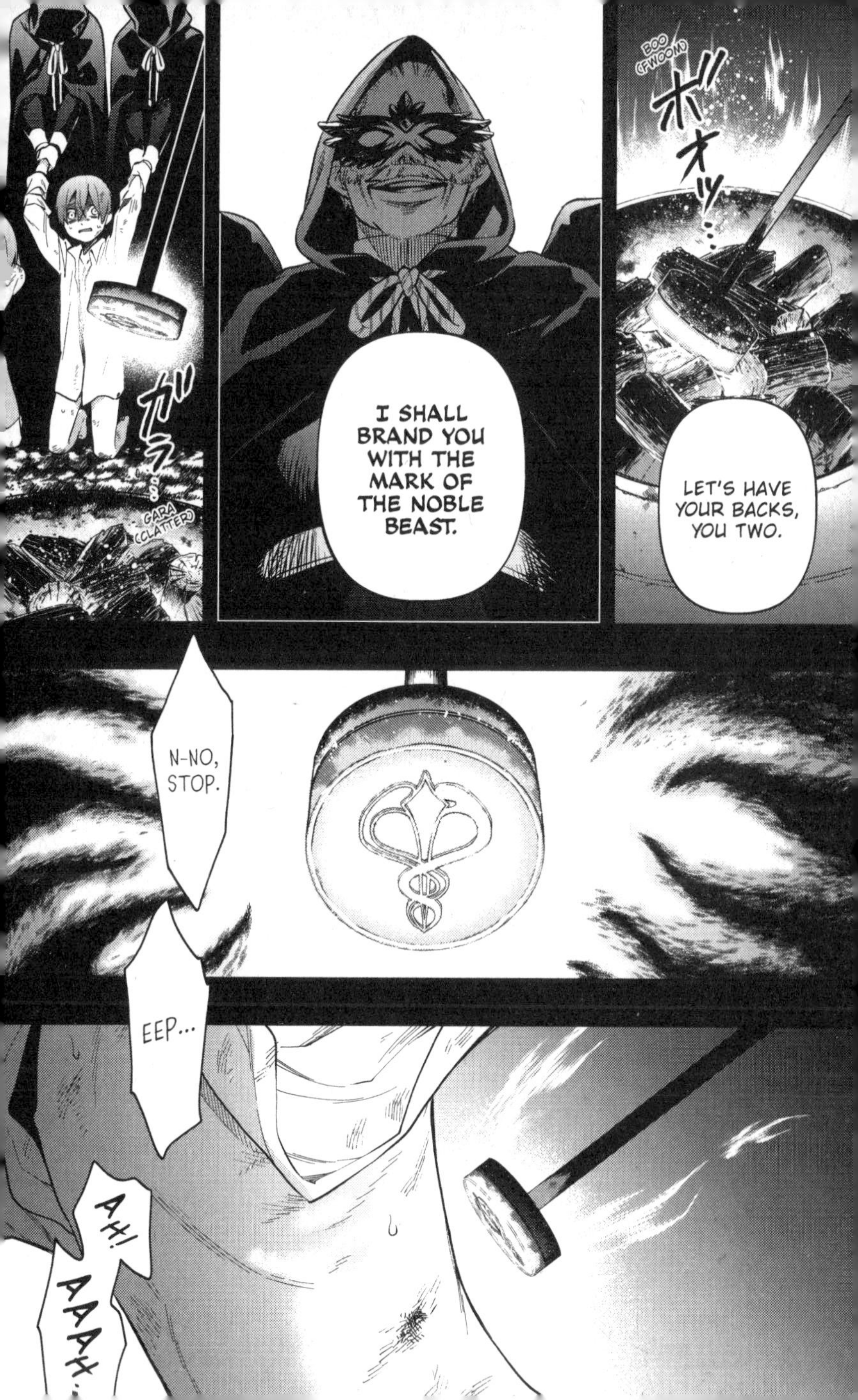
BOO (FWOOM)
LET'S HAVE YOUR BACKS, YOU TWO.
I SHALL BRAND YOU WITH THE MARK OF THE NOBLE BEAST.
GARA (CLATTER)
N-NO, STOP.
EEP...
AH!
AAAAH...

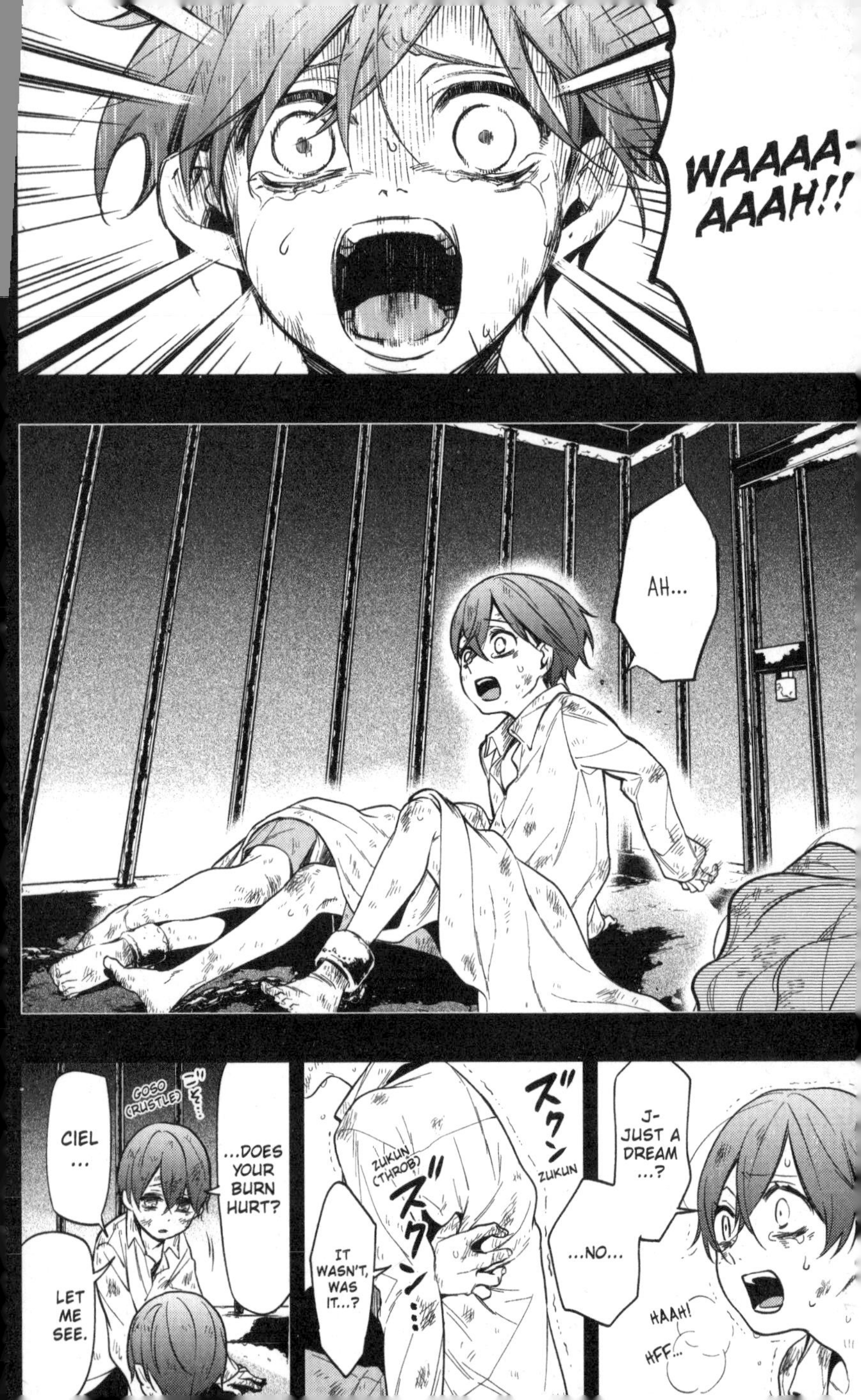
WAAAA-AAAH!!
AH...
J-JUST A DREAM...?
HAAH!
HFF...
...NO...
ZUKUN
ZUKUN (THROB)
IT WASN'T, WAS IT...?
...DOES YOUR BURN HURT?
GOSO (RUSTLE)
CIEL...
LET ME SEE.

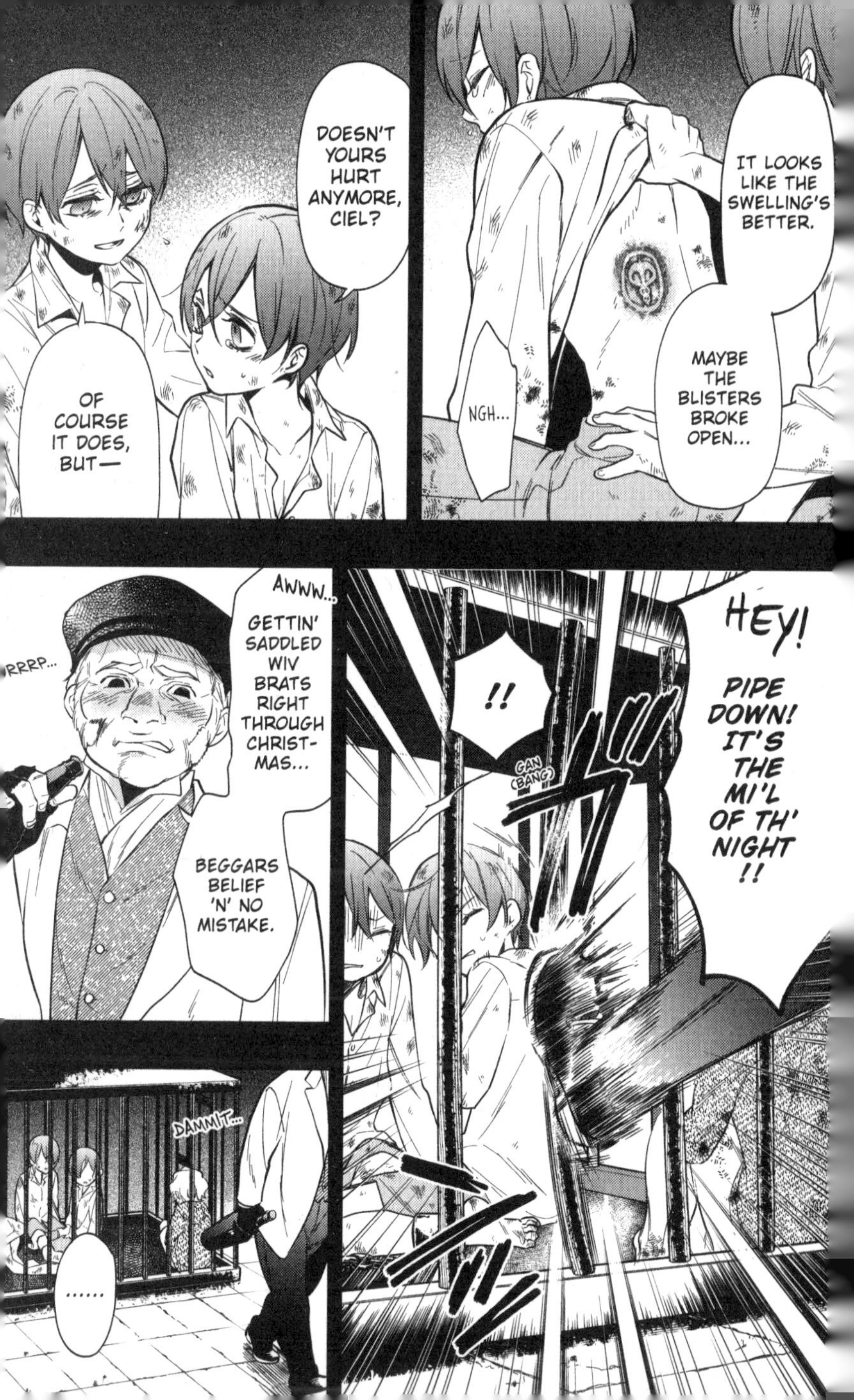
IT LOOKS LIKE THE SWELLING'S BETTER.
MAYBE THE BLISTERS BROKE OPEN...
NGH...
DOESN'T YOURS HURT ANYMORE, CIEL?
OF COURSE IT DOES, BUT—
HEY!
PIPE DOWN! IT'S THE MI'L OF TH' NIGHT!!
!!
GAN (BANG)
AWWW...
GETTIN' SADDLED WIV BRATS RIGHT THROUGH CHRIST-MAS...
RRRP...
BEGGARS BELIEF 'N' NO MISTAKE.
DAMMIT...
......

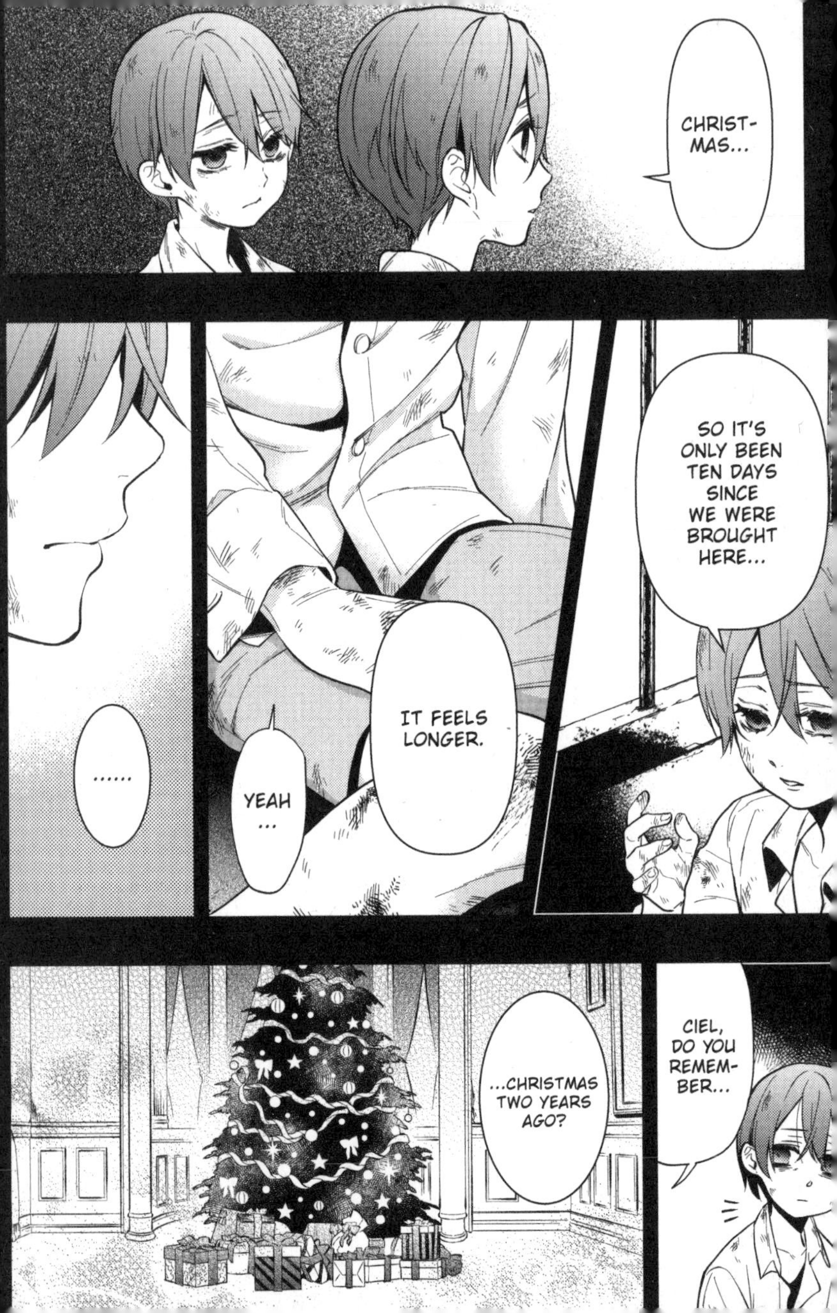
CHRIST-MAS...
SO IT'S ONLY BEEN TEN DAYS SINCE WE WERE BROUGHT HERE...
IT FEELS LONGER.
YEAH...
......
CIEL, DO YOU REMEM-BER...
...CHRISTMAS TWO YEARS AGO?

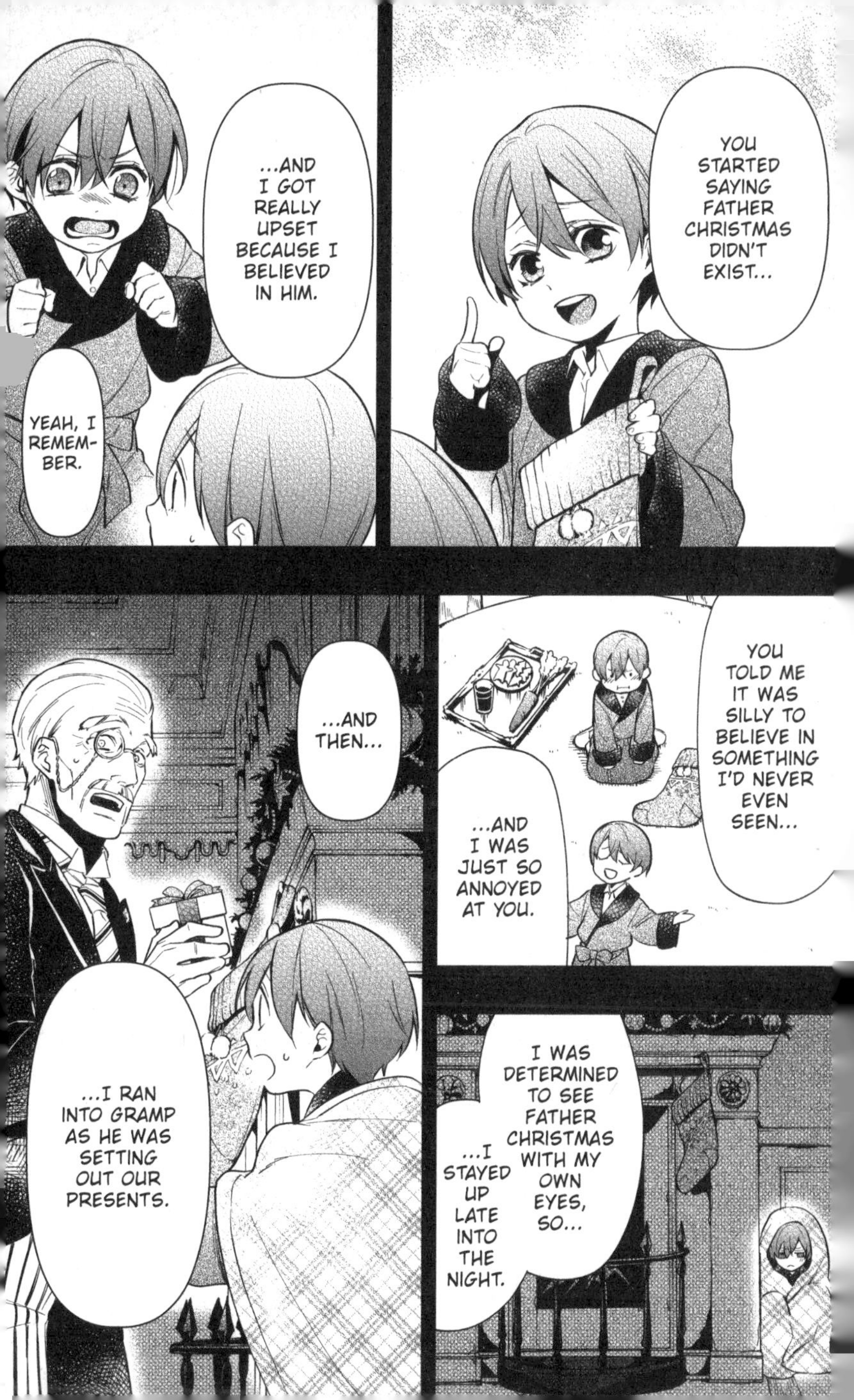
YOU STARTED SAYING FATHER CHRISTMAS DIDN'T EXIST...
...AND I GOT REALLY UPSET BECAUSE I BELIEVED IN HIM.
YEAH, I REMEMBER.
YOU TOLD ME IT WAS SILLY TO BELIEVE IN SOMETHING I'D NEVER EVEN SEEN...
...AND I WAS JUST SO ANNOYED AT YOU.
I WAS DETERMINED TO SEE FATHER CHRISTMAS WITH MY OWN EYES, SO...
...I STAYED UP LATE INTO THE NIGHT.
...AND THEN...
...I RAN INTO GRAMP AS HE WAS SETTING OUT OUR PRESENTS.

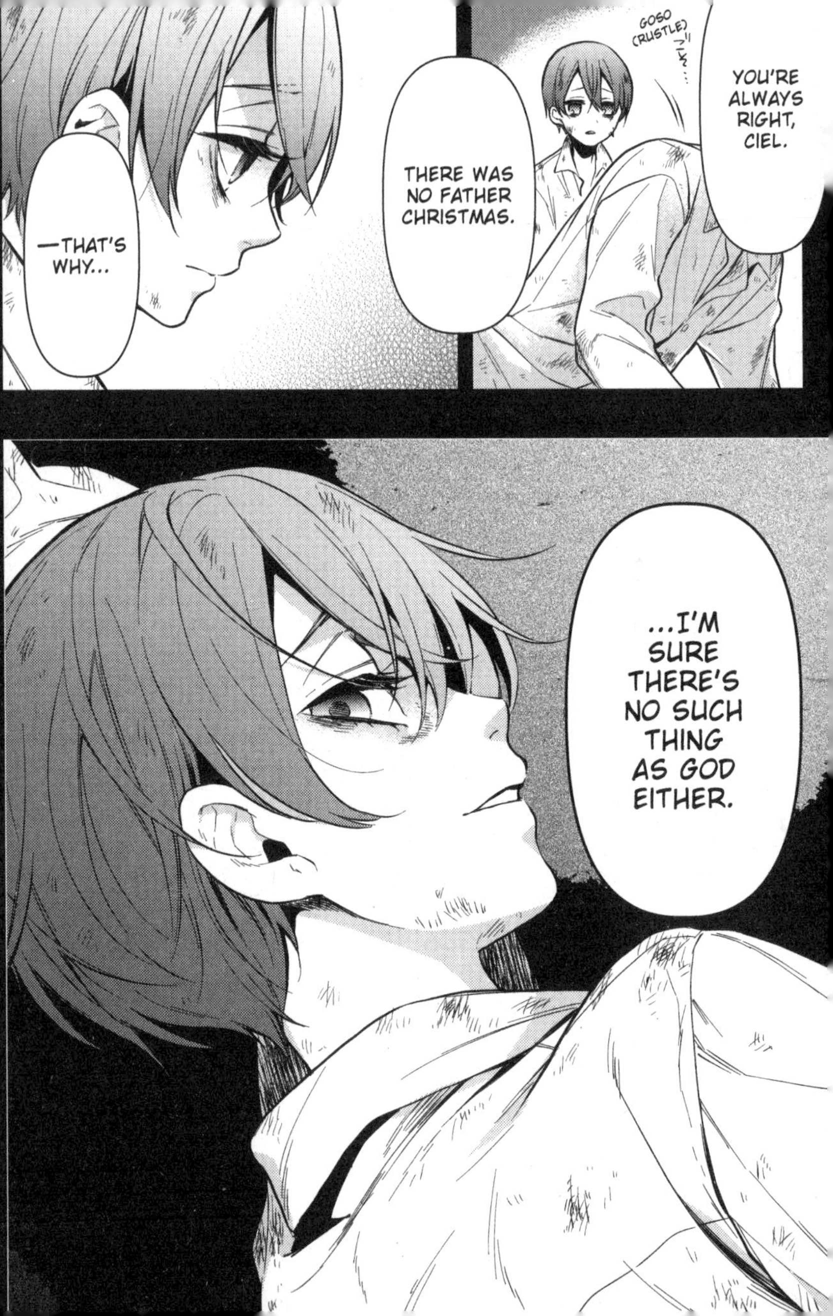
GOSO (RUSTLE)
YOU'RE ALWAYS RIGHT, CIEL.
THERE WAS NO FATHER CHRISTMAS.
—THAT'S WHY...
...I'M SURE THERE'S NO SUCH THING AS GOD EITHER.

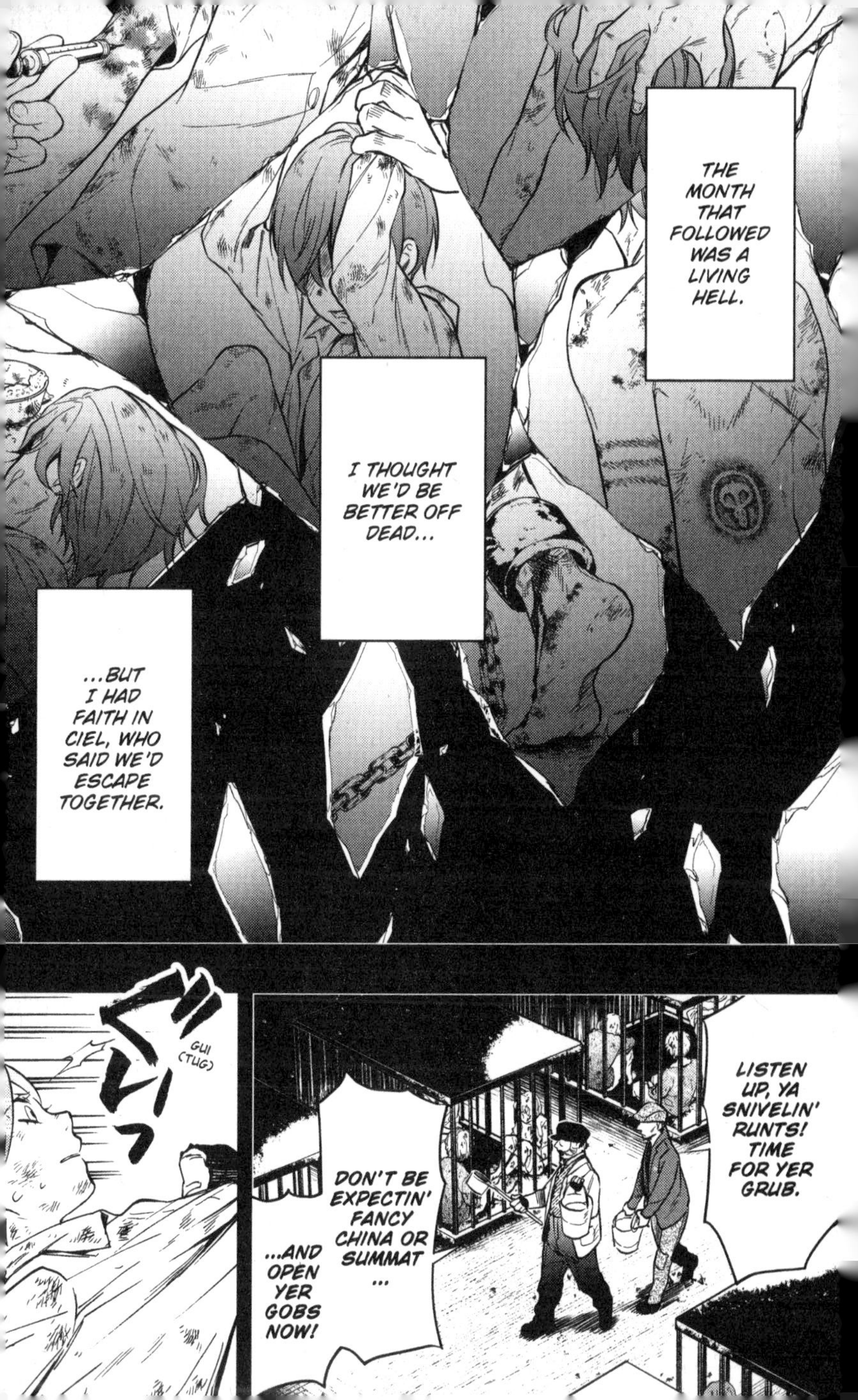
THE MONTH THAT FOLLOWED WAS A LIVING HELL.
I THOUGHT WE'D BE BETTER OFF DEAD...
...BUT I HAD FAITH IN CIEL, WHO SAID WE'D ESCAPE TOGETHER.
LISTEN UP, YA SNIVELIN' RUNTS! TIME FOR YER GRUB.
DON'T BE EXPECTIN' FANCY CHINA OR SUMMAT...
...AND OPEN YER GOBS NOW!
GUI (TUG)

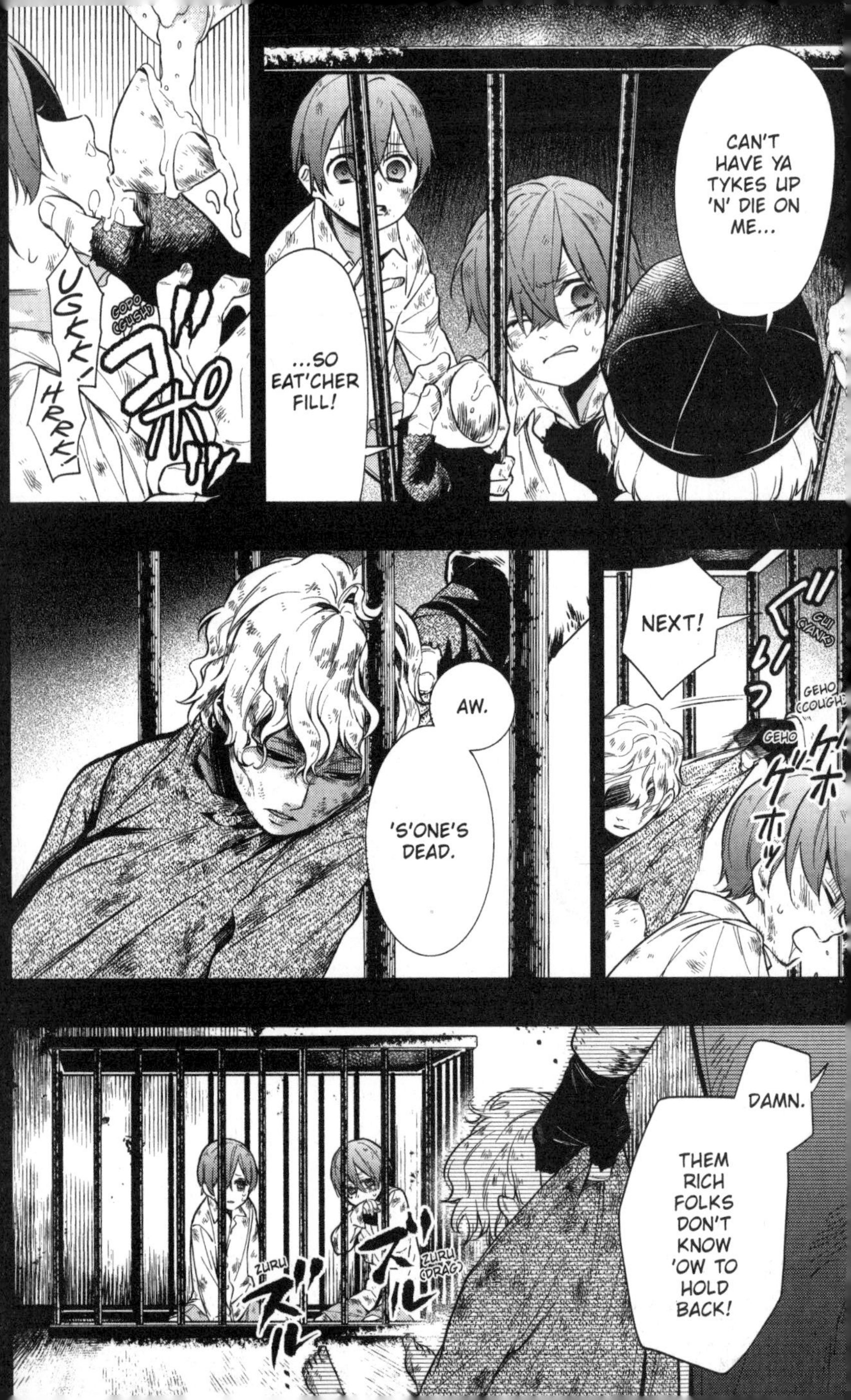
CAN'T HAVE YA TYKES UP 'N' DIE ON ME...
...SO EAT'CHER FILL!
GOPO (GUSH)
UGKK!
HRRK!
NEXT!
GUI (YANK)
GEHO (COUGH)
GEHO
AW.
'S'ONE'S DEAD.
DAMN.
THEM RICH FOLKS DON'T KNOW 'OW TO HOLD BACK!
ZURU (DRAG)
ZURU

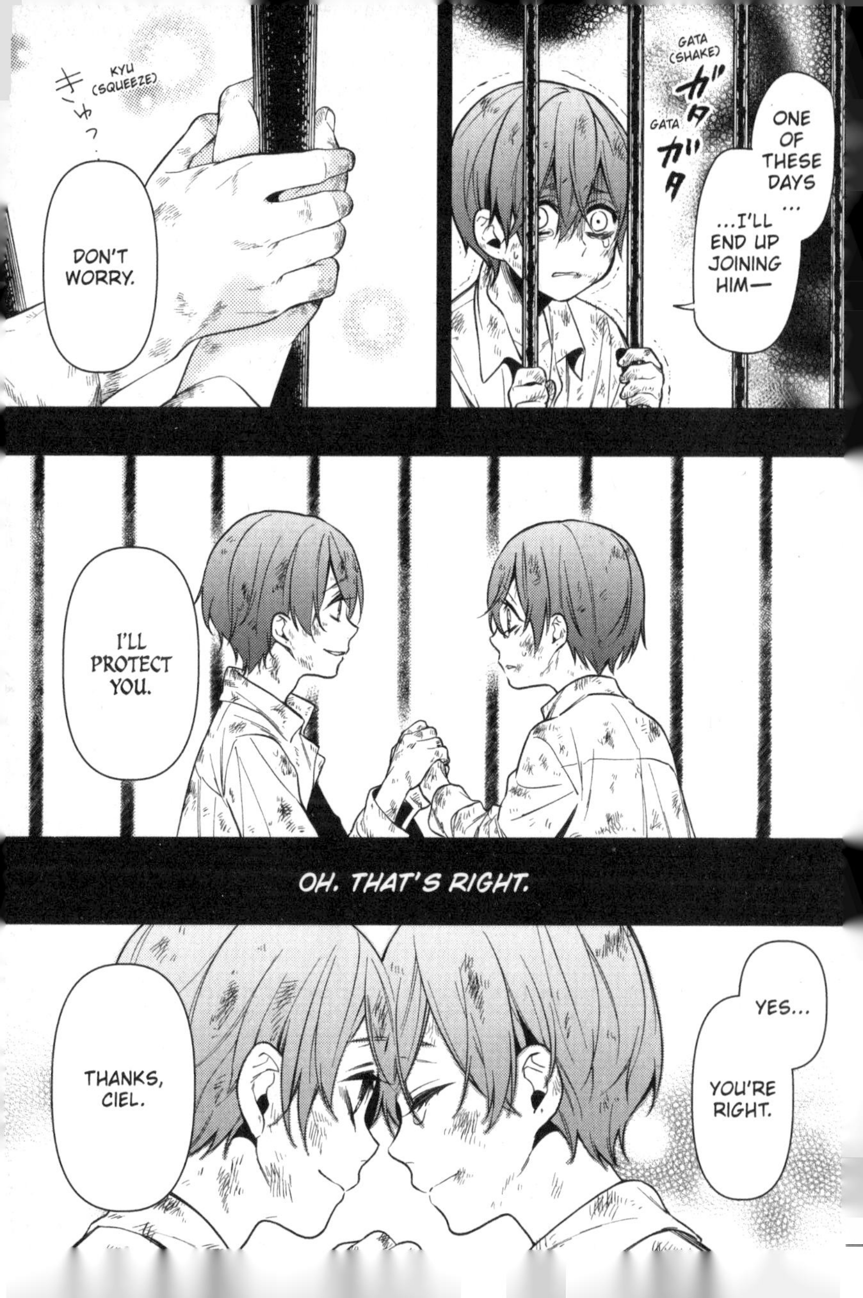
GATA (SHAKE)
GATA
ガタ ガタ
ONE OF THESE DAYS...
...I'LL END UP JOINING HIM—
KYU (SQUEEZE)
きゅっ
DON'T WORRY.
I'LL PROTECT YOU.
OH. THAT'S RIGHT.
YES...
YOU'RE RIGHT.
THANKS, CIEL.

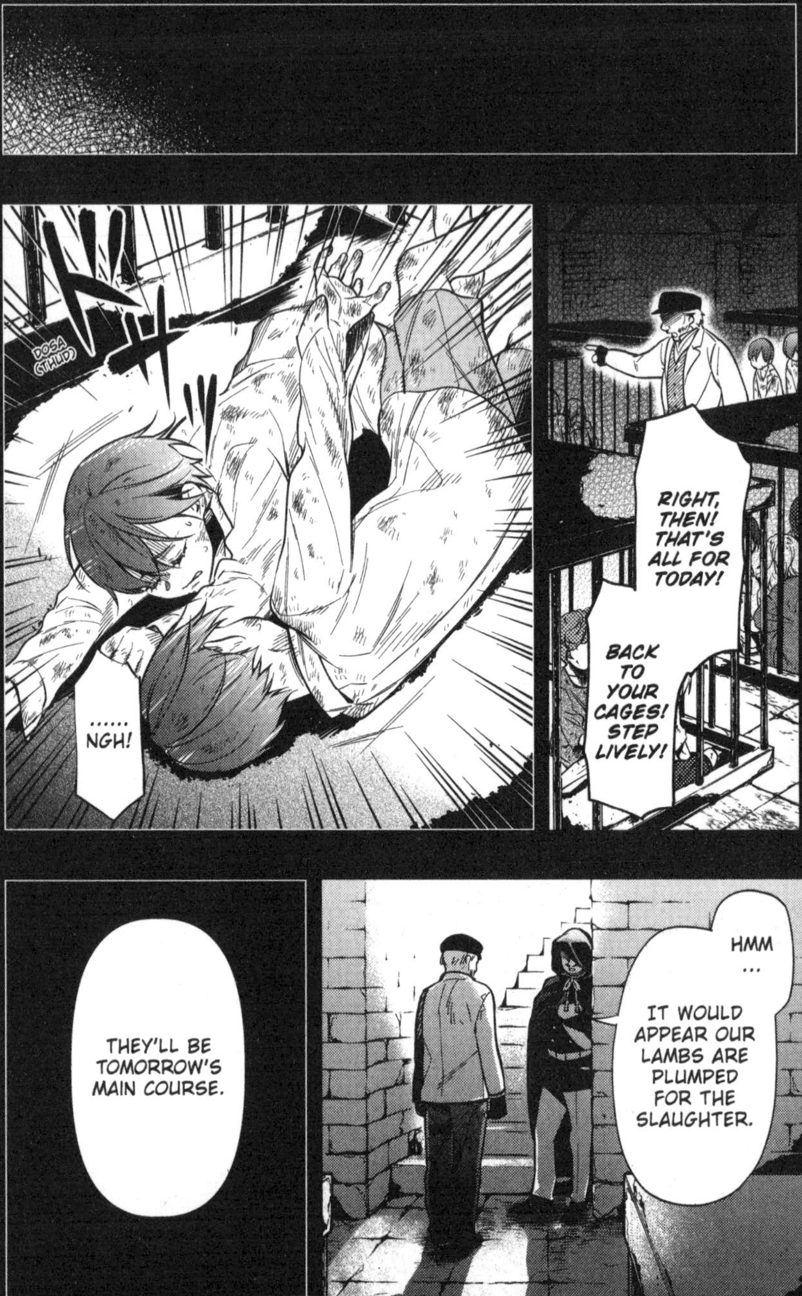
RIGHT, THEN! THAT'S ALL FOR TODAY!
BACK TO YOUR CAGES! STEP LIVELY!
DOSA (THUD)
......NGH!
HMM...
IT WOULD APPEAR OUR LAMBS ARE PLUMPED FOR THE SLAUGHTER.
THEY'LL BE TOMORROW'S MAIN COURSE.

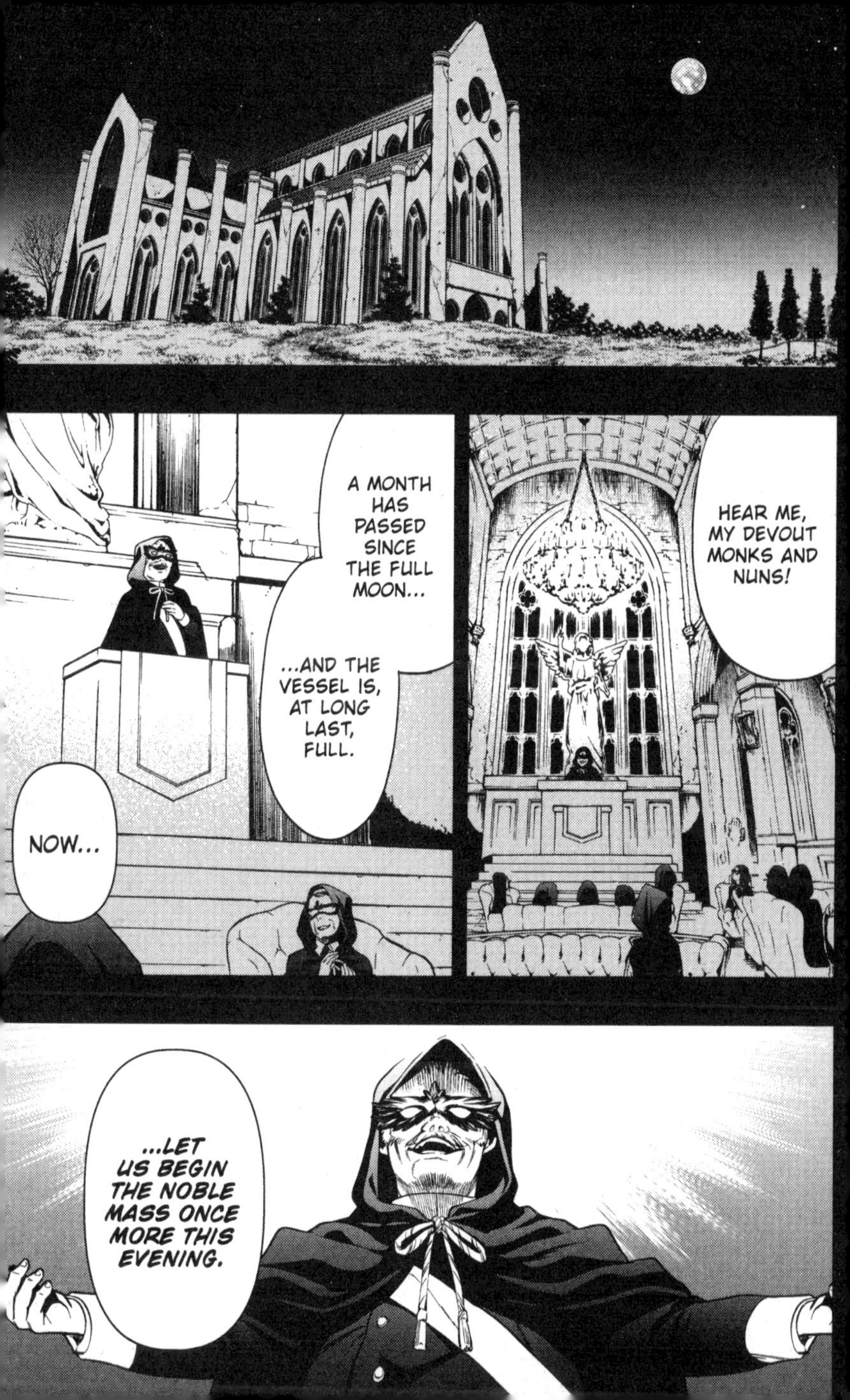
HEAR ME, MY DEVOUT MONKS AND NUNS!
A MONTH HAS PASSED SINCE THE FULL MOON...
...AND THE VESSEL IS, AT LONG LAST, FULL.
NOW...
...LET US BEGIN THE NOBLE MASS ONCE MORE THIS EVENING.

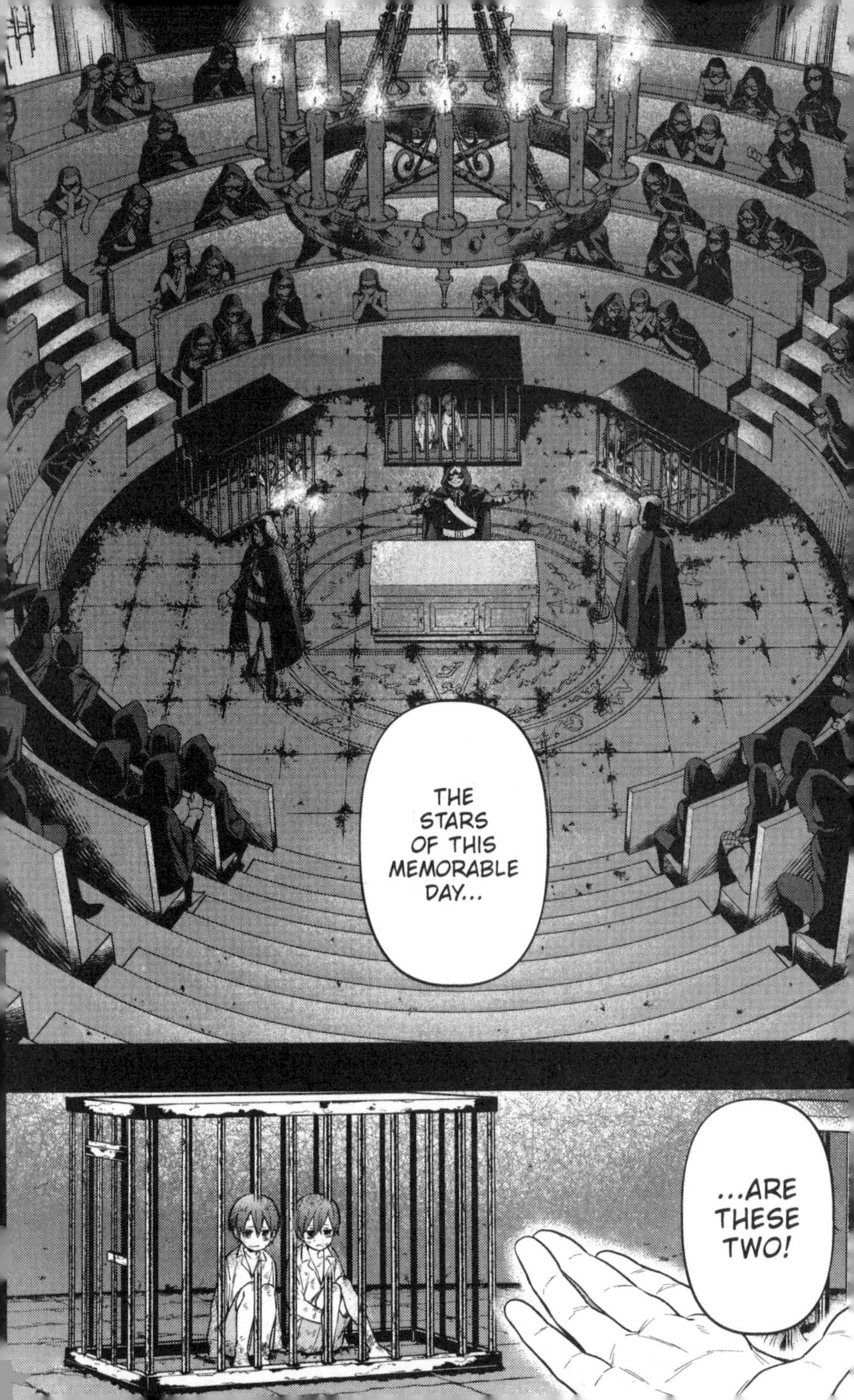
THE STARS OF THIS MEMORABLE DAY...
...ARE THESE TWO!

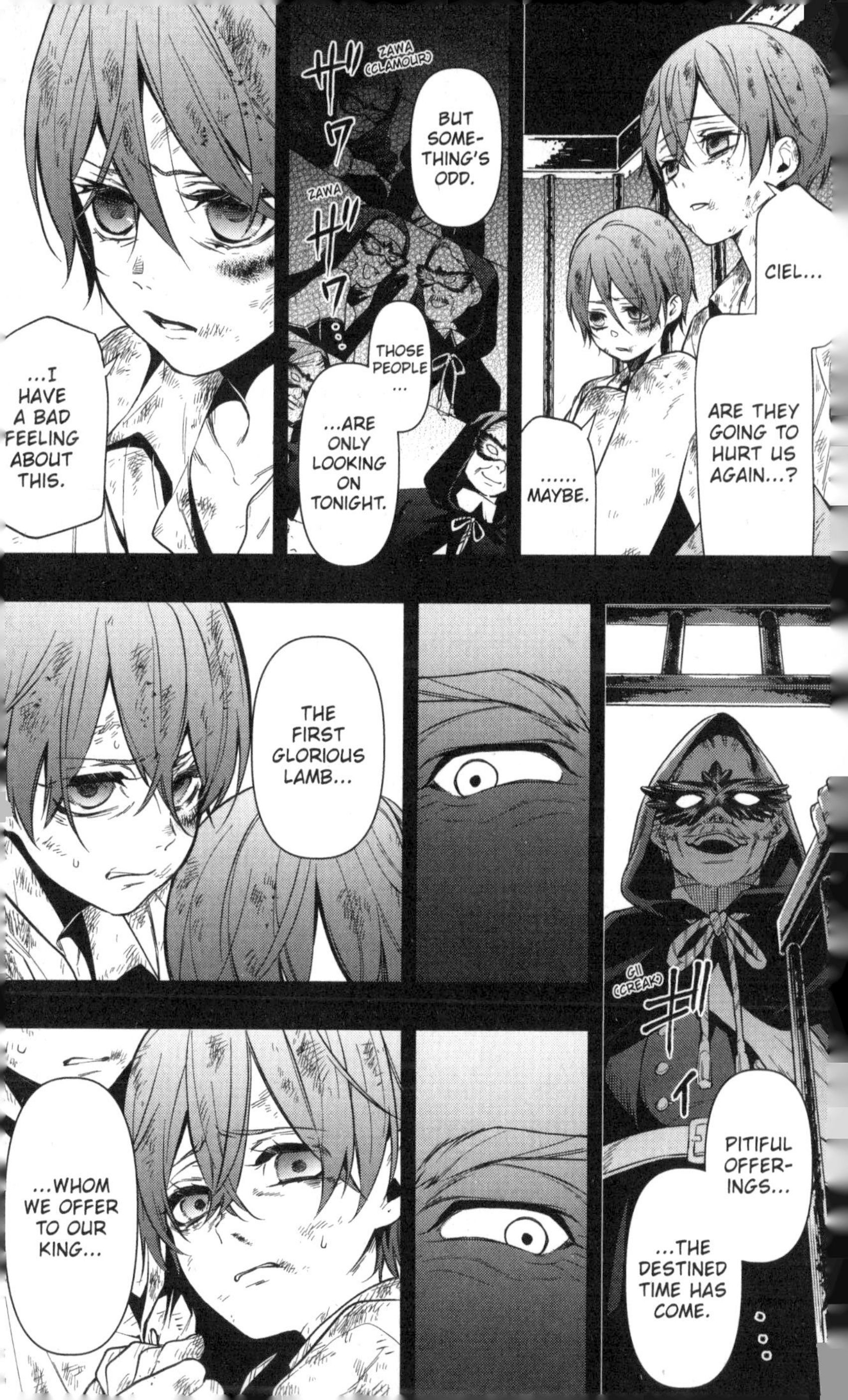
CIEL...
ARE THEY GOING TO HURT US AGAIN...?
...... MAYBE.
ZAWA (CLAMOUR)
BUT SOME-THING'S ODD.
ZAWA
THOSE PEOPLE...
...ARE ONLY LOOKING ON TONIGHT.
...I HAVE A BAD FEELING ABOUT THIS.
GII (CREAK)
PITIFUL OFFER-INGS...
...THE DESTINED TIME HAS COME.
THE FIRST GLORIOUS LAMB...
...WHOM WE OFFER TO OUR KING...

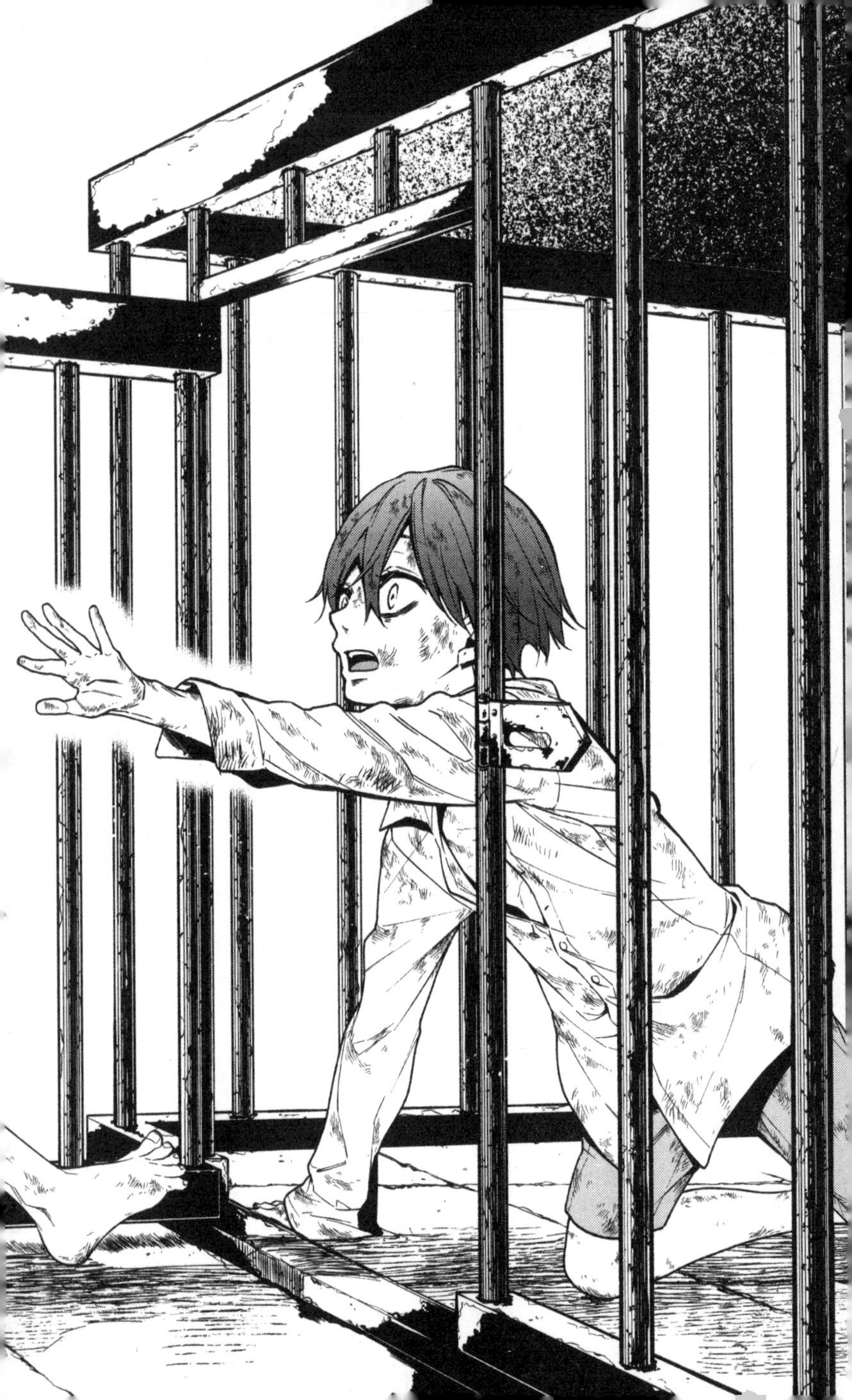

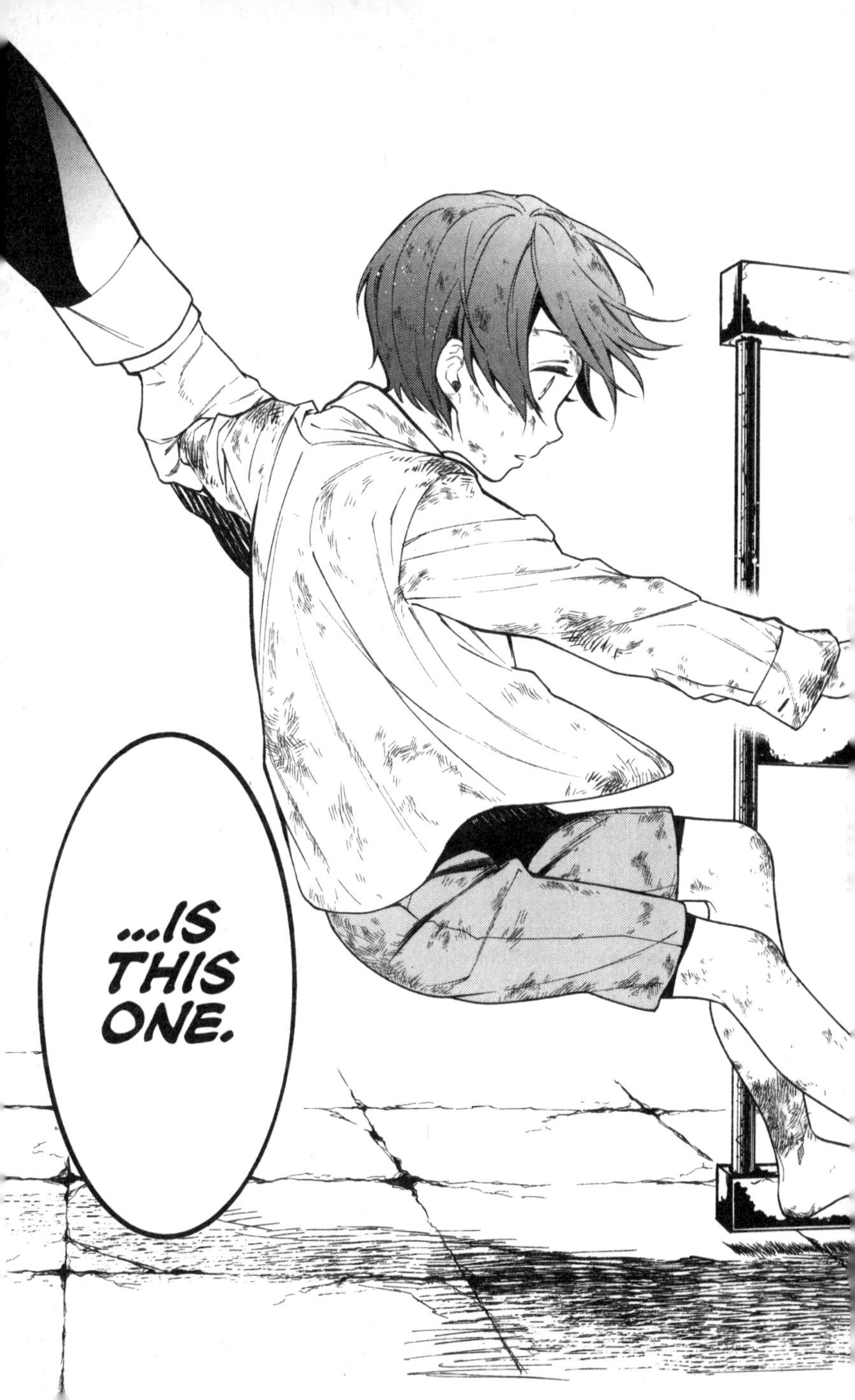
...IS THIS ONE.

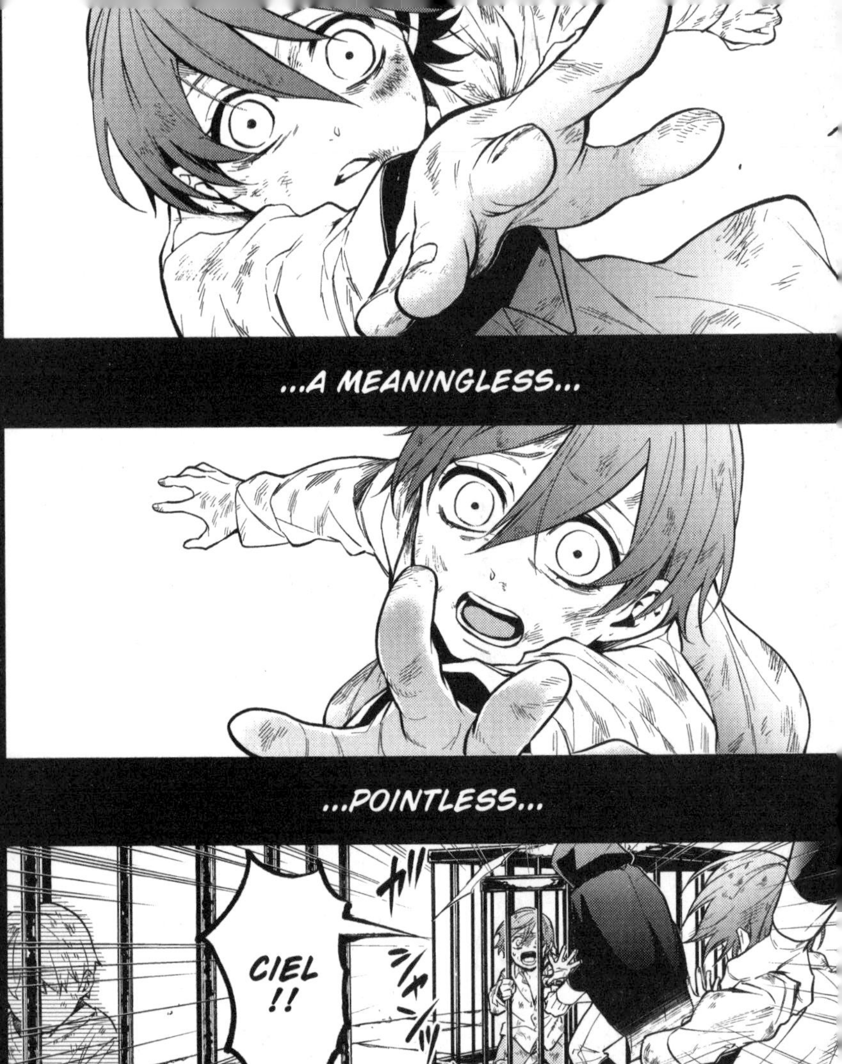
...A MEANINGLESS...
...POINTLESS...
CIEL !!
GASHAN (CLANG)

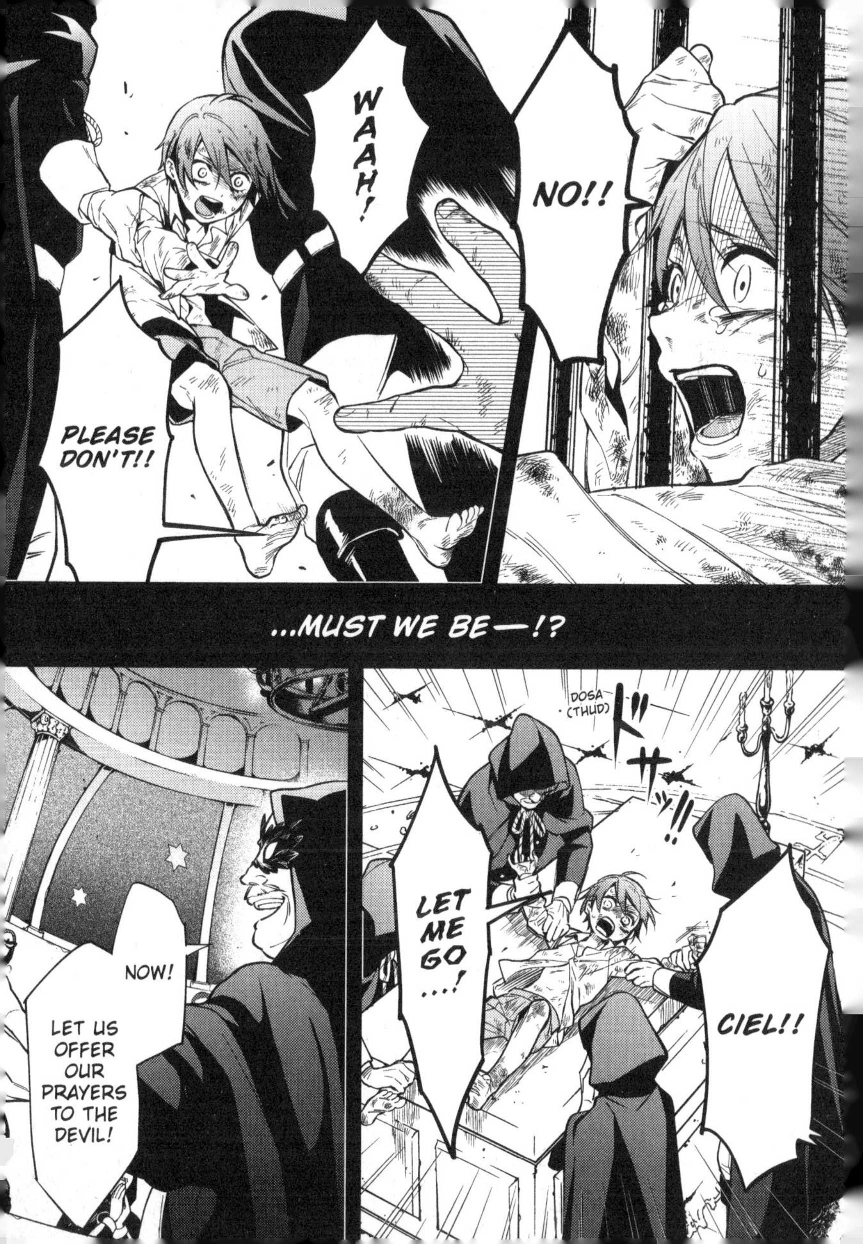
NO!!
WAAAH!
PLEASE DON'T!!
...MUST WE BE—!?
DOSA (THUD)
LET ME GO...!
CIEL!!
NOW!
LET US OFFER OUR PRAYERS TO THE DEVIL!

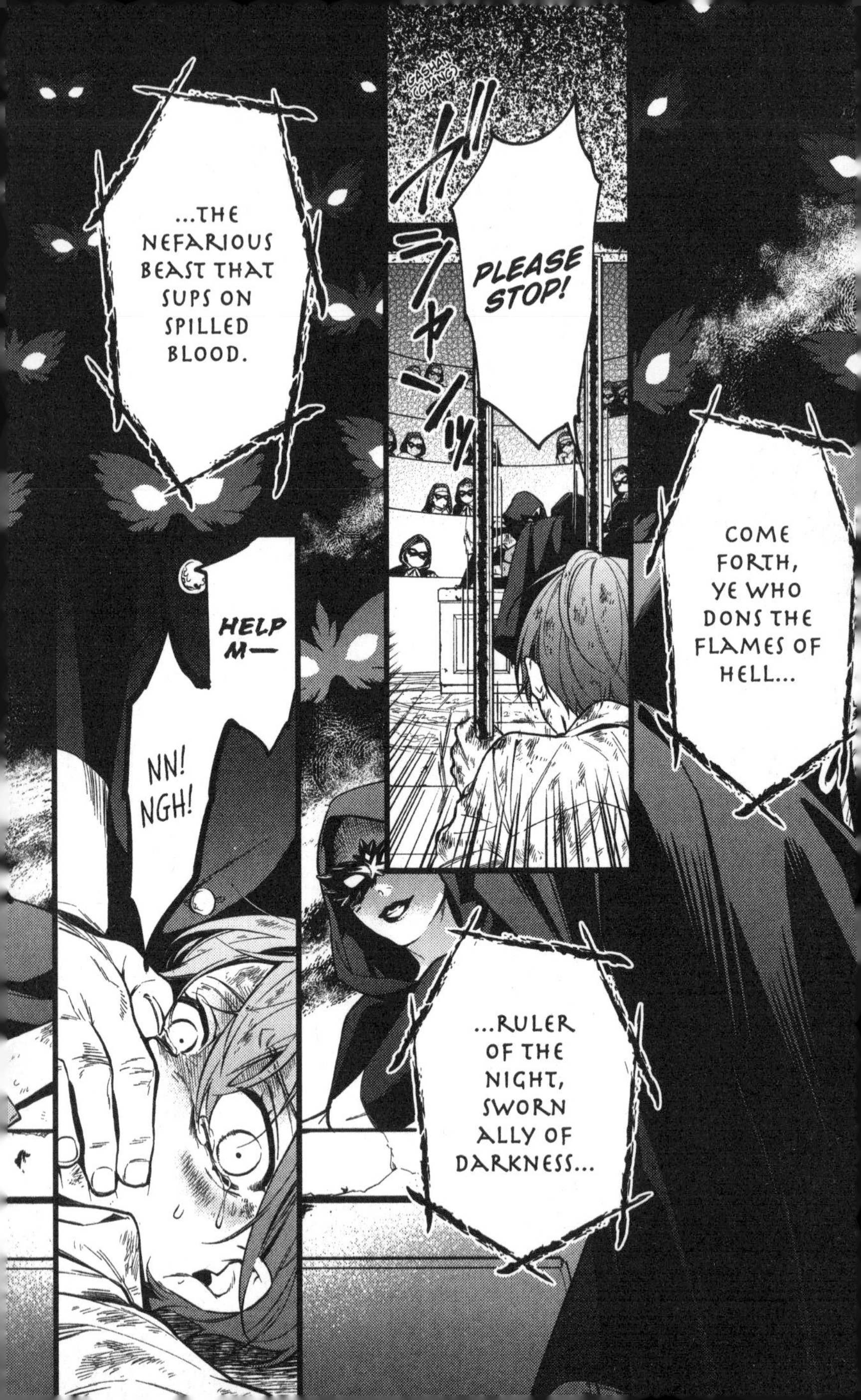
COME FORTH, YE WHO DONS THE FLAMES OF HELL...
...RULER OF THE NIGHT, SWORN ALLY OF DARKNESS...
GASHAN (CLANG)
PLEASE STOP!
...THE NEFARIOUS BEAST THAT SUPS ON SPILLED BLOOD.
HELP M—
NN! NGH!

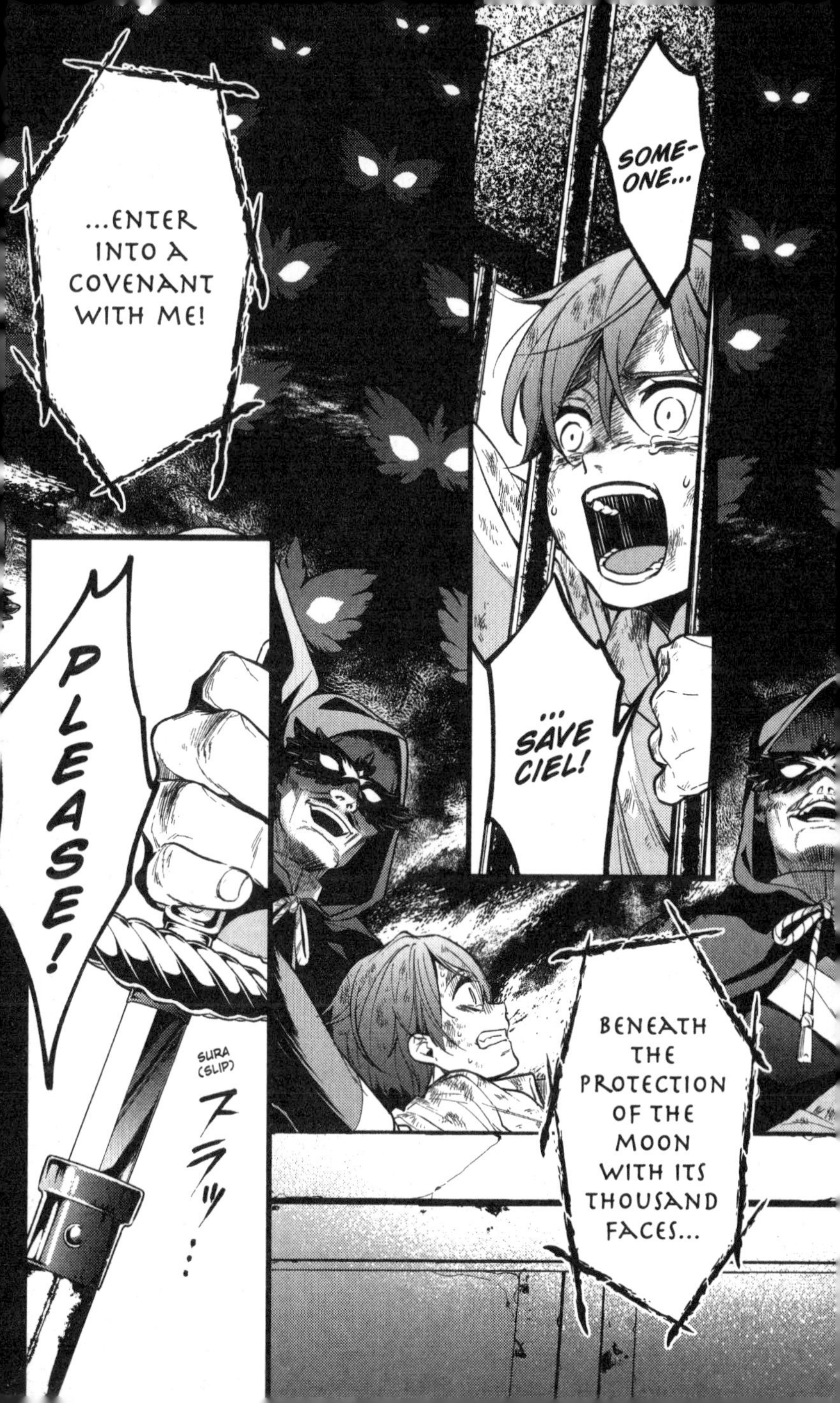
SOME-ONE...
...SAVE CIEL!
...ENTER INTO A COVENANT WITH ME!
BENEATH THE PROTECTION OF THE MOON WITH ITS THOUSAND FACES...
PLEASE!
SURA (SLIP)
スラッ...

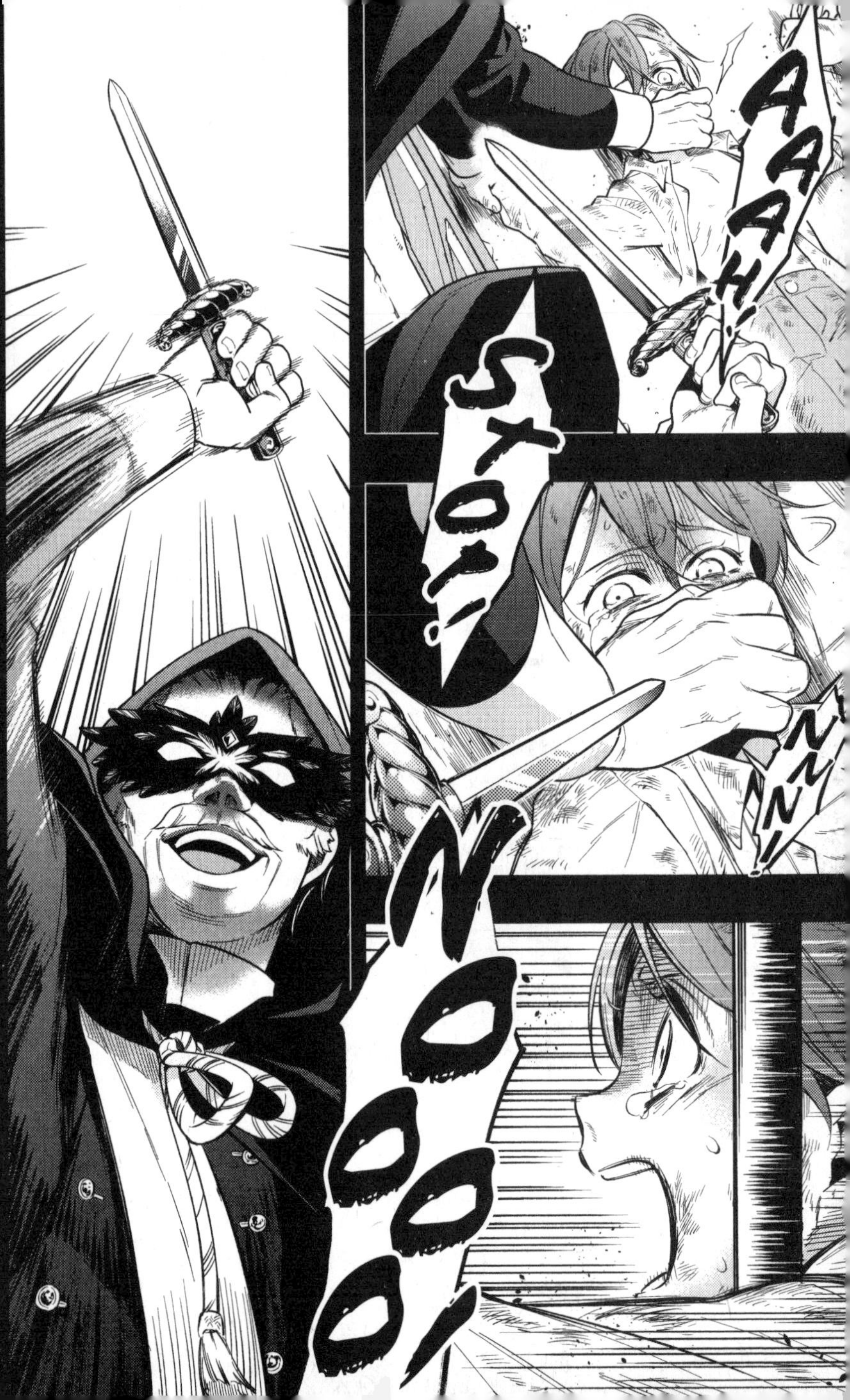
AAAH!!
STOP!!
NNN!!
NOOOO

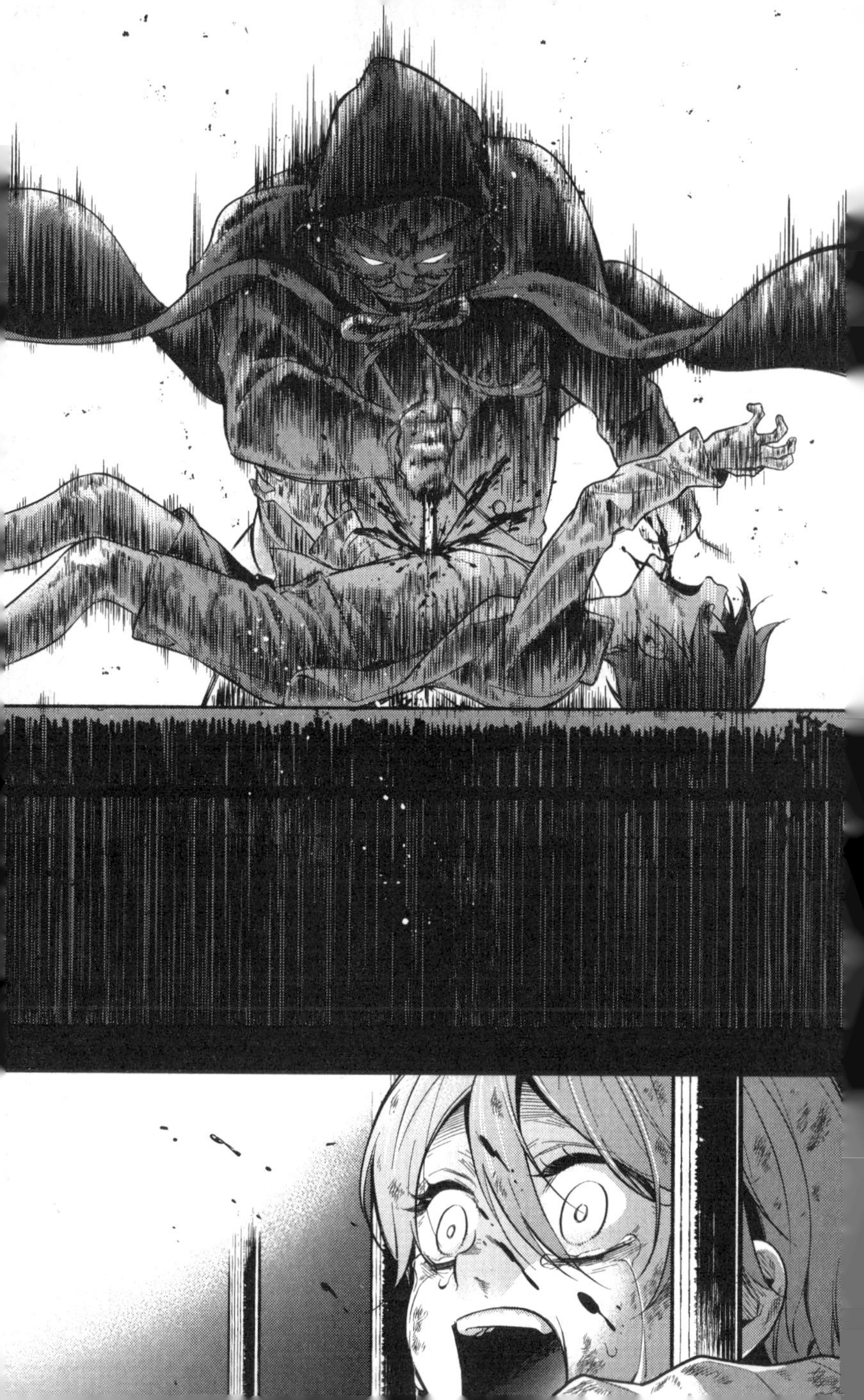

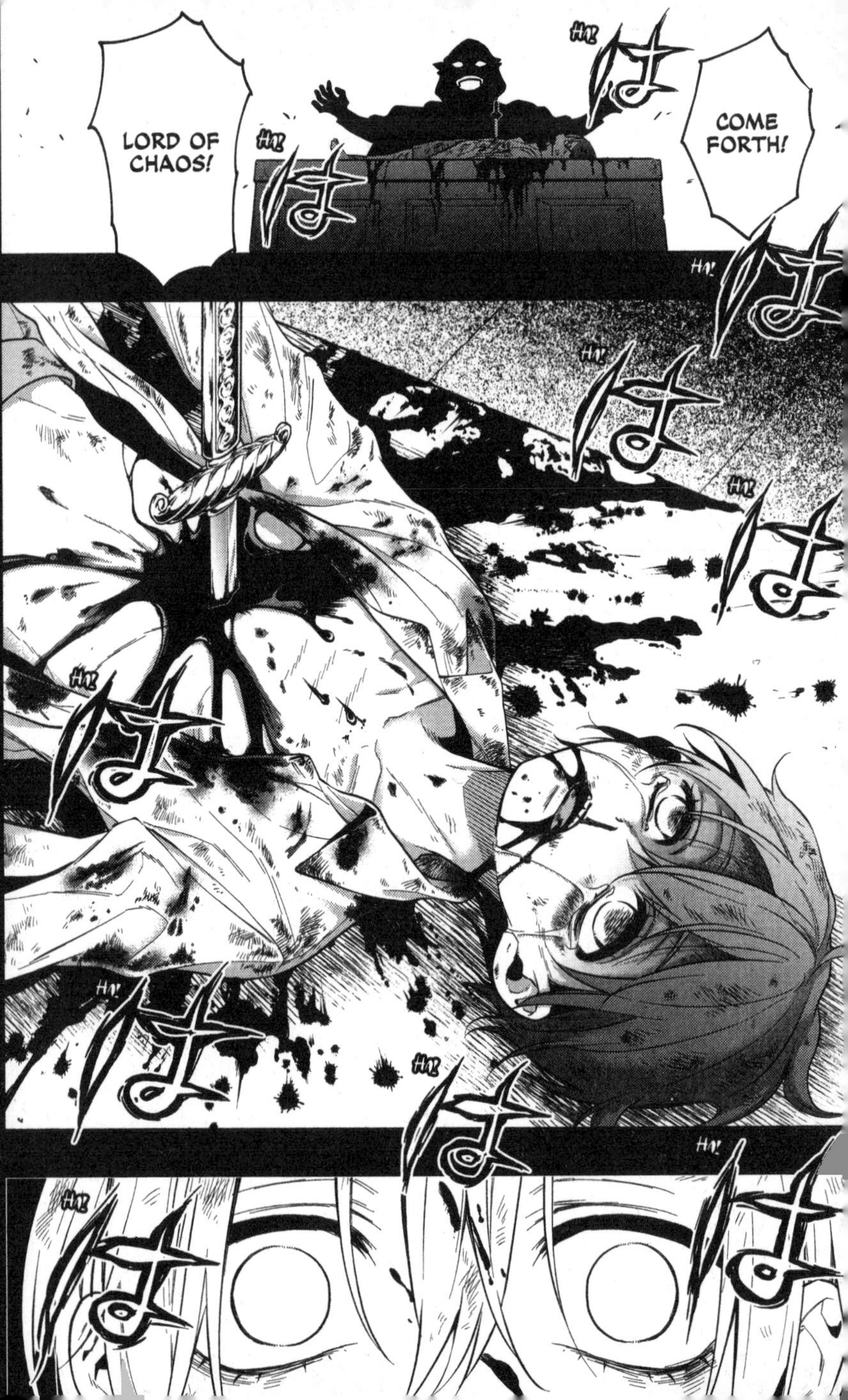
COME FORTH!
HA!
HA!
LORD OF CHAOS!
HA!
HA!
HA!
HA!
HA!
HA!
HA!
HA!

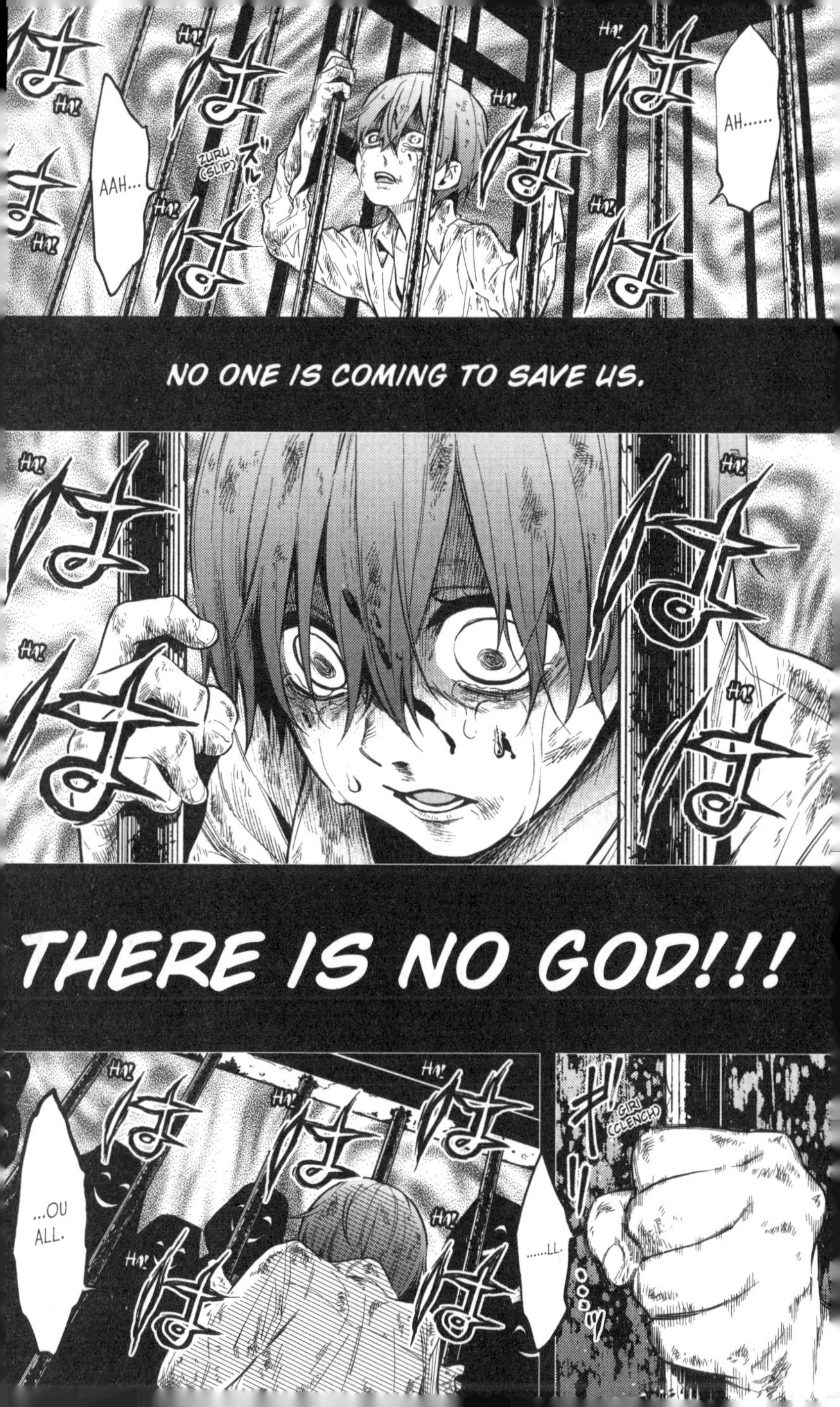

HA!
AH......
HA!
ZURU (SLIP)
AAH...
HA!
NO ONE IS COMING TO SAVE US.
HA!
HA!
HA!
THERE IS NO GOD!!!
GIRI (CLENCH)
HA!
......LL.
...OU ALL.

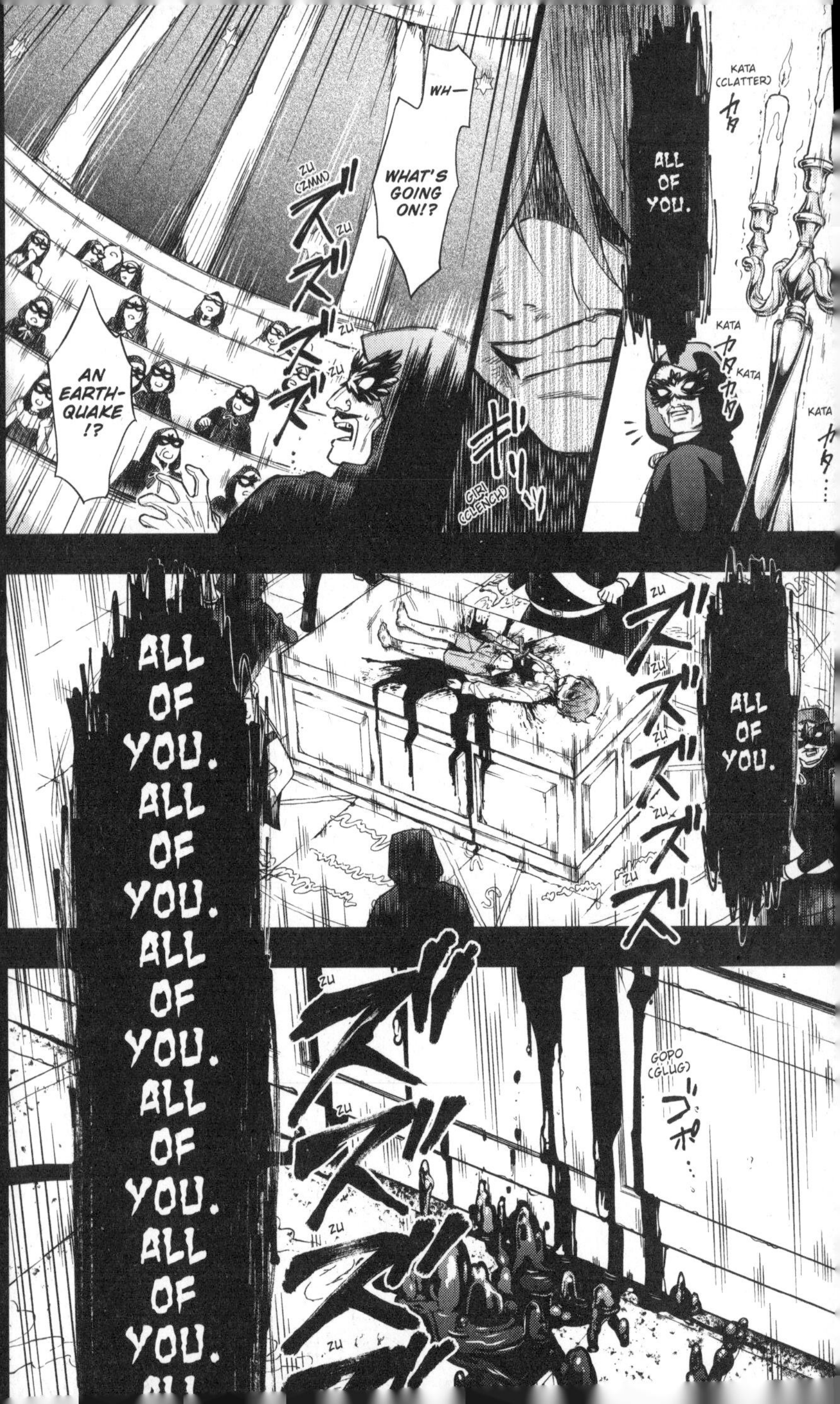
KATA (CLATTER)
ALL OF YOU.
KATA
KATA
KATA
GIRI (CLENCH)
WH—
WHAT'S GOING ON!?
ZU (ZMM)
ZU
ZU
ZU
AN EARTHQUAKE!?
ZU
ZU
ZU
ZU
ZU
ALL OF YOU.
GOPO (GLUG)
ZU
ZU
ZU
ZU
ALL OF YOU. ALL OF YOU. ALL OF YOU. ALL OF YOU. ALL OF YOU.

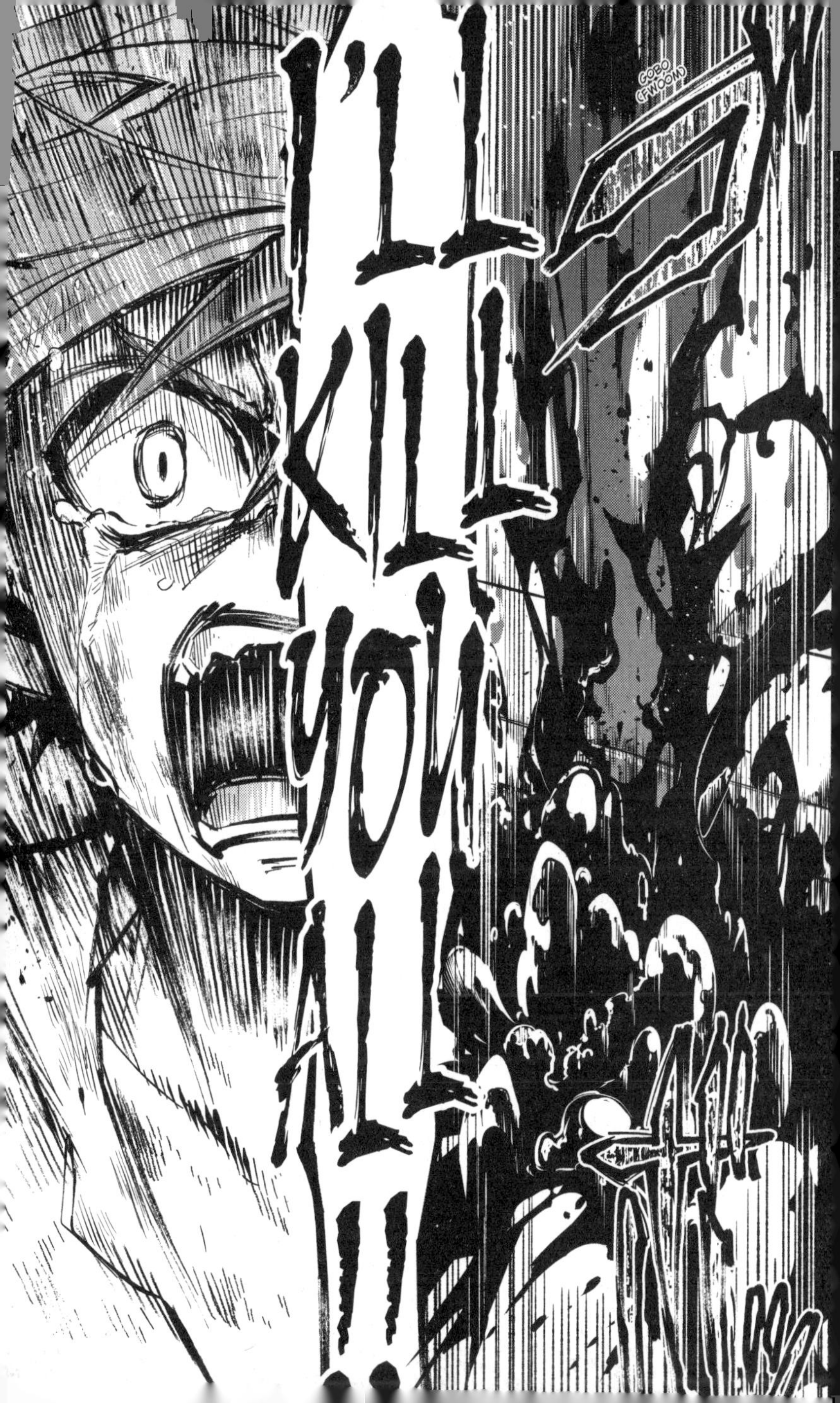
GOBO
(FWOOM)
I'LL KILL YOU ALL!!

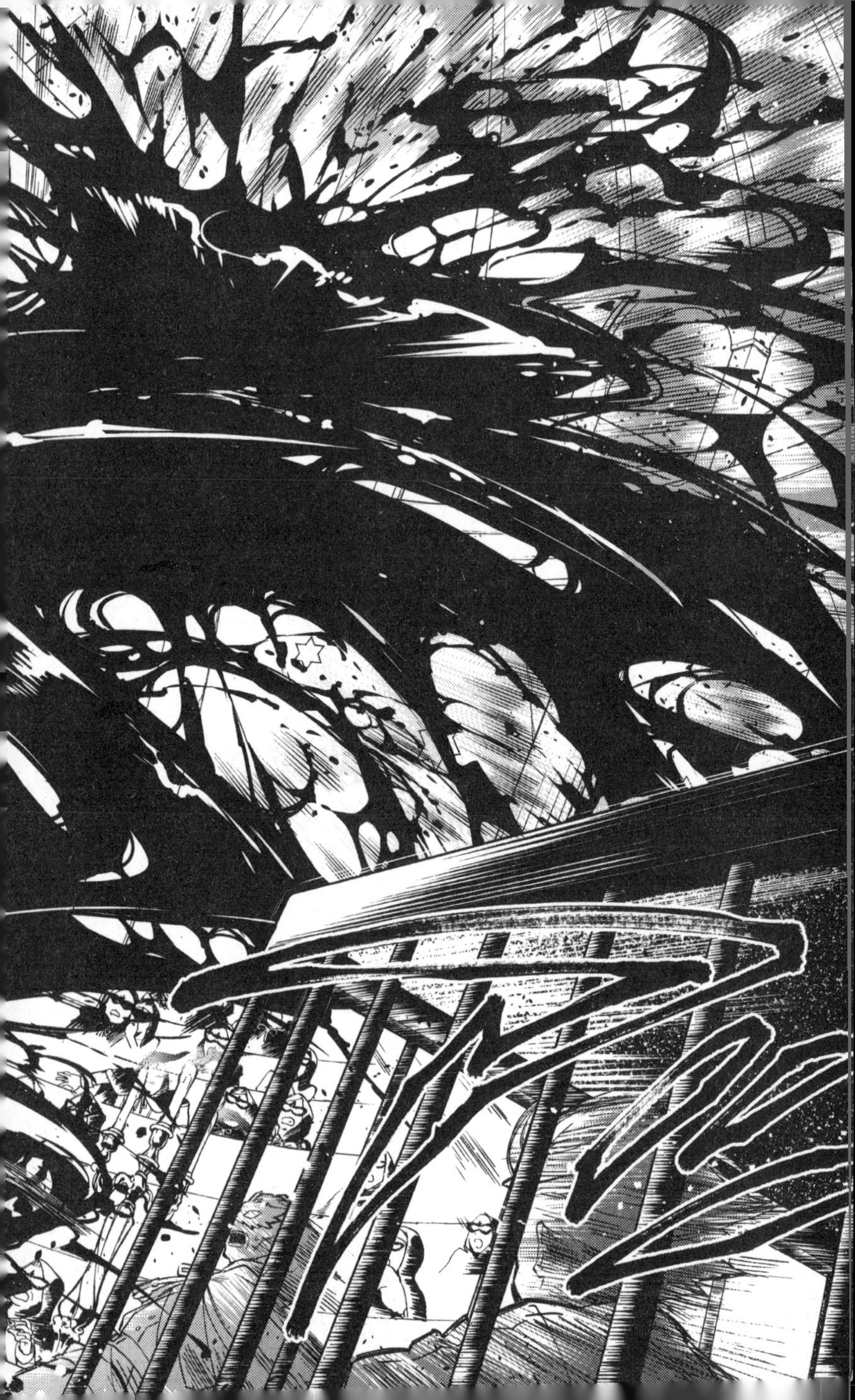

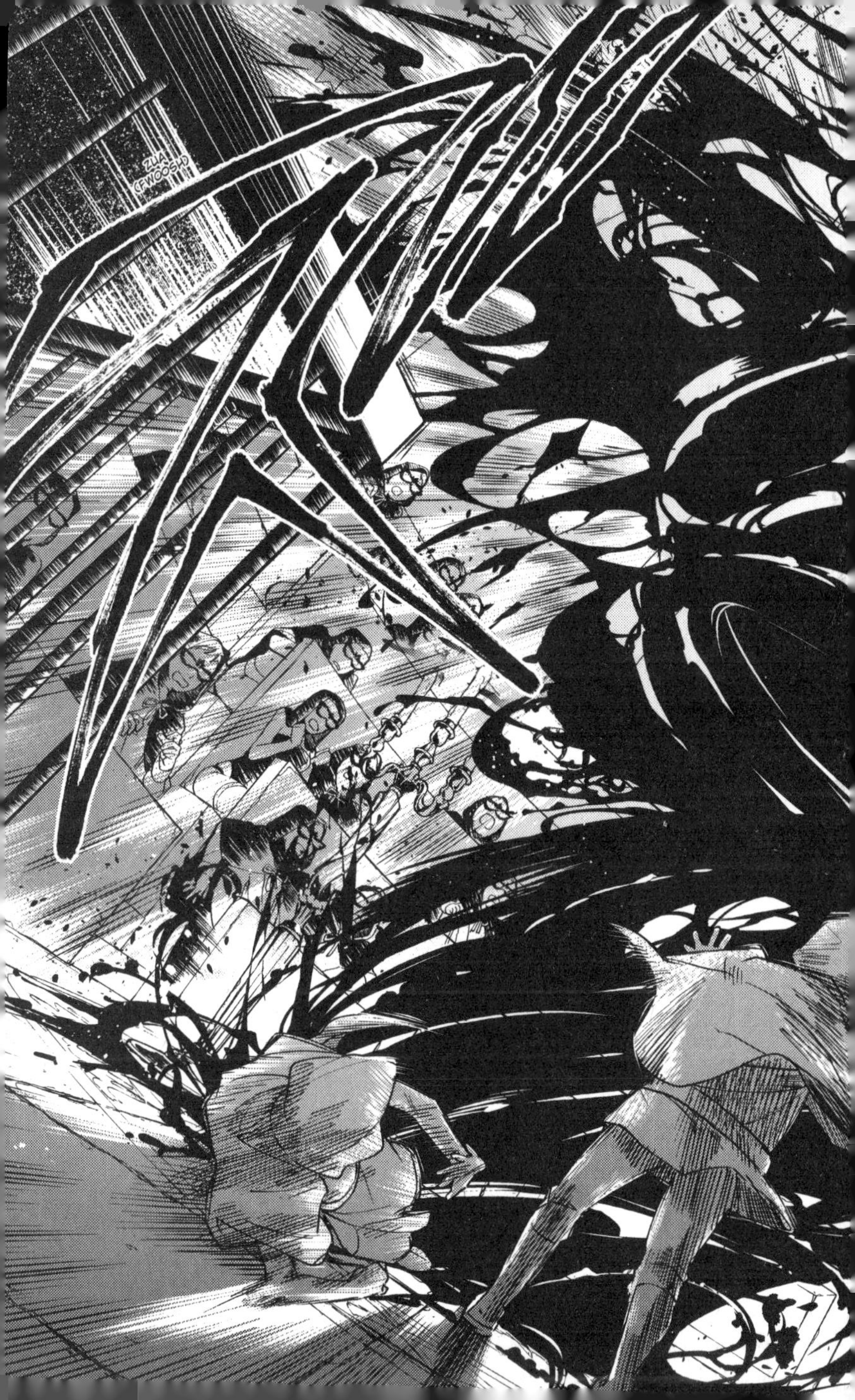
ZUA
(FWOOSH)

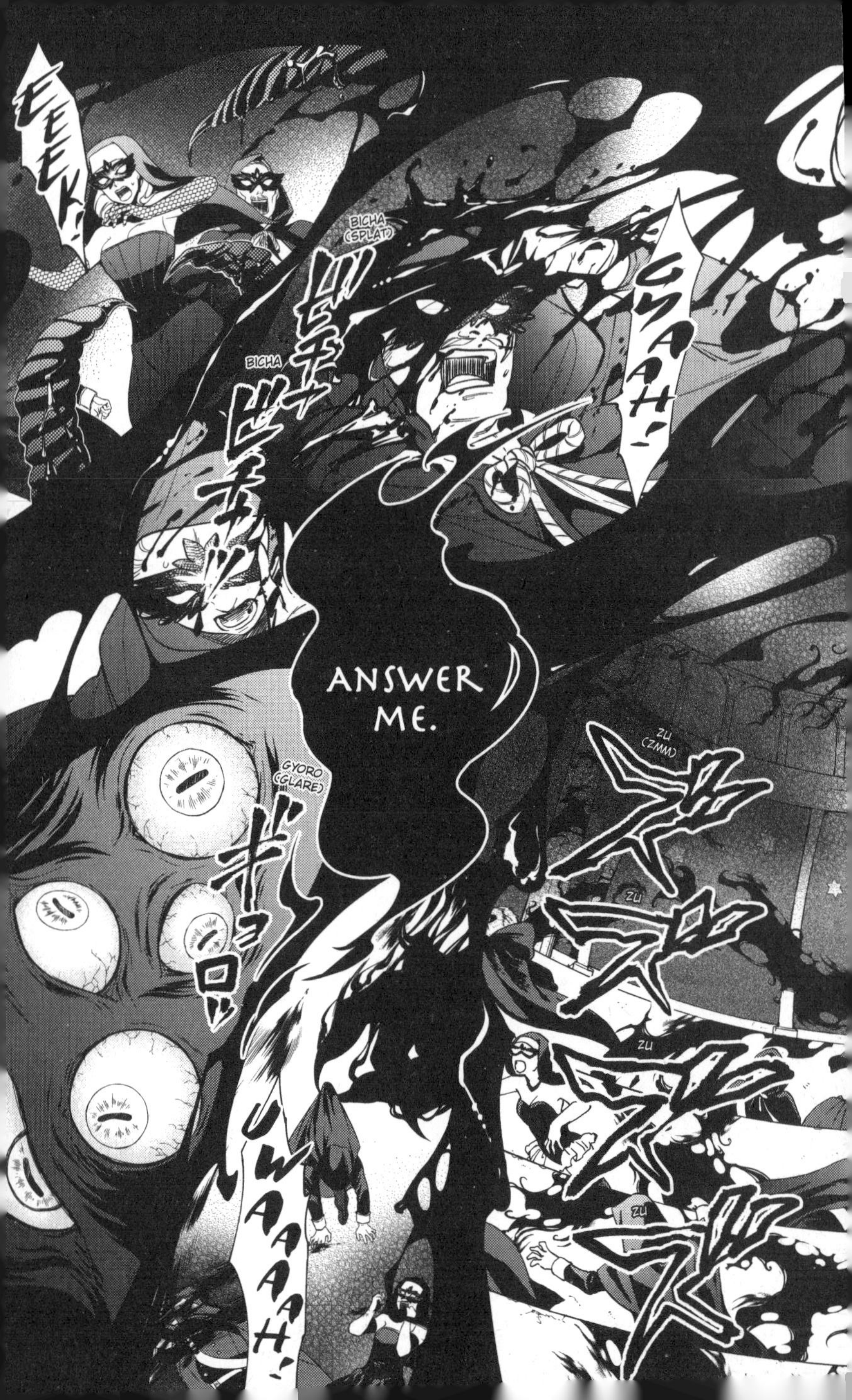
GYAAH!
BICHA (SPLAT)
BICHA
EEEEK!
ANSWER ME.
ZU (ZMM)
ZU
ZU
ZU
GYORO (GLARE)
UWAAAAH!

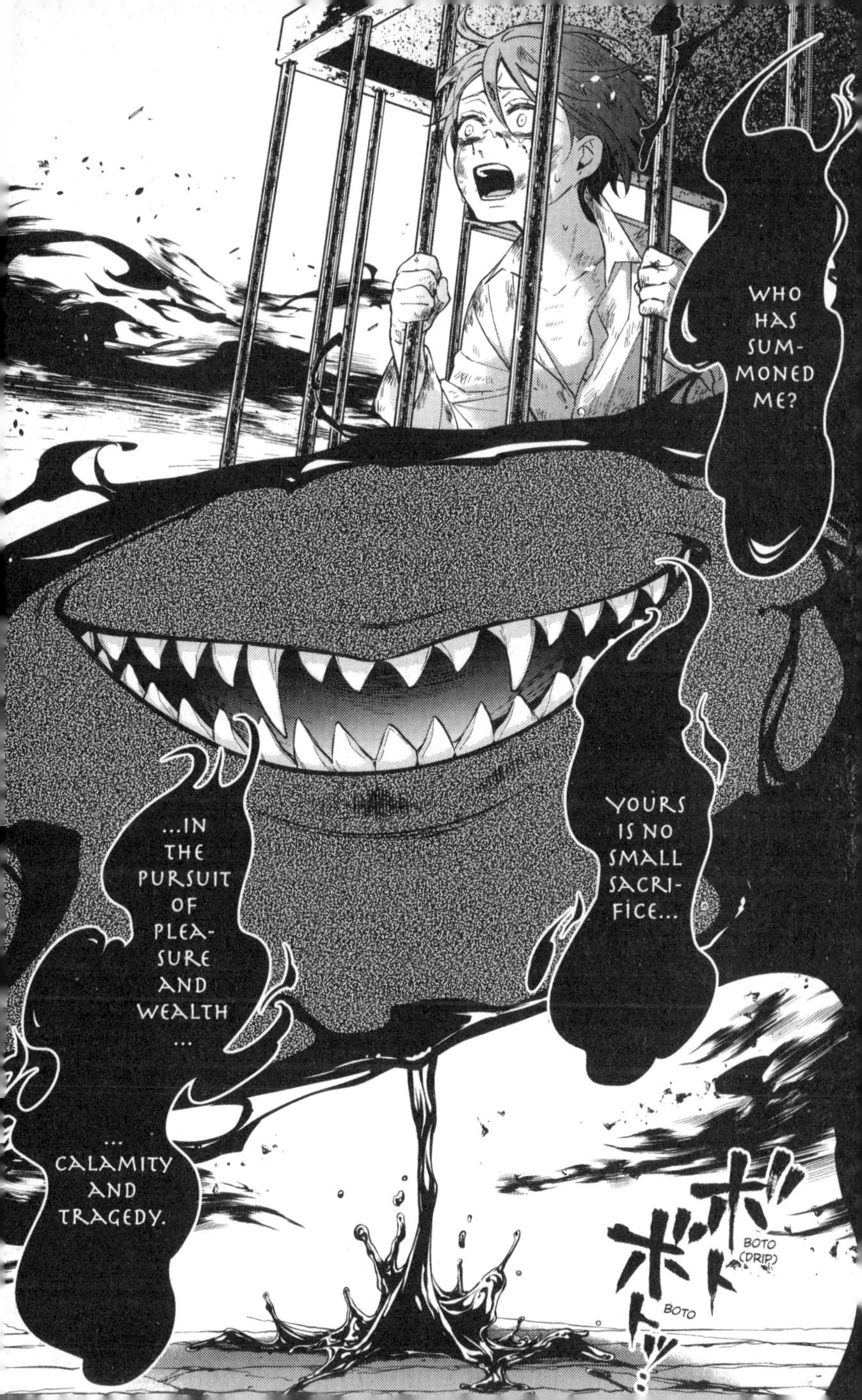
WHO HAS SUMMONED ME?
YOURS IS NO SMALL SACRIFICE...
...IN THE PURSUIT OF PLEASURE AND WEALTH...
...CALAMITY AND TRAGEDY.
ボトボトッ!!
BOTO (DRIP)
BOTO

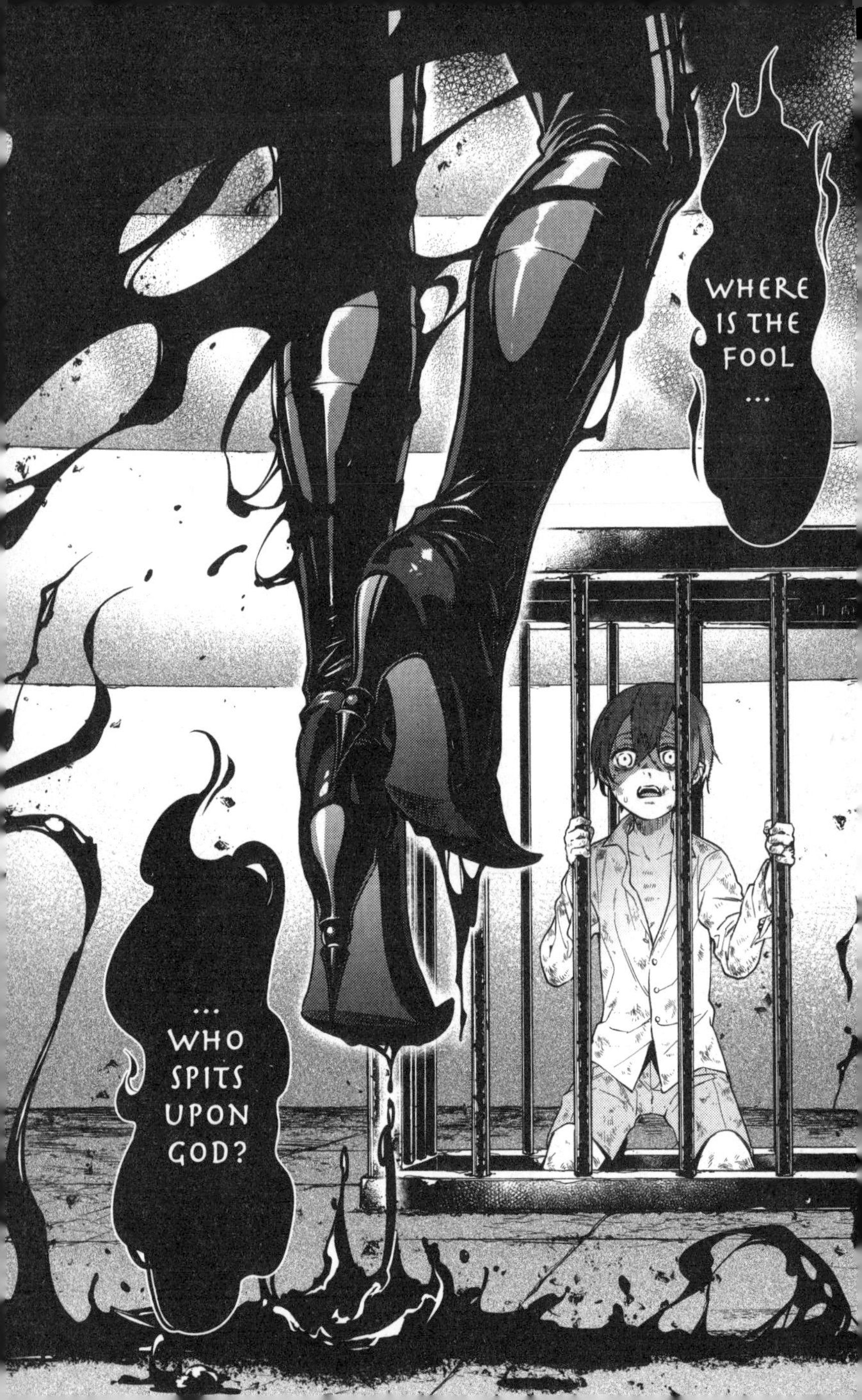
WHERE IS THE FOOL ...
... WHO SPITS UPON GOD?

**Black Butler**

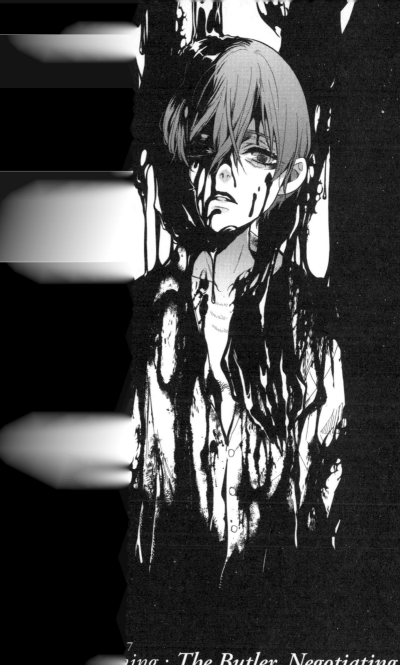

ing : *The Butler, Negotiating*

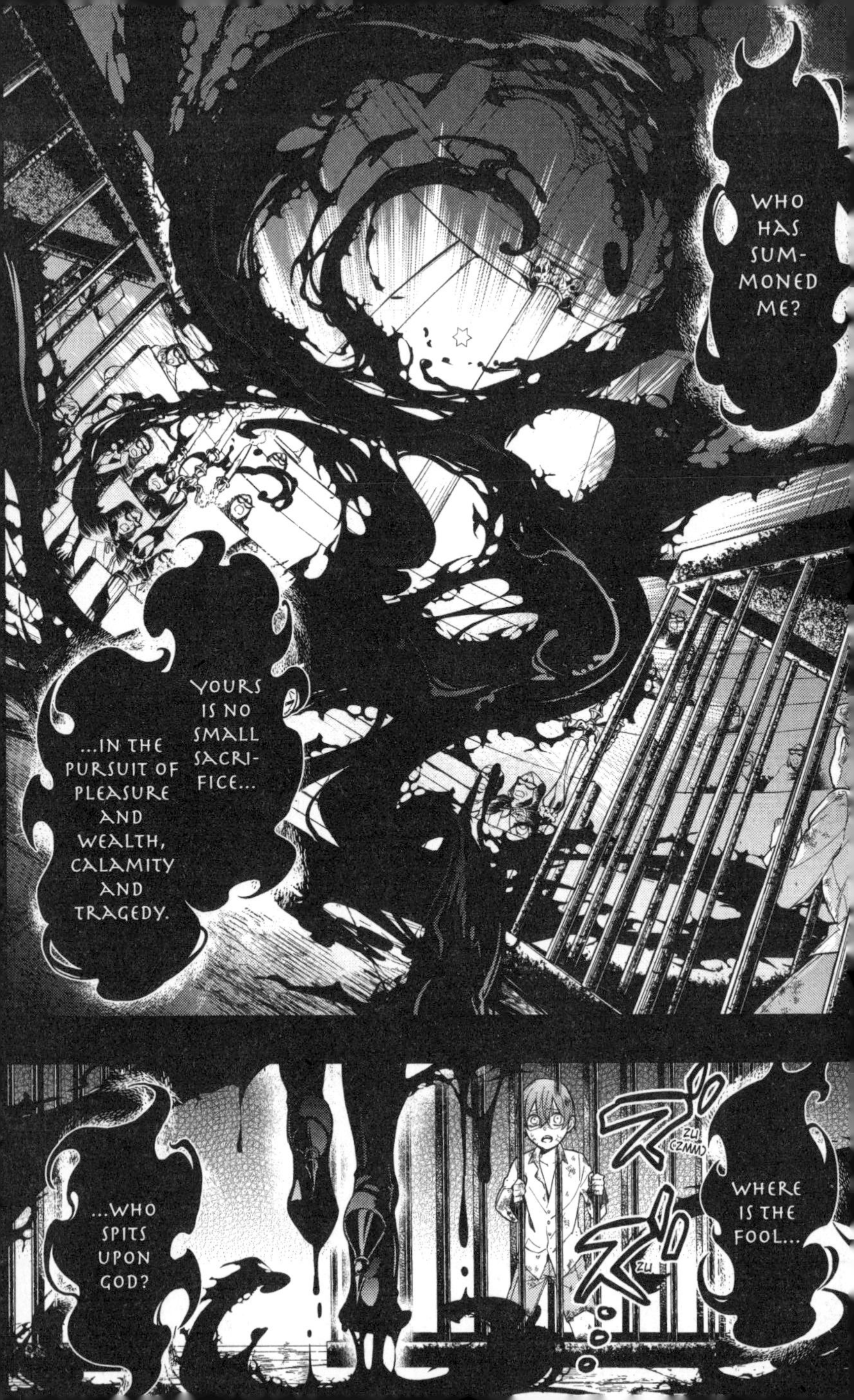
WHO HAS SUMMONED ME?
YOURS IS NO SMALL SACRIFICE...
...IN THE PURSUIT OF PLEASURE AND WEALTH, CALAMITY AND TRAGEDY.
ZU (ZMM)
ZU
WHERE IS THE FOOL...
...WHO SPITS UPON GOD?

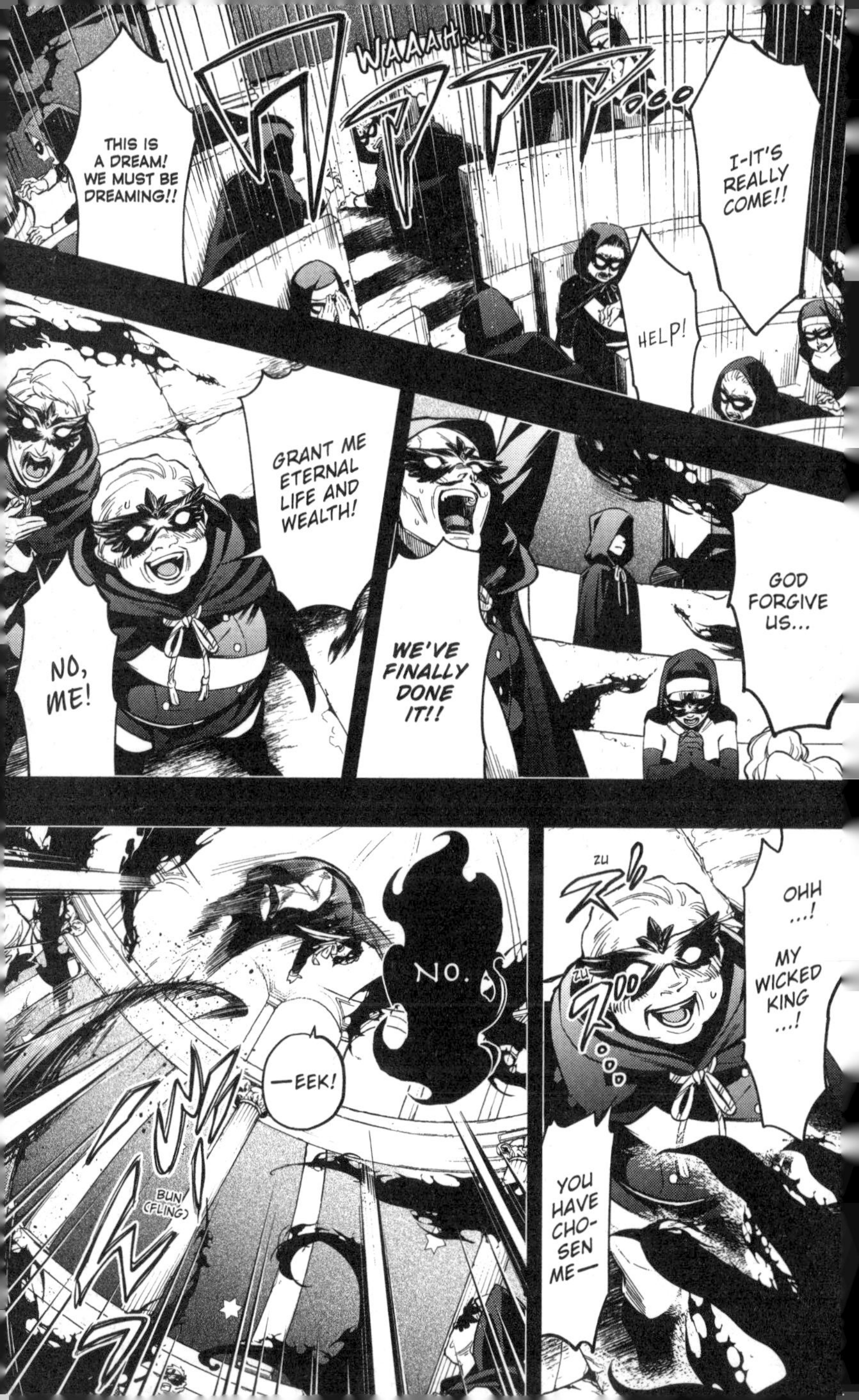
I-IT'S REALLY COME!!
WAAAH...
THIS IS A DREAM! WE MUST BE DREAMING!!
HELP!
GOD FORGIVE US...
WE'VE FINALLY DONE IT!!
GRANT ME ETERNAL LIFE AND WEALTH!
NO, ME!
ZU
ZU ZOO
OHH...! MY WICKED KING...!
YOU HAVE CHO-SEN ME—
NO.
—EEK!
BUN (FLING)

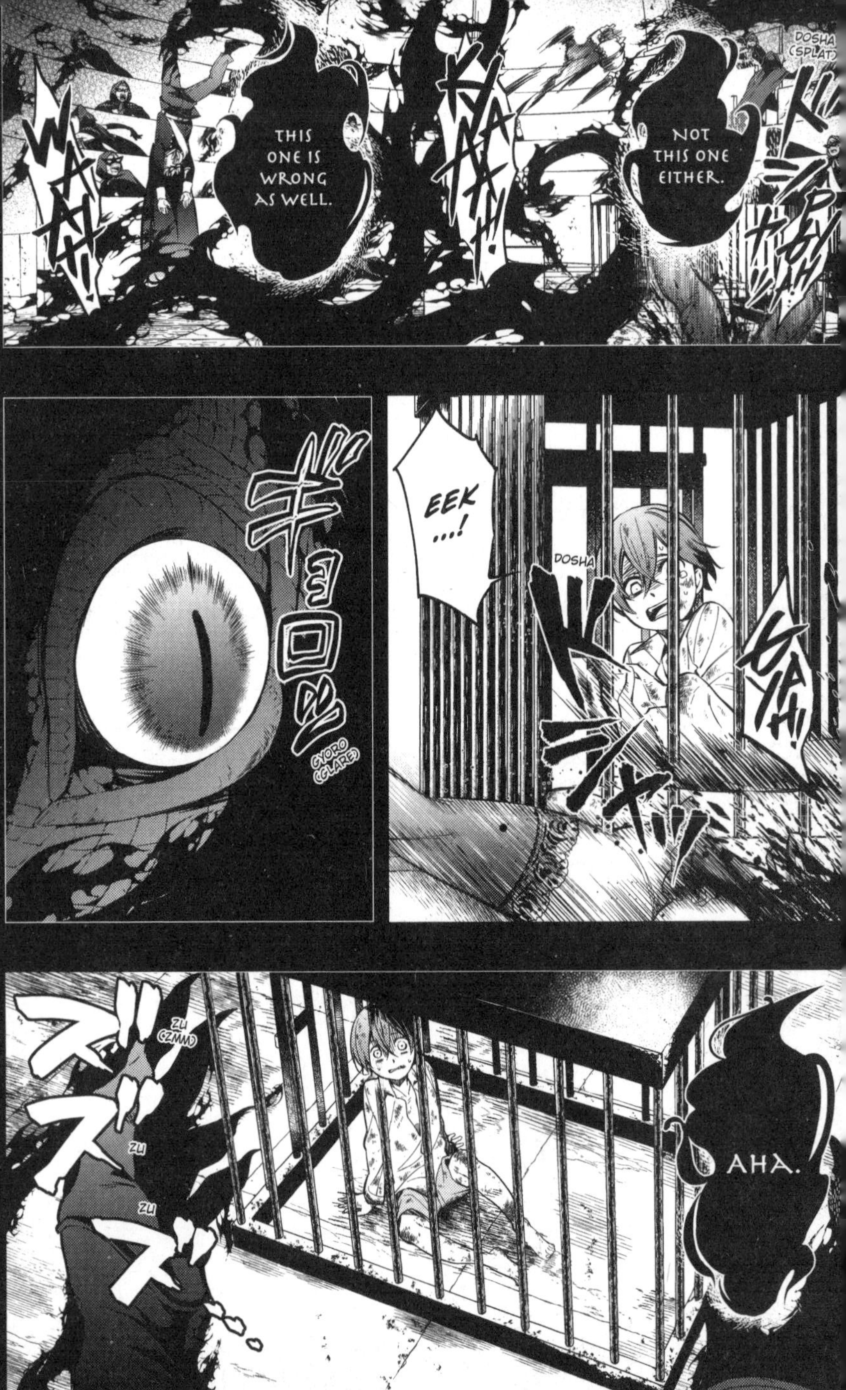
DOSHA (SPLAT)
NOT THIS ONE EITHER.
THIS ONE IS WRONG AS WELL.
EEK ...!
DOSHA
GYORO (GLARE)
AHA.
ZU (ZMM)
ZU
ZU

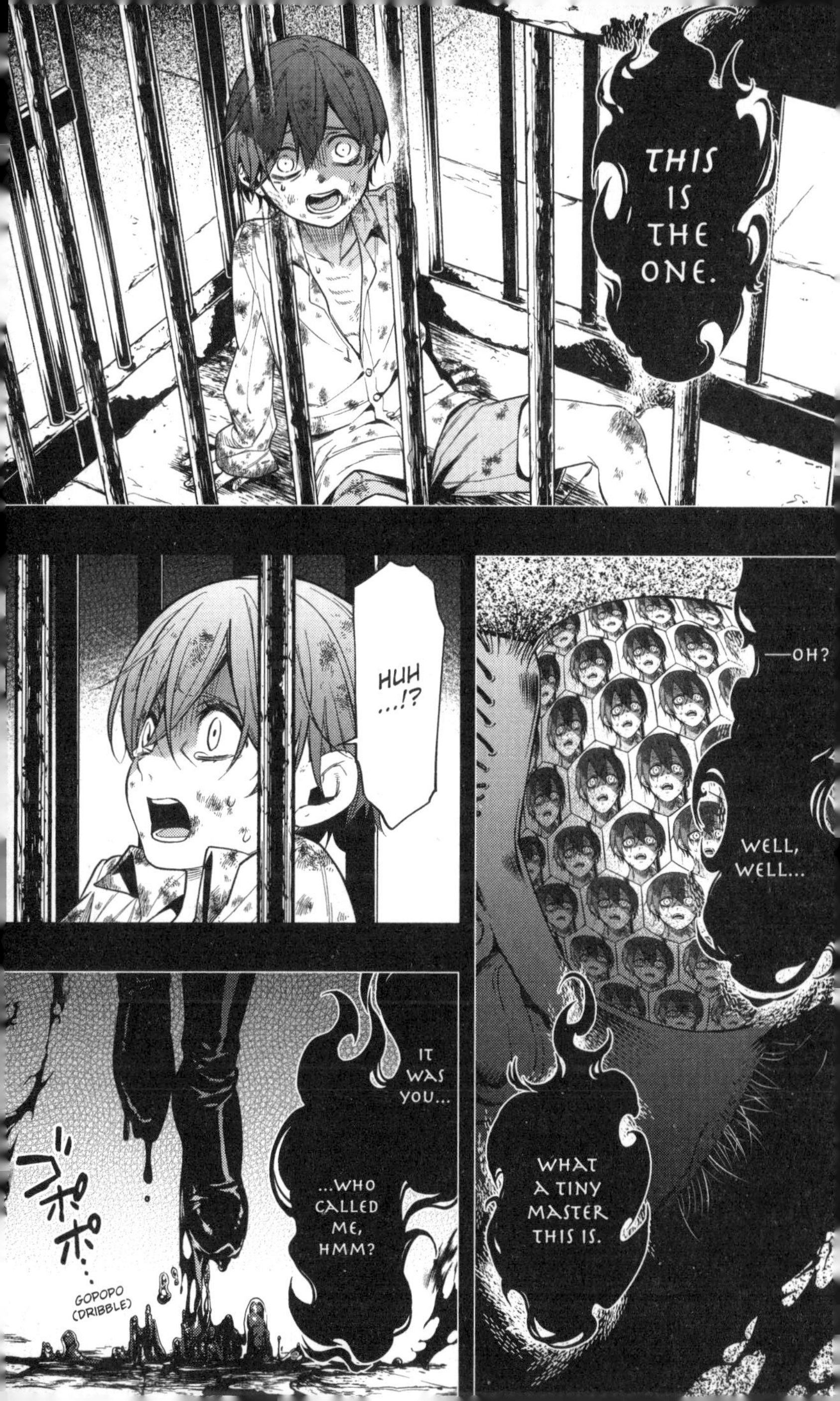
THIS IS THE ONE.
—OH?
WELL, WELL...
WHAT A TINY MASTER THIS IS.
HUH ...!?
IT WAS YOU...
...WHO CALLED ME, HMM?
ゴポポ...
GOPOPO (DRIBBLE)

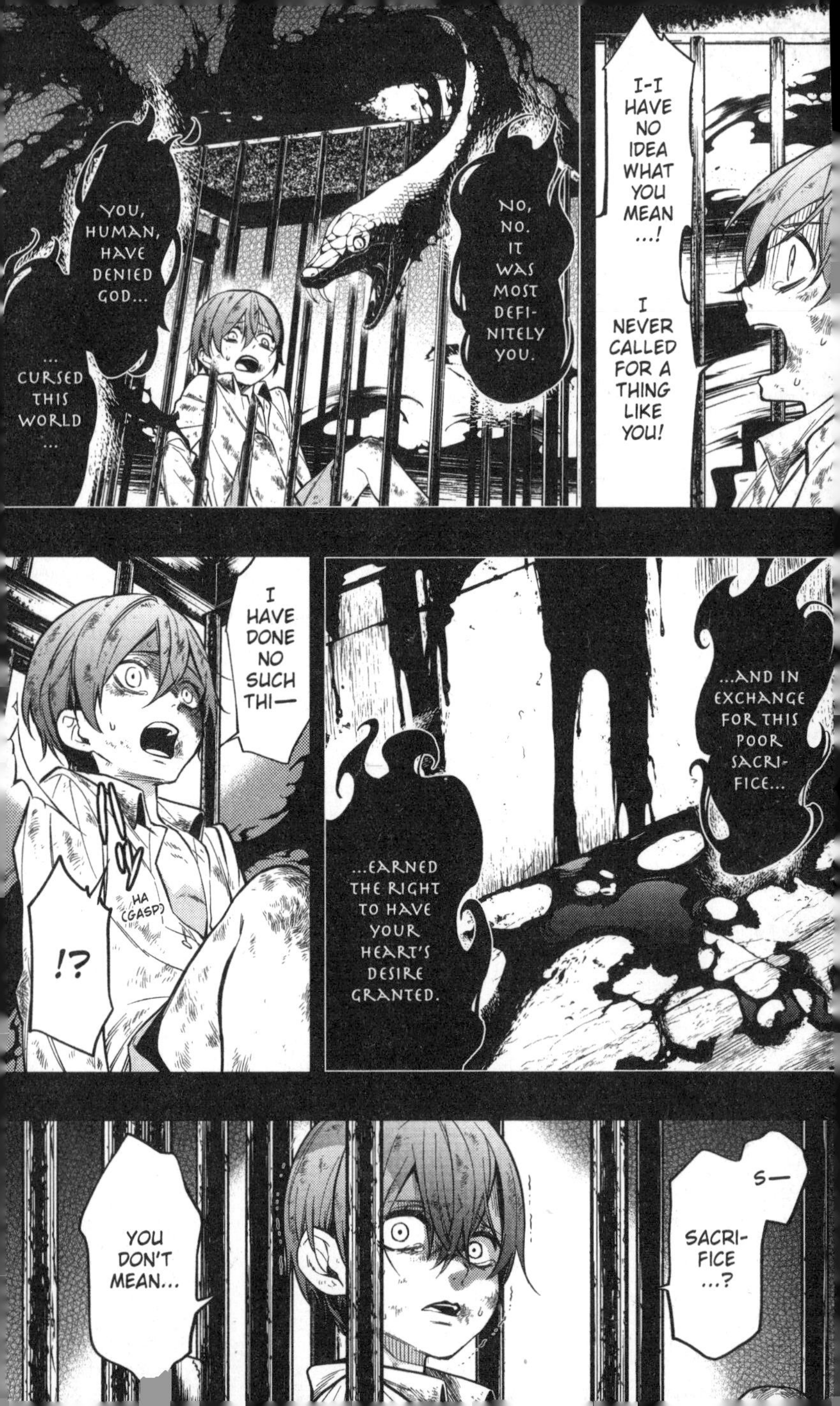
I-I HAVE NO IDEA WHAT YOU MEAN ...!
I NEVER CALLED FOR A THING LIKE YOU!
NO, NO. IT WAS MOST DEFI-NITELY YOU.
YOU, HUMAN, HAVE DENIED GOD...
...CURSED THIS WORLD ...
...AND IN EXCHANGE FOR THIS POOR SACRI-FICE...
...EARNED THE RIGHT TO HAVE YOUR HEART'S DESIRE GRANTED.
I HAVE DONE NO SUCH THI—
HA (GASP)
!?
S—
SACRI-FICE ...?
YOU DON'T MEAN...

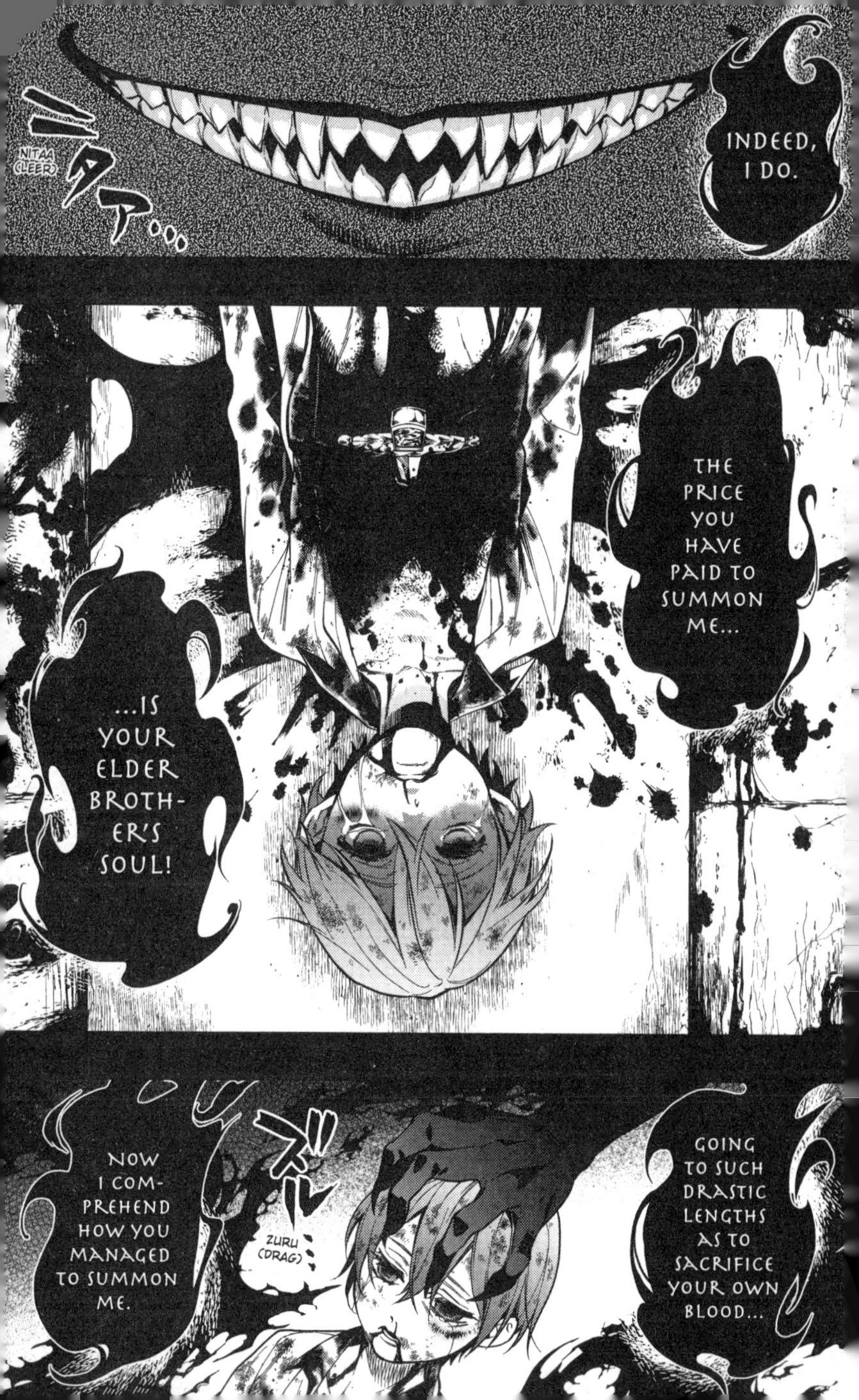
INDEED, I DO.
NITAA (LEER)
THE PRICE YOU HAVE PAID TO SUMMON ME...
...IS YOUR ELDER BROTH-ER'S SOUL!
GOING TO SUCH DRASTIC LENGTHS AS TO SACRIFICE YOUR OWN BLOOD...
ZURU (DRAG)
NOW I COM-PREHEND HOW YOU MANAGED TO SUMMON ME.

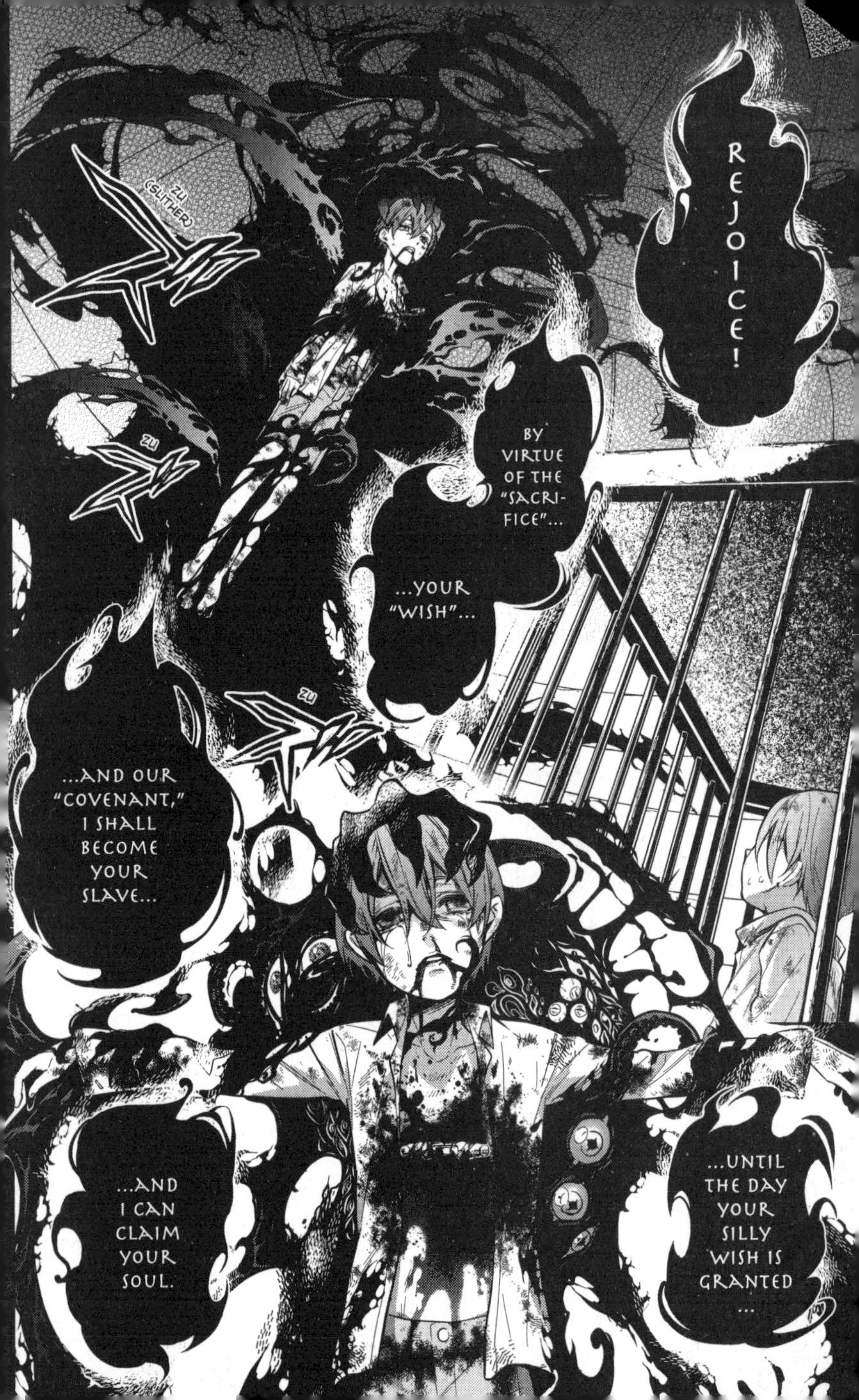
REJOICE!
ZU (SLITHER)
BY VIRTUE OF THE "SACRIFICE"...
...YOUR "WISH"...
ZU
ZU
...AND OUR "COVENANT," I SHALL BECOME YOUR SLAVE...
...UNTIL THE DAY YOUR SILLY WISH IS GRANTED ...
...AND I CAN CLAIM YOUR SOUL.

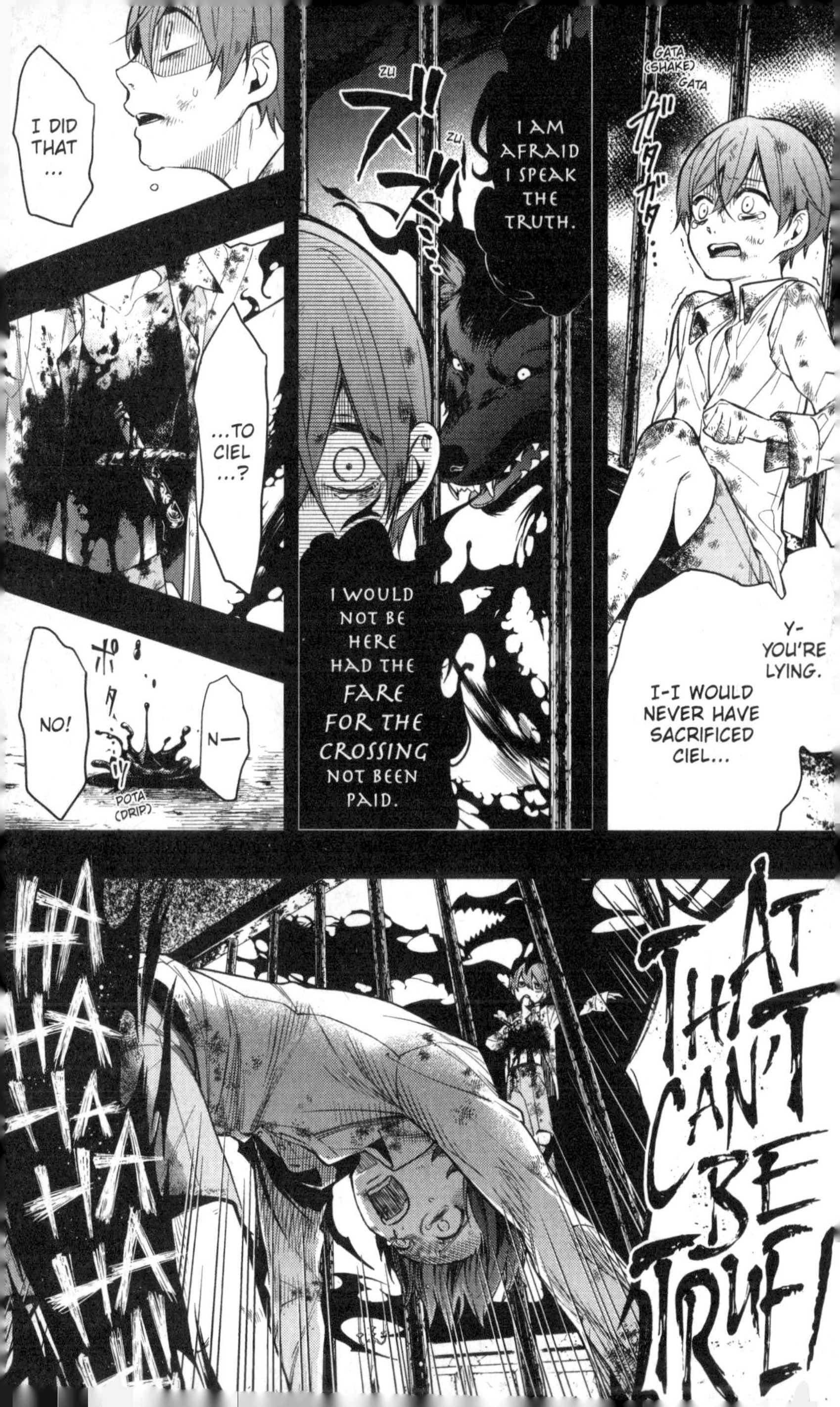
GATA (SHAKE) GATA
Y-YOU'RE LYING.
I-I WOULD NEVER HAVE SACRIFICED CIEL...
ZU
ZU
I AM AFRAID I SPEAK THE TRUTH.
I WOULD NOT BE HERE HAD THE FARE FOR THE CROSSING NOT BEEN PAID.
I DID THAT...
...TO CIEL...?
N—
NO!
POTA (DRIP)
THAT CAN'T BE TRUE!
HAHAHAHAHA

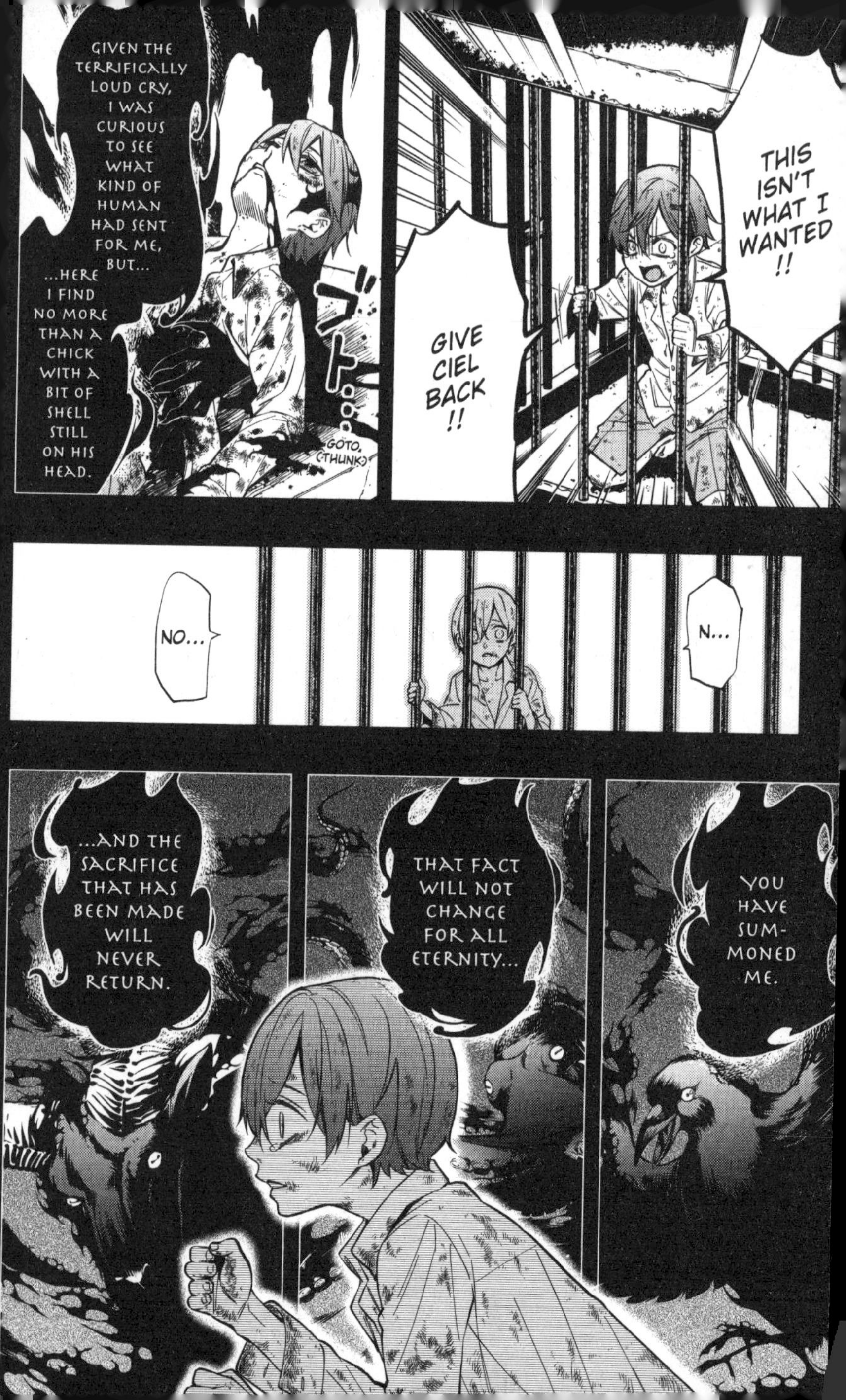
THIS ISN'T WHAT I WANTED!!
GIVE CIEL BACK!!
GIVEN THE TERRIFICALLY LOUD CRY, I WAS CURIOUS TO SEE WHAT KIND OF HUMAN HAD SENT FOR ME, BUT...
...HERE I FIND NO MORE THAN A CHICK WITH A BIT OF SHELL STILL ON HIS HEAD.
GOTO (THUNK)
N...
NO...
YOU HAVE SUM-MONED ME.
THAT FACT WILL NOT CHANGE FOR ALL ETERNITY...
...AND THE SACRIFICE THAT HAS BEEN MADE WILL NEVER RETURN.

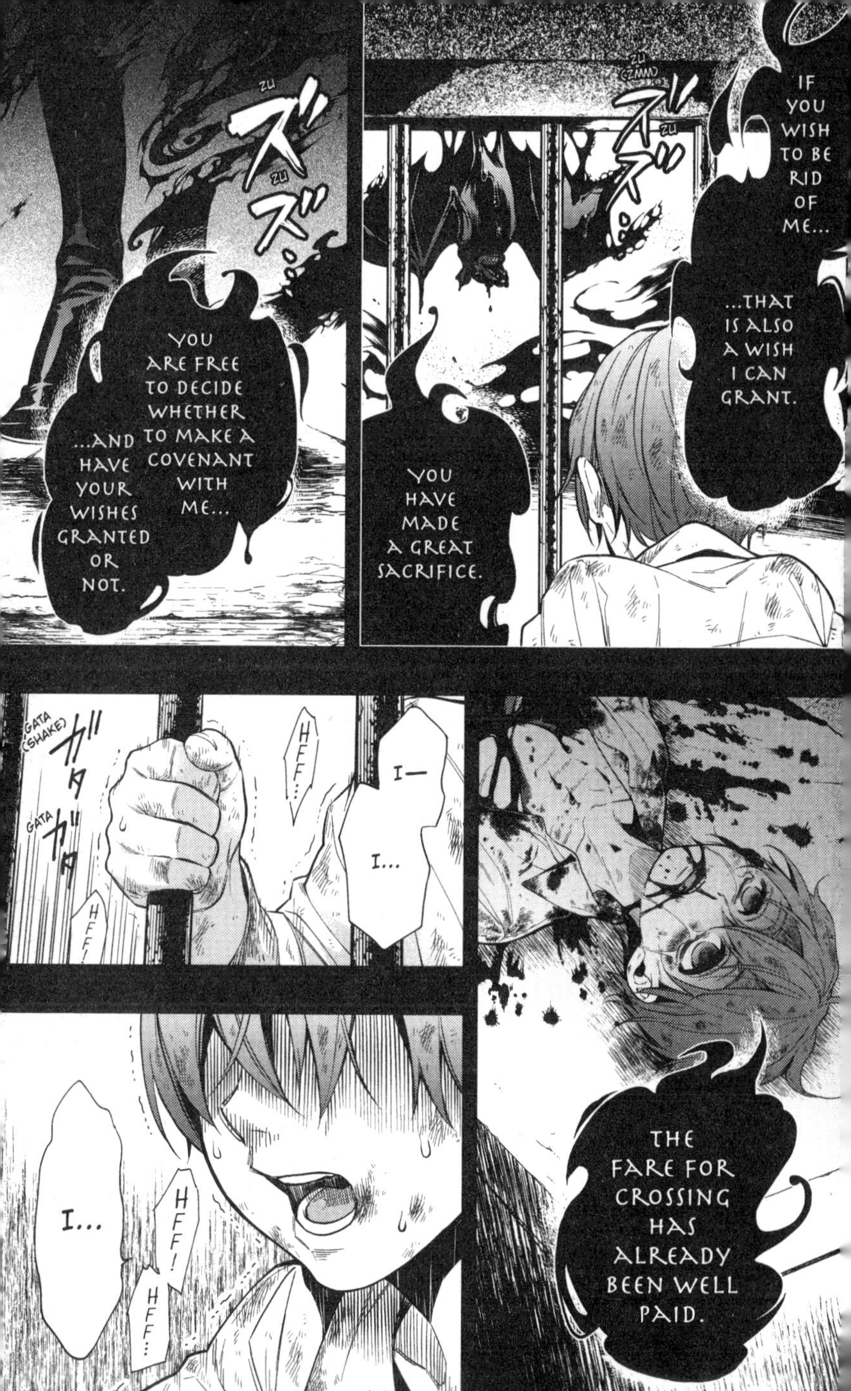
ZU (ZMM)
ズズ
ZU
IF YOU WISH TO BE RID OF ME...
...THAT IS ALSO A WISH I CAN GRANT.
YOU HAVE MADE A GREAT SACRIFICE.
ZU
ズ
ZU
ズ
YOU ARE FREE TO DECIDE WHETHER TO MAKE A COVENANT WITH ME...
...AND HAVE YOUR WISHES GRANTED OR NOT.
THE FARE FOR CROSSING HAS ALREADY BEEN WELL PAID.
HFF...
I—
I...
GATA (SHAKE)
ガタ
GATA
ガタ
HFF!
HFF!
HFF...
I...

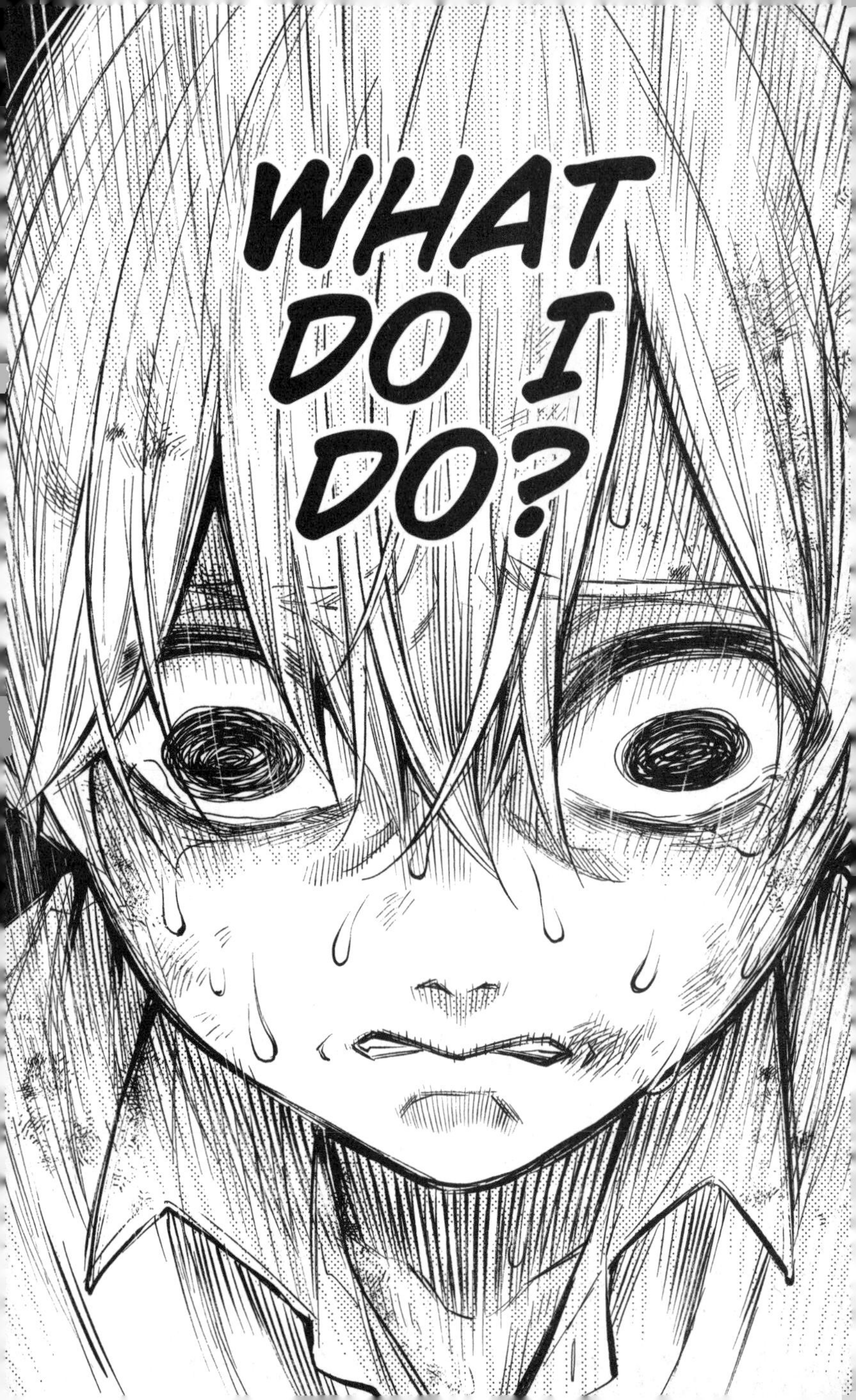
WHAT DO I DO?

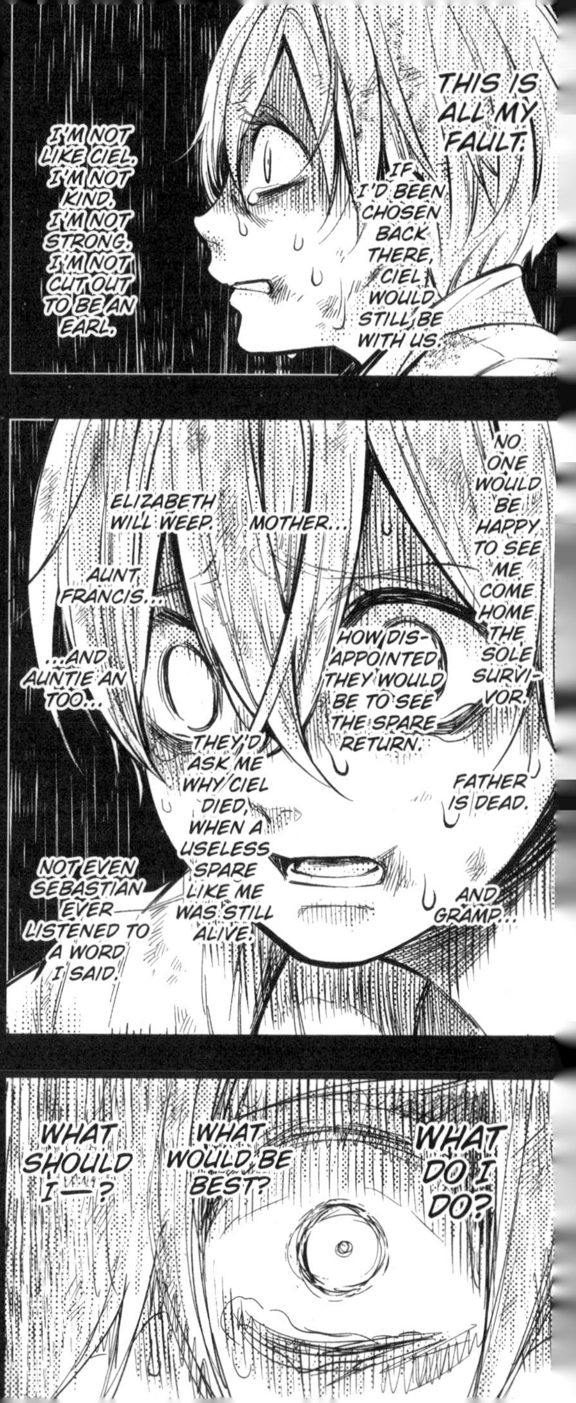
THIS IS ALL MY FAULT.
IF I'D BEEN CHOSEN BACK THERE, CIEL WOULD STILL BE WITH US.
I'M NOT LIKE CIEL. I'M NOT KIND. I'M NOT STRONG. I'M NOT CUT OUT TO BE AN EARL.
NO ONE WOULD BE HAPPY TO SEE ME COME HOME THE SOLE SURVIVOR.
HOW DIS-APPOINTED THEY WOULD BE TO SEE THE SPARE RETURN.
MOTHER...
ELIZABETH WILL WEEP.
AUNT FRANCIS...
...AND AUNTIE AN TOO...
FATHER IS DEAD.
AND GRAMP...
THEY'D ASK ME WHY CIEL DIED, WHEN A USELESS SPARE LIKE ME WAS STILL ALIVE.
NOT EVEN SEBASTIAN EVER LISTENED TO A WORD I SAID.
WHAT DO I DO?
WHAT WOULD BE BEST?
WHAT SHOULD I—?

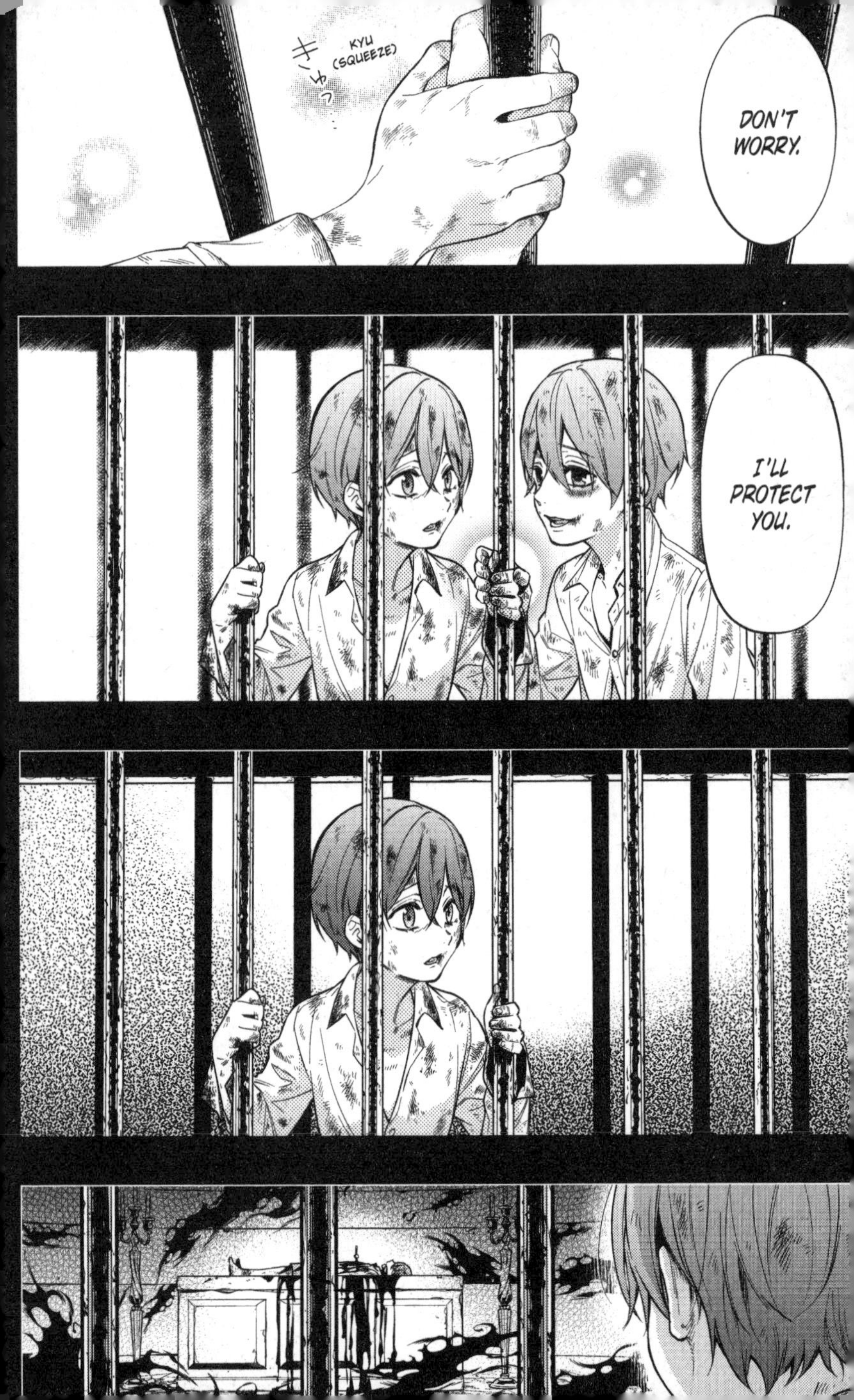
DON'T WORRY.
きゅっ
KYU (SQUEEZE)
I'LL PROTECT YOU.

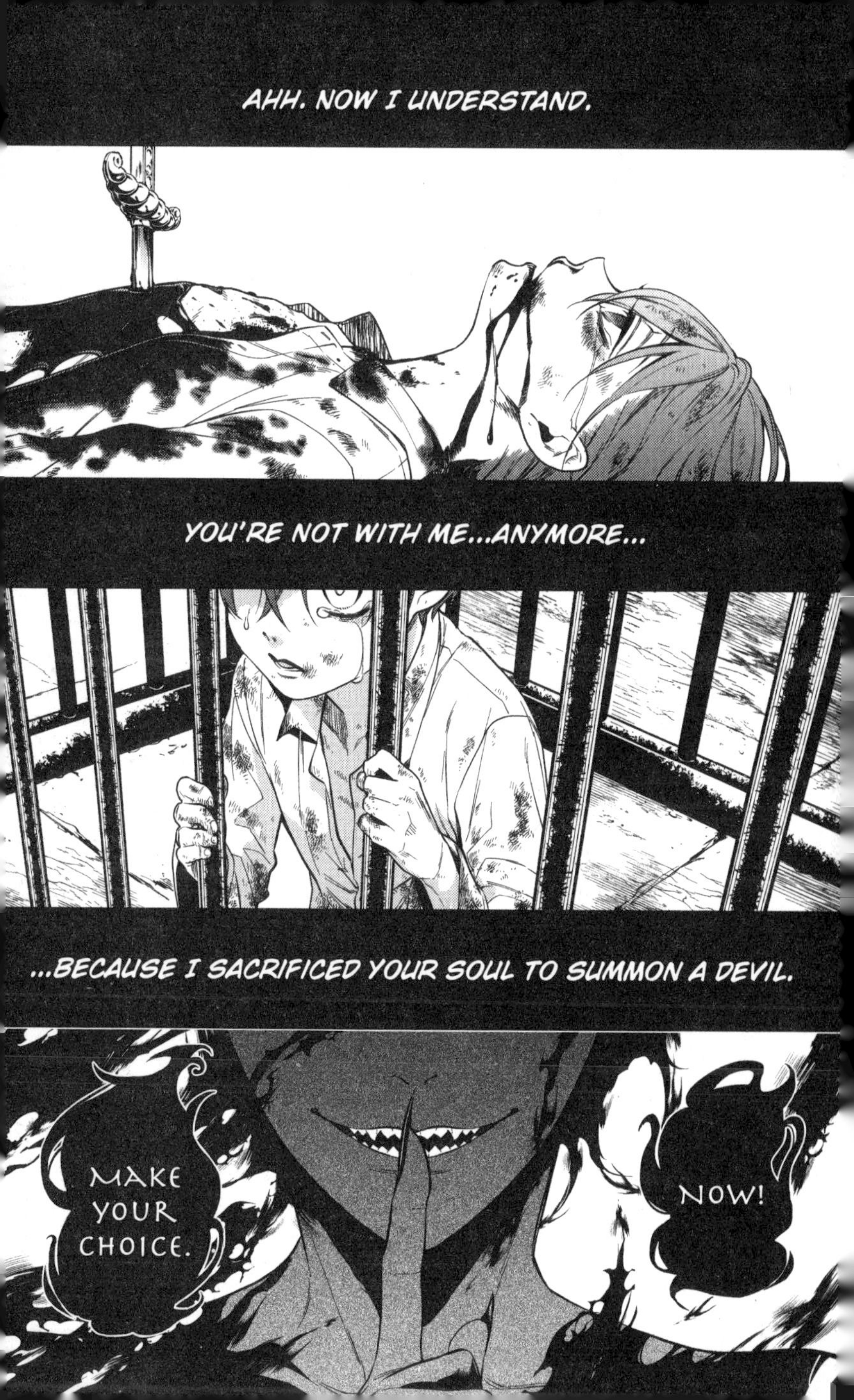
AHH. NOW I UNDERSTAND.
YOU'RE NOT WITH ME...ANYMORE...
...BECAUSE I SACRIFICED YOUR SOUL TO SUMMON A DEVIL.
NOW!
MAKE YOUR CHOICE.

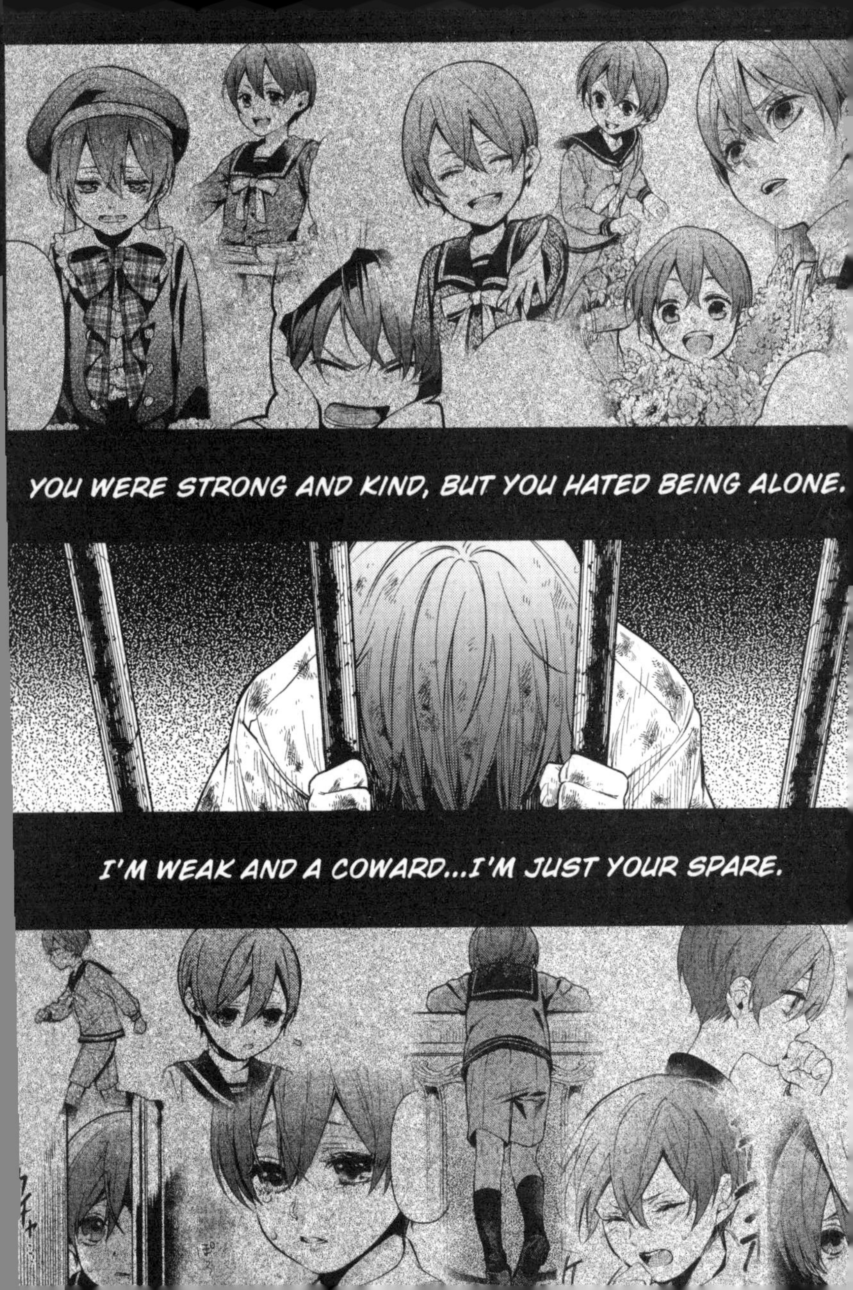
YOU WERE STRONG AND KIND, BUT YOU HATED BEING ALONE.
I'M WEAK AND A COWARD...I'M JUST YOUR SPARE.

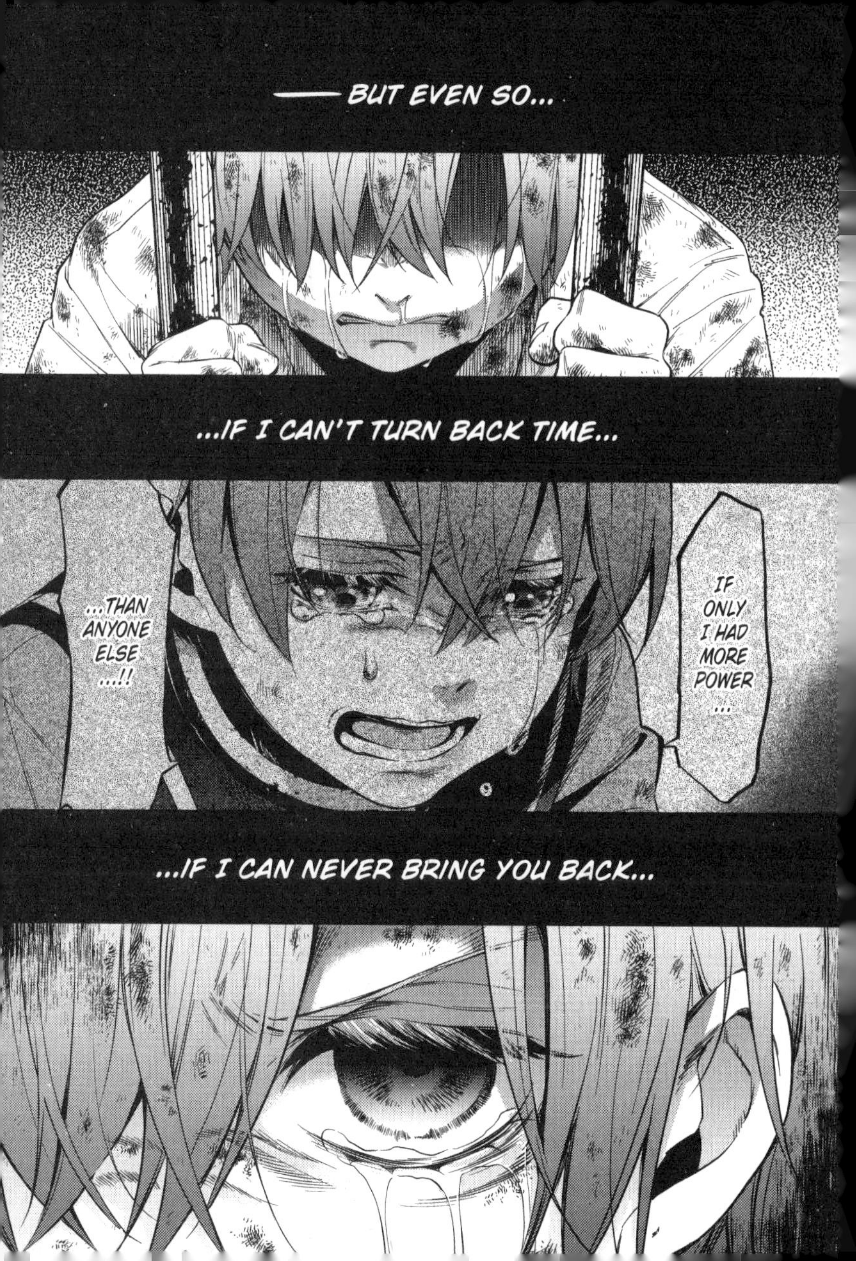
——BUT EVEN SO...
...IF I CAN'T TURN BACK TIME...
IF ONLY I HAD MORE POWER ...
...THAN ANYONE ELSE ...!!
...IF I CAN NEVER BRING YOU BACK...

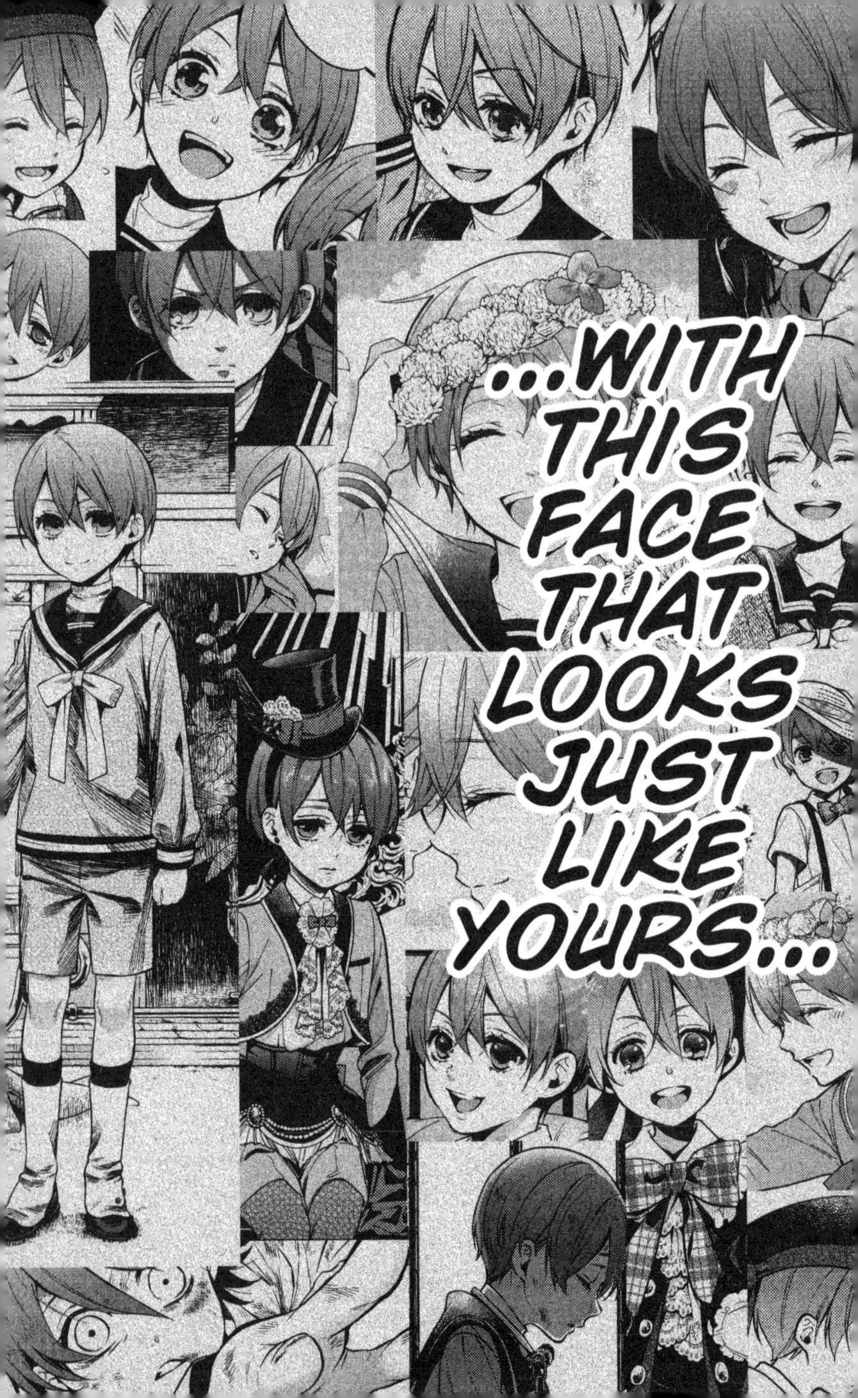
...WITH THIS FACE THAT LOOKS JUST LIKE YOURS...

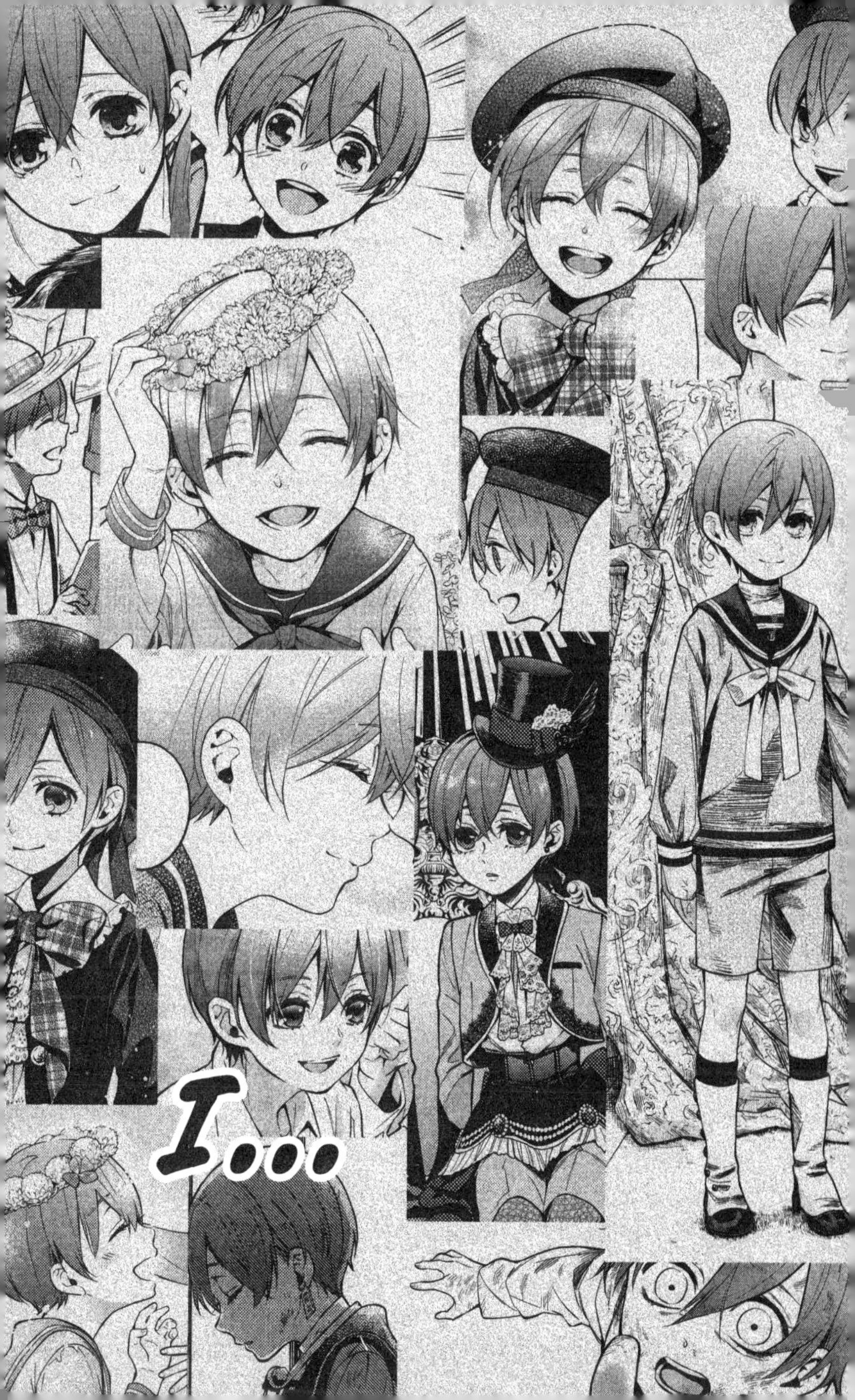
Iooo

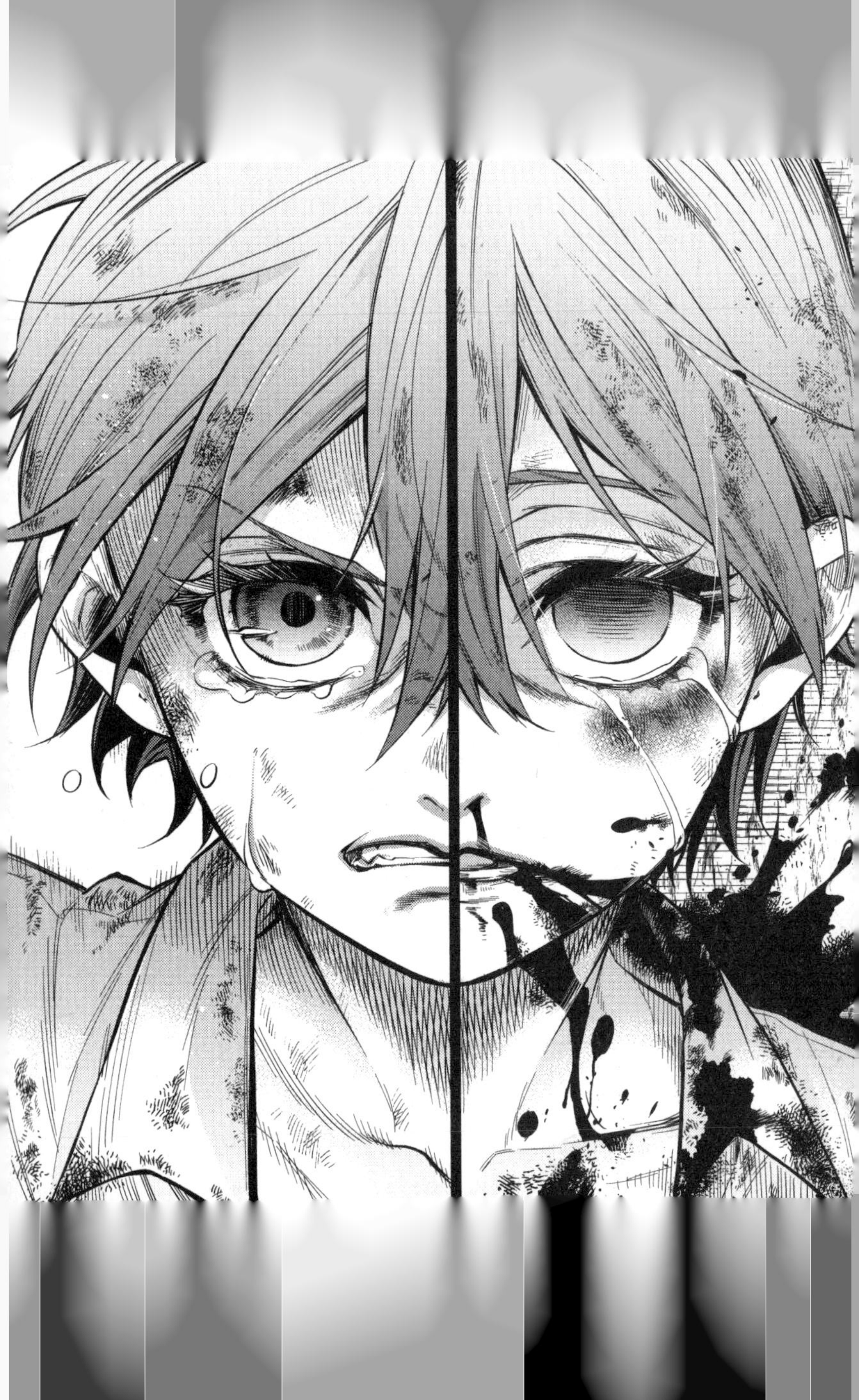

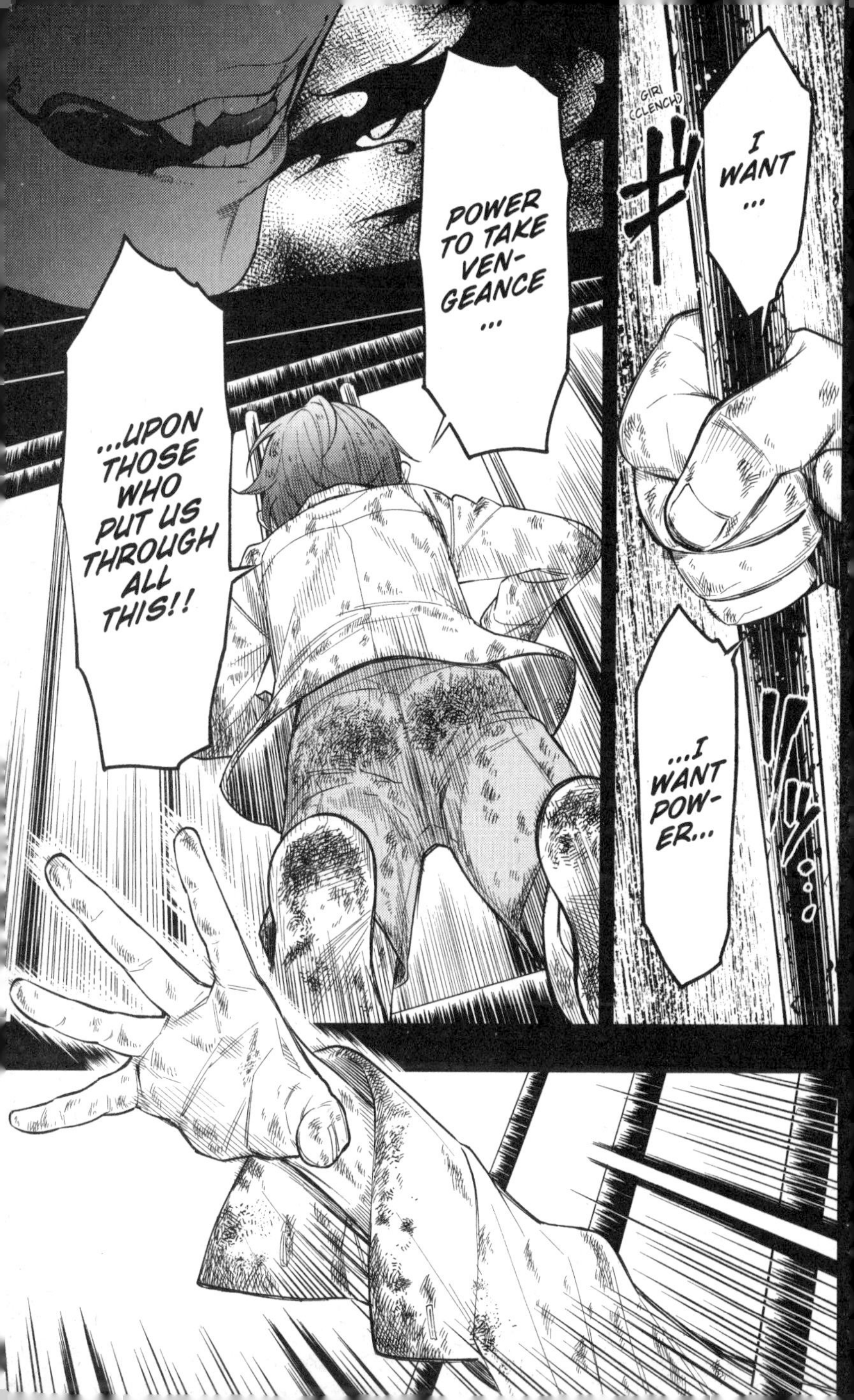
GIRI (CLENCH)
I WANT...
...I WANT POWER...
POWER TO TAKE VENGEANCE...
...UPON THOSE WHO PUT US THROUGH ALL THIS!!

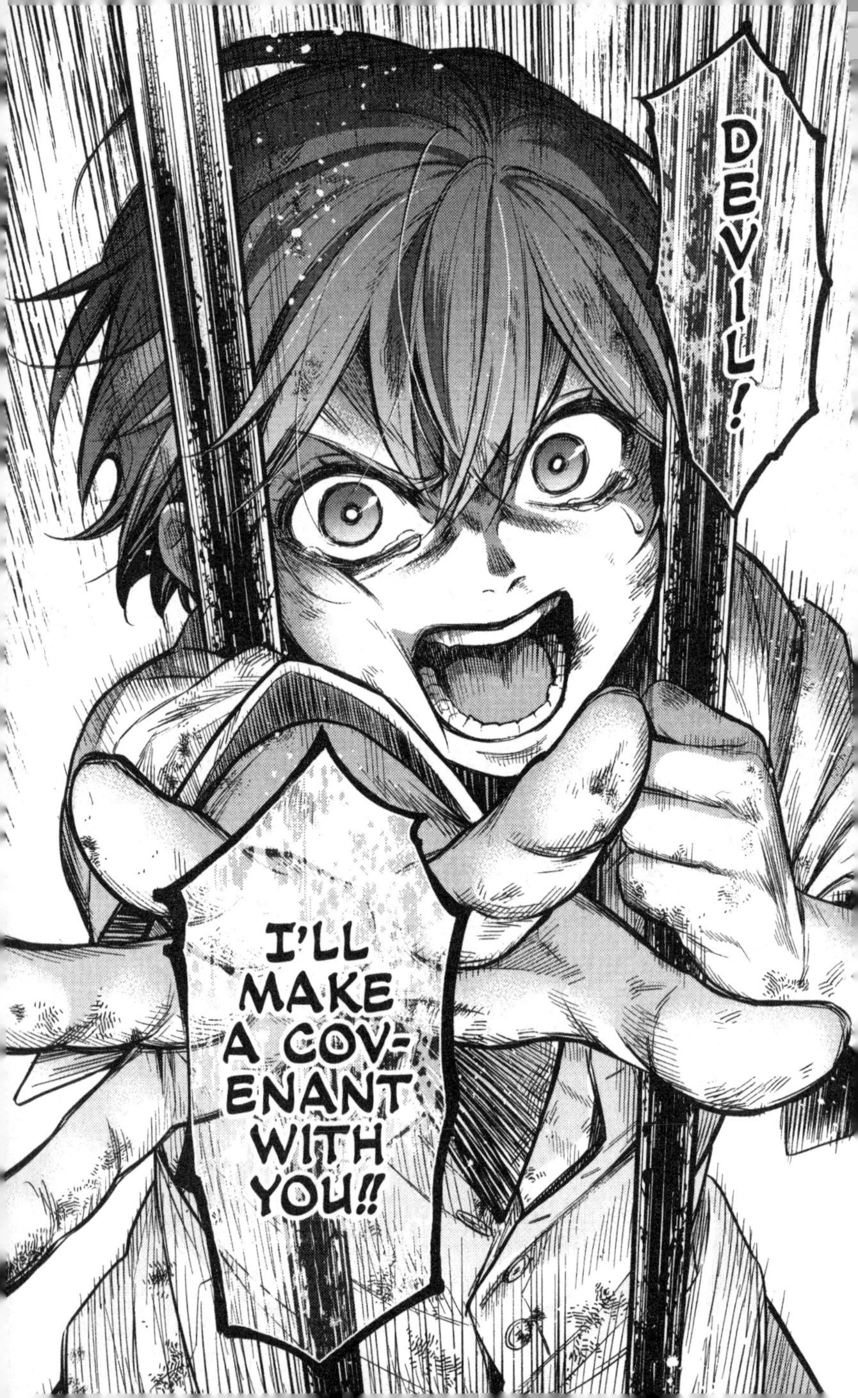
DEVIL!
I'LL MAKE A COV-ENANT WITH YOU!!

**Black Butler**

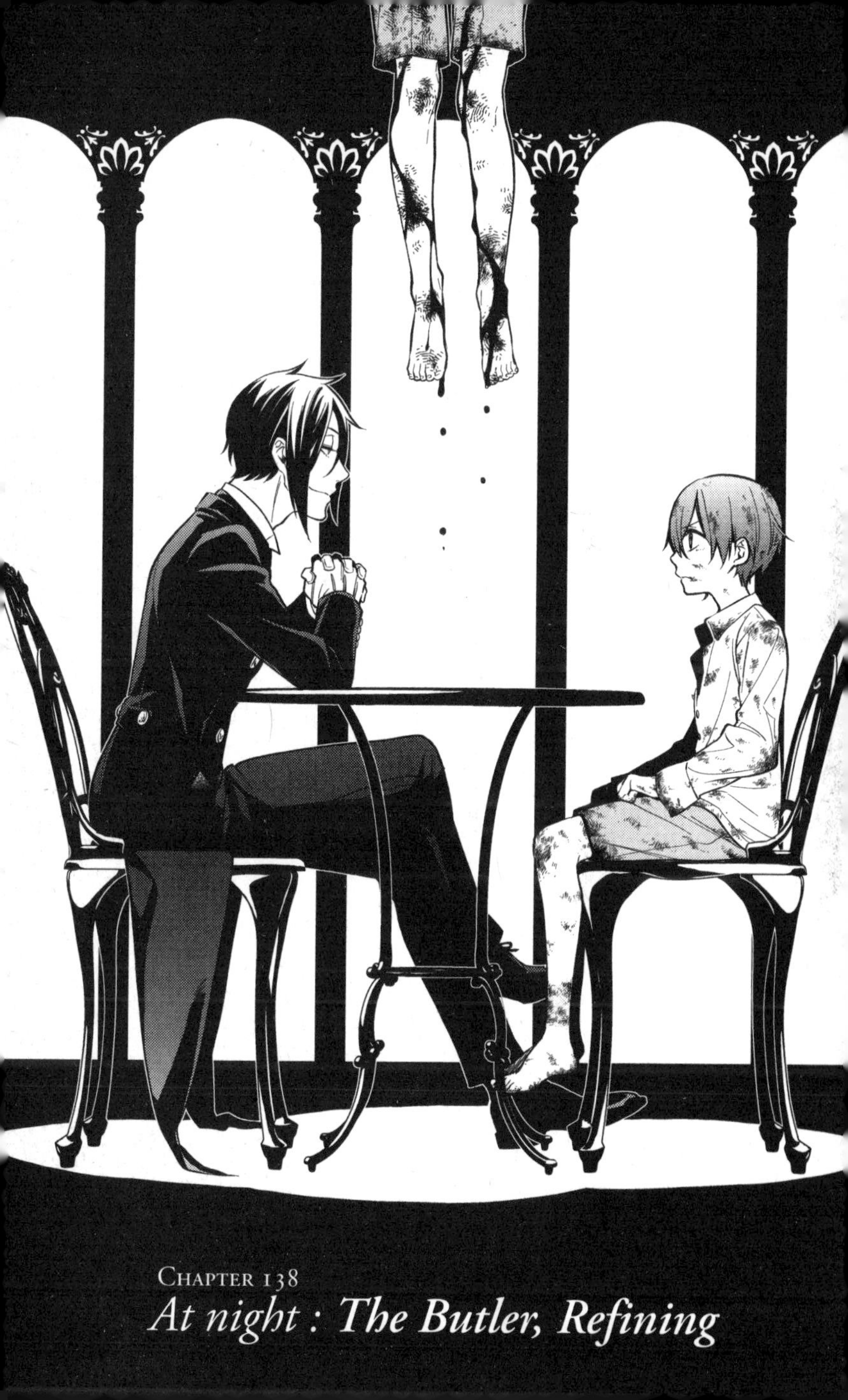

Chapter 138

# At night : The Butler, Refining

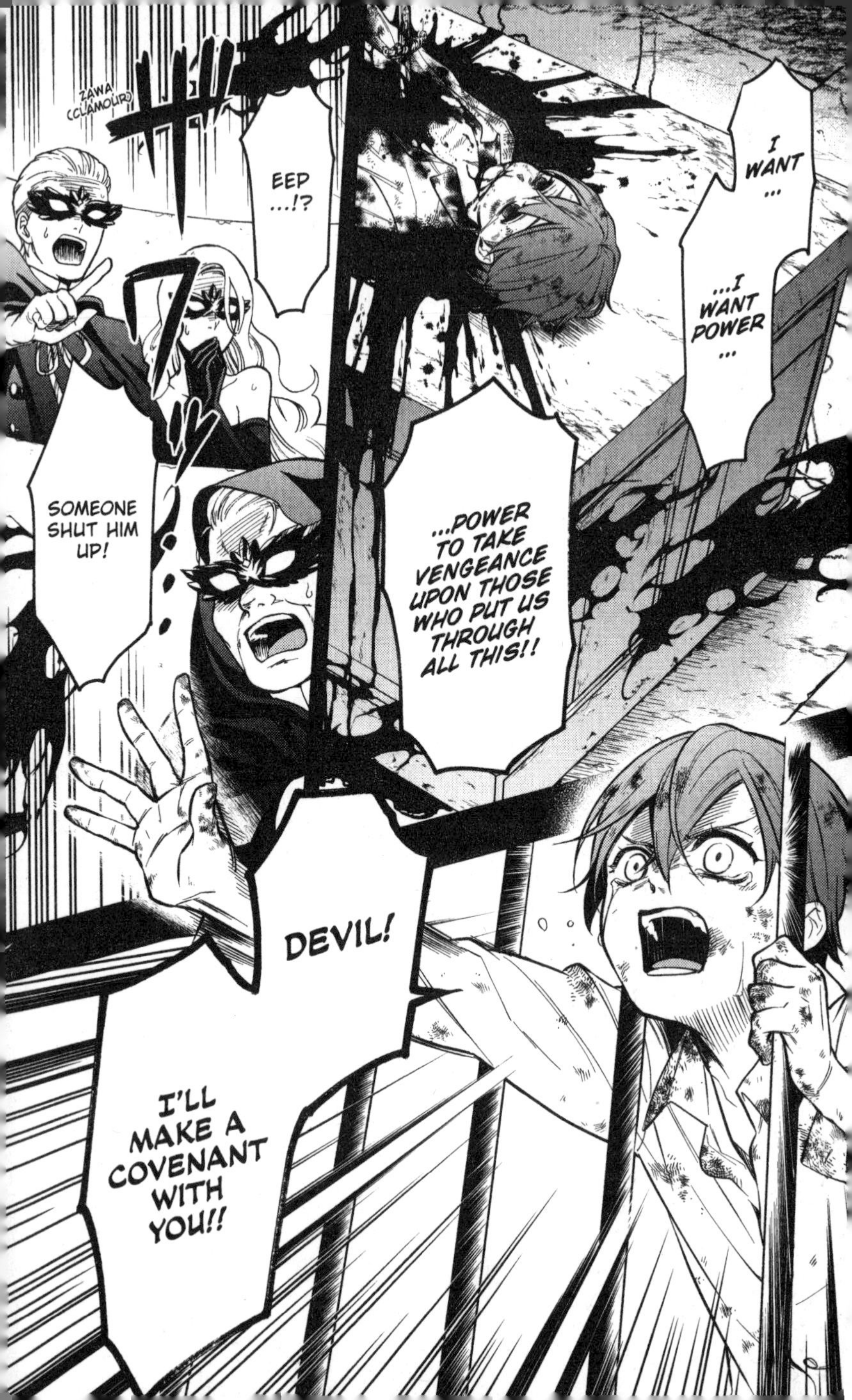
I WANT...
...I WANT POWER...
EEP...!?
ZAWA (CLAMOUR)
...POWER TO TAKE VENGEANCE UPON THOSE WHO PUT US THROUGH ALL THIS!!
SOMEONE SHUT HIM UP!
DEVIL!
I'LL MAKE A COVENANT WITH YOU!!

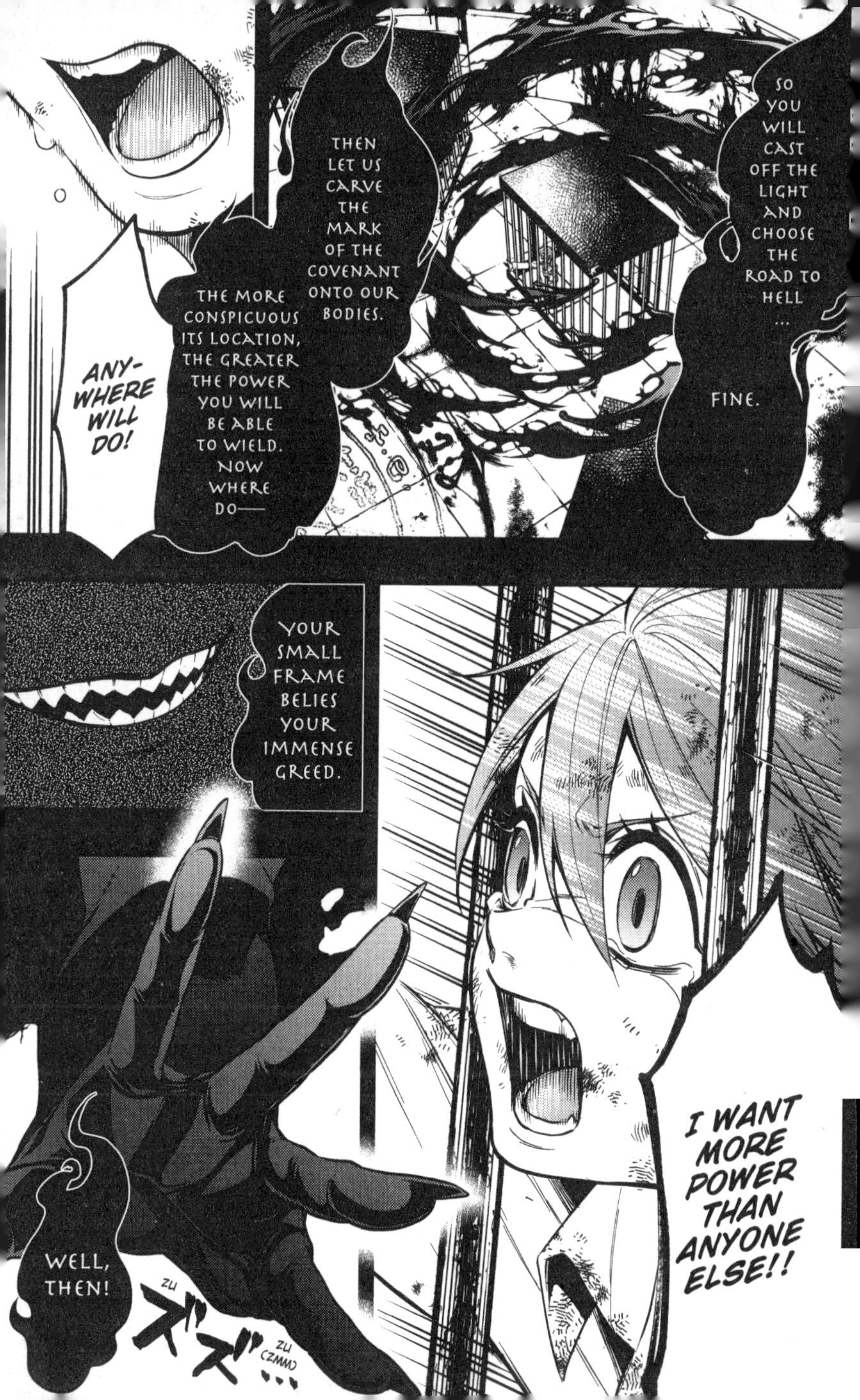
SO YOU WILL CAST OFF THE LIGHT AND CHOOSE THE ROAD TO HELL ...
FINE.
THEN LET US CARVE THE MARK OF THE COVENANT ONTO OUR BODIES.
THE MORE CONSPICUOUS ITS LOCATION, THE GREATER THE POWER YOU WILL BE ABLE TO WIELD. NOW WHERE DO—
ANY-WHERE WILL DO!
I WANT MORE POWER THAN ANYONE ELSE!!
YOUR SMALL FRAME BELIES YOUR IMMENSE GREED.
WELL, THEN!
ZU
ZU (ZMM)

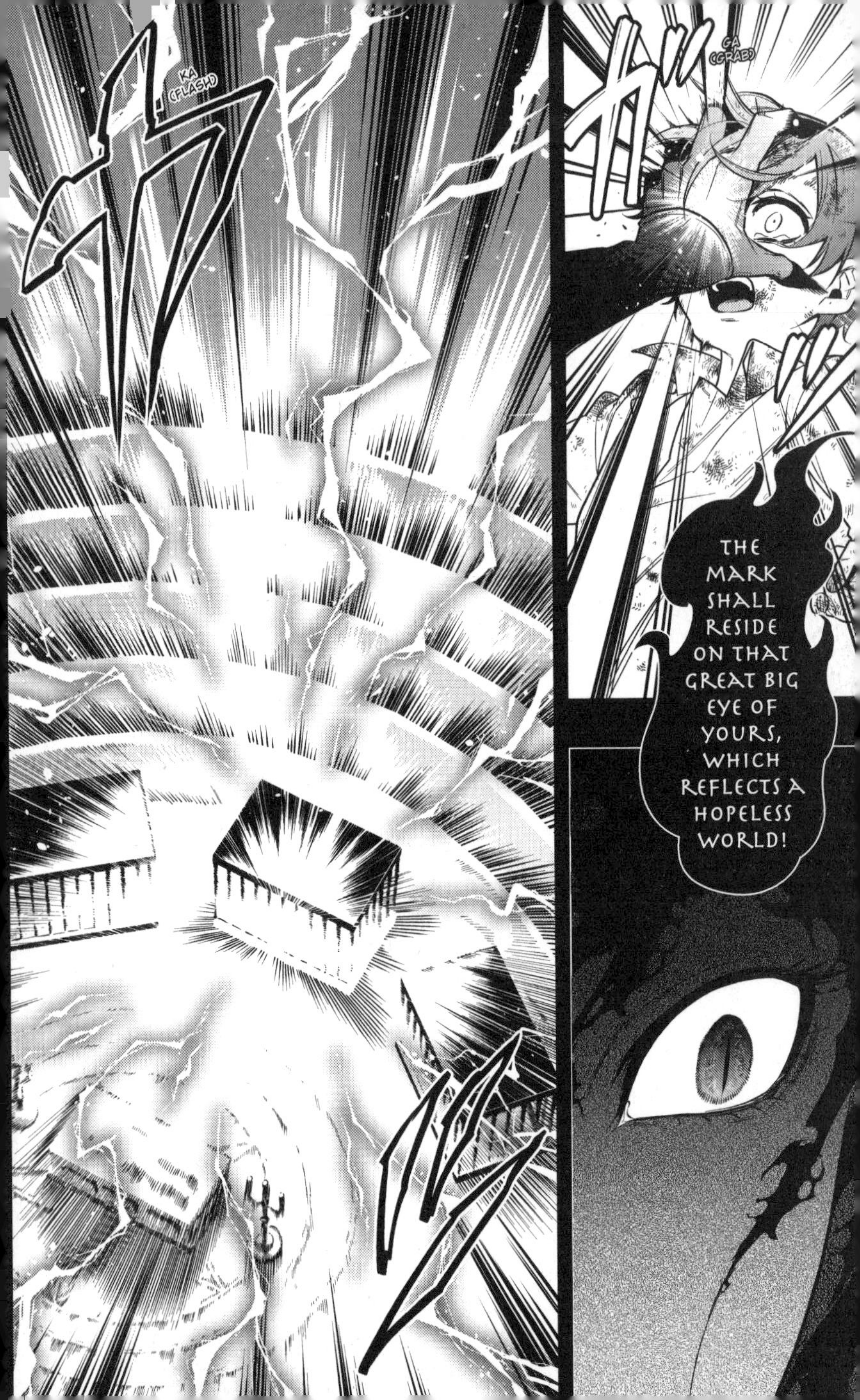
GA (GRAB)
THE MARK SHALL RESIDE ON THAT GREAT BIG EYE OF YOURS, WHICH REFLECTS A HOPELESS WORLD!
KA (FLASH)

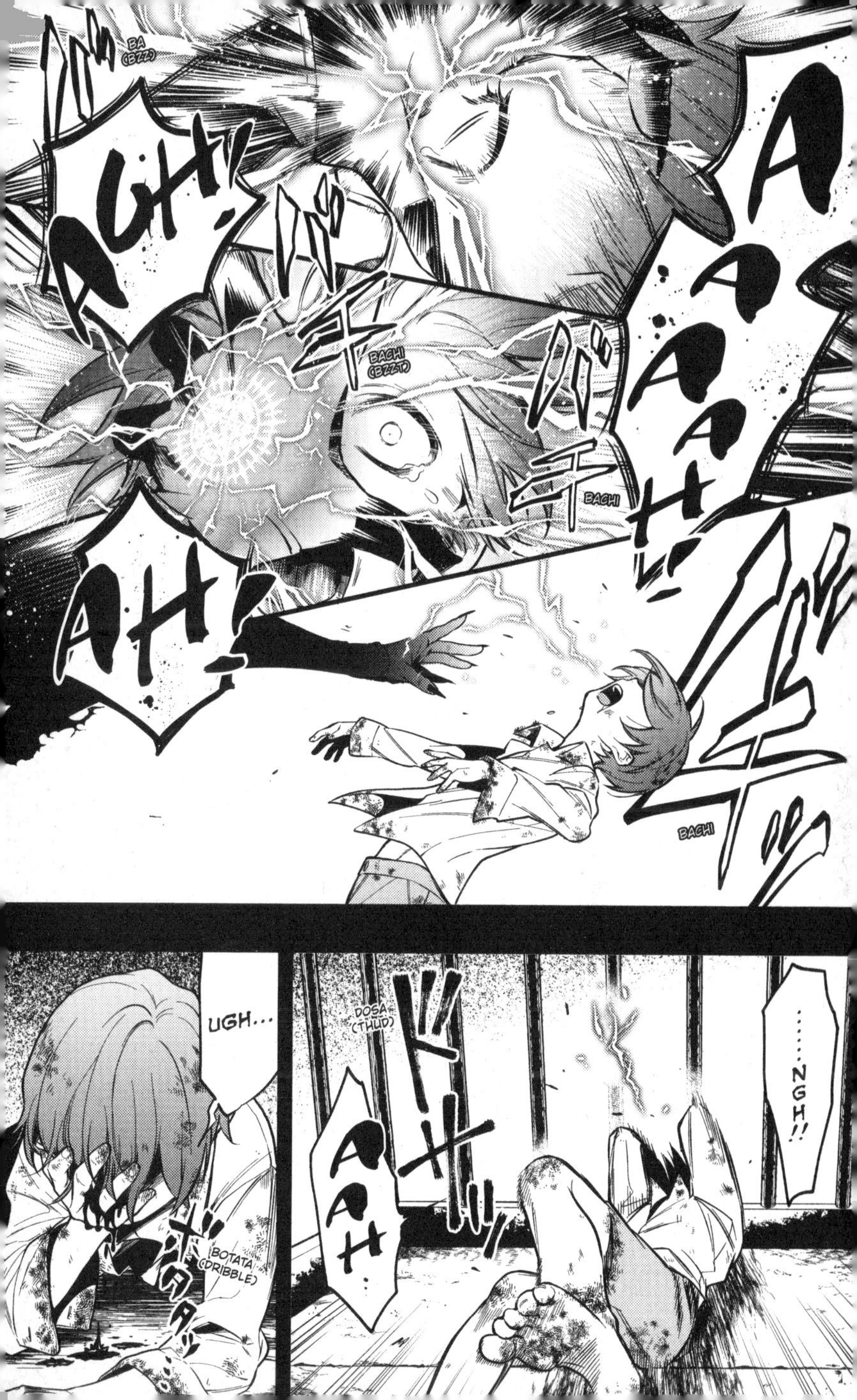
AAAAH
BA (BZZ)
AGH!
BACHI (BZZT)
BACHI
AH!
BACHI
......NGH!!
DOSA (THUD)
AAH
UGH...
BOTATA (DRIBBLE)

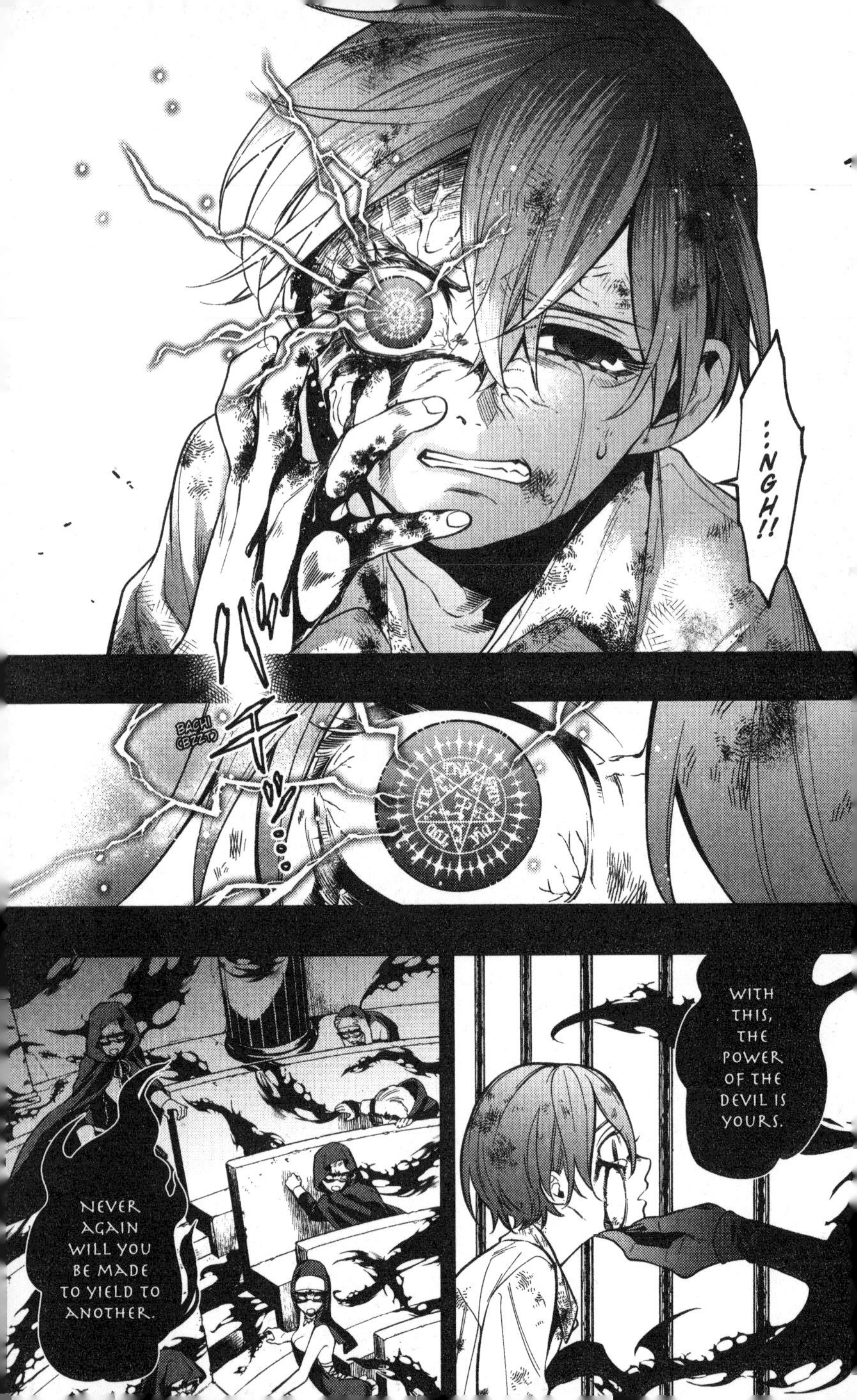
...NGH!!
BACHI (BZZT)
...
WITH THIS, THE POWER OF THE DEVIL IS YOURS.
NEVER AGAIN WILL YOU BE MADE TO YIELD TO ANOTHER.

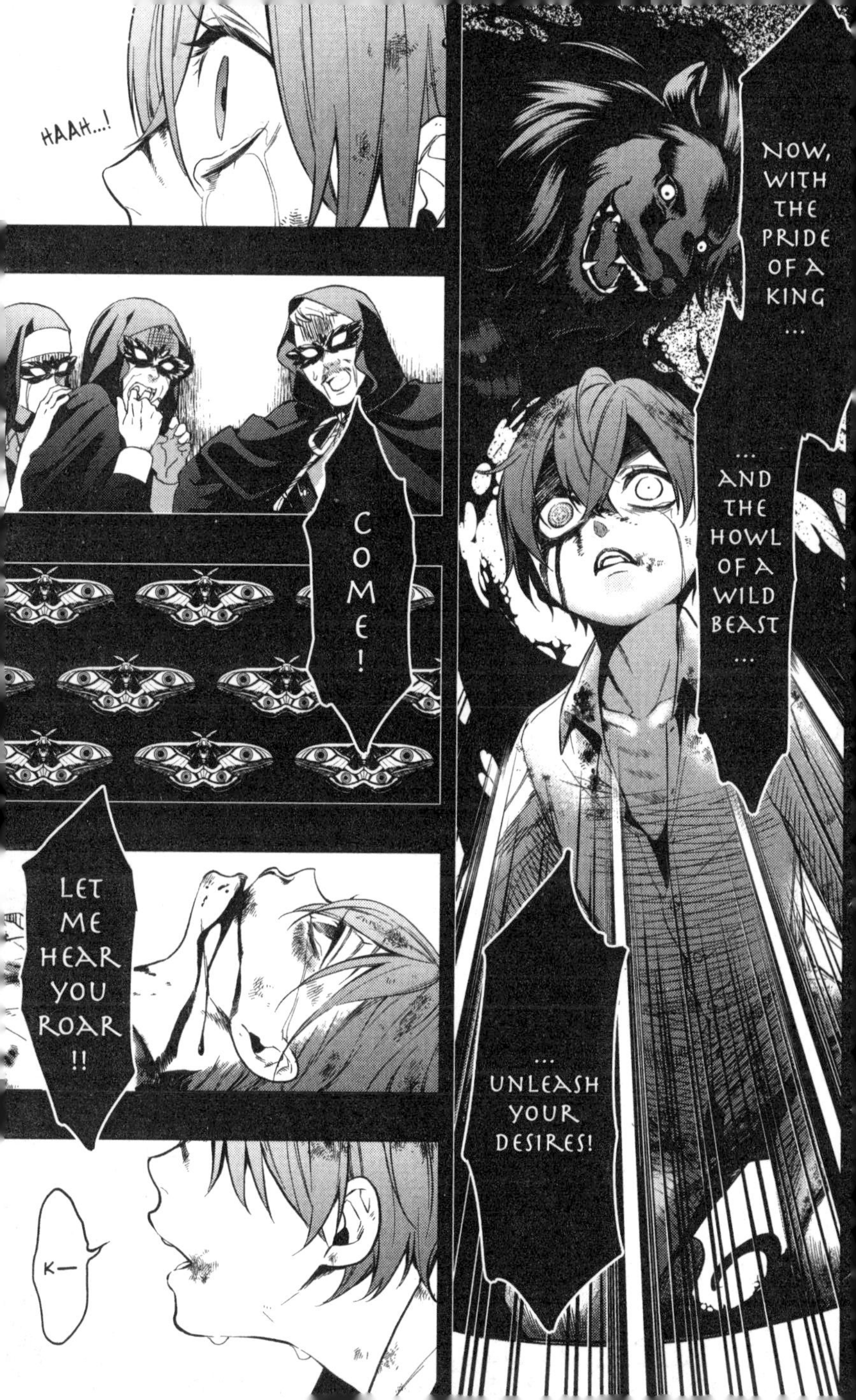
NOW, WITH THE PRIDE OF A KING...
...AND THE HOWL OF A WILD BEAST...
...UNLEASH YOUR DESIRES!
HAAH...!
COME!
LET ME HEAR YOU ROAR!!
K—

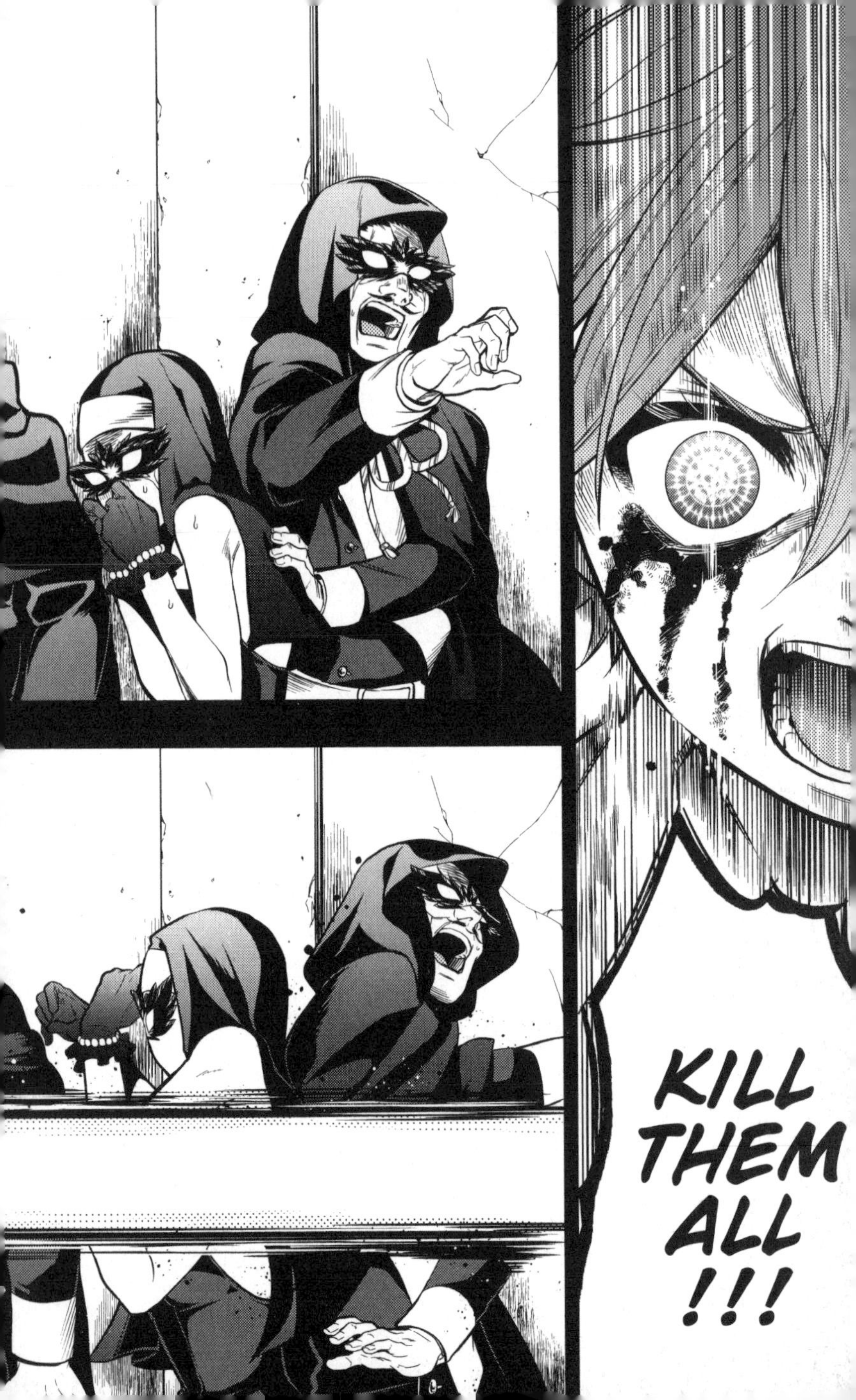
KILL THEM ALL!!!

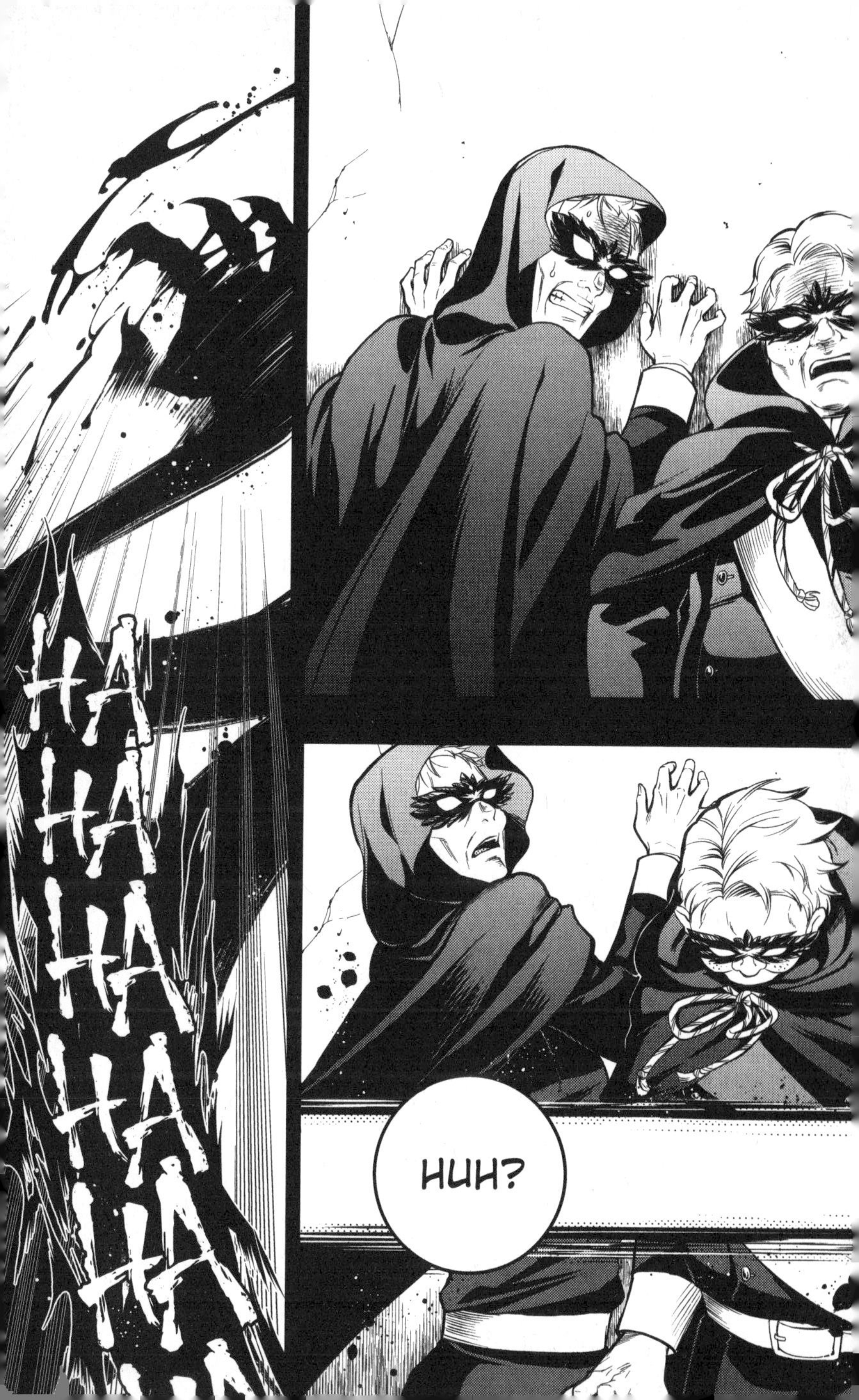
HUH?
HA HA HA HA HA

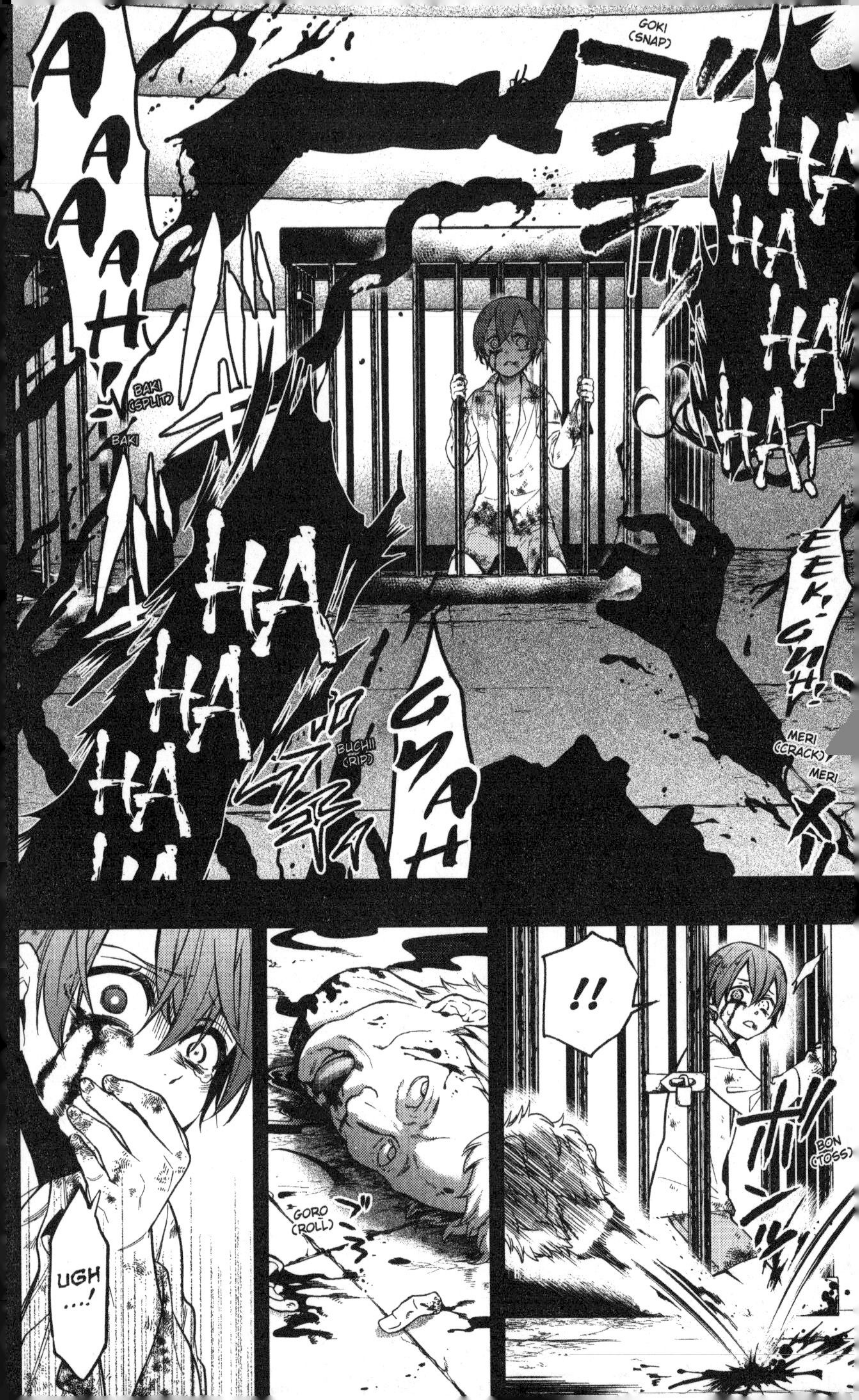

GOKI (SNAP)
HA HA HA HA HA!
EEK! GUH!
MERI (CRACK)
MERI
GYAAH
BUCHII (RIP)
AAAAAH!!
BAKI (SPLIT)
BAKI
HA HA HA HA
!!
BON (TOSS)
GORO (ROLL)
UGH...!

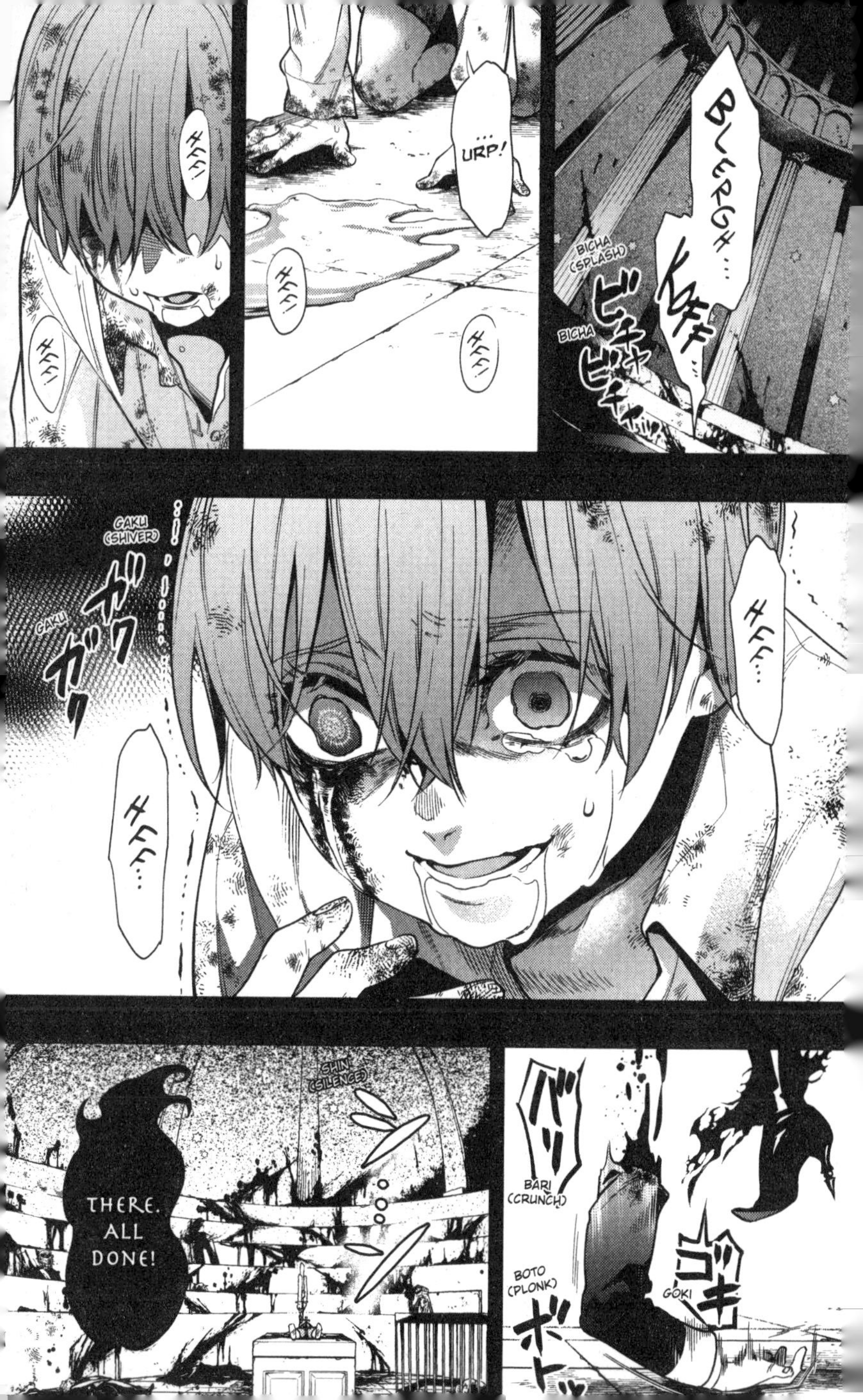
BLERGH...
KOFF...
BICHA (SPLASH)
BICHA
...URP!
HFF!
HFF!
HFF!
HFF!
HFF...
GAKU (SHIVER)
GAKU
HFF...
BARI (CRUNCH)
GOKI
BOTO (PLONK)
SHIN (SILENCE)
THERE. ALL DONE!

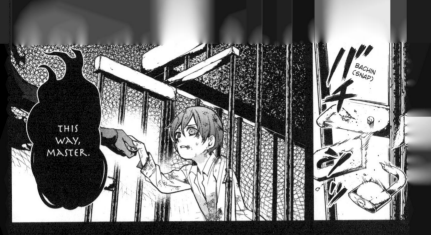

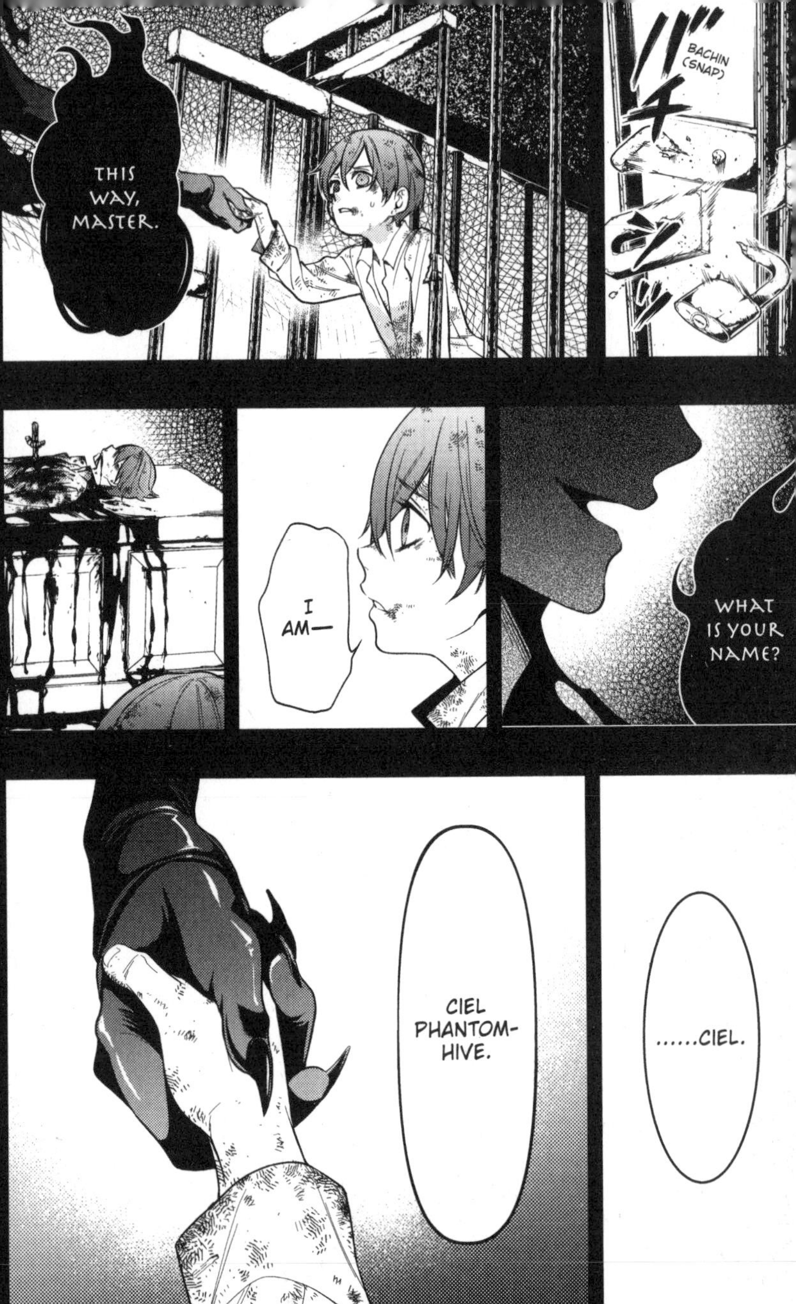
BACHIN (SNAP)
THIS WAY, MASTER.
WHAT IS YOUR NAME?
I AM—
......CIEL.
CIEL PHANTOM-HIVE.

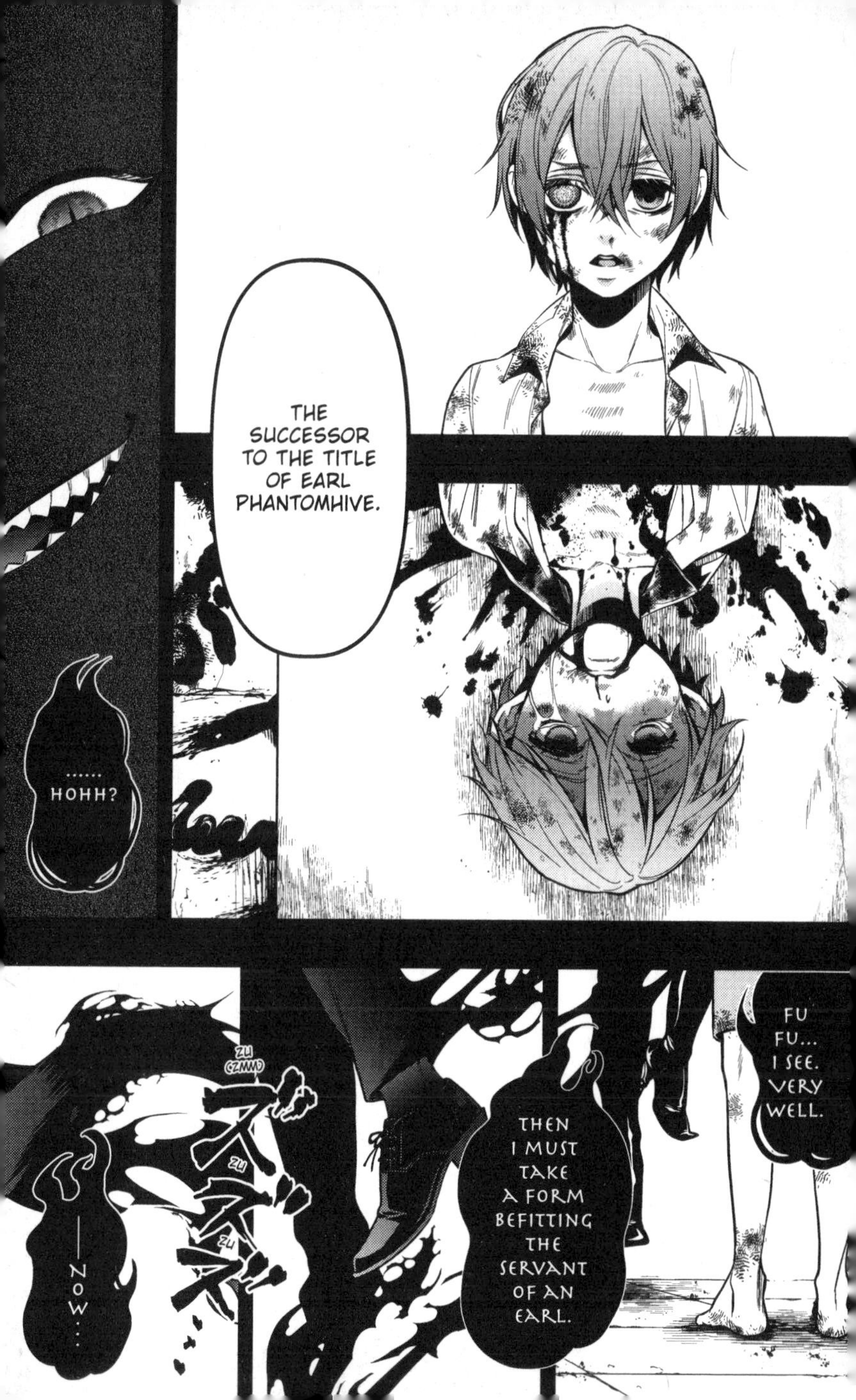
THE SUCCESSOR TO THE TITLE OF EARL PHANTOMHIVE.
......HOHH?
FU FU... I SEE. VERY WELL.
THEN I MUST TAKE A FORM BEFITTING THE SERVANT OF AN EARL.
ZU (ZMM)
ZU
ZU
——NOW...

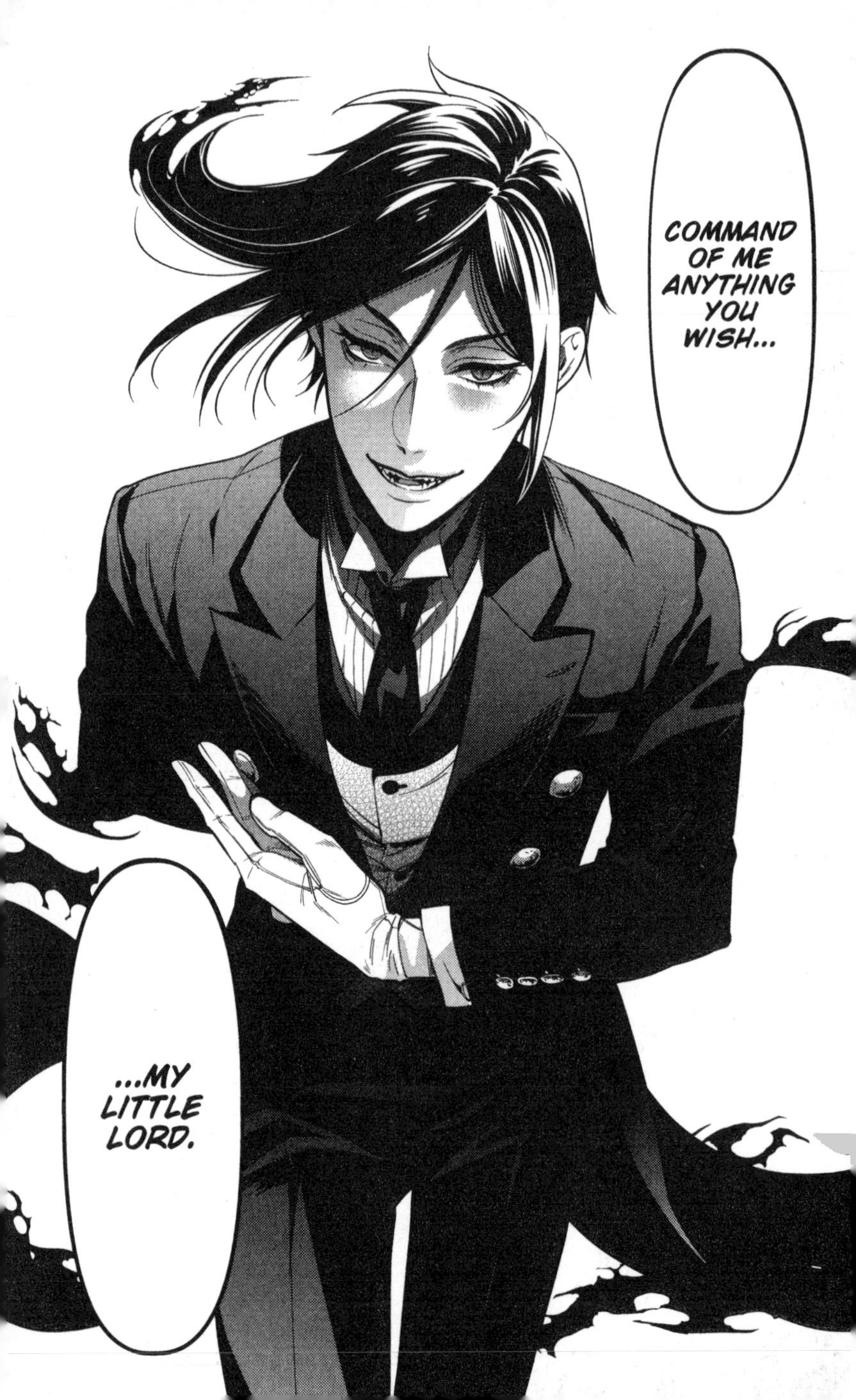
COMMAND OF ME ANYTHING YOU WISH...
...MY LITTLE LORD.

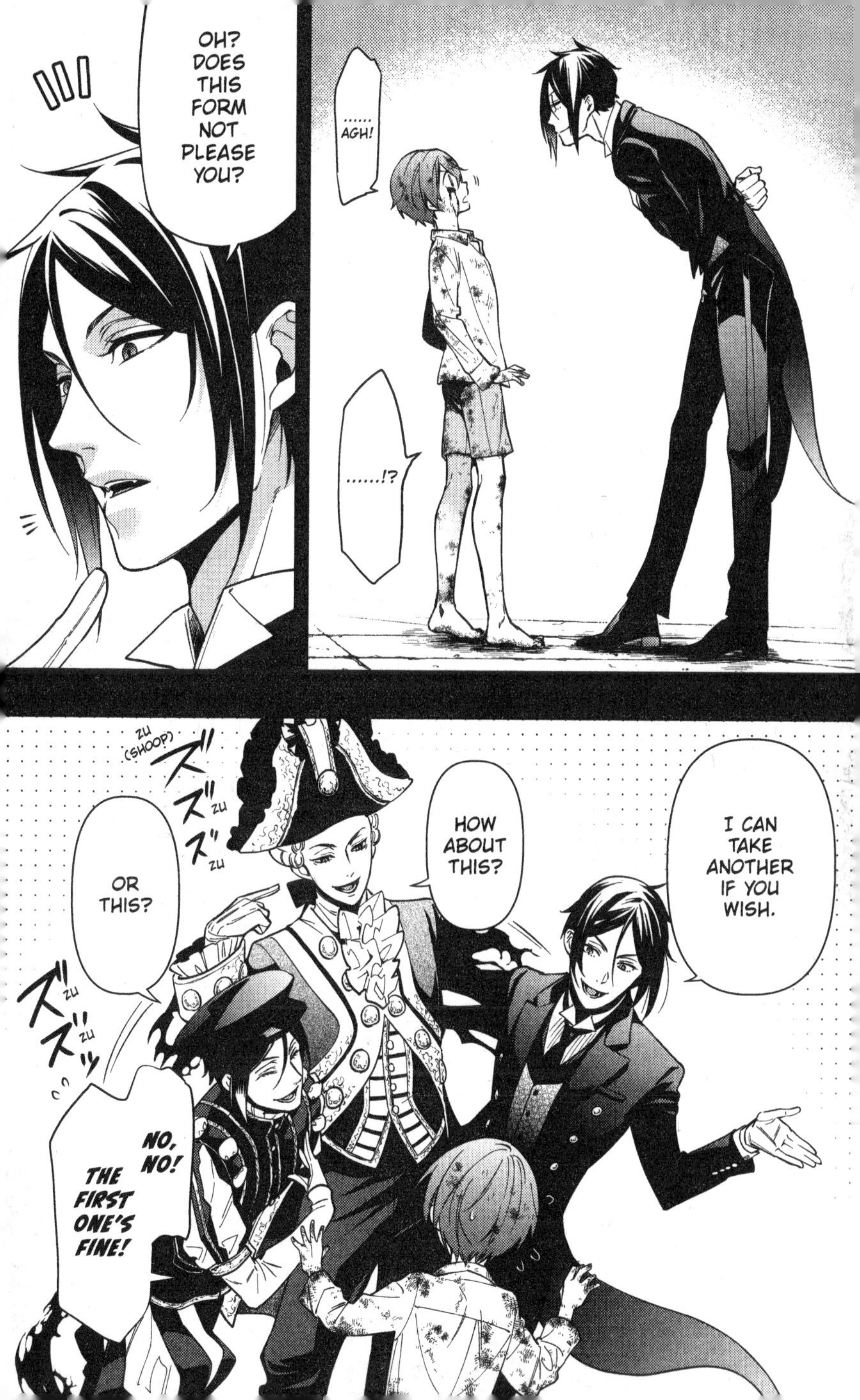
......AGH!
......!?
OH? DOES THIS FORM NOT PLEASE YOU?
I CAN TAKE ANOTHER IF YOU WISH.
HOW ABOUT THIS?
ZU (SHOOP)
ZU
ZU
OR THIS?
ZU
ZU
NO, NO! THE FIRST ONE'S FINE!

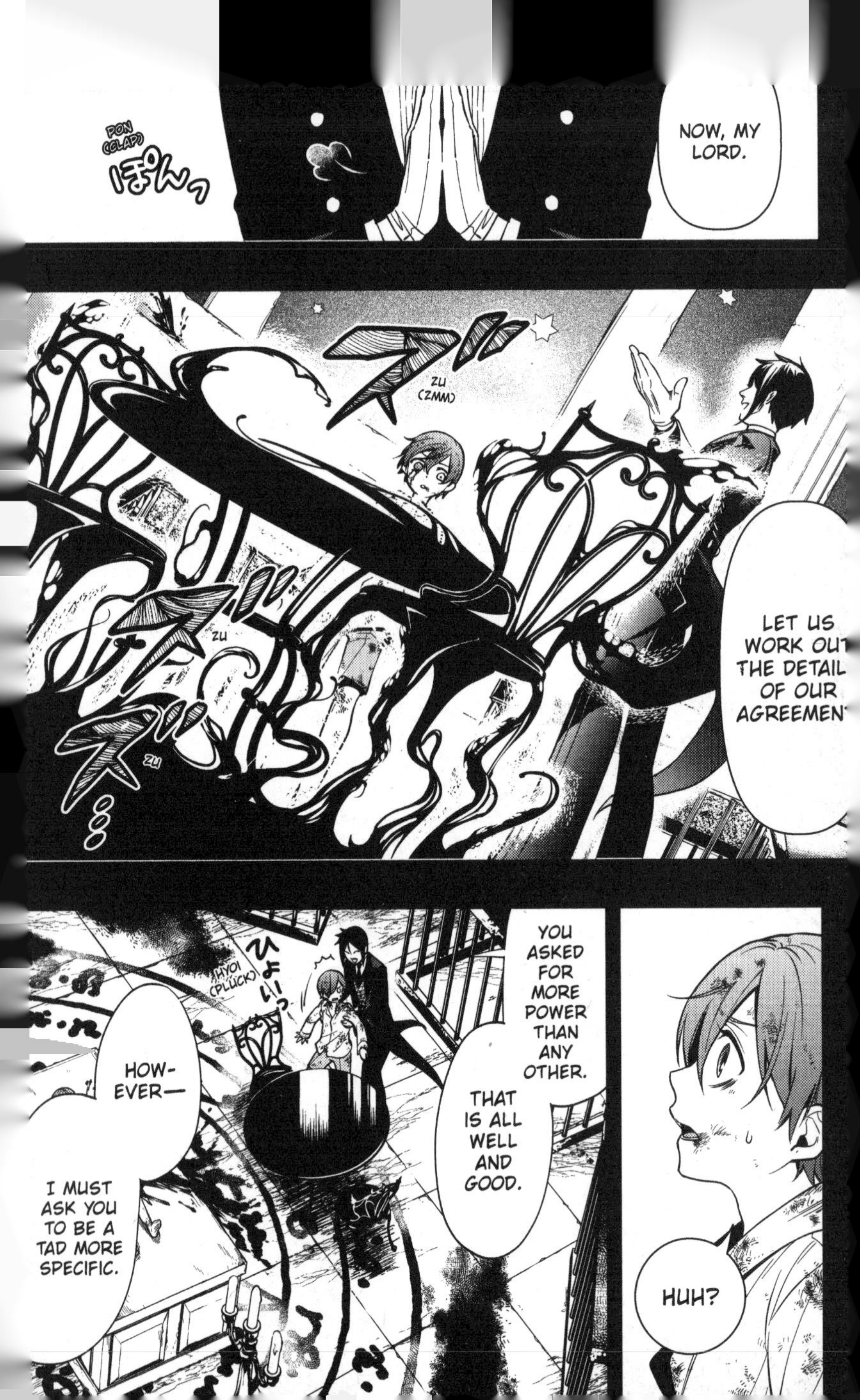
NOW, MY LORD.
PON (CLAP)
ぽんっ
LET US WORK OUT THE DETAIL OF OUR AGREEMEN
ズッ
ZU (ZMM)
ズッ
ZU
ズ…
ZU
HUH?
YOU ASKED FOR MORE POWER THAN ANY OTHER.
THAT IS ALL WELL AND GOOD.
ひょいっ
HYOI (PLUCK)
HOW-EVER—
I MUST ASK YOU TO BE A TAD MORE SPECIFIC.

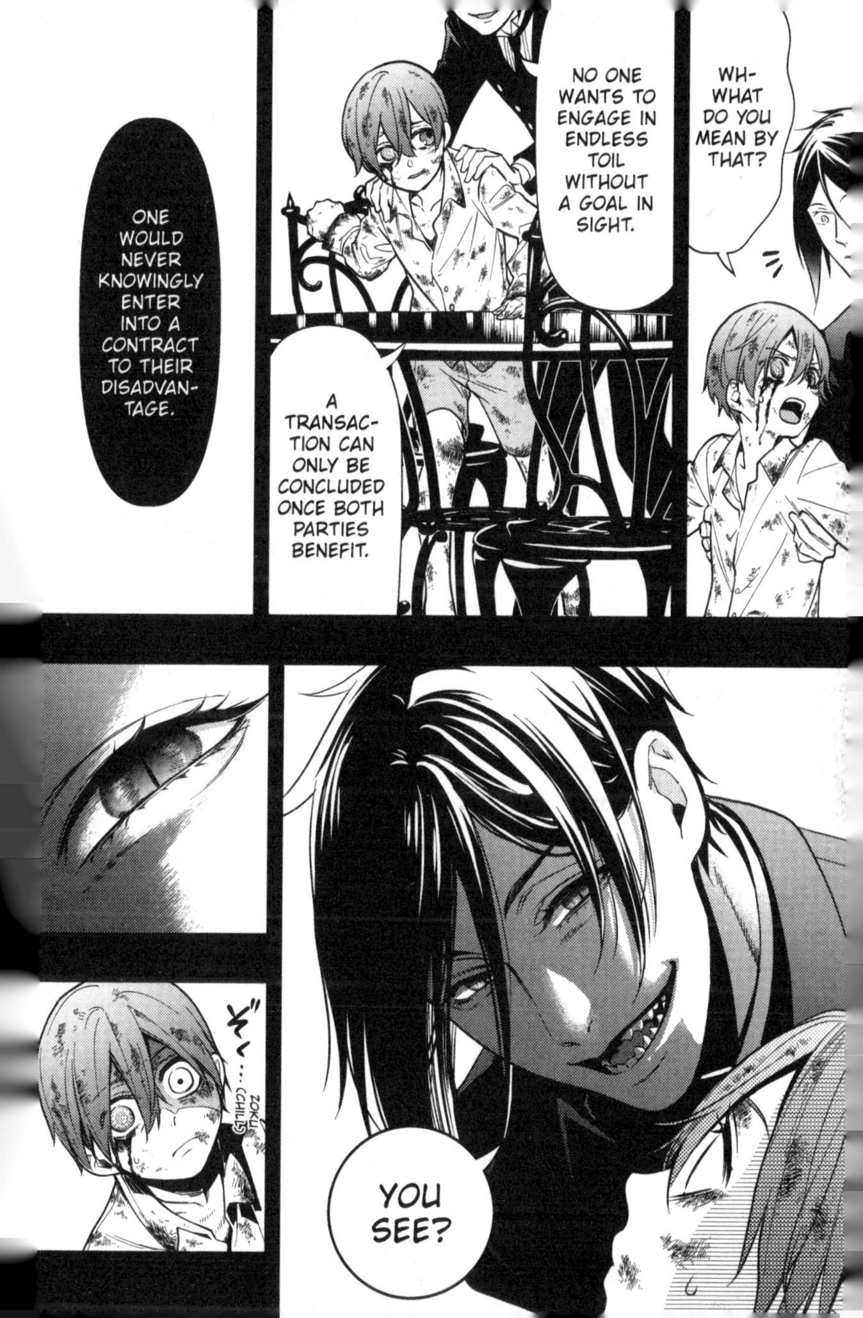
WH- WHAT DO YOU MEAN BY THAT?
NO ONE WANTS TO ENGAGE IN ENDLESS TOIL WITHOUT A GOAL IN SIGHT.
A TRANSACTION CAN ONLY BE CONCLUDED ONCE BOTH PARTIES BENEFIT.
ONE WOULD NEVER KNOWINGLY ENTER INTO A CONTRACT TO THEIR DISADVANTAGE.
YOU SEE?
ZOKU... (CHILL)

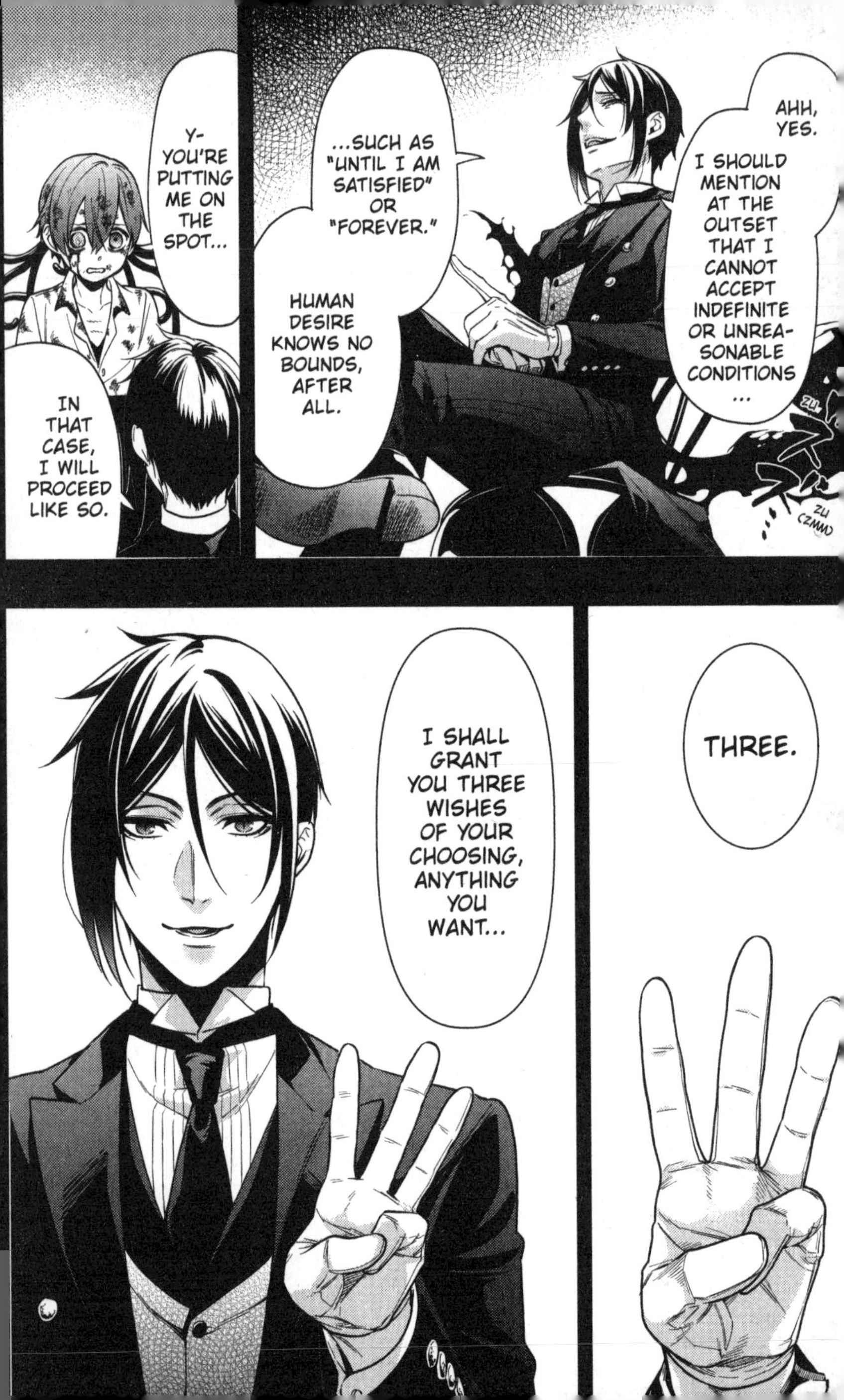
AHH, YES.
I SHOULD MENTION AT THE OUTSET THAT I CANNOT ACCEPT INDEFINITE OR UNREA-SONABLE CONDITIONS...
ZU
ZU (ZMM)
...SUCH AS "UNTIL I AM SATISFIED" OR "FOREVER."
HUMAN DESIRE KNOWS NO BOUNDS, AFTER ALL.
Y-YOU'RE PUTTING ME ON THE SPOT...
IN THAT CASE, I WILL PROCEED LIKE SO.
THREE.
I SHALL GRANT YOU THREE WISHES OF YOUR CHOOSING, ANYTHING YOU WANT...

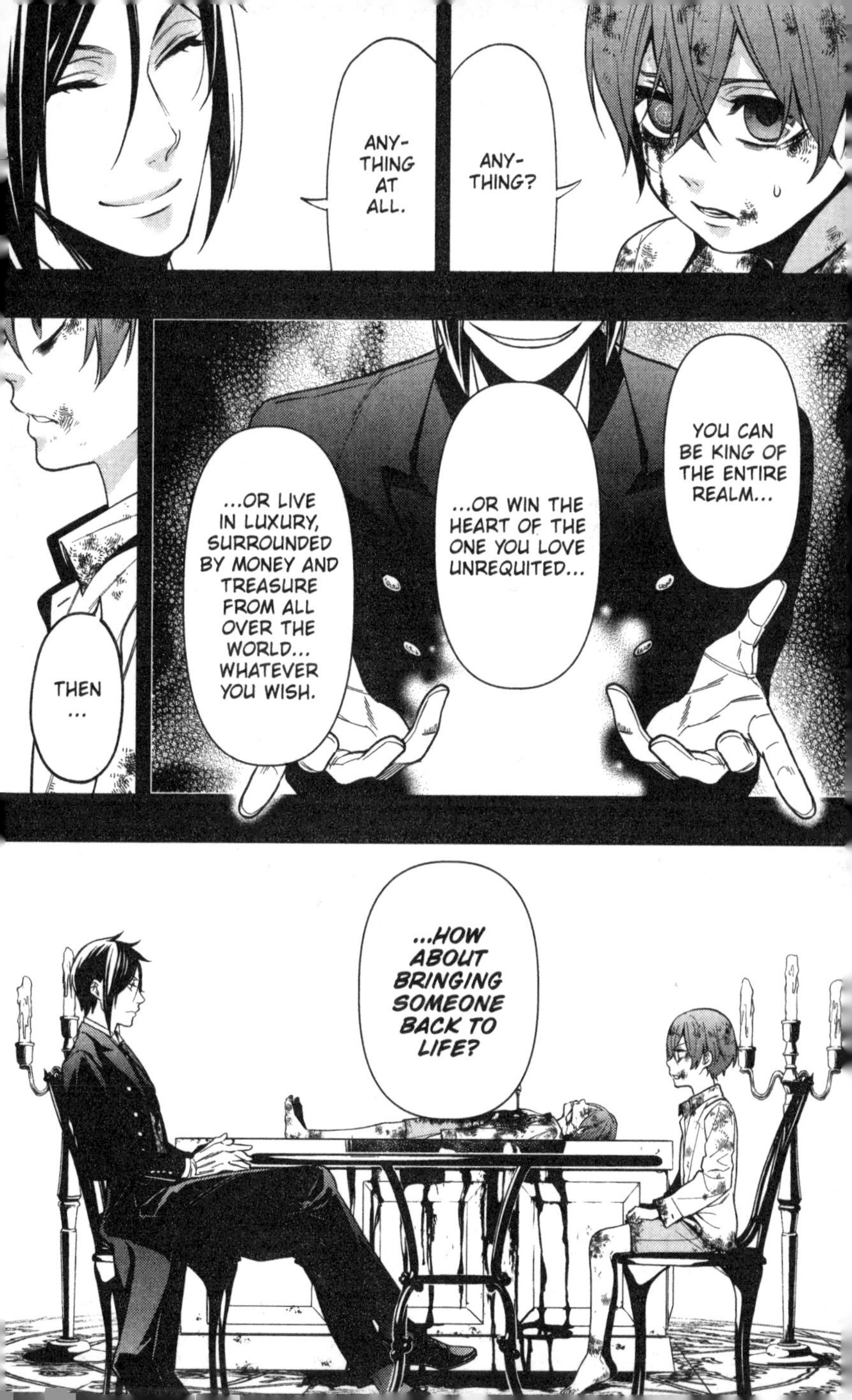
ANY-THING?
ANY-THING AT ALL.
YOU CAN BE KING OF THE ENTIRE REALM...
...OR WIN THE HEART OF THE ONE YOU LOVE UNREQUITED...
...OR LIVE IN LUXURY, SURROUNDED BY MONEY AND TREASURE FROM ALL OVER THE WORLD... WHATEVER YOU WISH.
THEN ...
...HOW ABOUT BRINGING SOMEONE BACK TO LIFE?

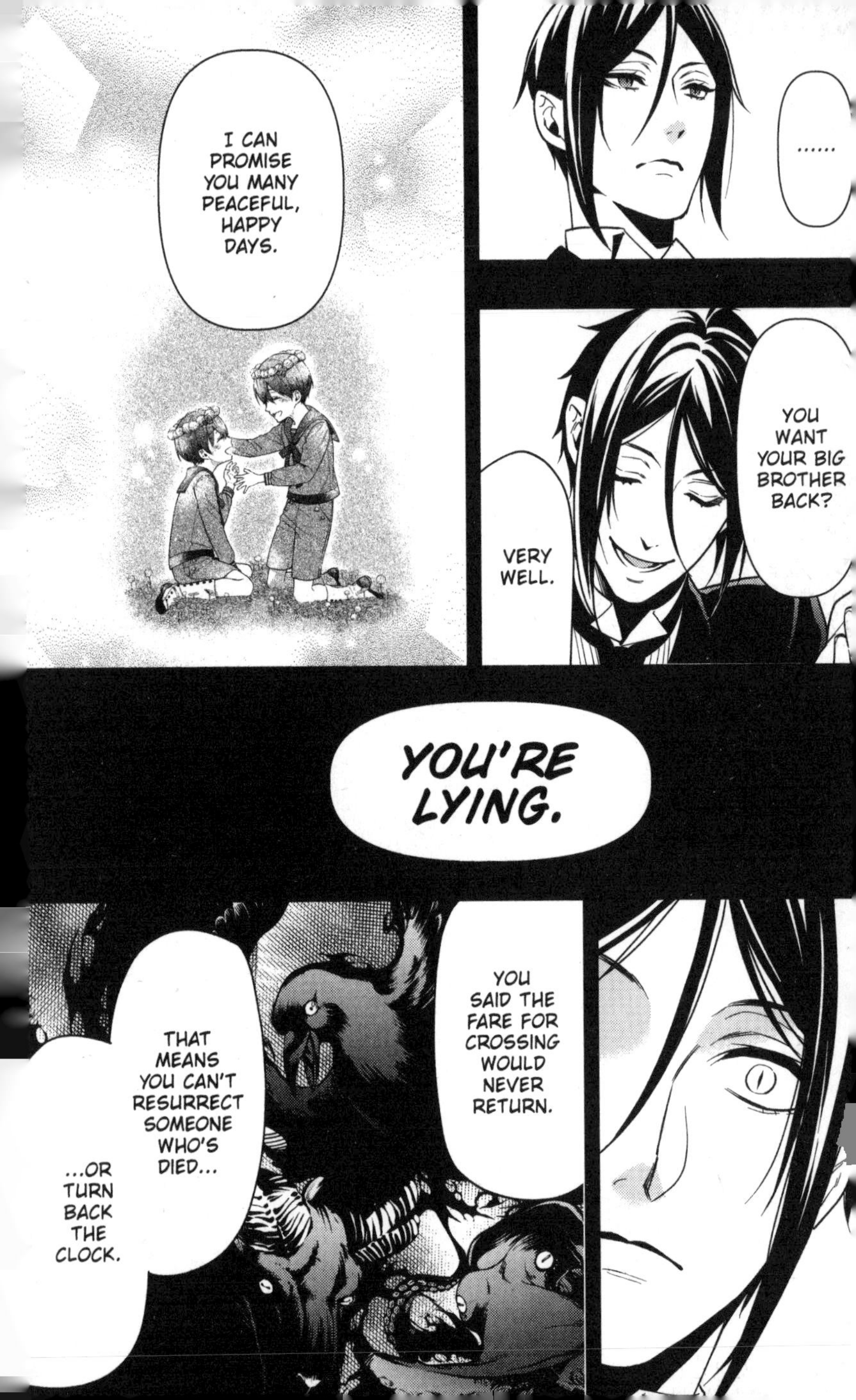
......
YOU WANT YOUR BIG BROTHER BACK?
VERY WELL.
I CAN PROMISE YOU MANY PEACEFUL, HAPPY DAYS.
YOU'RE LYING.
YOU SAID THE FARE FOR CROSSING WOULD NEVER RETURN.
THAT MEANS YOU CAN'T RESURRECT SOMEONE WHO'S DIED...
...OR TURN BACK THE CLOCK.

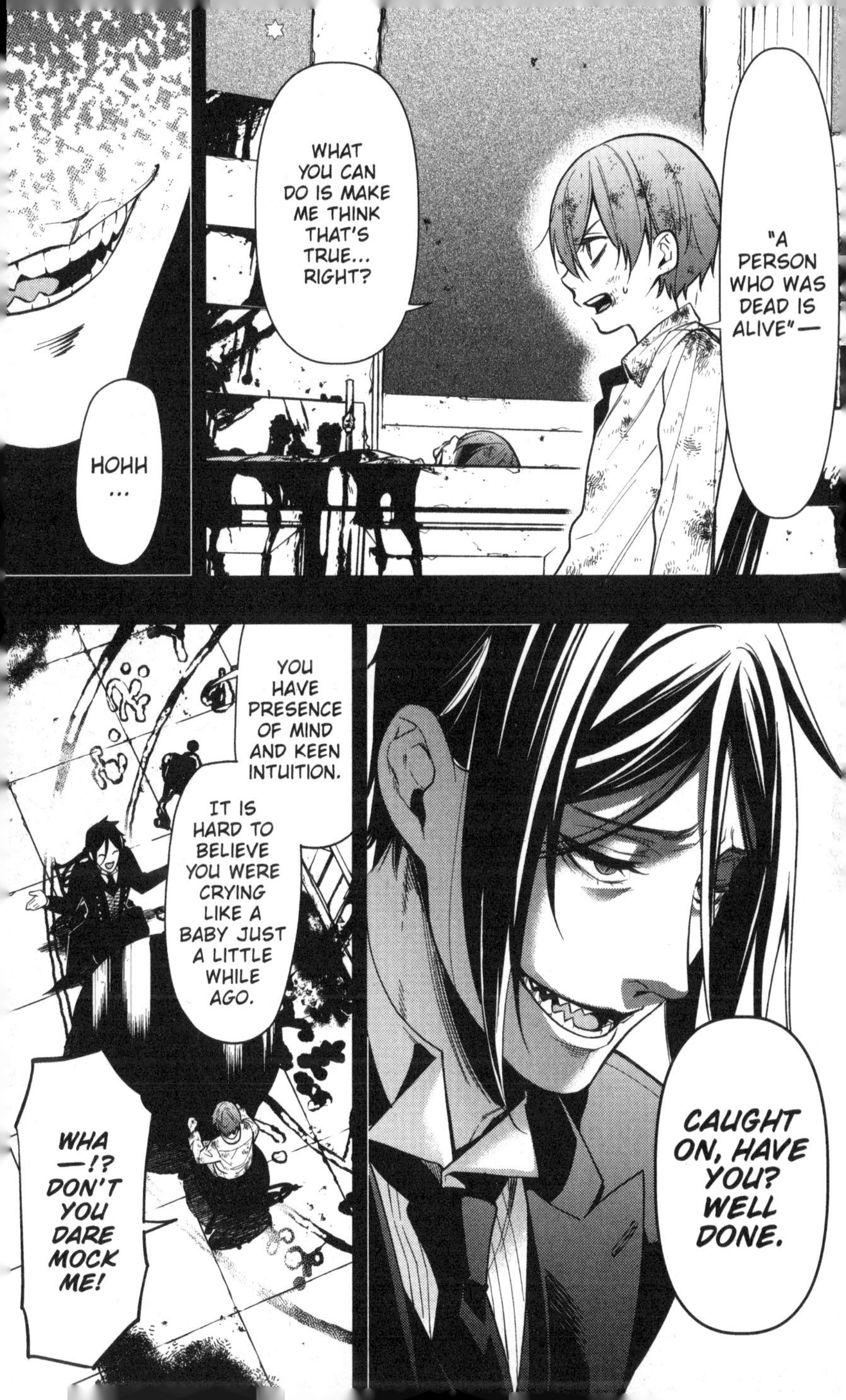
"A PERSON WHO WAS DEAD IS ALIVE"—
WHAT YOU CAN DO IS MAKE ME THINK THAT'S TRUE... RIGHT?
HOHH ...
CAUGHT ON, HAVE YOU? WELL DONE.
YOU HAVE PRESENCE OF MIND AND KEEN INTUITION.
IT IS HARD TO BELIEVE YOU WERE CRYING LIKE A BABY JUST A LITTLE WHILE AGO.
WHA—!? DON'T YOU DARE MOCK ME!

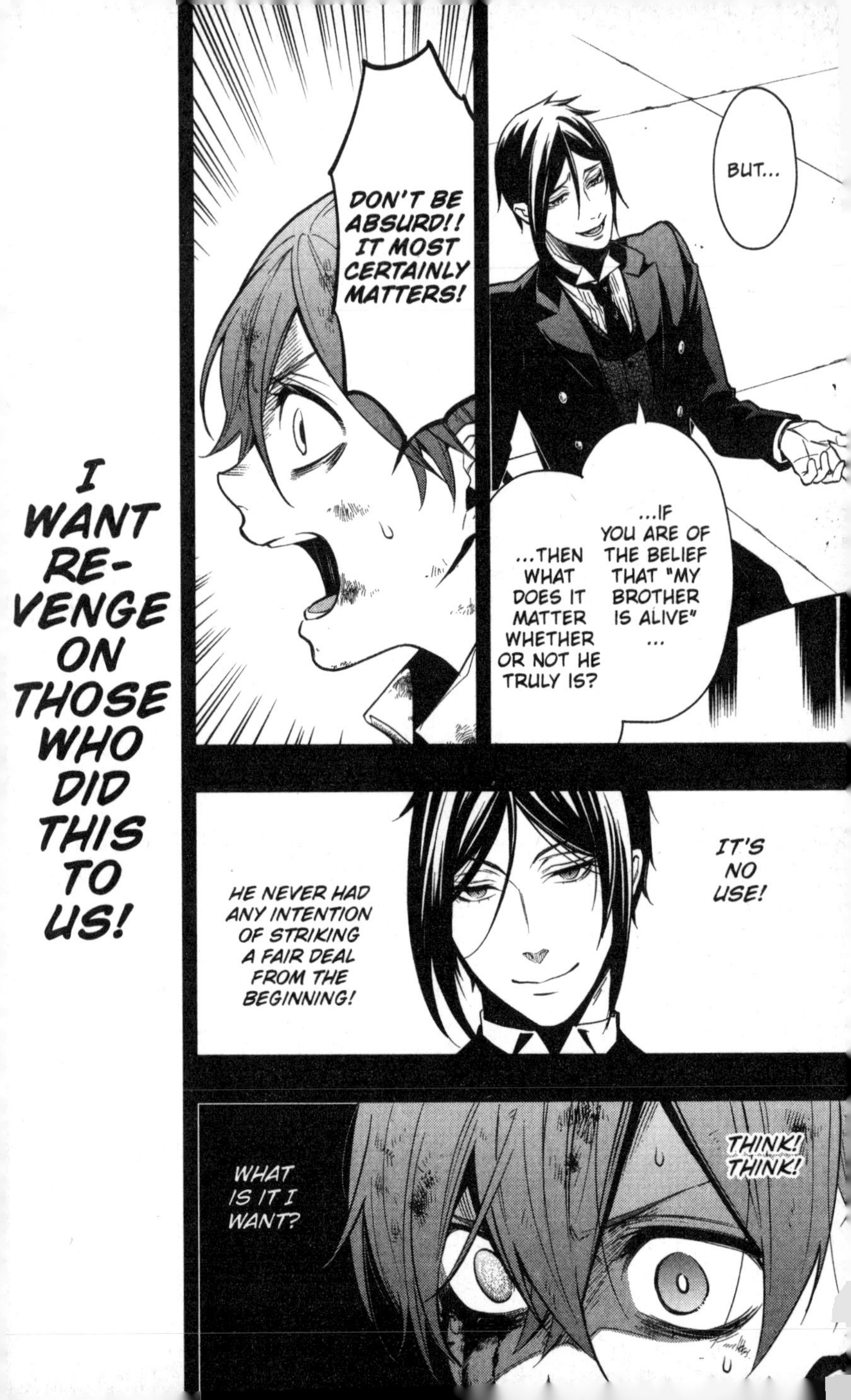
BUT...
...IF YOU ARE OF THE BELIEF THAT "MY BROTHER IS ALIVE" ...
...THEN WHAT DOES IT MATTER WHETHER OR NOT HE TRULY IS?
DON'T BE ABSURD!! IT MOST CERTAINLY MATTERS!
IT'S NO USE!
HE NEVER HAD ANY INTENTION OF STRIKING A FAIR DEAL FROM THE BEGINNING!
THINK! THINK!
WHAT IS IT I WANT?
I WANT RE-VENGE ON THOSE WHO DID THIS TO US!

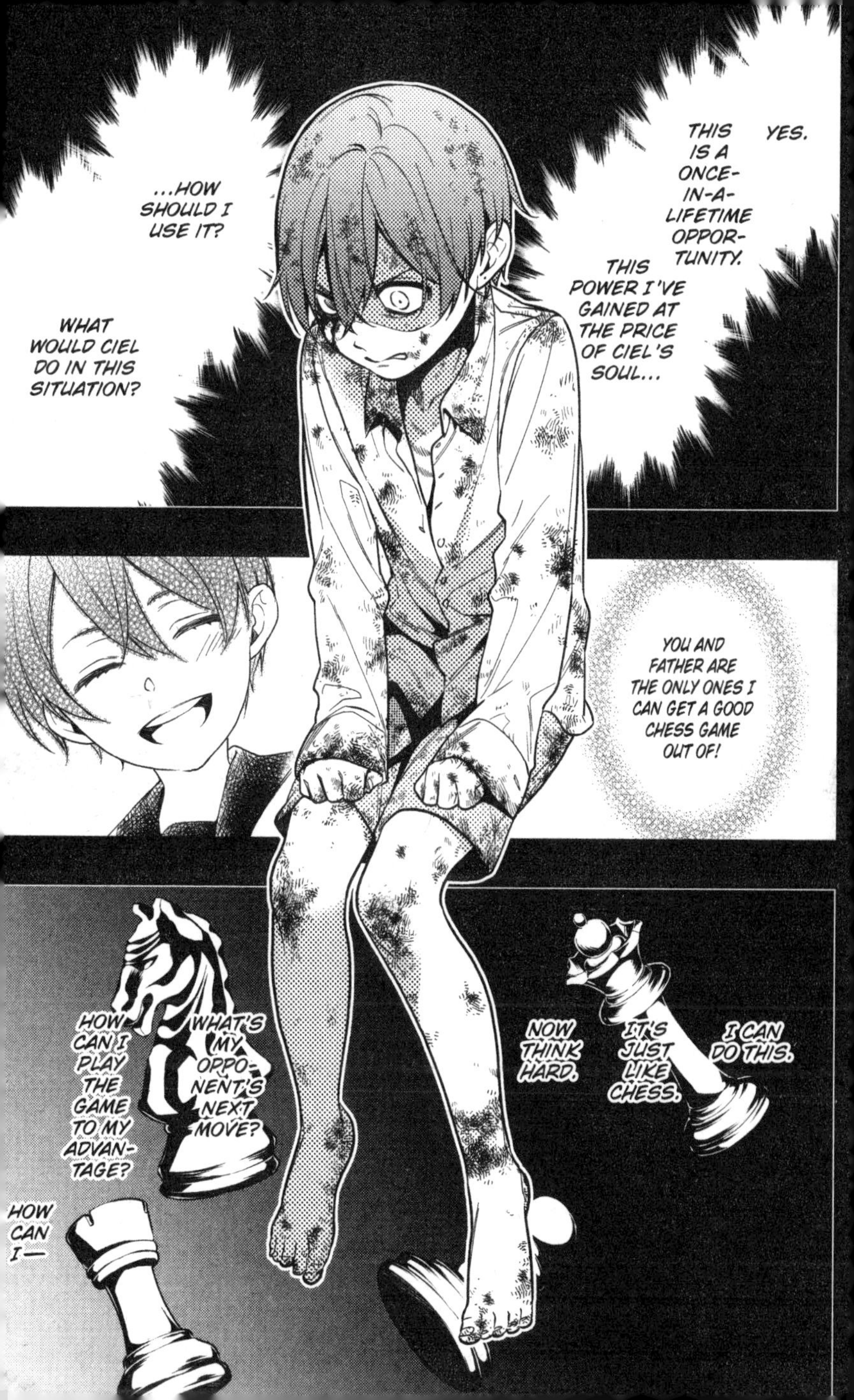
YES.
THIS IS A ONCE-IN-A-LIFETIME OPPORTUNITY.
THIS POWER I'VE GAINED AT THE PRICE OF CIEL'S SOUL...
...HOW SHOULD I USE IT?
WHAT WOULD CIEL DO IN THIS SITUATION?
YOU AND FATHER ARE THE ONLY ONES I CAN GET A GOOD CHESS GAME OUT OF!
I CAN DO THIS.
IT'S JUST LIKE CHESS.
NOW THINK HARD.
WHAT'S MY OPPONENT'S NEXT MOVE?
HOW CAN I PLAY THE GAME TO MY ADVANTAGE?
HOW CAN I—

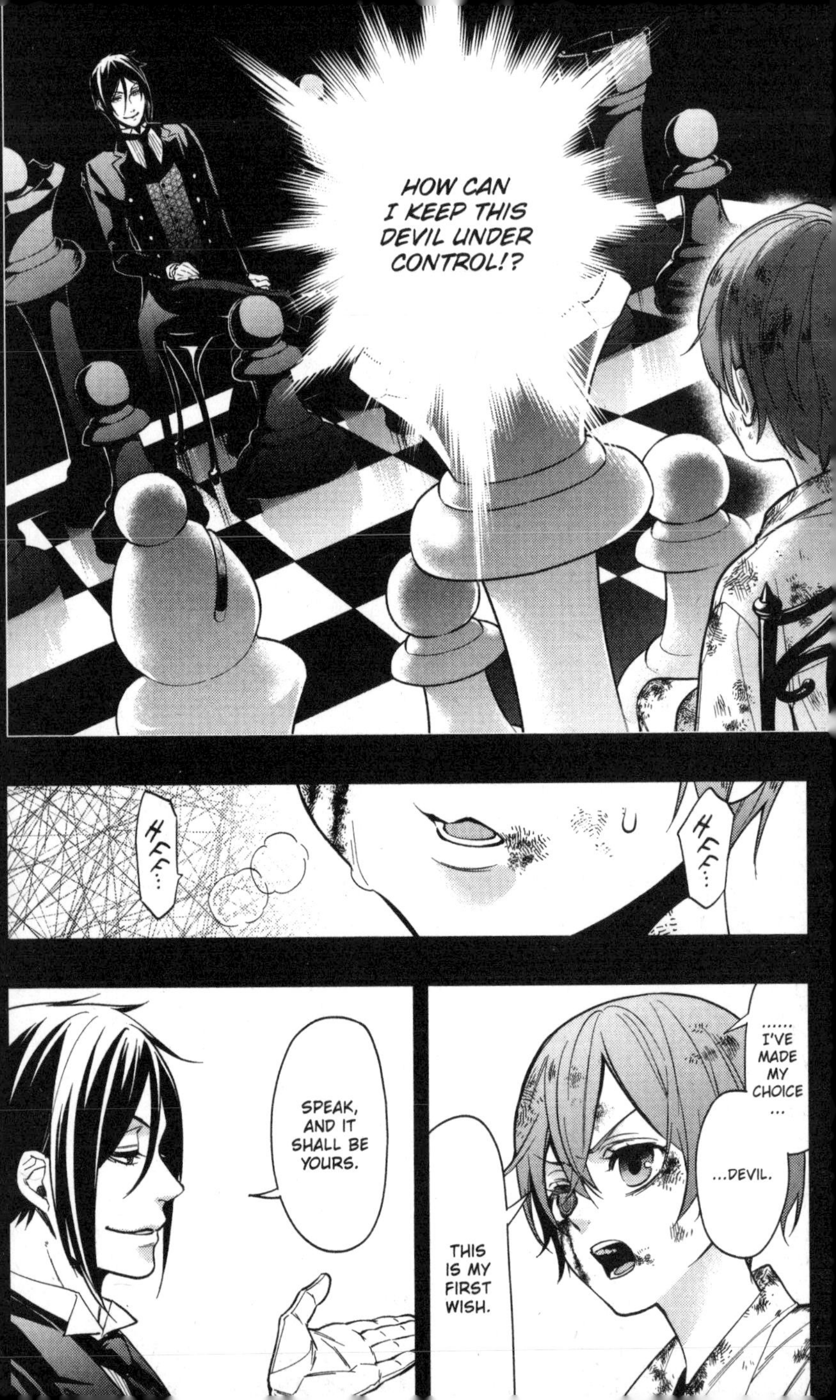
HOW CAN I KEEP THIS DEVIL UNDER CONTROL!?
HFF...
HFF...
......I'VE MADE MY CHOICE...
...DEVIL.
THIS IS MY FIRST WISH.
SPEAK, AND IT SHALL BE YOURS.

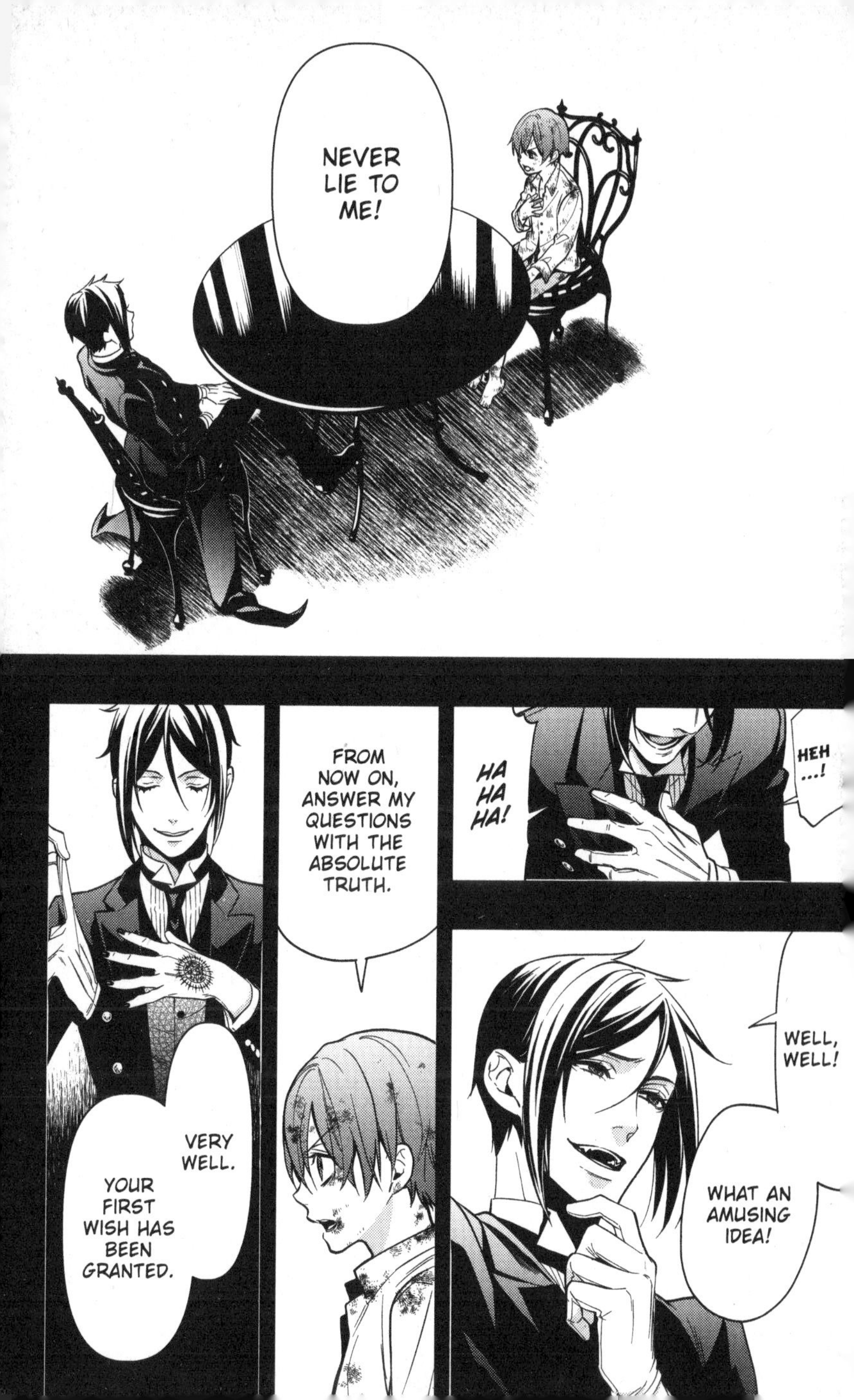
NEVER LIE TO ME!
HEH ...!
HA HA HA!
WELL, WELL!
WHAT AN AMUSING IDEA!
FROM NOW ON, ANSWER MY QUESTIONS WITH THE ABSOLUTE TRUTH.
VERY WELL.
YOUR FIRST WISH HAS BEEN GRANTED.

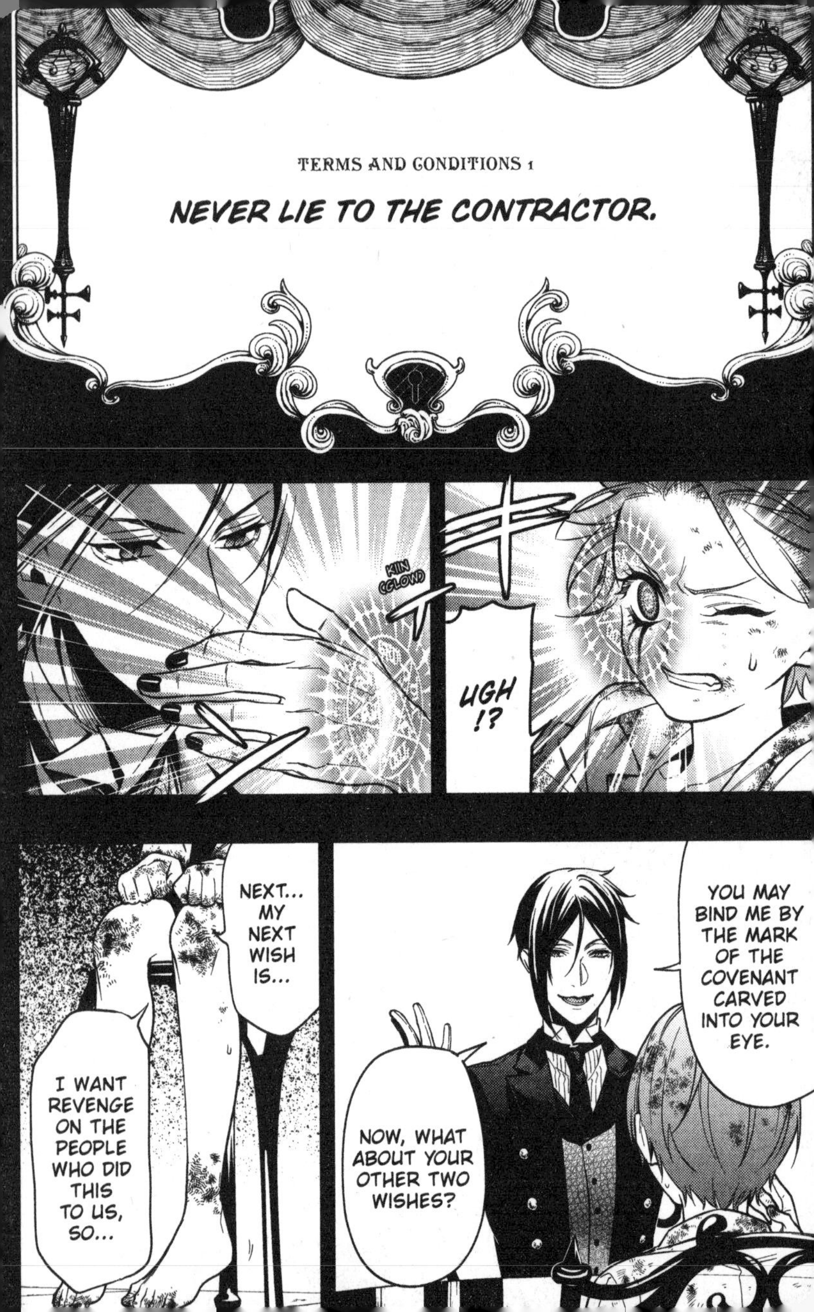
TERMS AND CONDITIONS 1
NEVER LIE TO THE CONTRACTOR.
UGH !?
KIIN (GLOW)
YOU MAY BIND ME BY THE MARK OF THE COVENANT CARVED INTO YOUR EYE.
NOW, WHAT ABOUT YOUR OTHER TWO WISHES?
NEXT... MY NEXT WISH IS...
I WANT REVENGE ON THE PEOPLE WHO DID THIS TO US, SO...

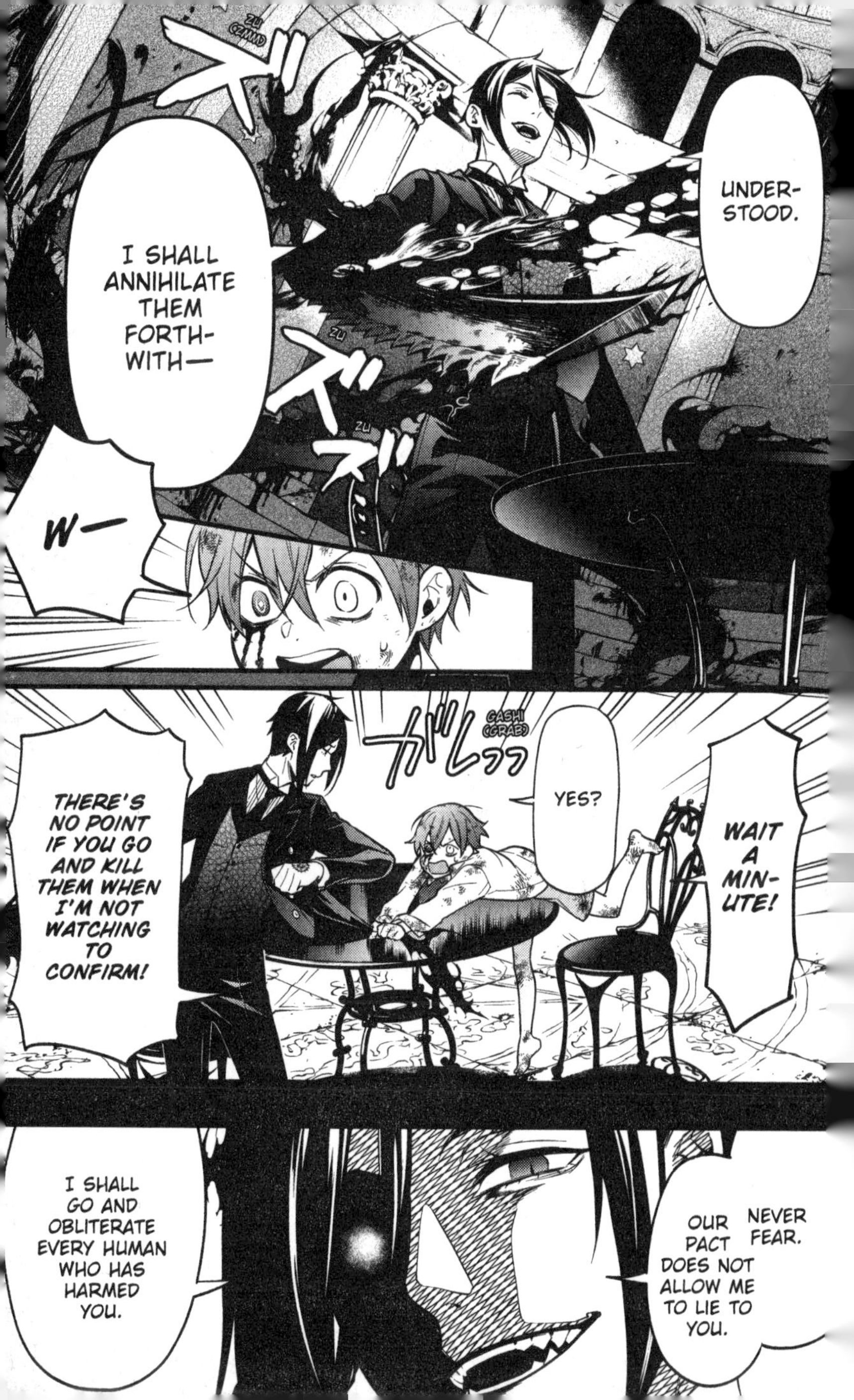
UNDER-STOOD.
ZU (ZWMM)
I SHALL ANNIHILATE THEM FORTH-WITH—
ZU
ZU
W—
WAIT A MIN-UTE!
GASHI (GRAB)
YES?
THERE'S NO POINT IF YOU GO AND KILL THEM WHEN I'M NOT WATCHING TO CONFIRM!
NEVER FEAR.
OUR PACT DOES NOT ALLOW ME TO LIE TO YOU.
I SHALL GO AND OBLITERATE EVERY HUMAN WHO HAS HARMED YOU.

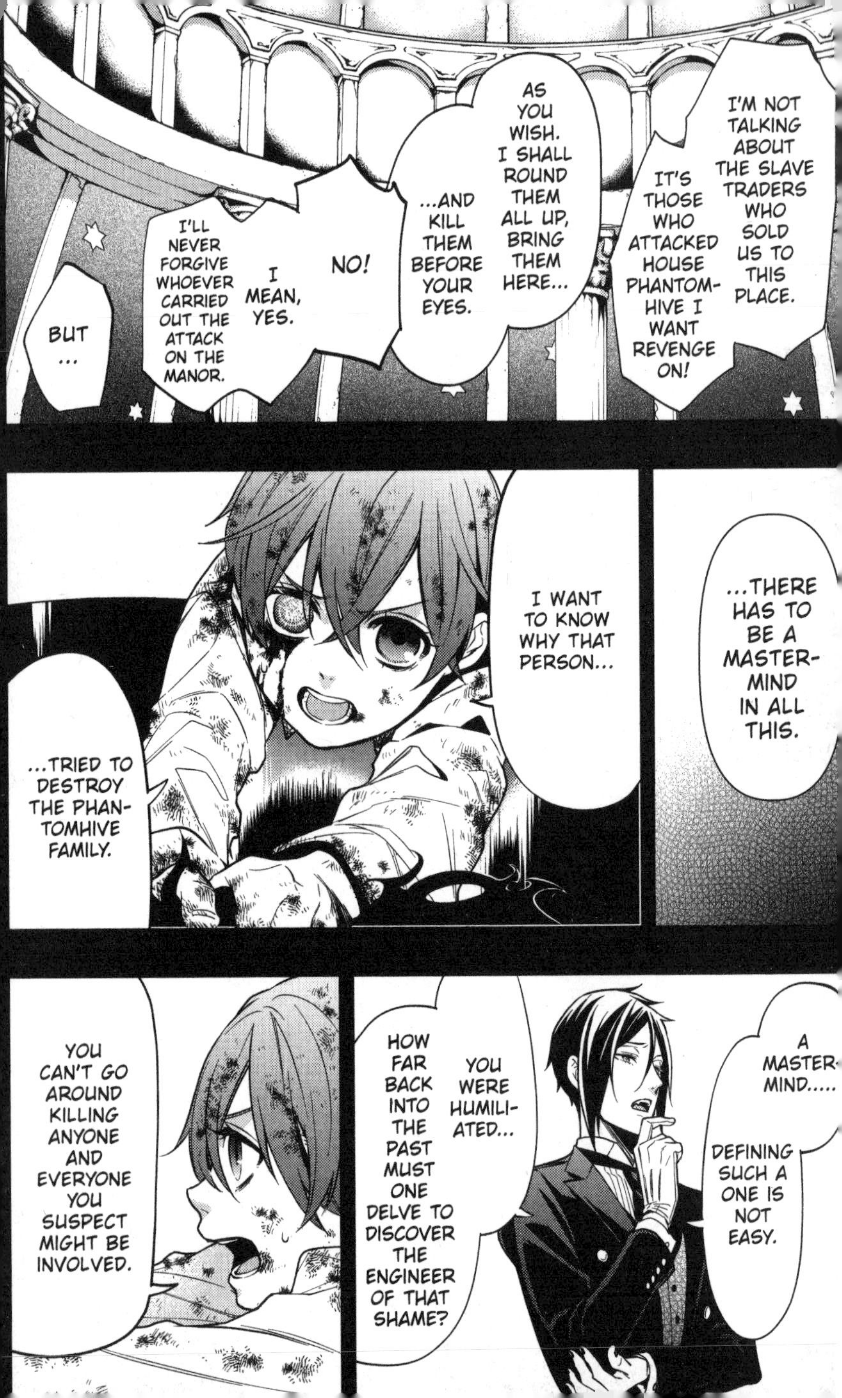
I'M NOT TALKING ABOUT THE SLAVE TRADERS WHO SOLD US TO THIS PLACE.
IT'S THOSE WHO ATTACKED HOUSE PHANTOMHIVE I WANT REVENGE ON!
AS YOU WISH. I SHALL ROUND THEM ALL UP, BRING THEM HERE...
...AND KILL THEM BEFORE YOUR EYES.
NO!
I MEAN, YES.
I'LL NEVER FORGIVE WHOEVER CARRIED OUT THE ATTACK ON THE MANOR.
BUT ...
...THERE HAS TO BE A MASTERMIND IN ALL THIS.
I WANT TO KNOW WHY THAT PERSON...
...TRIED TO DESTROY THE PHANTOMHIVE FAMILY.
A MASTERMIND.....
DEFINING SUCH A ONE IS NOT EASY.
YOU WERE HUMILIATED...
HOW FAR BACK INTO THE PAST MUST ONE DELVE TO DISCOVER THE ENGINEER OF THAT SHAME?
YOU CAN'T GO AROUND KILLING ANYONE AND EVERYONE YOU SUSPECT MIGHT BE INVOLVED.

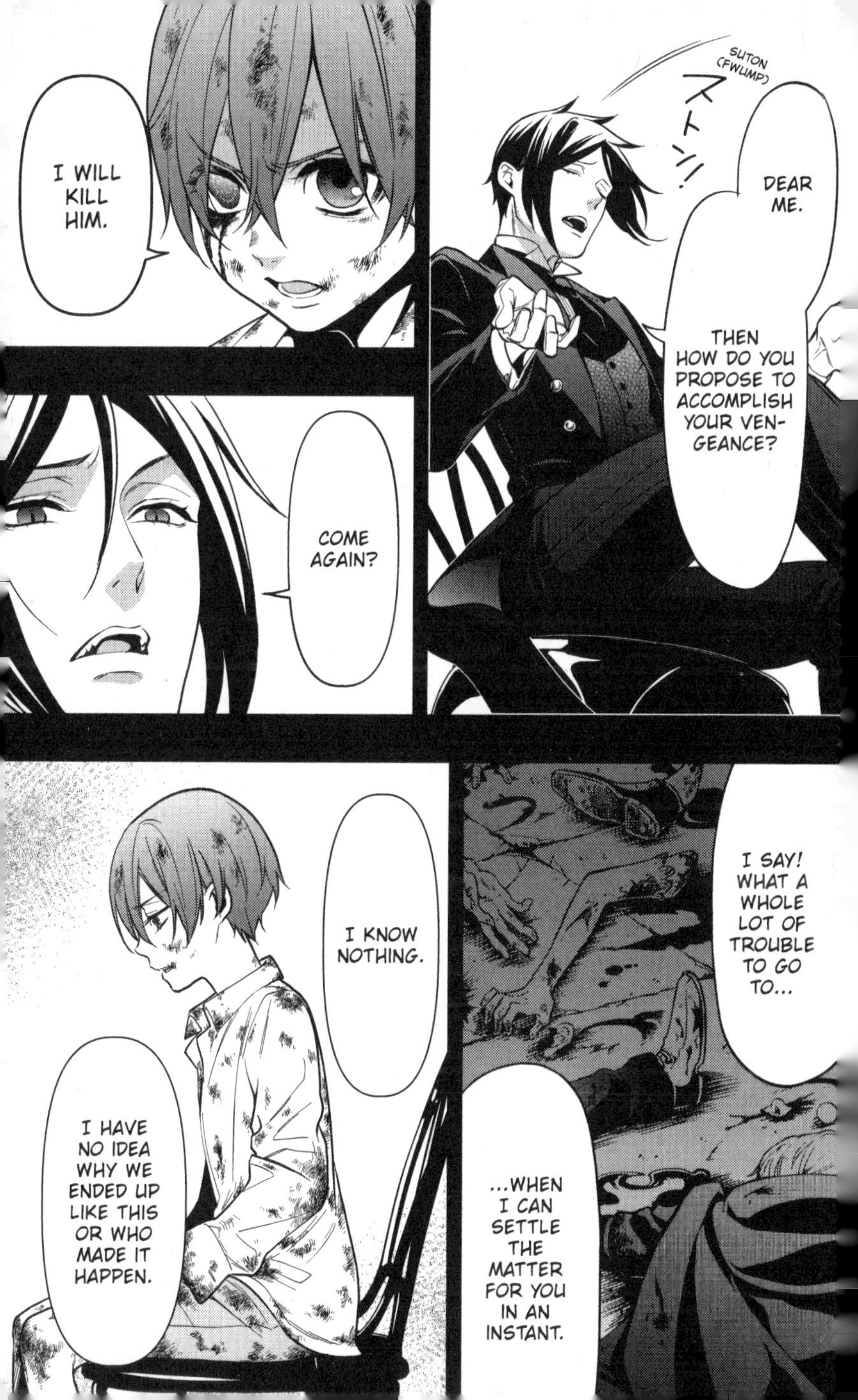
SUTON (FWUMP)
DEAR ME.
THEN HOW DO YOU PROPOSE TO ACCOMPLISH YOUR VEN-GEANCE?
I WILL KILL HIM.
COME AGAIN?
I SAY! WHAT A WHOLE LOT OF TROUBLE TO GO TO...
...WHEN I CAN SETTLE THE MATTER FOR YOU IN AN INSTANT.
I KNOW NOTHING.
I HAVE NO IDEA WHY WE ENDED UP LIKE THIS OR WHO MADE IT HAPPEN.

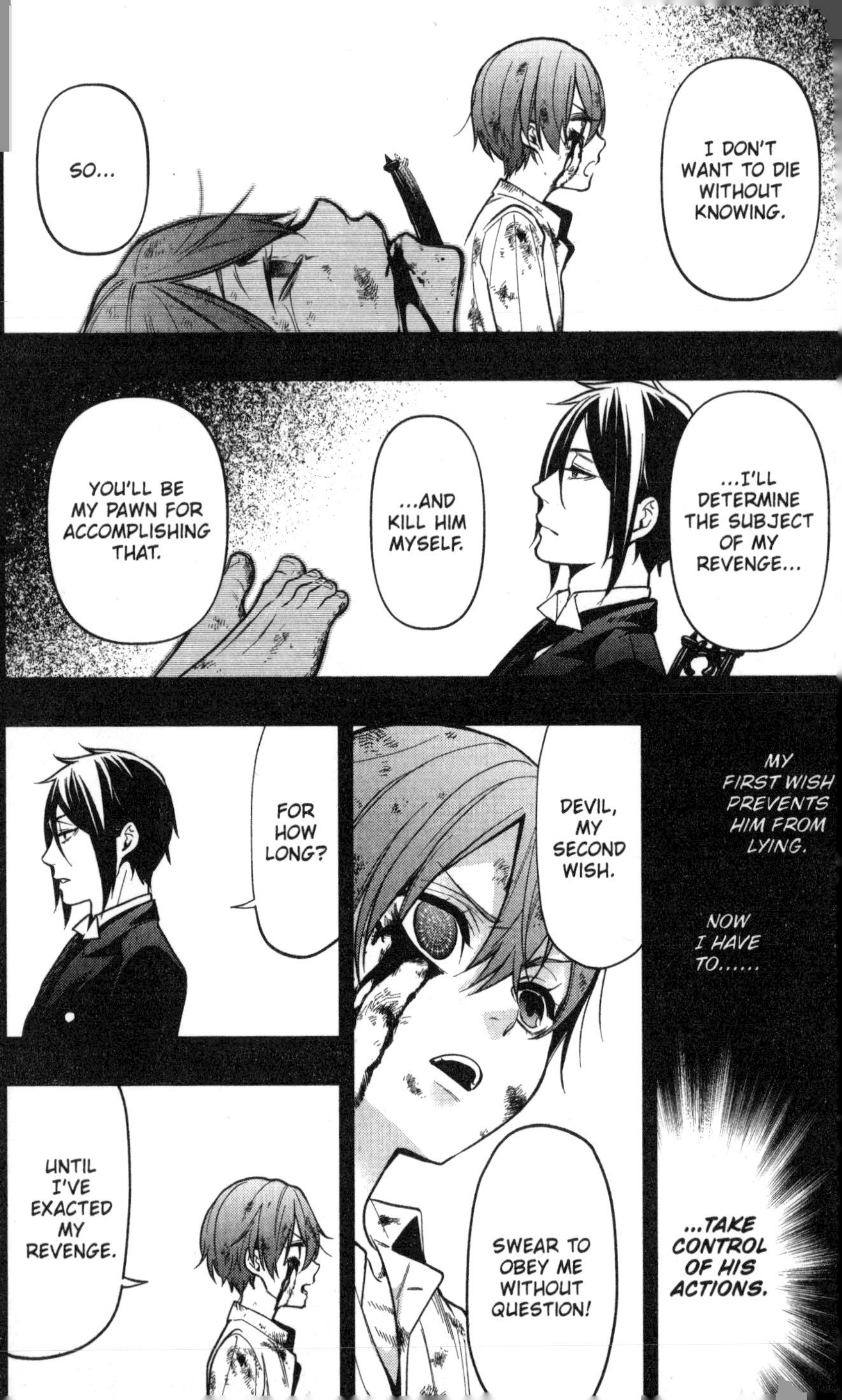
I DON'T WANT TO DIE WITHOUT KNOWING.
SO...
...I'LL DETERMINE THE SUBJECT OF MY REVENGE...
...AND KILL HIM MYSELF.
YOU'LL BE MY PAWN FOR ACCOMPLISHING THAT.
MY FIRST WISH PREVENTS HIM FROM LYING.
NOW I HAVE TO......
...TAKE CONTROL OF HIS ACTIONS.
DEVIL, MY SECOND WISH.
SWEAR TO OBEY ME WITHOUT QUESTION!
FOR HOW LONG?
UNTIL I'VE EXACTED MY REVENGE.

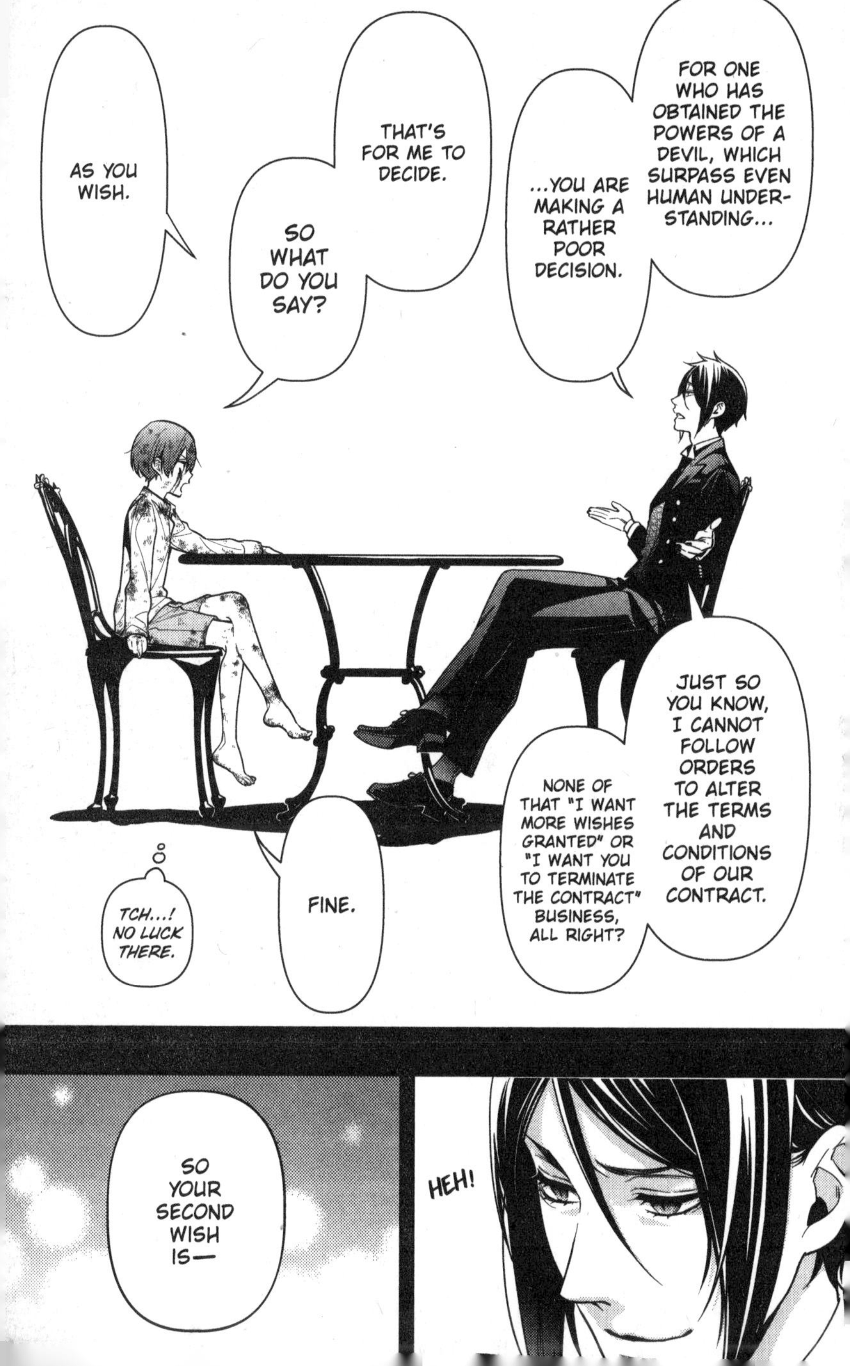
FOR ONE WHO HAS OBTAINED THE POWERS OF A DEVIL, WHICH SURPASS EVEN HUMAN UNDER-STANDING...
...YOU ARE MAKING A RATHER POOR DECISION.
THAT'S FOR ME TO DECIDE.
SO WHAT DO YOU SAY?
AS YOU WISH.
JUST SO YOU KNOW, I CANNOT FOLLOW ORDERS TO ALTER THE TERMS AND CONDITIONS OF OUR CONTRACT.
NONE OF THAT "I WANT MORE WISHES GRANTED" OR "I WANT YOU TO TERMINATE THE CONTRACT" BUSINESS, ALL RIGHT?
FINE.
TCH...! NO LUCK THERE.
HEH!
SO YOUR SECOND WISH IS—

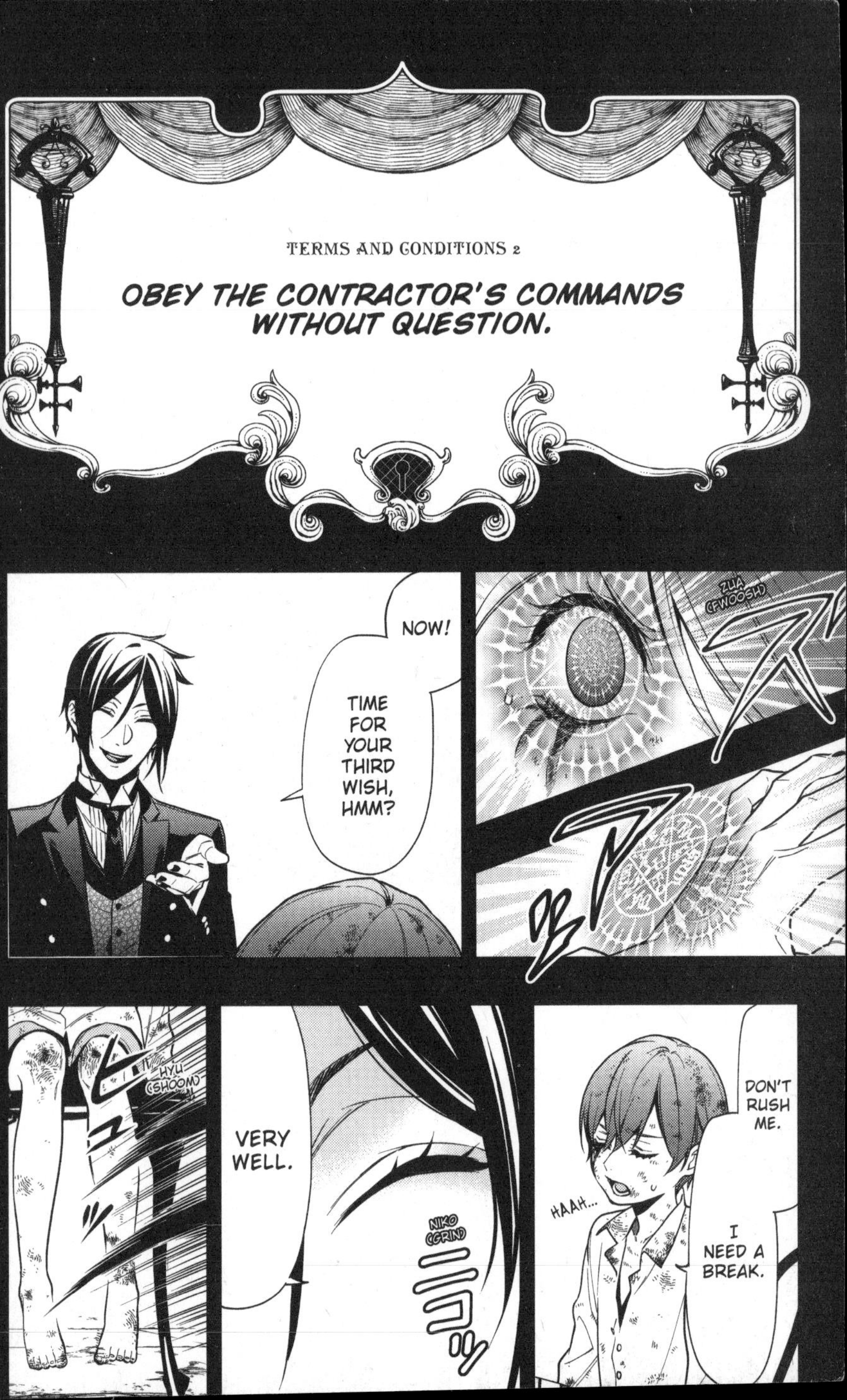
TERMS AND CONDITIONS 2
OBEY THE CONTRACTOR'S COMMANDS WITHOUT QUESTION.
ZUA (FWOOSH)
NOW!
TIME FOR YOUR THIRD WISH, HMM?
DON'T RUSH ME.
HAAH...
I NEED A BREAK.
VERY WELL.
NIKO (GRIND)
HYU (SHOOM)

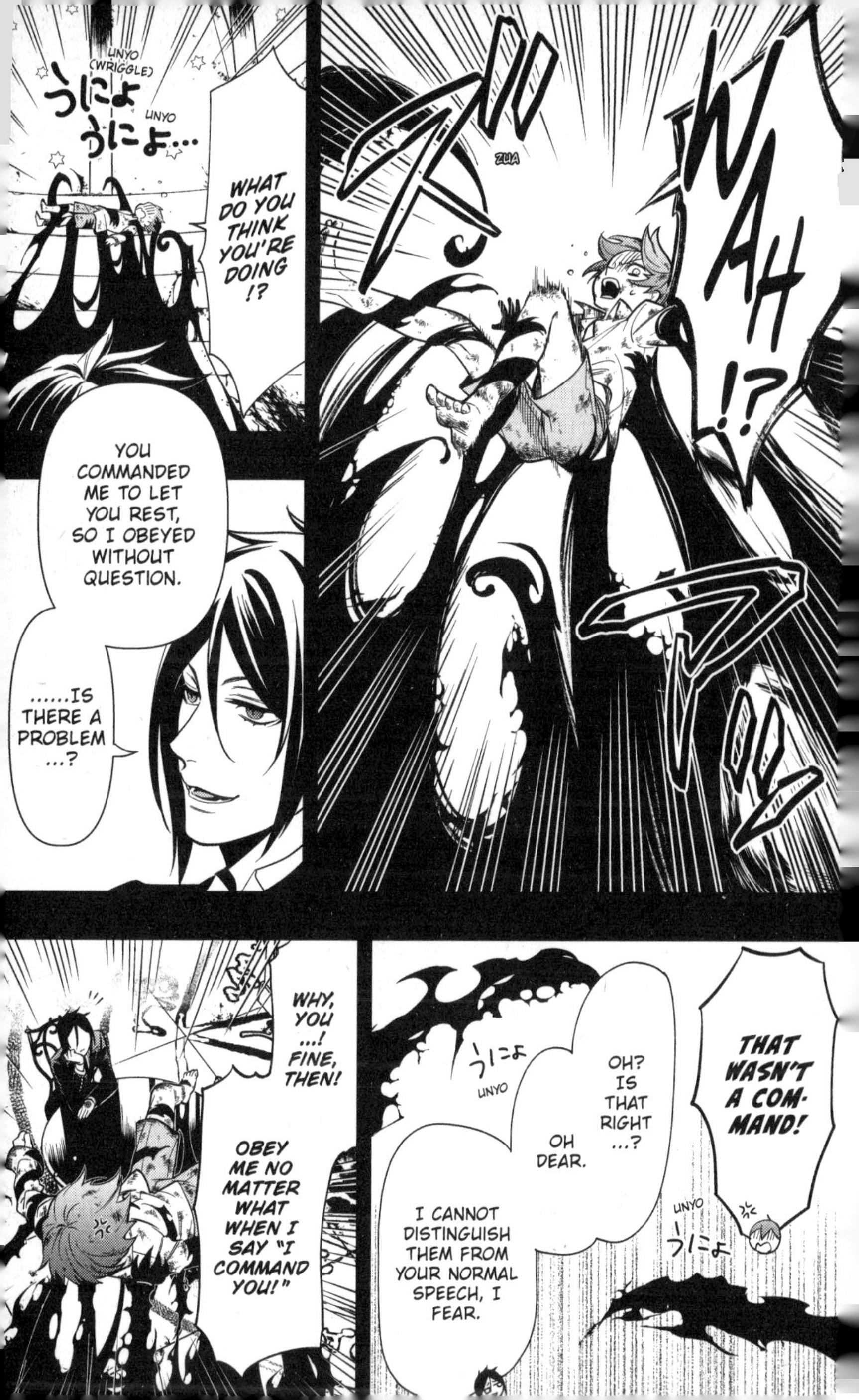

ZUA
WAAH!?
うにょ うにょ…
UNYO (WRIGGLE)
UNYO
WHAT DO YOU THINK YOU'RE DOING!?
YOU COMMANDED ME TO LET YOU REST, SO I OBEYED WITHOUT QUESTION.
……IS THERE A PROBLEM …?
THAT WASN'T A COMMAND!
うにょ
UNYO
OH? IS THAT RIGHT …?
OH DEAR.
I CANNOT DISTINGUISH THEM FROM YOUR NORMAL SPEECH, I FEAR.
うにょ
UNYO
WHY, YOU …! FINE, THEN!
OBEY ME NO MATTER WHAT WHEN I SAY "I COMMAND YOU!"

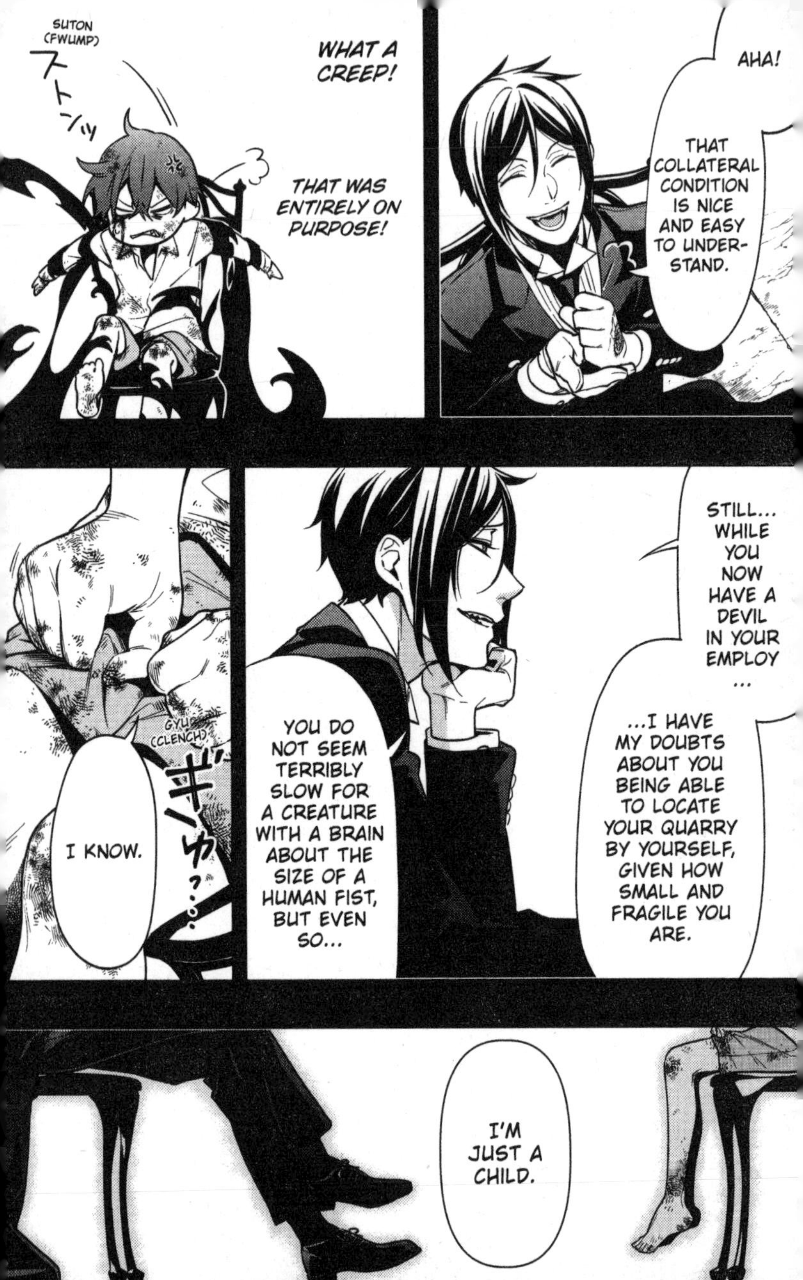
AHA!
THAT COLLATERAL CONDITION IS NICE AND EASY TO UNDER-STAND.
SUTON (FWUMP)
WHAT A CREEP!
THAT WAS ENTIRELY ON PURPOSE!
STILL... WHILE YOU NOW HAVE A DEVIL IN YOUR EMPLOY...
...I HAVE MY DOUBTS ABOUT YOU BEING ABLE TO LOCATE YOUR QUARRY BY YOURSELF, GIVEN HOW SMALL AND FRAGILE YOU ARE.
YOU DO NOT SEEM TERRIBLY SLOW FOR A CREATURE WITH A BRAIN ABOUT THE SIZE OF A HUMAN FIST, BUT EVEN SO...
GYU (CLENCH)
I KNOW.
I'M JUST A CHILD.

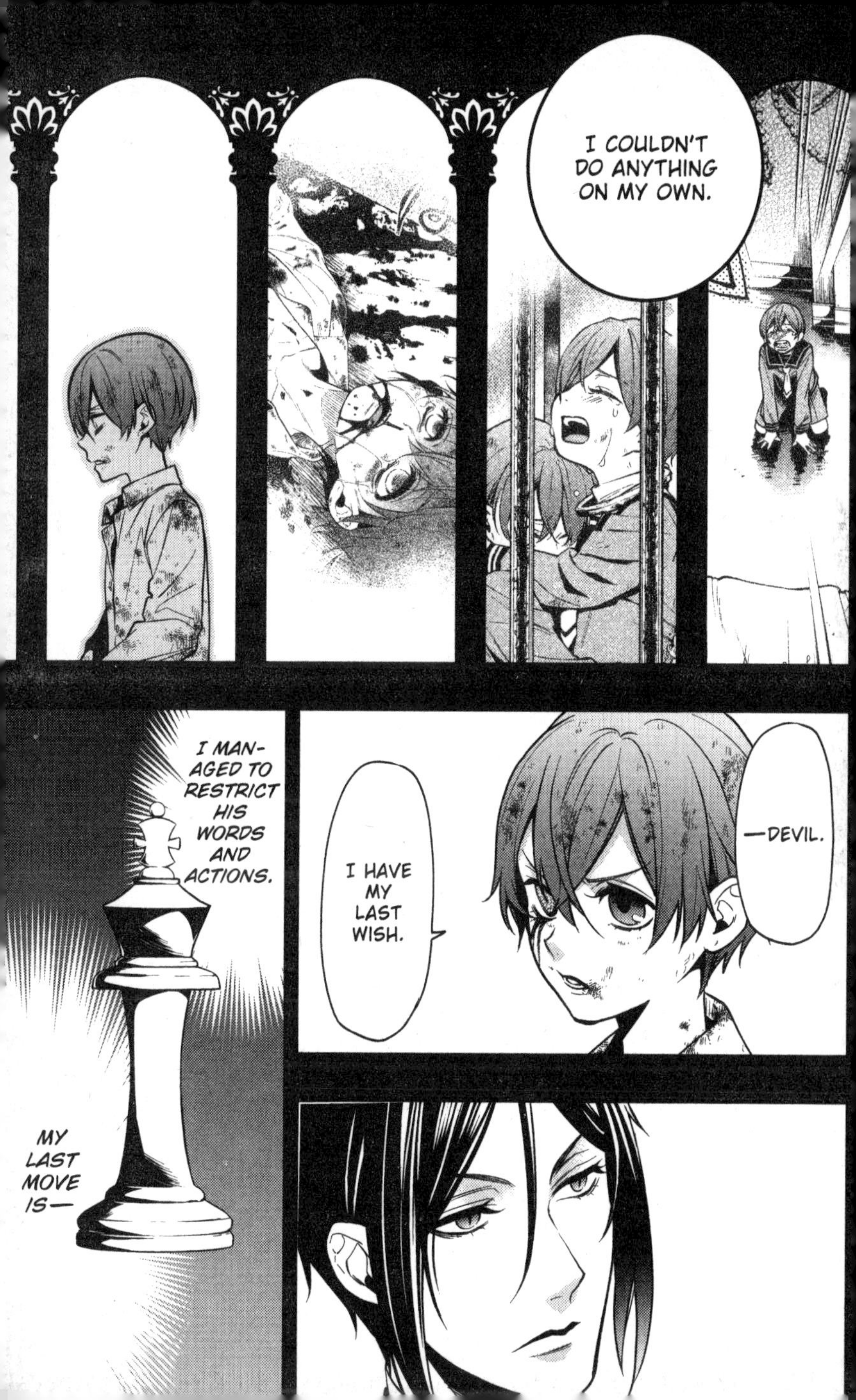
I COULDN'T DO ANYTHING ON MY OWN.
—DEVIL.
I HAVE MY LAST WISH.
I MAN-AGED TO RESTRICT HIS WORDS AND ACTIONS.
MY LAST MOVE IS—

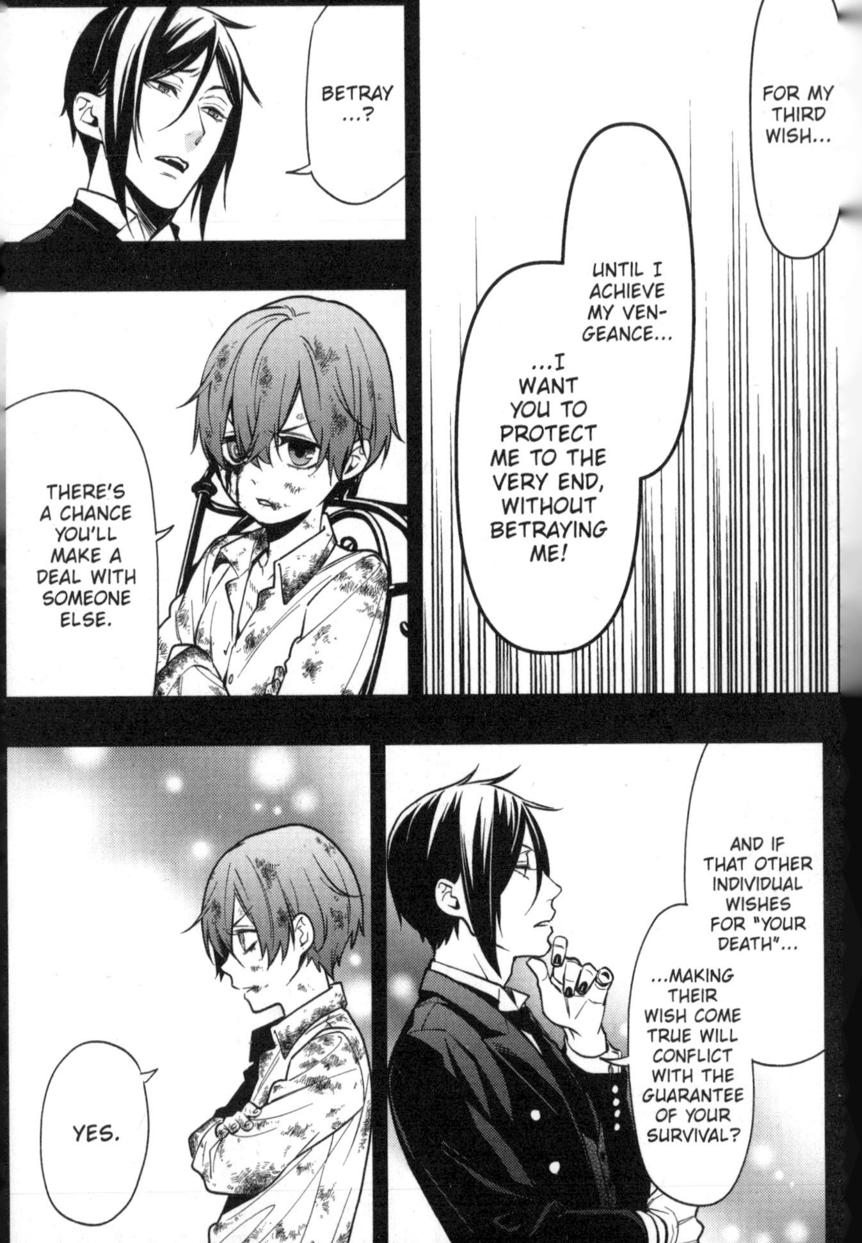
FOR MY THIRD WISH...
UNTIL I ACHIEVE MY VEN-GEANCE...
...I WANT YOU TO PROTECT ME TO THE VERY END, WITHOUT BETRAYING ME!
BETRAY ...?
THERE'S A CHANCE YOU'LL MAKE A DEAL WITH SOMEONE ELSE.
AND IF THAT OTHER INDIVIDUAL WISHES FOR "YOUR DEATH"...
...MAKING THEIR WISH COME TRUE WILL CONFLICT WITH THE GUARANTEE OF YOUR SURVIVAL?
YES.

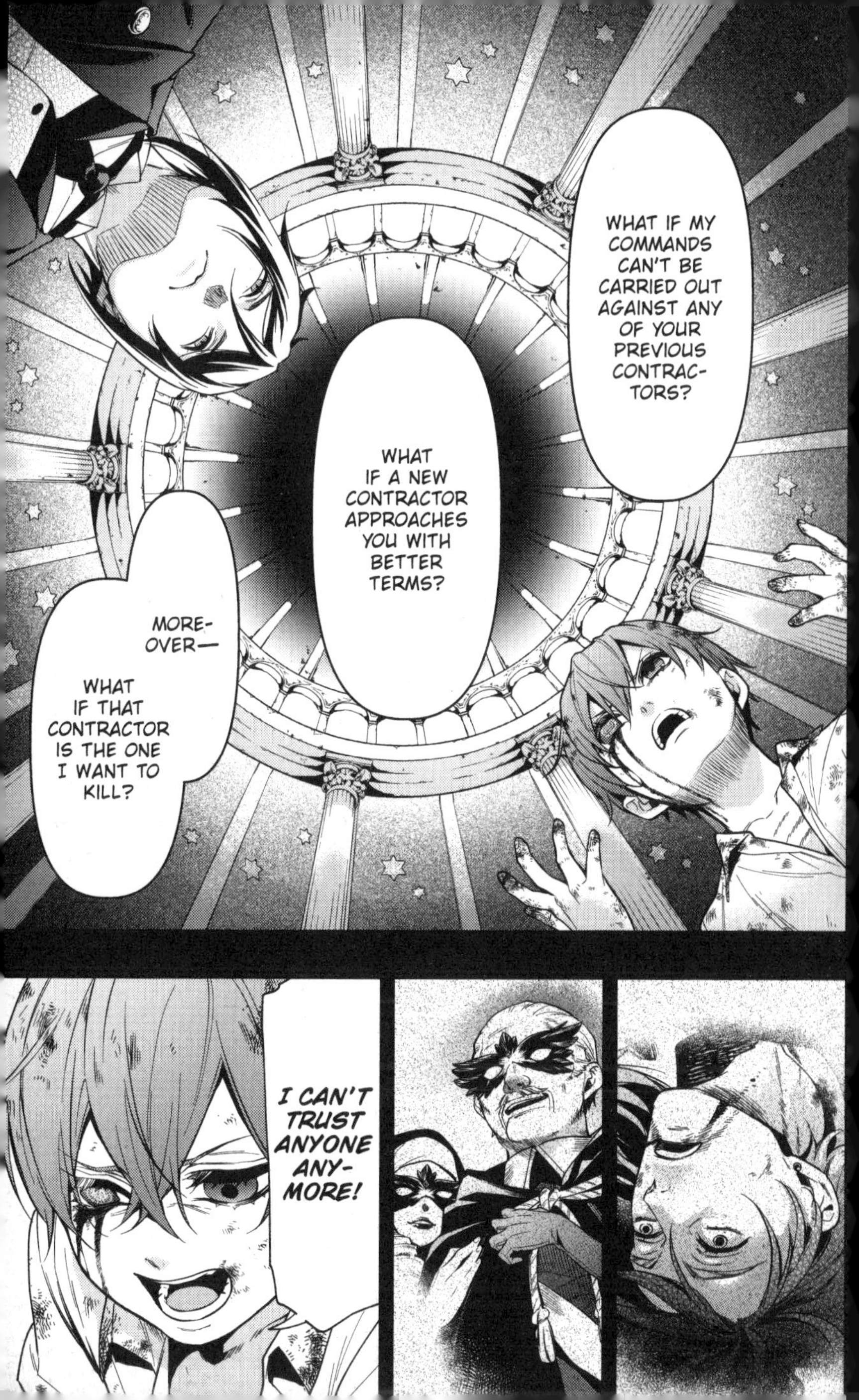
WHAT IF MY COMMANDS CAN'T BE CARRIED OUT AGAINST ANY OF YOUR PREVIOUS CONTRAC-TORS?
WHAT IF A NEW CONTRACTOR APPROACHES YOU WITH BETTER TERMS?
MORE-OVER—
WHAT IF THAT CONTRACTOR IS THE ONE I WANT TO KILL?
I CAN'T TRUST ANYONE ANY-MORE!

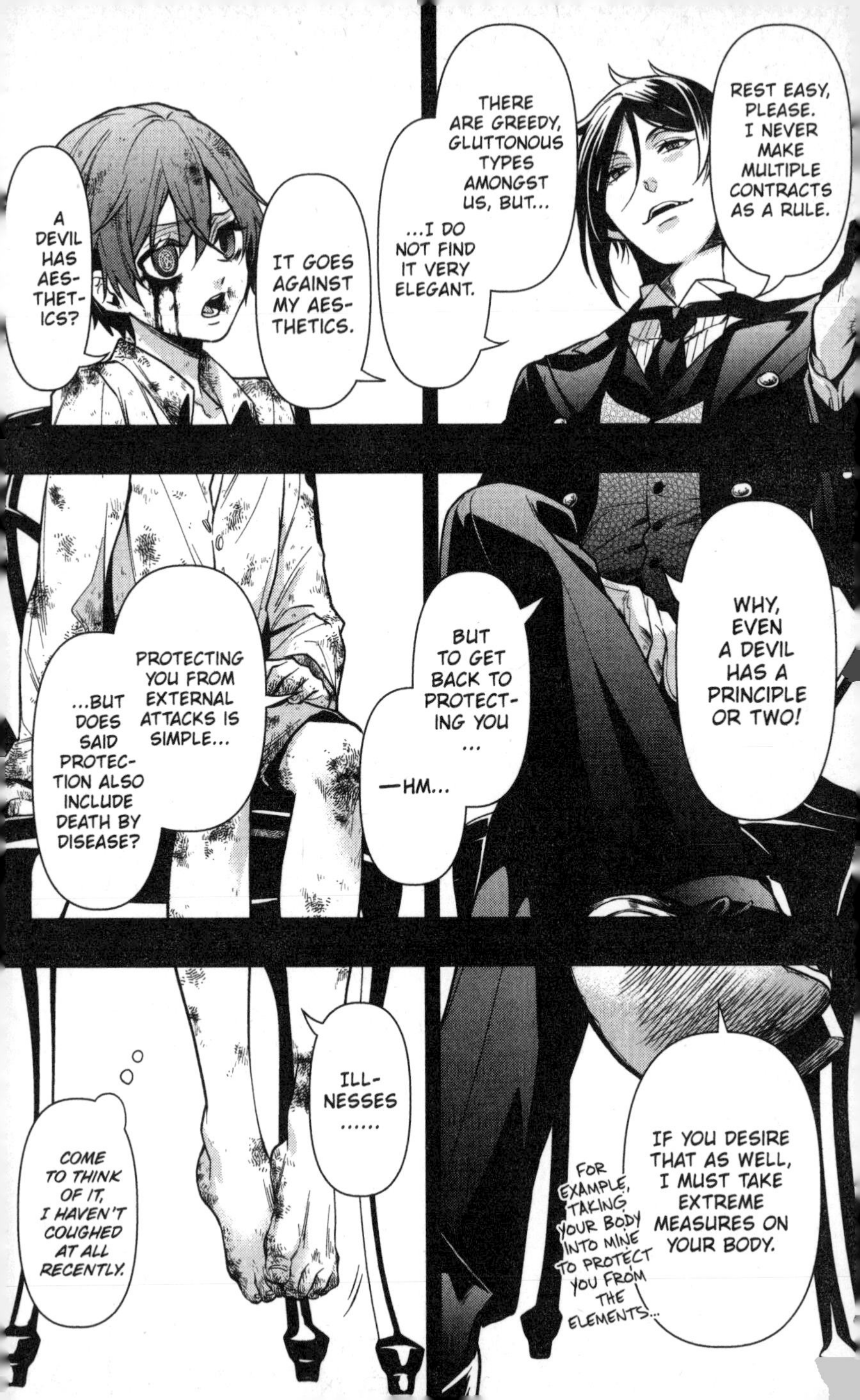
REST EASY, PLEASE. I NEVER MAKE MULTIPLE CONTRACTS AS A RULE.
THERE ARE GREEDY, GLUTTONOUS TYPES AMONGST US, BUT...
...I DO NOT FIND IT VERY ELEGANT.
IT GOES AGAINST MY AES-THETICS.
A DEVIL HAS AES-THET-ICS?
WHY, EVEN A DEVIL HAS A PRINCIPLE OR TWO!
BUT TO GET BACK TO PROTECT-ING YOU ...
—HM...
PROTECTING YOU FROM EXTERNAL ATTACKS IS SIMPLE...
...BUT DOES SAID PROTEC-TION ALSO INCLUDE DEATH BY DISEASE?
IF YOU DESIRE THAT AS WELL, I MUST TAKE EXTREME MEASURES ON YOUR BODY.
FOR EXAMPLE, TAKING YOUR BODY INTO MINE TO PROTECT YOU FROM THE ELEMENTS...
ILL-NESSES ......
COME TO THINK OF IT, I HAVEN'T COUGHED AT ALL RECENTLY.

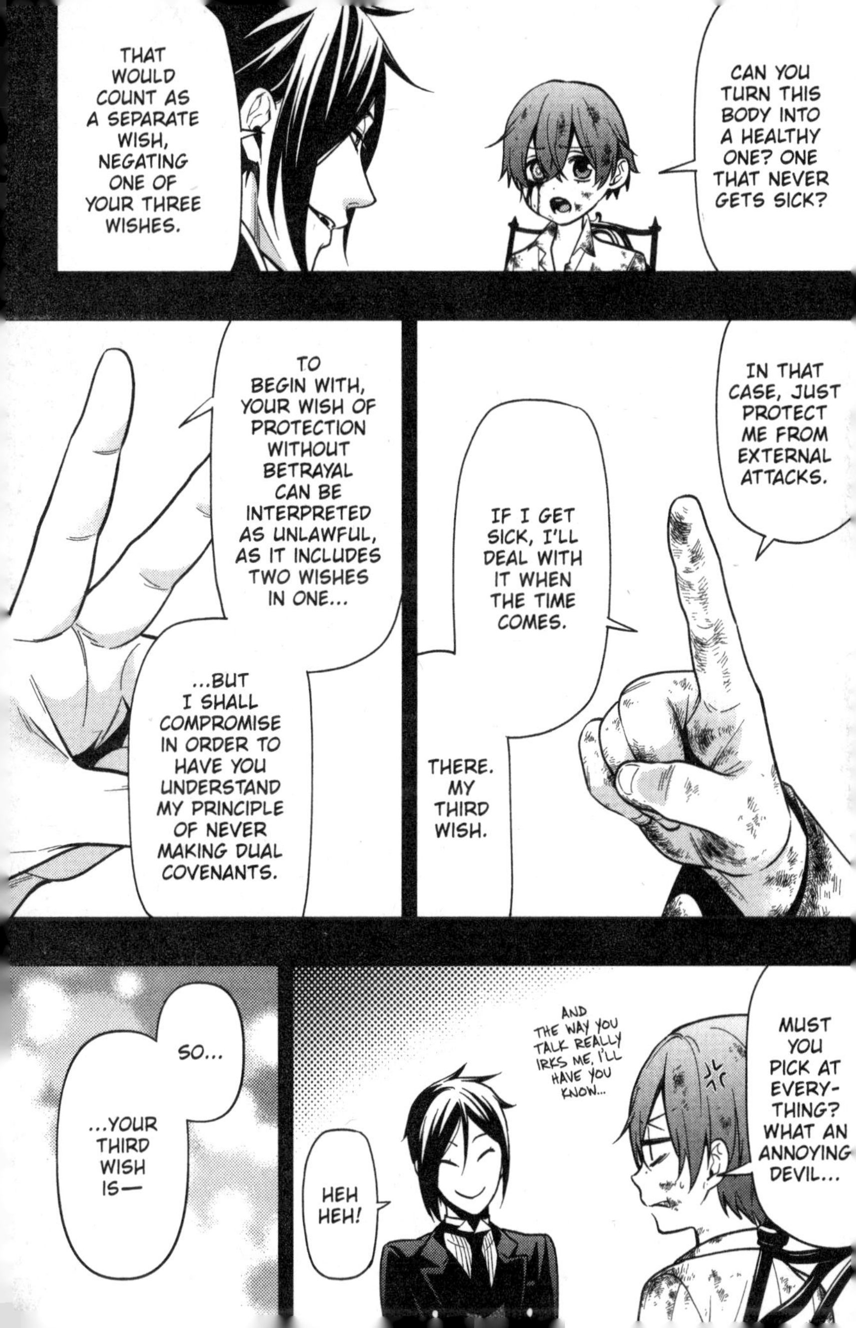
CAN YOU TURN THIS BODY INTO A HEALTHY ONE? ONE THAT NEVER GETS SICK?
THAT WOULD COUNT AS A SEPARATE WISH, NEGATING ONE OF YOUR THREE WISHES.
IN THAT CASE, JUST PROTECT ME FROM EXTERNAL ATTACKS.
IF I GET SICK, I'LL DEAL WITH IT WHEN THE TIME COMES.
THERE. MY THIRD WISH.
TO BEGIN WITH, YOUR WISH OF PROTECTION WITHOUT BETRAYAL CAN BE INTERPRETED AS UNLAWFUL, AS IT INCLUDES TWO WISHES IN ONE...
...BUT I SHALL COMPROMISE IN ORDER TO HAVE YOU UNDERSTAND MY PRINCIPLE OF NEVER MAKING DUAL COVENANTS.
MUST YOU PICK AT EVERYTHING? WHAT AN ANNOYING DEVIL...
AND THE WAY YOU TALK REALLY IRKS ME, I'LL HAVE YOU KNOW...
HEH HEH!
SO...
...YOUR THIRD WISH IS—

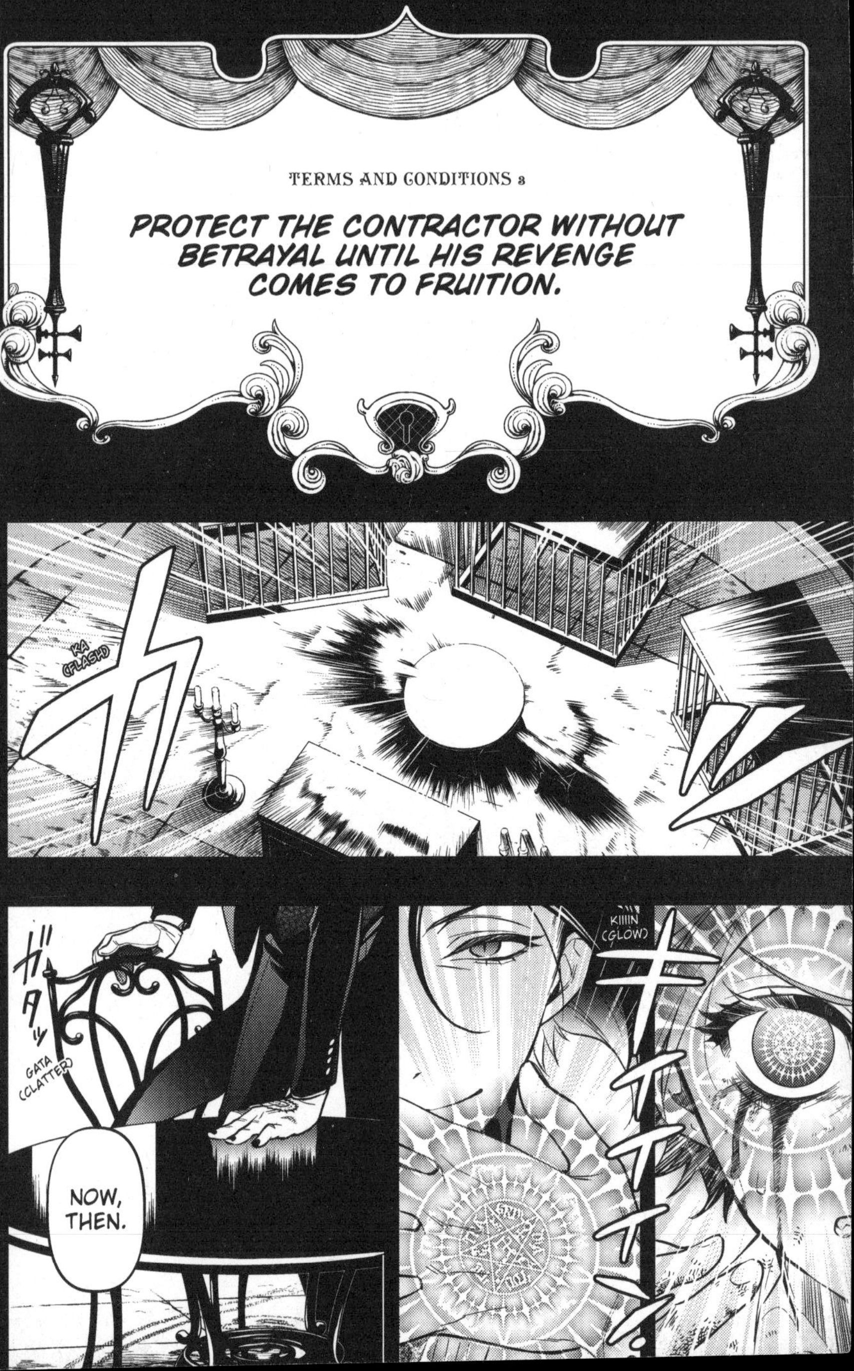
TERMS AND CONDITIONS 3
PROTECT THE CONTRACTOR WITHOUT BETRAYAL UNTIL HIS REVENGE COMES TO FRUITION.
KA (FLASH)
KIIIN (GLOW)
GATA (CLATTER)
NOW, THEN.

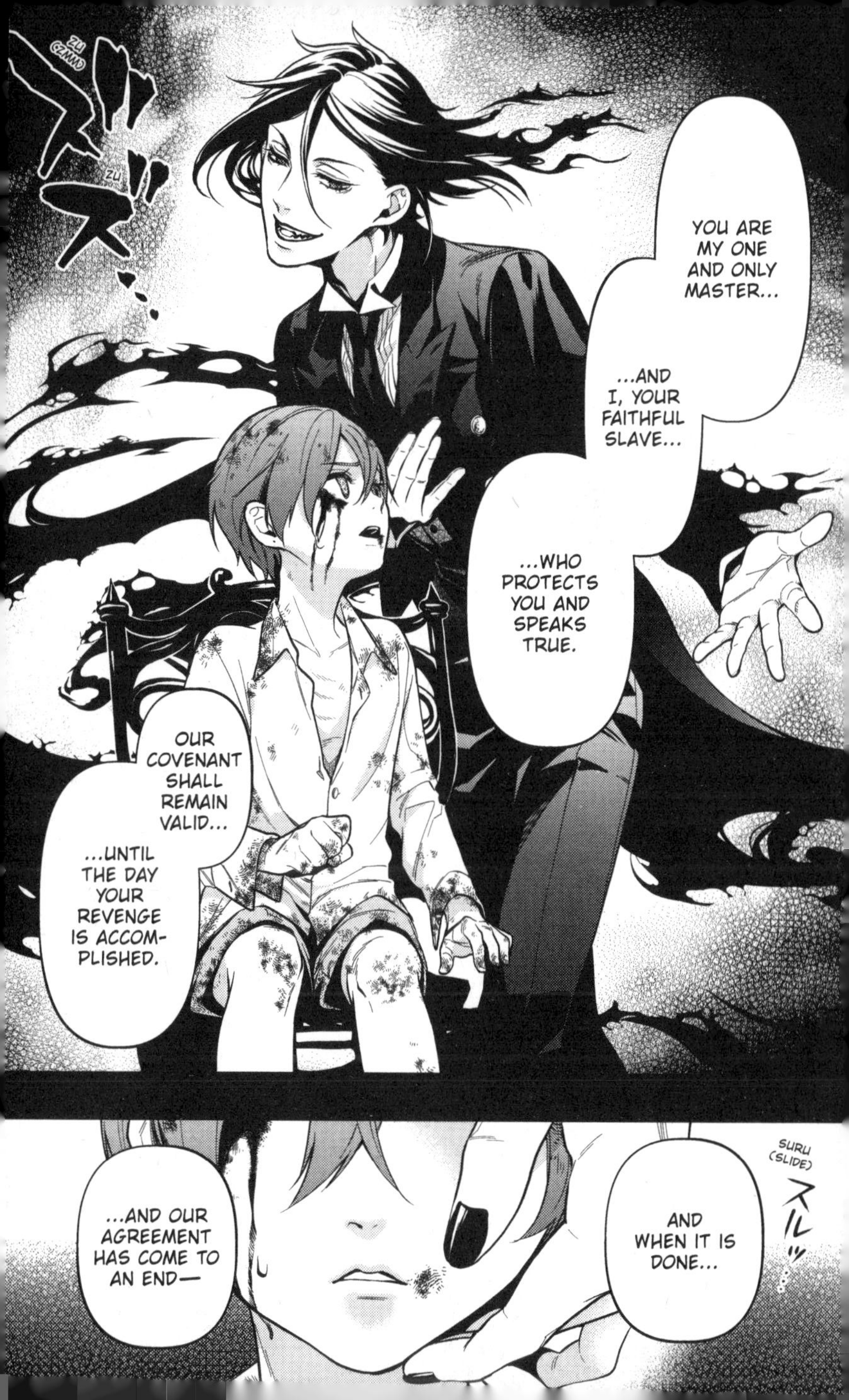
YOU ARE MY ONE AND ONLY MASTER...
...AND I, YOUR FAITHFUL SLAVE...
...WHO PROTECTS YOU AND SPEAKS TRUE.
ZU (ZWMM) ZU
OUR COVENANT SHALL REMAIN VALID...
...UNTIL THE DAY YOUR REVENGE IS ACCOM-PLISHED.
SURU (SLIDE)
AND WHEN IT IS DONE...
...AND OUR AGREEMENT HAS COME TO AN END—

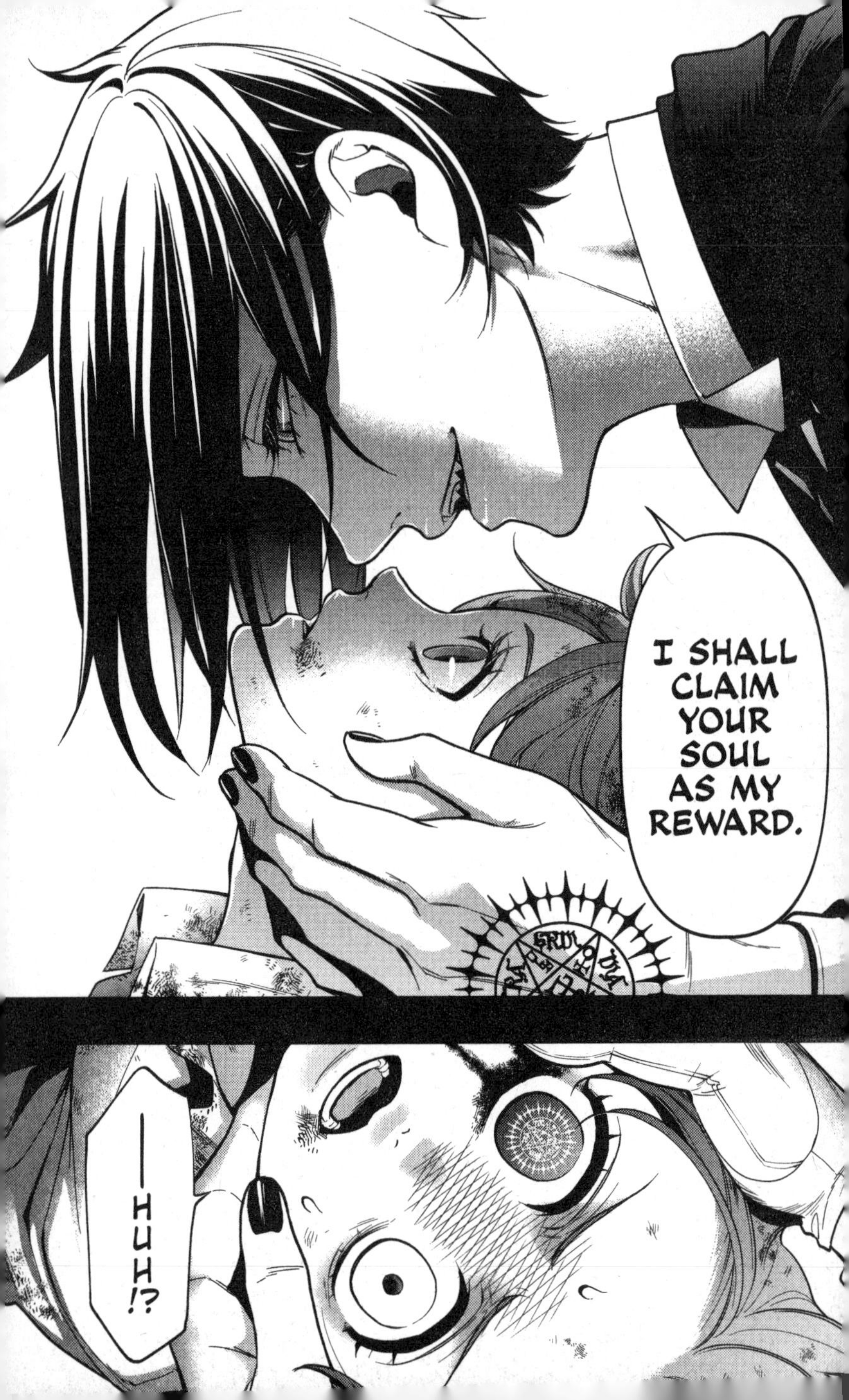
I SHALL CLAIM YOUR SOUL AS MY REWARD.
—HUH!?

**Black Butler**

## Chapter 139

# *At midnight : The Butler, Incising*

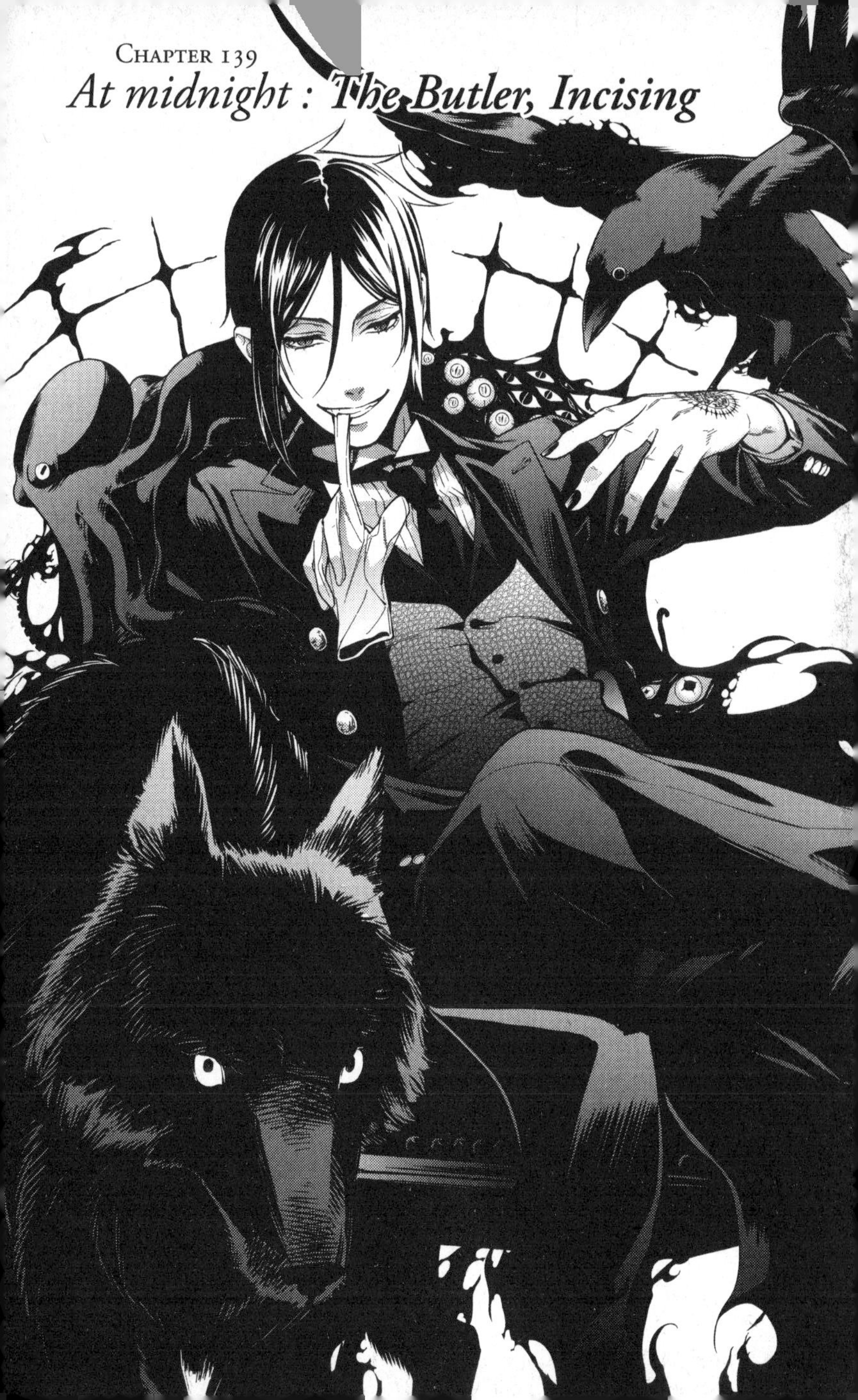

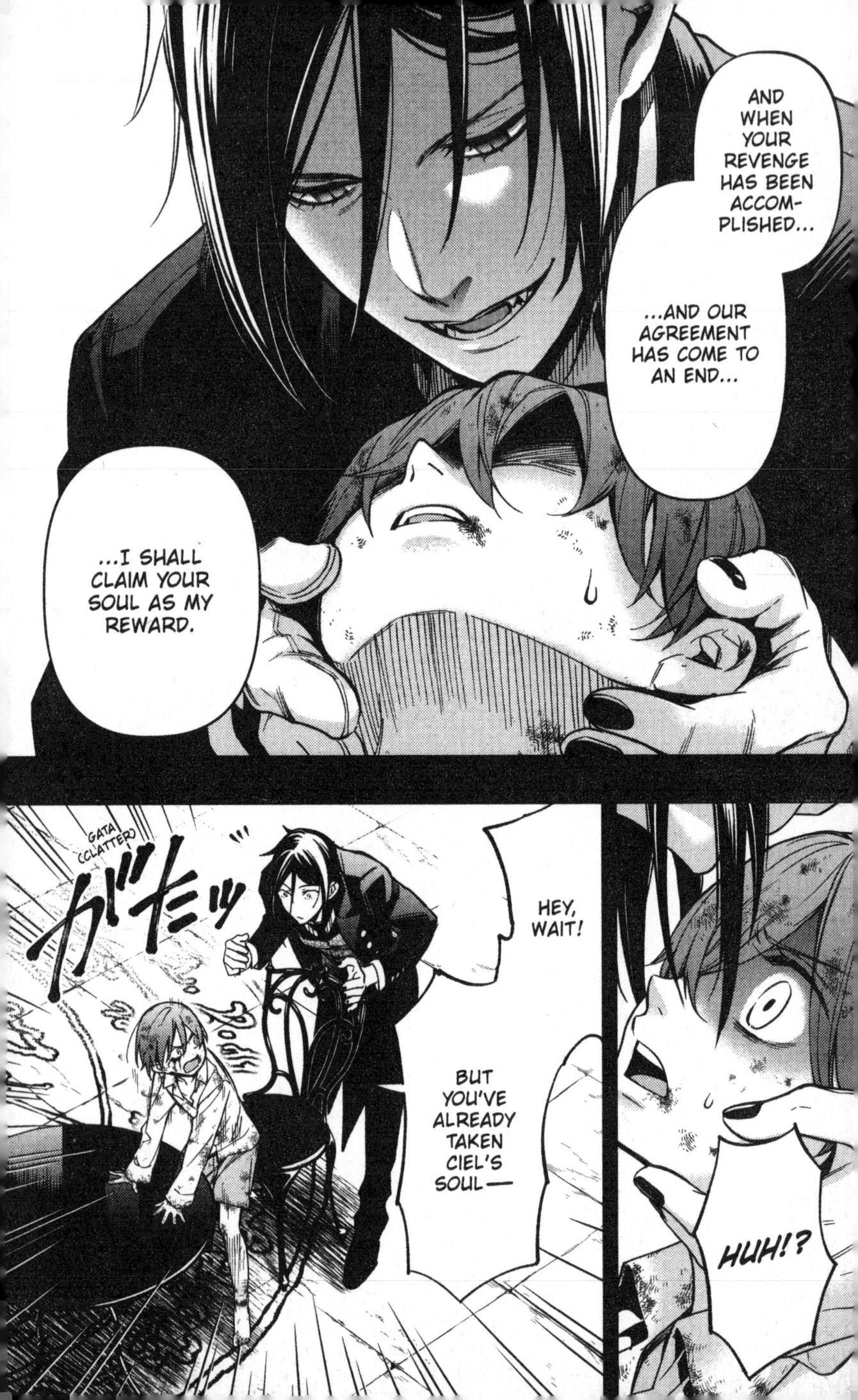
AND WHEN YOUR REVENGE HAS BEEN ACCOMPLISHED...
...AND OUR AGREEMENT HAS COME TO AN END...
...I SHALL CLAIM YOUR SOUL AS MY REWARD.
HUH!?
HEY, WAIT!
GATA (CLATTER)
ガタッ
BUT YOU'VE ALREADY TAKEN CIEL'S SOUL—

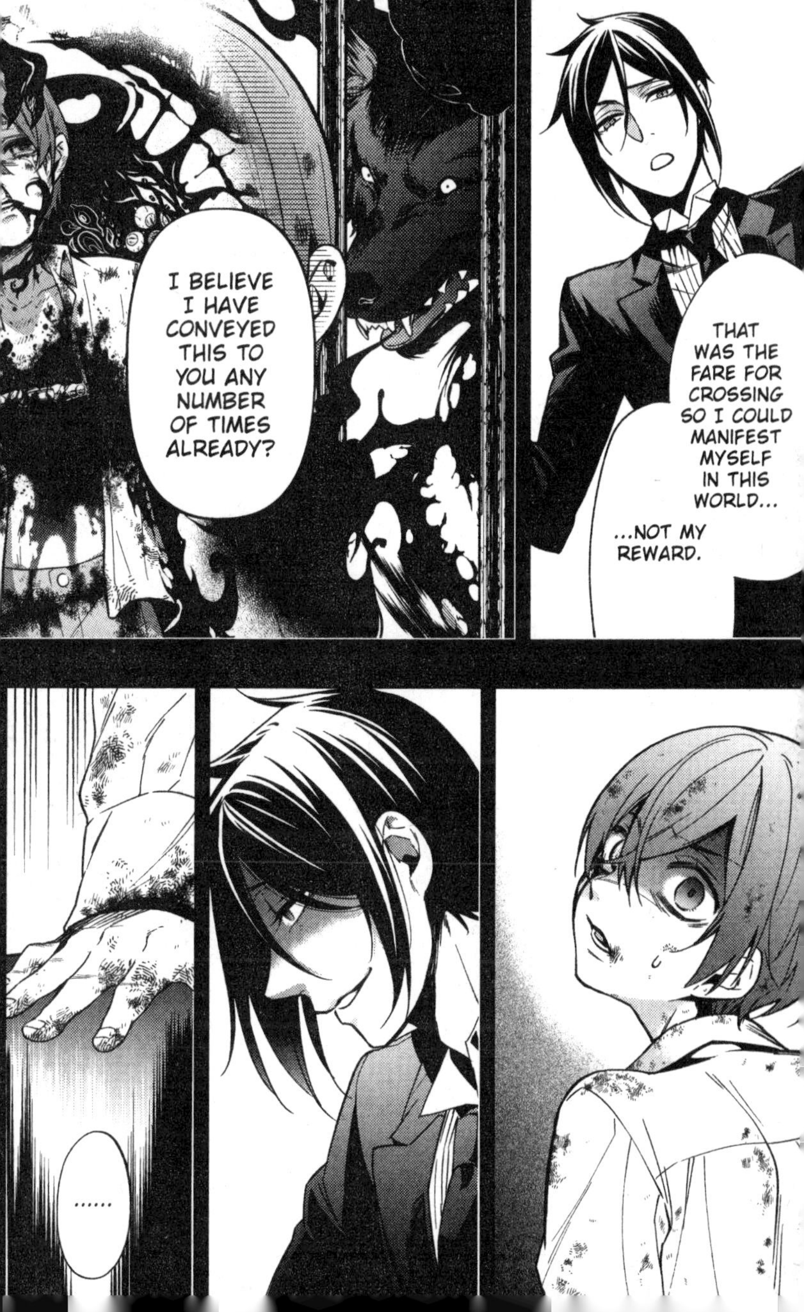
THAT WAS THE FARE FOR CROSSING SO I COULD MANIFEST MYSELF IN THIS WORLD...
...NOT MY REWARD.
I BELIEVE I HAVE CONVEYED THIS TO YOU ANY NUMBER OF TIMES ALREADY?
......

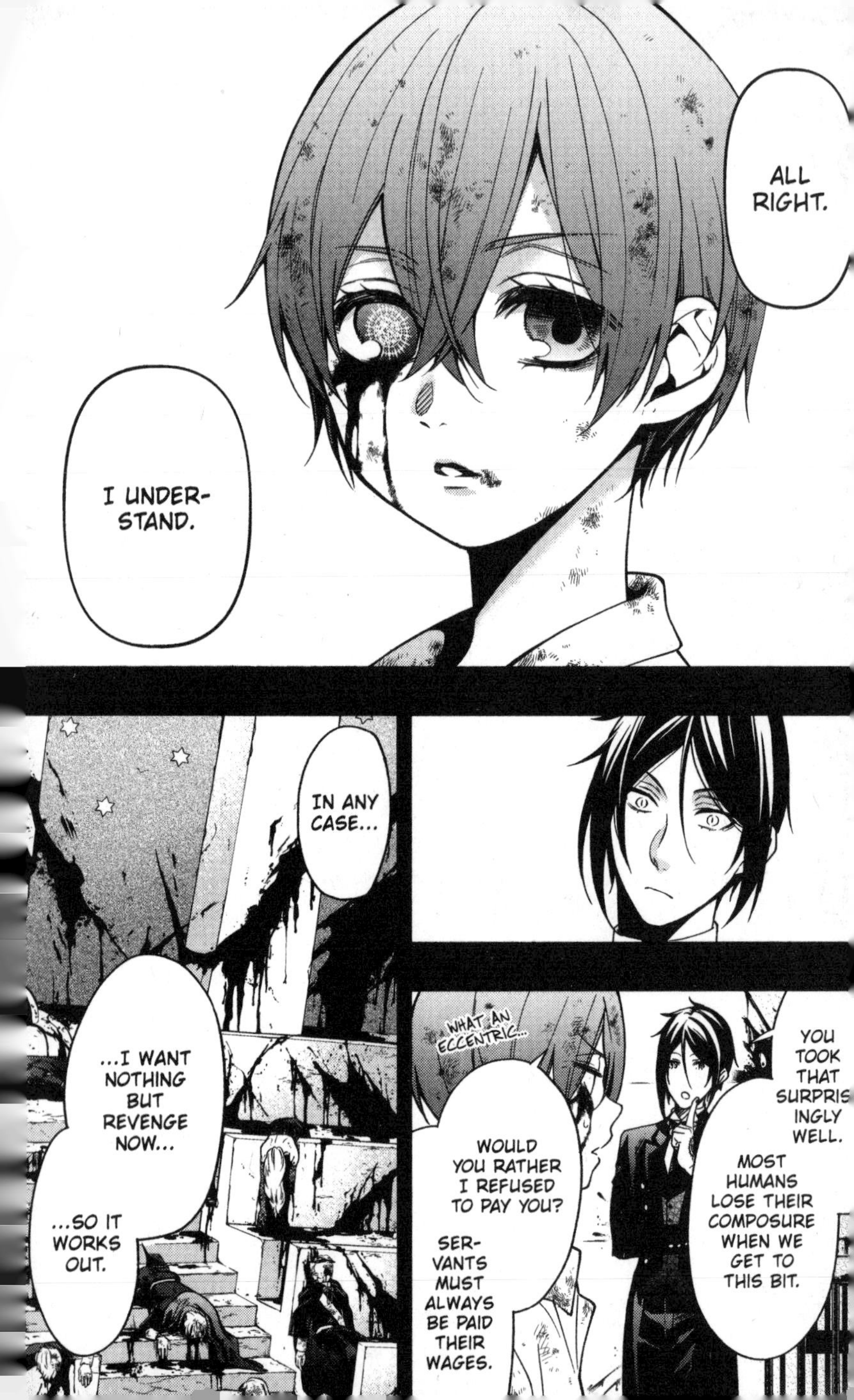
ALL RIGHT.
I UNDERSTAND.
YOU TOOK THAT SURPRISINGLY WELL.
MOST HUMANS LOSE THEIR COMPOSURE WHEN WE GET TO THIS BIT.
WHAT AN ECCENTRIC...
WOULD YOU RATHER I REFUSED TO PAY YOU?
SERVANTS MUST ALWAYS BE PAID THEIR WAGES.
IN ANY CASE...
...I WANT NOTHING BUT REVENGE NOW...
...SO IT WORKS OUT.

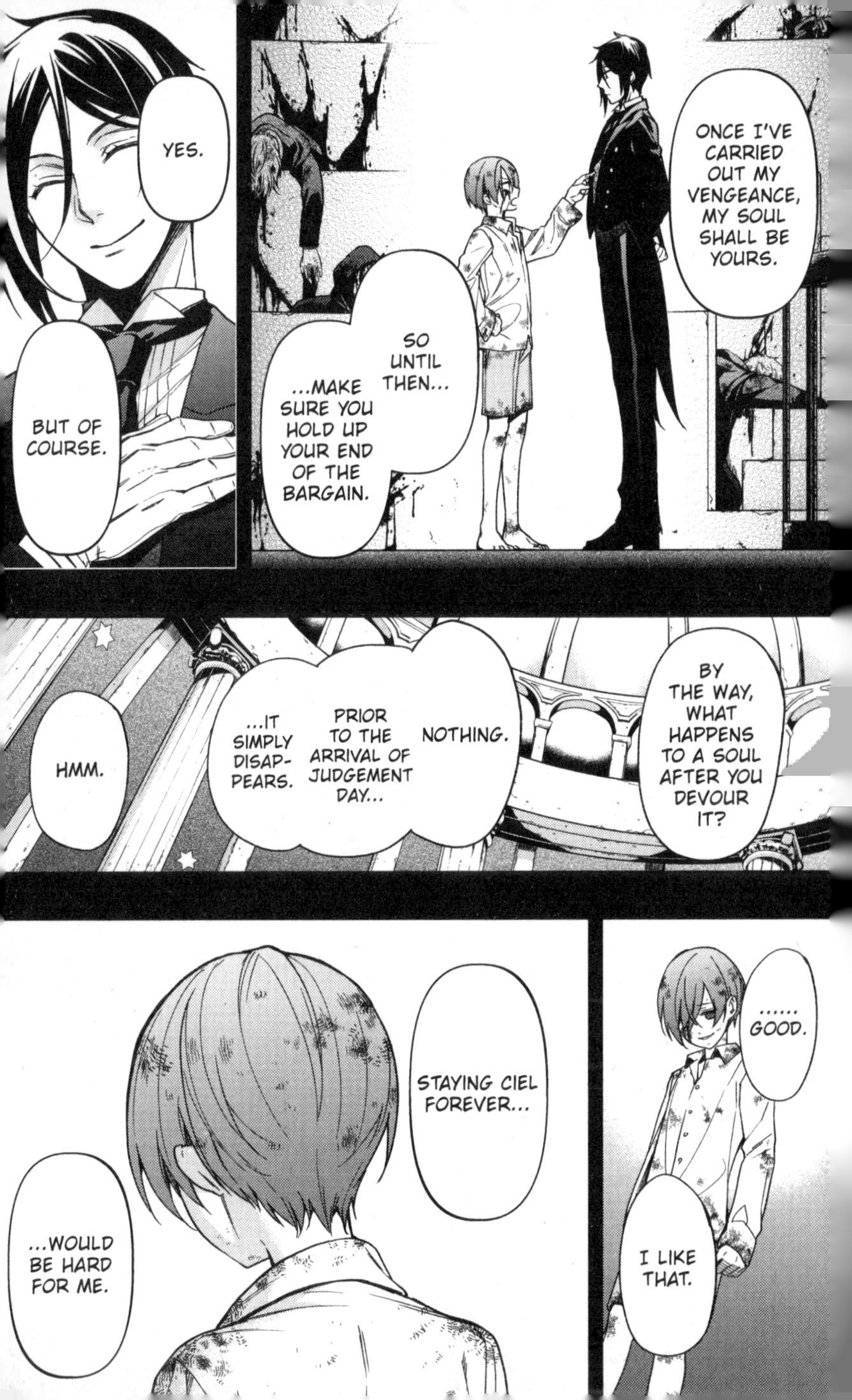
ONCE I'VE CARRIED OUT MY VENGEANCE, MY SOUL SHALL BE YOURS.
SO UNTIL THEN...
...MAKE SURE YOU HOLD UP YOUR END OF THE BARGAIN.
YES.
BUT OF COURSE.
BY THE WAY, WHAT HAPPENS TO A SOUL AFTER YOU DEVOUR IT?
NOTHING.
PRIOR TO THE ARRIVAL OF JUDGEMENT DAY...
...IT SIMPLY DISAP-PEARS.
HMM.
......GOOD.
I LIKE THAT.
STAYING CIEL FOREVER...
...WOULD BE HARD FOR ME.

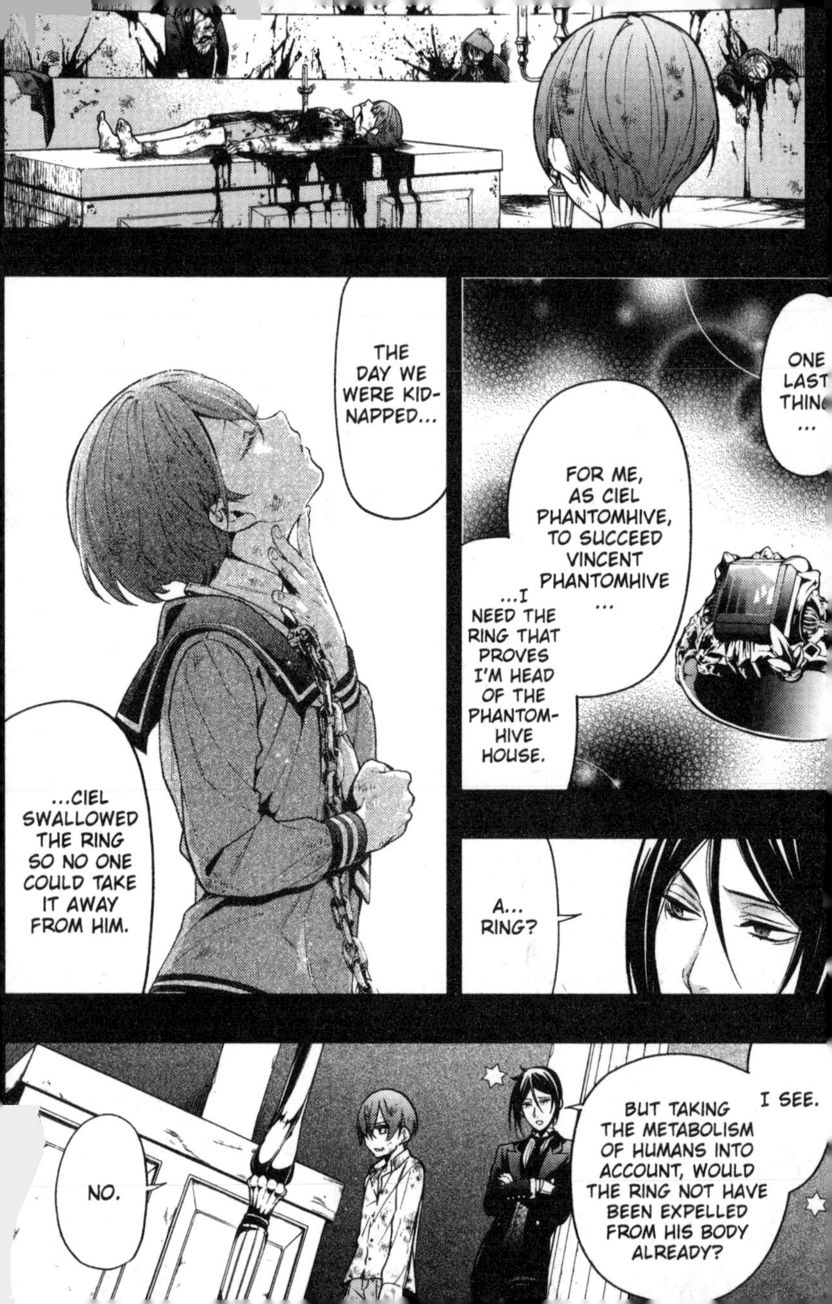
ONE LAST THIN ...
FOR ME, AS CIEL PHANTOMHIVE, TO SUCCEED VINCENT PHANTOMHIVE ...
...I NEED THE RING THAT PROVES I'M HEAD OF THE PHANTOM-HIVE HOUSE.
A... RING?
THE DAY WE WERE KID-NAPPED...
...CIEL SWALLOWED THE RING SO NO ONE COULD TAKE IT AWAY FROM HIM.
I SEE.
BUT TAKING THE METABOLISM OF HUMANS INTO ACCOUNT, WOULD THE RING NOT HAVE BEEN EXPELLED FROM HIS BODY ALREADY?
NO.

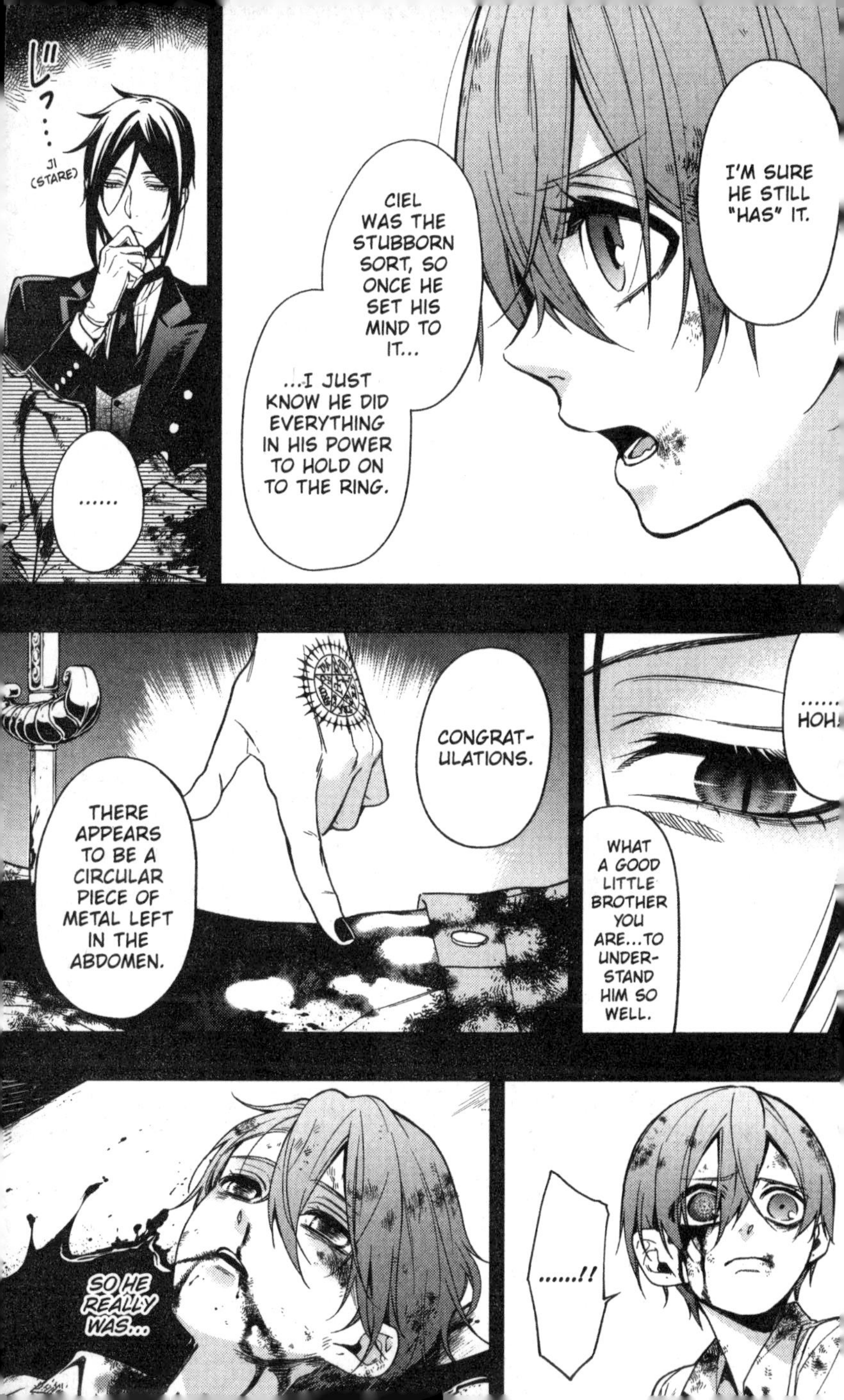

I'M SURE HE STILL "HAS" IT.
CIEL WAS THE STUBBORN SORT, SO ONCE HE SET HIS MIND TO IT...
...I JUST KNOW HE DID EVERYTHING IN HIS POWER TO HOLD ON TO THE RING.
JI (STARE)
......
......HOH
WHAT A GOOD LITTLE BROTHER YOU ARE...TO UNDER-STAND HIM SO WELL.
CONGRAT-ULATIONS.
THERE APPEARS TO BE A CIRCULAR PIECE OF METAL LEFT IN THE ABDOMEN.
......!!
SO HE REALLY WAS...

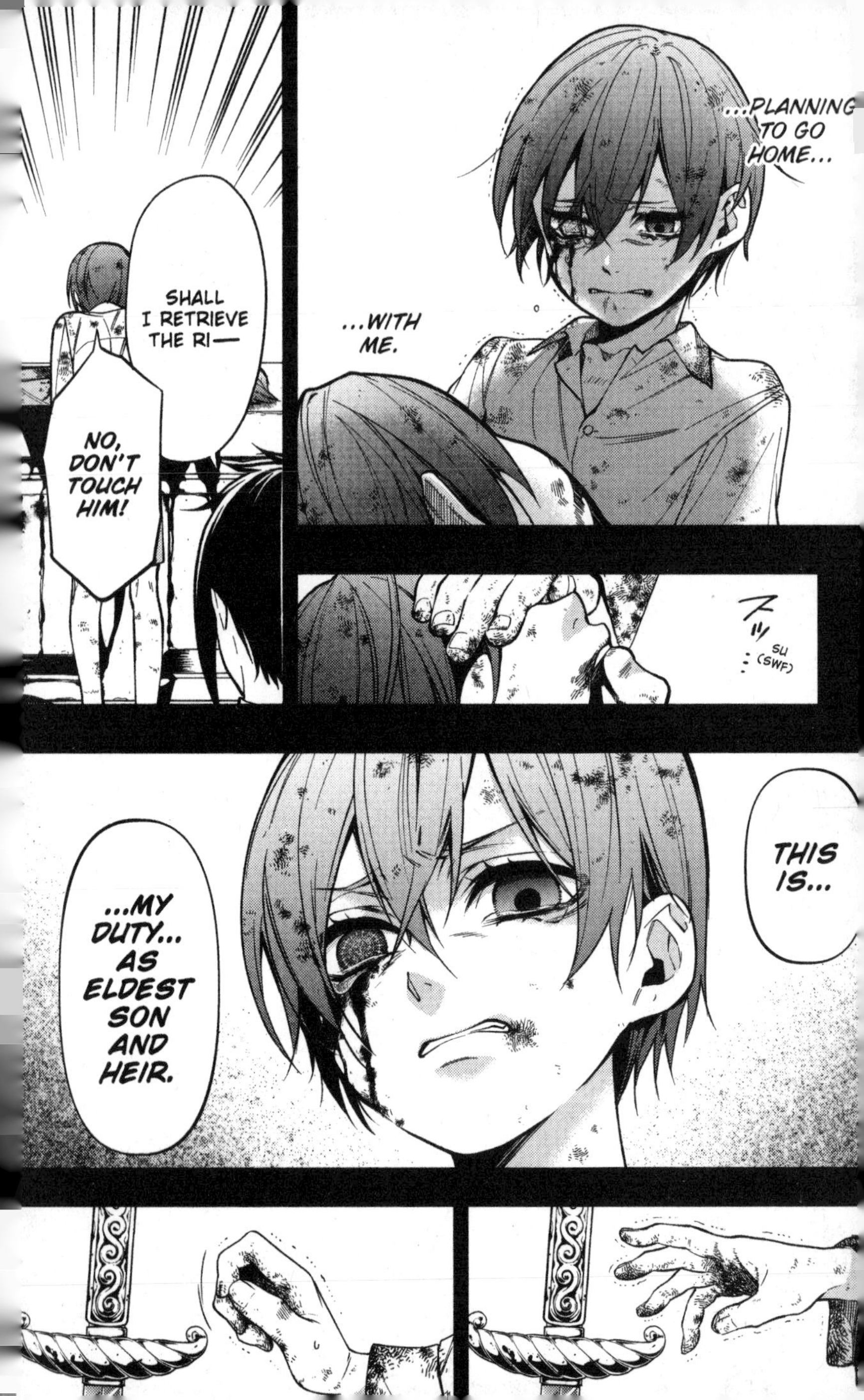
...PLANNING TO GO HOME...
...WITH ME.
スッ
SU (SWF)
SHALL I RETRIEVE THE RI—
NO, DON'T TOUCH HIM!
THIS IS...
...MY DUTY... AS ELDEST SON AND HEIR.

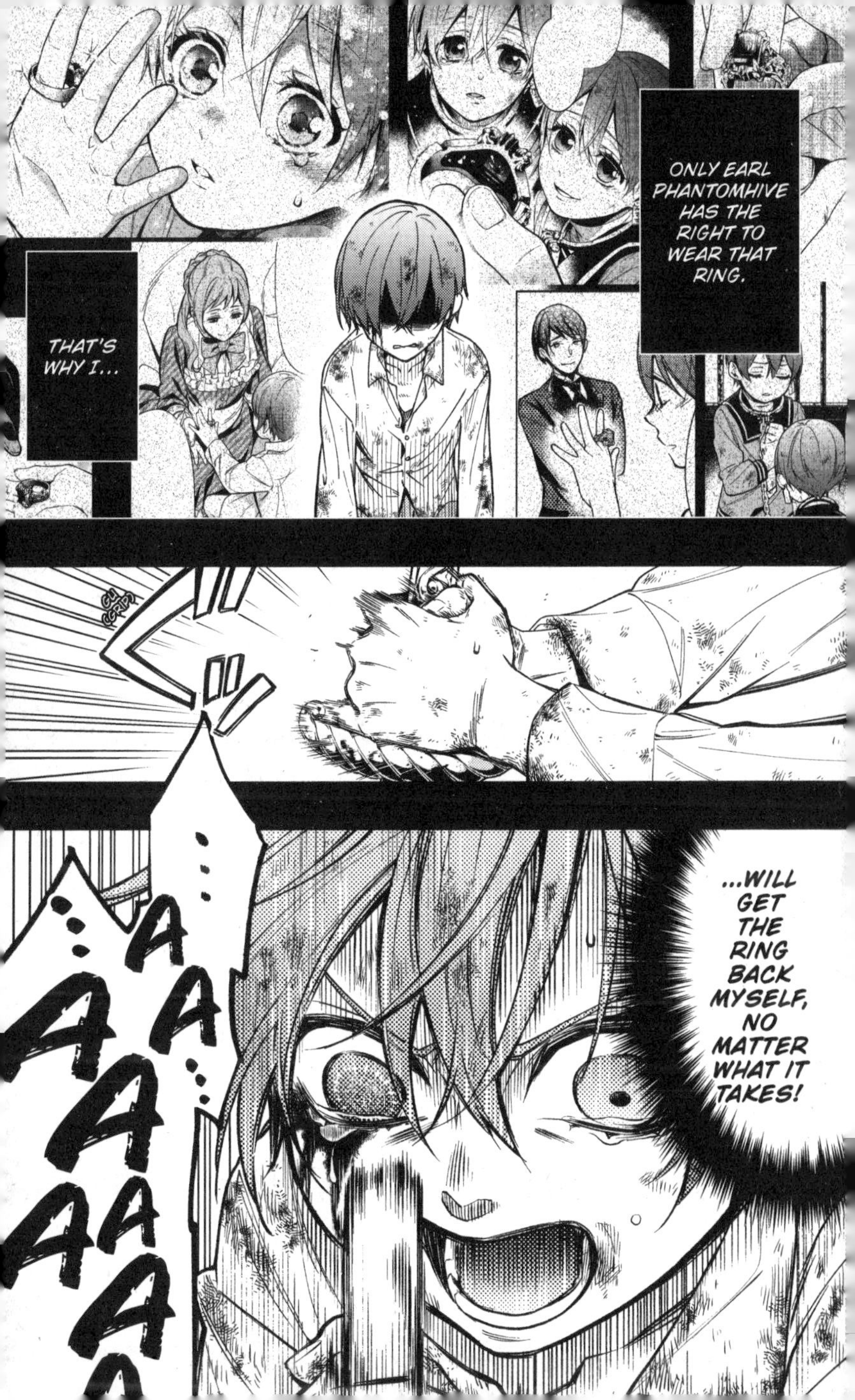
ONLY EARL PHANTOMHIVE HAS THE RIGHT TO WEAR THAT RING.
THAT'S WHY I...
GU (GRIP)
...WILL GET THE RING BACK MYSELF, NO MATTER WHAT IT TAKES!
...
...AAAAAAAAAA...

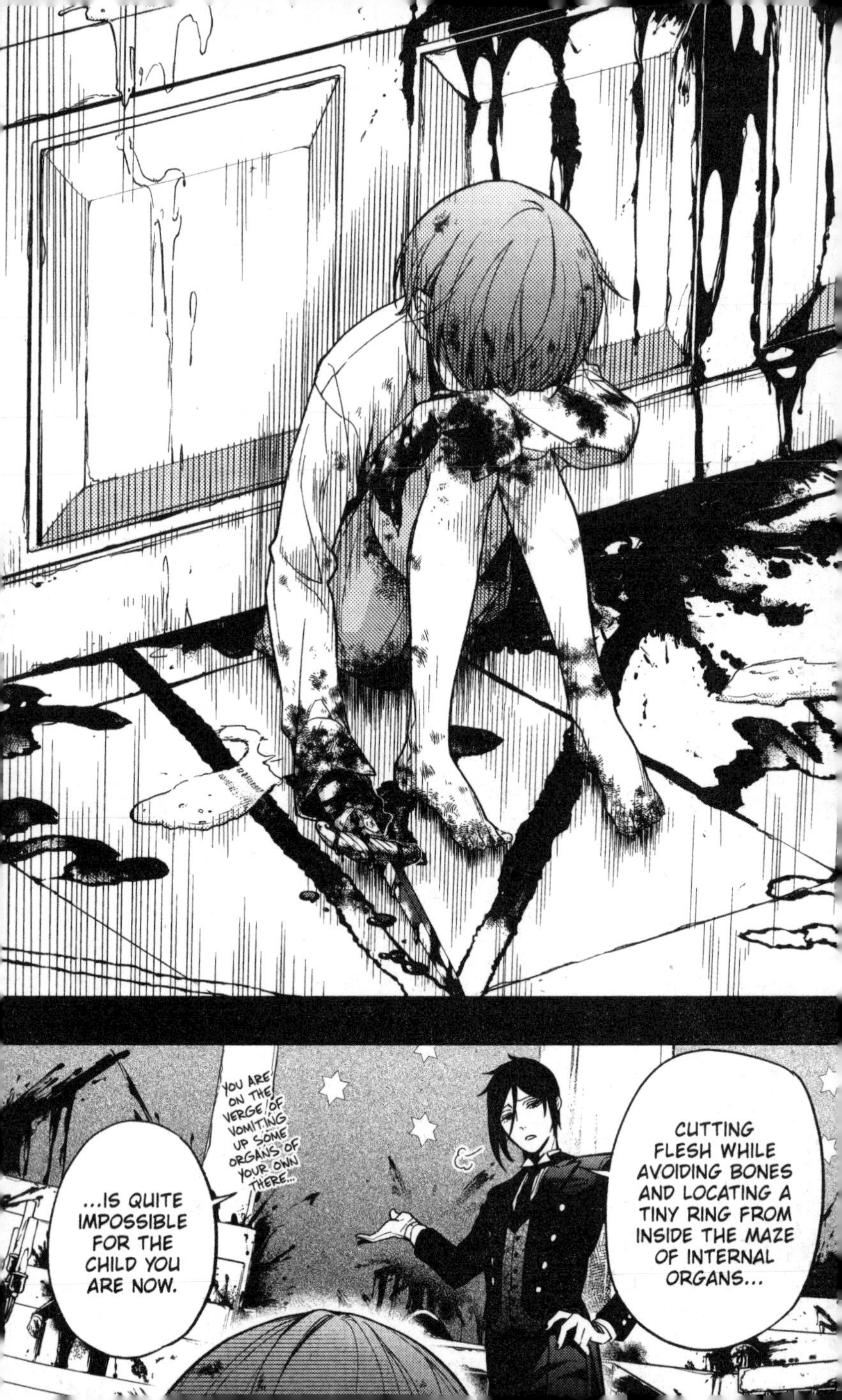
CUTTING FLESH WHILE AVOIDING BONES AND LOCATING A TINY RING FROM INSIDE THE MAZE OF INTERNAL ORGANS...
YOU ARE ON THE VERGE OF VOMITING UP SOME ORGANS OF YOUR OWN THERE...
...IS QUITE IMPOSSIBLE FOR THE CHILD YOU ARE NOW.

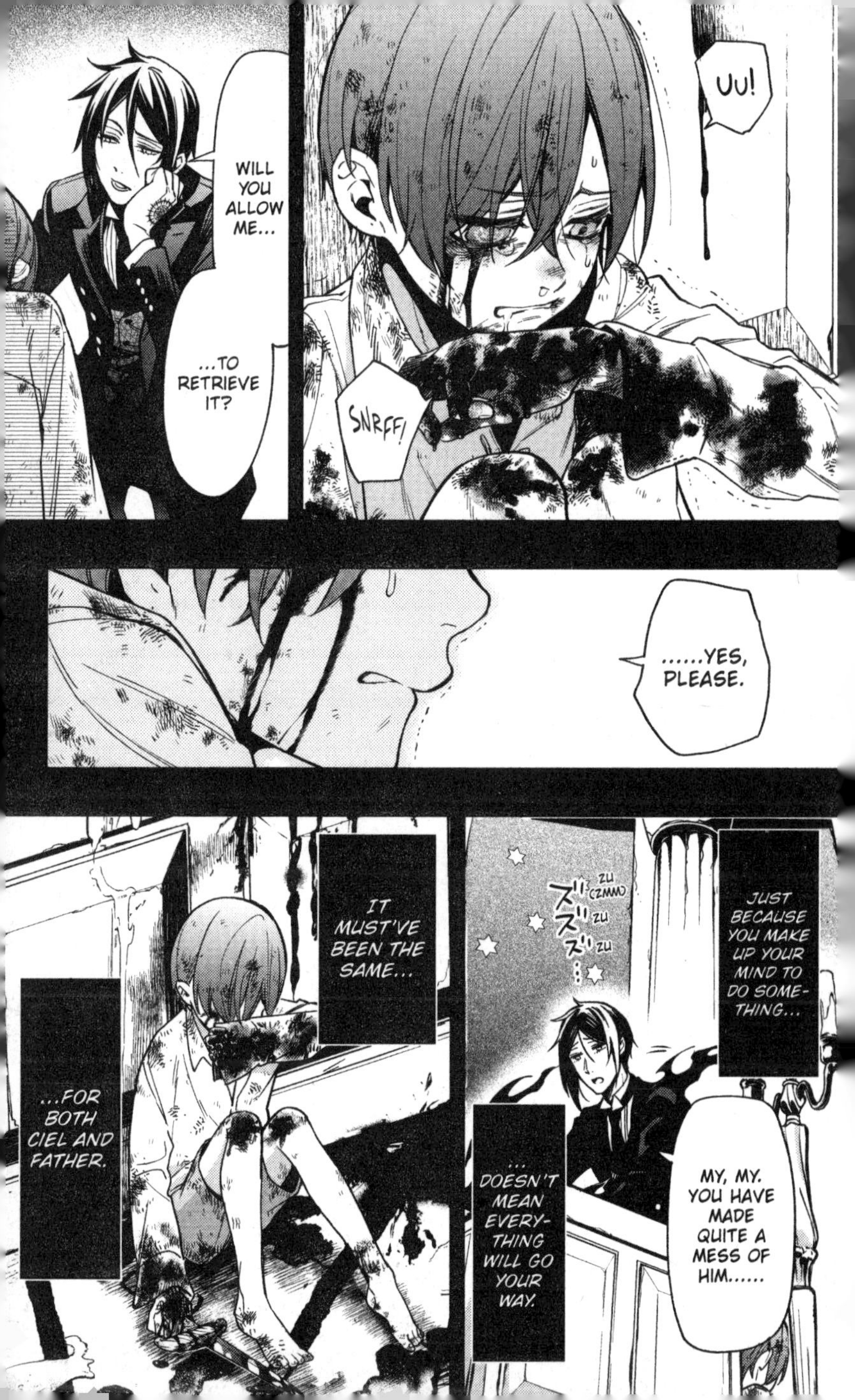
UU!
SNRFF!
WILL YOU ALLOW ME...
...TO RETRIEVE IT?
......YES, PLEASE.
JUST BECAUSE YOU MAKE UP YOUR MIND TO DO SOME-THING...
ズズズ...
ZU (ZMM) ZU ZU
MY, MY. YOU HAVE MADE QUITE A MESS OF HIM......
...DOESN'T MEAN EVERY-THING WILL GO YOUR WAY.
IT MUST'VE BEEN THE SAME...
...FOR BOTH CIEL AND FATHER.

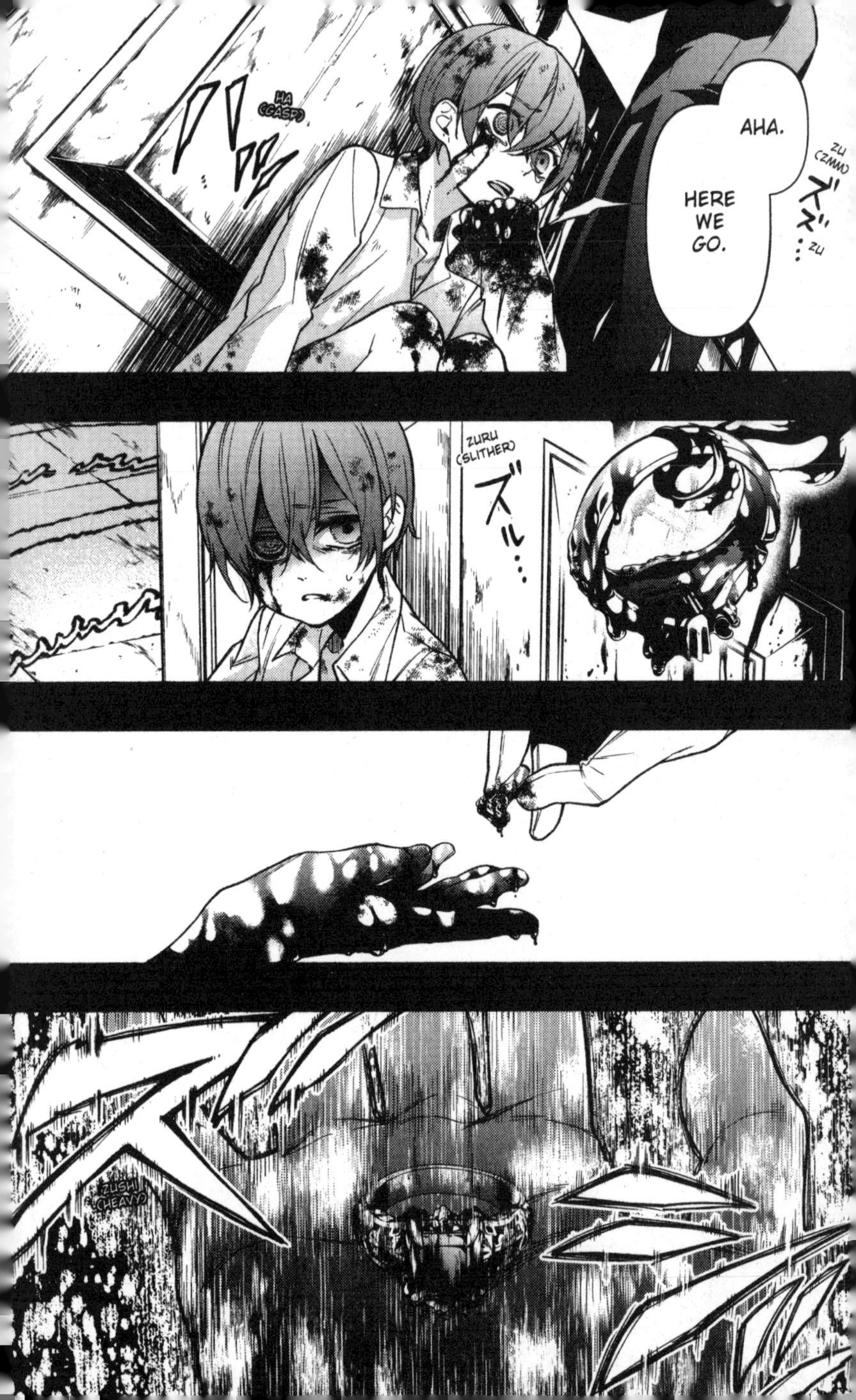
ZU (ZMM)
ズズ…ZU
AHA.
HERE WE GO.
HA (GASP)
ZURU (SLITHER)
ズル…
ZUSHI (HEAVY)

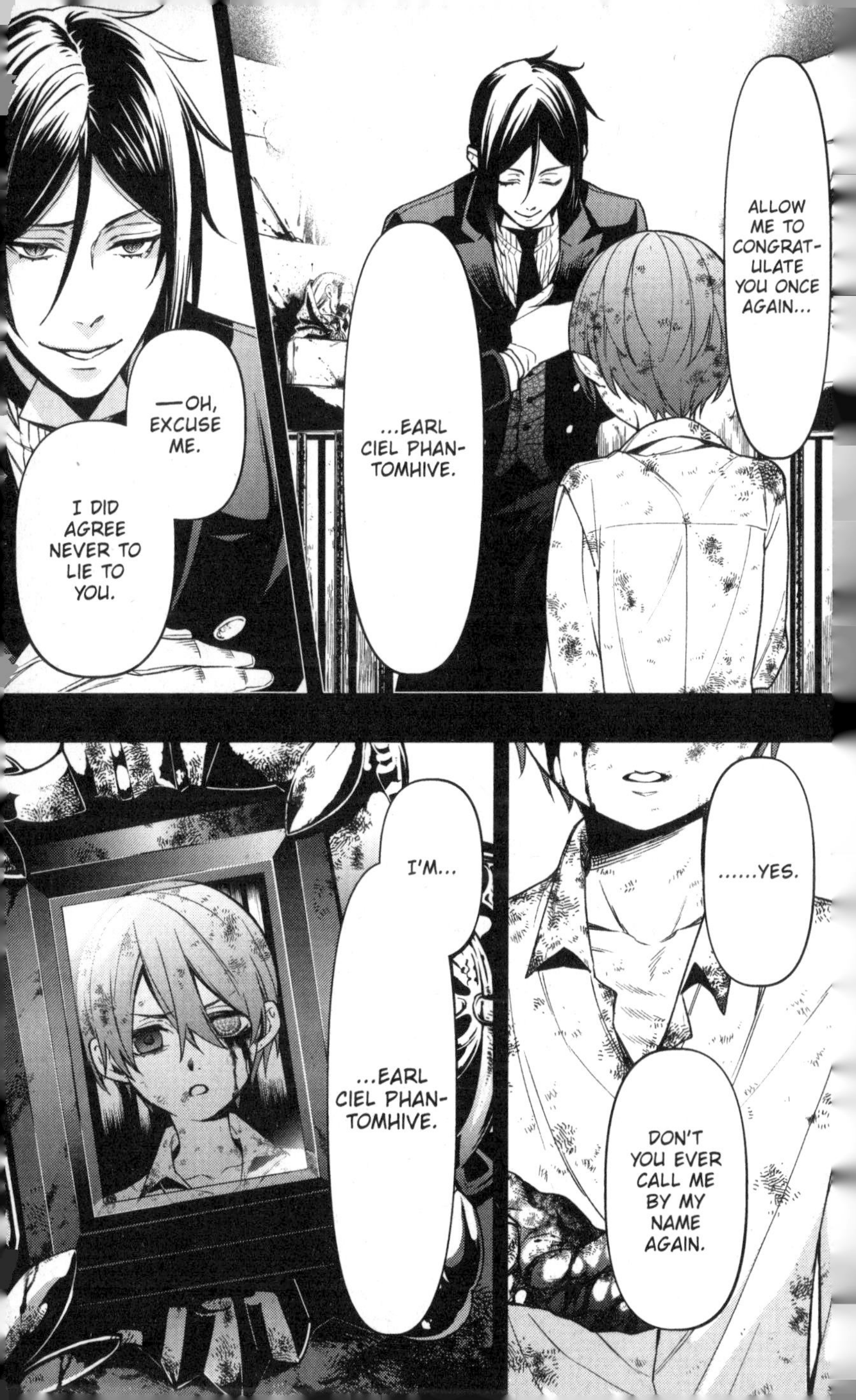
ALLOW ME TO CONGRATULATE YOU ONCE AGAIN...
...EARL CIEL PHANTOMHIVE.
—OH, EXCUSE ME.
I DID AGREE NEVER TO LIE TO YOU.
......YES.
DON'T YOU EVER CALL ME BY MY NAME AGAIN.
I'M...
...EARL CIEL PHANTOMHIVE.

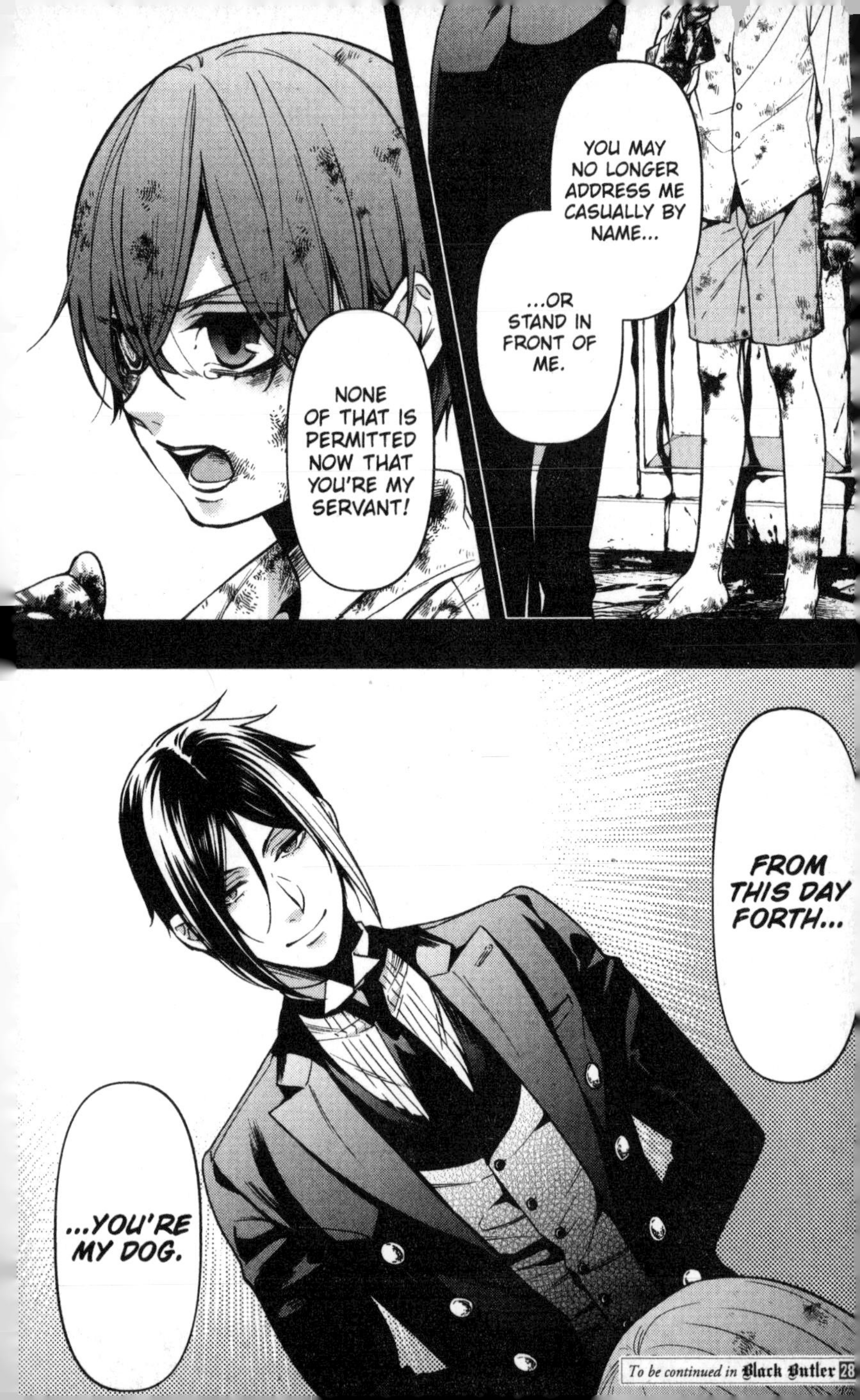
YOU MAY NO LONGER ADDRESS ME CASUALLY BY NAME...
...OR STAND IN FRONT OF ME.
NONE OF THAT IS PERMITTED NOW THAT YOU'RE MY SERVANT!
FROM THIS DAY FORTH...
...YOU'RE MY DOG.

*To be continued in* Black Butler 28

# ⇒ Black Butler ⇐
## 黒執事

# Downstairs

Wakana Haduki
7
Tsuki Sorano
Chiaki Nagaoka
Sanihiko
Seira
Urai
Natsume
*
Takeshi Kuma
*
Yana Toboso

Adviser

Rico Murakami

## Special thanks to You!

# Translation Notes

INSIDE BACK COVER
**Tanaka's sweets**
Tanaka is making *nerikiri*, Japanese sweets
made of white bean paste and a thickening
agent, such as rice flour or taro. The paste is
colored and shaped into seasonal objects like
flowers and fruits or items depicting themes
from classical literature. *Nerikiri* are often
served at tea ceremonies and celebrations.

PAGE 49
**"*Fais ce que voudras*"**
Meaning "Do what thou wilt" in French,
this phrase is the motto of the monks who
reside in the Abbey of Thélème, a utopia
whose residents are bound by no other laws
or rules. It appears in 16th century French
humanist François Rabelais's *Gargantua*
novel. The English occultist Aleister Crowley
(1875–1947) also wrote on the subject and is
the founder of the Thelema religion.

# Yana Toboso

AUTHOR'S NOTE

When I was drawing the cover illustration, I opened up the files for the Volume 6 cover because I wanted to use the same palette. The files were such a mess that I couldn't help but smile wryly. It was obvious I was really struggling back then.

I was also smiling wryly while drawing this volume, since I had to look back into the past.

And so, this is Volume 27. Sorry to keep you waiting.

# BLACK BUTLER ㉗

FEB 1 2 2019

Indian Prairie Library
401 Plainfield Road
Darien, IL 60561

YANA TOBOSO

**Translation: Tomo Kimura**
**Lettering: Bianca Pistillo, Rochelle Gancio**

KUROSHITSUJI Vol. 27 © 2018 Yana Toboso / SQUARE ENIX CO., LTD. First published in Japan in 2018 by SQUARE ENIX CO., LTD. English translation rights arranged with SQUARE ENIX CO., LTD. and Yen Press, LLC through Tuttle-Mori Agency, Inc.

English translation © 2019 by SQUARE ENIX CO., LTD.

Yen Press
1290 Avenue of the Americas
New York, NY 10104

Visit us!
† yenpress.com
† facebook.com/yenpress
† twitter.com/yenpress
† yenpress.tumblr.com
† instagram.com/yenpress

First Yen Press Edition: January 2019
The chapters in this volume were originally published as ebooks by Yen Press.

Yen Press is an imprint of Yen Press, LLC.
The Yen Press name and logo are trademarks of Yen Press, LLC.

The publisher is not responsible for websites (or their content) that are not owned by the publisher.

Library of Congress Control Number: 2010525567

ISBNs: 978-1-9753-8361-9 (paperback)
       978-1-9753-8362-6 (ebook)

10  9  8  7  6  5  4  3  2  1

WOR

Printed in the United States of America